Angelomorphic Pneumatology

Supplements
to
Vigiliae Christianae

Texts and Studies of
Early Christian Life and Language

Editors

J. den Boeft – B.D. Ehrman – J. van Oort
D.T. Runia – C. Scholten – J.C.M. van Winden

VOLUME 95

Angelomorphic Pneumatology

Clement of Alexandria and Other Early Christian Witnesses

By

Bogdan Gabriel Bucur

BRILL

LEIDEN • BOSTON
2009

This book is printed on acid-free paper.

Library of Congress Cataloging-in-Publication-Data

Bucur, Bogdan Gabriel.
  Angelomorphic pneumatology : Clement of Alexandria and other early Christian witnesses / by Bogdan Gabriel Bucur.
    p. cm. — (Supplements to Vigiliae Christianae, ISSN 0920-623X ; v. 95)
  Includes bibliographical references.
  ISBN 978-90-04-17414-6 (hardback : alk. paper) 1. Holy Spirit—History of doctrines—Early church, ca. 30–600. 2. Clement, of Alexandria, Saint, ca. 150–ca. 215. I. Title. II. Series.

  BT119.B83 2009
  231'.309015—dc22

                                                              2009006447

ISSN 0920-623x
ISBN 978 90 04 17414 6

Copyright 2009 by Koninklijke Brill NV, Leiden, The Netherlands.
Koninklijke Brill NV incorporates the imprints Brill, Hotei Publishing,
IDC Publishers, Martinus Nijhoff Publishers and VSP.

PRINTED IN THE NETHERLANDS

CONTENTS

Preface ix
Acknowledgments xiii
Abbreviations xvii
Introduction xxi

PART ONE

ANGELOMORPHIC PNEUMATOLOGY IN
CLEMENT OF ALEXANDRIA

Chapter One:
"The Other Clement" and Angelomorphic Pneumatology   3
  1. Prolegomena: The Place of the *Hypotyposeis* in the
     Clementine Corpus   6
     Protreptikos—Paidagogos—Didaskalos   11
     Ethics—Physics—Epoptics   18
     Physics to *Epoptics*: Ma'asse Bereshīt to Ma'asse
       Merkavah   21
     The *Hypotyposeis* and Later Orthodoxy   25
     Conclusions   27
  2. Clement on Divine Unity and the Cosmic Multiplicity ...   28
     Unity and Multiplicity in the Logos   28
     Unity and Multiplicity in the Spirit   30
  3. Clement's "Celestial Hierarchy"   32
     The Principles of the Hierarchy   36
     The Function of the Hierarchy   41
     Clement on the Interior Ascent   42
  4. Clement's Theory of Prophetic Inspiration   52
  5. Clement's Understanding of "Spirit of Christ" and
     "Paraclete"   54
     "Spirit of Christ"   54
     "Paraclete"   56
  6. Angelic or Angelomorphic Pneumatology?   59
     Excursus: Matt 18:10 and Clement's *Protoctists*   61

Chapter Two:
The Larger Theological Framework for Clement's
Angelomorphic Pneumatology 73
  1. Binitarian Monotheism in Clement of Alexandria 73
  2. Spirit Christology in Clement of Alexandria 75
  3. A Final Look at Clement's Speculations on Unity and
     Diversity 79
     Conclusions 80

PART TWO

ANGELOMORPHIC PNEUMATOLOGY IN
CLEMENT'S PREDECESSORS

Introduction 87

Chapter Three:
Angelomorphic Pneumatology in the Book of Revelation 89
Introduction 89
  1. The "Seven Spirits" in Revelation and Clement's
     Protoctists 91
     Who are the "Seven Spirits"? 98
  2. Binitarianism and Spirit Christology in Revelation 100
  3. The Phenomenon of Prophecy in Revelation 104
     Conclusions 110

Chapter Four:
Angelomorphic Pneumatology in the Shepherd of Hermas 113
  Introduction 113
  1. Πνεῦμα as an Angelic Being 115
  2. Πνεῦμα as the Son of God 120
  3. Πνεῦμα in the Fifth Similitude 126
     Excursus: "Flesh" in the Fifth Similitude 134
  4. Further Clarifications on the Shepherd's Angelomorphic
     Pneumatology 136
     Conclusions 137

Chapter Five:
The Son of God and the Angelomorphic Holy Spirit in Justin
    Martyr 139
Introduction 139
    1. Difficulties with Justin Martyr's Use of πνεῦμα 141
    2. Justin Martyr on "the Powers of the Spirit" 148
    Conclusions 155

PART THREE

A WITNESS FROM THE EAST:
APHRAHAT THE PERSIAN SAGE

Chapter Six:
Angelomorphic Pneumatology in Aphrahat 159
Introduction 159
    1. Aphrahat's Views: "Many Aberrations and Very Crass
       Statements" 161
    2. The Seven Operations of the Spirit are Six 163
    3. "The Spirit is not always found with those that
       receive it..." 165
    4. An Older Exegetical Tradition 169
       Cramer versus Kretschmar 169
    5. The Larger Theological Framework for Aphrahat's
       Angelomorphic Pneumatology 174
       Difficulties of Aphrahat's Pneumatology 175
       The Holy Spirit and the Move from Unity to
          Multiplicity 180
       Excursus: "Wisdom" and "Power" as Pneumatological
          Terms 181
    6. The "Fragmentary" Gift of the Spirit and Angelomorphic
       Pneumatology 185
       Conclusions 186

General Conclusions 189
    "The Other Clement"... 189
    Angelomorphic Pneumatology and the History of Christian
       Thought 190
    Brief Theological Assessment 191

Bibliography 195
    Primary Sources 195
    Secondary Sources 198

Index of Terms 217
Index of Sources 219
    A. Hebrew Bible 219
    B. New Testament 220
    C. Early Christian Writings 222
    D. Dead Sea Scrolls, Targums, Philo, Pseudepigrapha, and
       Apocrypha 227
    E. Mishna, Talmud, Hekhalot and Later Jewish
       Literature 228
Index of Modern Authors 229

PREFACE

This monograph is the fruit of a long period of accumulations and research, which started as early as my first semester of graduate courses at Marquette University, in the Fall of 2000. It is now a study that starts with Clement of Alexandria and deals extensively with his theological thought. Yet Clement was chronologically the last stop on my very meandering *via inventionis*.

In 2000, when I came from Romania to the United States to study at Marquette University with Fr. Alexander Golitzin, I was determined to focus my research on Irenaeus of Lyon. I gave up the project very soon after my arrival, discouraged because all the issues I had had in mind had already been raised and solved in the scholarship of the past five or six decades, which had not been available to me in Bucharest. I moved to earlier writings, especially the *Shepherd of Hermas*. I discovered with delight that the questions I brought to this text were still valid, because, as one scholar wrote a few years ago, "there are many puzzles in this puzzling little book." One of the persistent puzzles of the *Shepherd*, whose theological views appear so strange to modern scholarship, is that it fared so well in the early Church. Both Irenaeus and Clement, for instance, treat it with the utmost respect; Clement especially is most enthusiastic about the *Shepherd*. My own solution to the christological and pneumatological puzzles in the *Shepherd* came after reading John Levison's work on "angelic Spirit in early Judaism" and Philippe Henne's literary analysis of the Similitudes. After arriving at an understanding of the *Shepherd* that answered the most important questions I had, it became important to document the existence of similar views in other early Christian writings.

The next stage consisted of classroom discussion and research for course papers on early Christian writers who have a strong, all-pervasive Logos-theology—writers such as Justin Martyr, Eusebius of Cesarea, and Ps.-Dionysius. The question was to make sense of the fact that the all-encompassing Logos-theology of these authors leaves almost no room for a theology of the Holy Spirit, and to make sense of instances when "spirit" is used as a christological term—such as in second-century interpretations of Luke 1:35, where the overshadowing Spirit is, in fact, the Logos. To compound the problem, these authors also assume, like most people in Late Antiquity, a hierarchically ordered universe, in which the presence of the divinity is conveyed by Logos through successive levels of angelic beings. This, again, makes it rather difficult to construct a robust pneumatology.

Gradually, I came to the conclusion that for much of early Christian literature the *functional taxis* was "Father-Son and holy angels". I later learned that Georg Kretschmar had argued this extensively in the nineteen fifties. I started toying with the idea that this insight should be combined with the above-mentioned overlapping and occasional identification of Logos and Spirit. This led me naturally to ask how early Christians viewed the relationship between angels and the Holy Spirit.

It is with this set of questions and these working hypotheses in mind that I started reading Clement of Alexandria. Considered from this perspective, which had by now become obsessive, Clement started to look more and more interesting. I *did* consider the danger of *eisegesis*: was this really Clement, or was I increasingly reading into the Clementine texts my own views on the *Shepherd*, Justin, and Ps.-Dionysius? As I was finishing a paper on the topic of Spirit and Logos and angels in Clement, I stumbled upon a reference, buried in the footnotes of an article on Justin, about a booklet written in 1967 by a German scholar, Christian Oeyen, which was entitled "An Angel Pneumatology in Clement of Alexandria." This booklet, it turned out, could not be obtained through any library channels. Only one copy existed in public circulation, at the University of Bern, where the author had taught for a while. Later I learned that it was a reprint, with some expansions, of an article published in a rather obscure journal. Christian Oeyen had studied in Rome with Antonio Orbe, the renowned specialist on Irenaeus and on Gnostic literature; but his work, although very positively reviewed by Jean Daniélou, found almost no echo in mainstream patristic scholarship. Oeyen eventually moved to the study of nineteenth-century Old Catholic ecclesiology and ecumenical involvement.

The encounter with Oeyen's scholarship on Clement and Justin Martyr was the decisive moment. Oeyen provided insights into deserted areas of research—Clement of Alexandria's pneumatology and his lesser-known works, *Eclogae propheticae*, *Adumbrationes*, and *Excerpta ex Theodoto*. I was glad to find that all the seemingly "odd" and "marginal" elements that I had been investigating in the *Stromateis* were stated here in a much more direct and open manner than in the *Stromateis*. Oeyen also mentioned, without expanding on this point, however, that Clement's use of Matt 18:10 (the angels of the little ones) as a pneumatological proof-text, also occurs in Aphrahat. This triggered my interest in the history of reception of Matt 18:10 and sent me to Aphrahat.

As the title indicates, this monograph is about Clement only inasmuch as I use certain writings of his as an entry-point into a larger early Christian tradition. My interest is to study a number of early Christian texts exemplifiying what I call "angelomorphic pneumatology," and to prove that this tradition was fairly vigorous and widespread in early Christianity. I see my study as a complement to Charles Gieschen's work on angelomorphic Christology and to John Levison's work on the angelic spirit in early Judaism.

ACKNOWLEDGMENTS

I would like to express my gratitude to the members of the editorial board of the Supplements to Vigiliae Christianae, especially to Professor Jan den Boeft, for agreeing to publish my book in this prestigious series at Brill, as well as to the anonymous reviewers of the manuscript, whose suggestions have significantly improved this work. A word of thanks is also due to Mrs. Renate de Vries for her careful, thorough, and speedy handling of the production of the book.

This monograph is a revised and amplified version of my doctoral dissertation, defended in May of 2007 at Marquette University. Over the past two years, I have benefited from the stimulating atmosphere at Duquesne University, and the generous and cheerful encouragement of my colleagues in the Department of Theology. I was greatly helped, especially during the spring, summer, and fall of 2008, by a generous grant from the Wimmer Family Foundation and the McAnulty College of Liberal Arts at Duquesne University. I welcome the opportunity to give special thanks to Dr. George Worgul, the chair of the Department of Theology, and to Dr. Albert Labriola, the dean of the McAnulty College of Liberal Arts, for their unfailing trust and support. Many thanks also to Mr. Daniel Lattier, whom I was fortunate to have as my graduate assistant, for his attentive proofreading of the final draft of this book and for compiling the index.

During my years of theological training in Romania, academic books and journals were luxury items; their procurement, when at all possible, required sacrifices of money and time unimaginable to students in the West. I hope never to forget the overwhelming and dizzying excitement that I experienced when I first walked through the library stacks and learned about the electronic databases of Marquette University's Memorial Library. I shall not forget that free access to these treasures came as a gift, and that my seven years of Master's and doctoral studies would not have been possible without generous funding from Marquette's Department of Theology.

I came to the United States, and specifically to Marquette University, with the definite purpose of studying with Fr. Alexander Golitzin, after having read some of his studies published in Romanian translation. From him I have learned *et multa et multum*, seeing him embody both Martha's and Mary's ways of "doing theology." Even after graduation, I remain his student.

I owe the greatest debt of gratitude to Dr. Julian Hills, the co-director of my dissertation. In one of his classes I produced seminar papers on the pneumatology of the *Shepherd of Hermas* and that of the *Epistula apostolorum*. Another independent study was devoted to translating and discussing Clement's *Eclogae propheticae*. His numerous corrections, suggestions, and observations on so many of my drafts—an expense in time and energy that speaks not only of professionalism, but also of genuine personal care—dramatically improved its overall arrangement and prose, and helped me clarify some of the arguments.

My research on early Christian views of the Holy Spirit owes very much to the courses and seminars in early Christian literature that Dr. Michel René Barnes celebrated almost liturgically as a banquet for the intellect and the imagination. Thank you!

Dr. Deirdre Dempsey has shepherded me through the Syriac passages in Aphrahat and George of the Arabs. Her boundless generosity and patience all these years has never ceased to amaze and humble me.

I am grateful to Dr. Charles Gieschen and Dr. Dale C. Allison, who read the entire manuscript at different stages, and provided very valuable feedback. Many thanks are also due to Fr. Michael Slusser and Dr. Christian Oeyen, who read and provided valuable criticism of earlier drafts of the sections on Revelation, Justin, and Clement.

It is with special gratitude that I mention Dr. Andrei Orlov. The very project of this study owes much to his suggestions. In fact, my entire scholarly development has been shaped by the friendship and generous mentorship of my senior colleagues at Marquette, and now esteemed colleagues in academia, Andrei Orlov and Silviu Bunta.

Seven years of studies and stress, spent far from my parents and my home country, would have been much more difficult to bear without the warm presence of friends. Heartfelt thanks to all: Fr. Thomas and Gina Mueller, Fr. Elijah Mueller and Rebecca Luft, Silviu and Maria Bunta, Andrei Orlov, Dragos Giulea, Mihaela Deselnicu, Iulia Corduneanu (now Curtright), Marius and Aura Costache, Fr. Radu and Loredana Bordeianu, Vlad Niculescu, James and Tatiana Miller, Symeon Magnusson, Adrian and Anca Guiu.

Above all, I thank my closest and dearest friends for bearing with me all this time and surrounding me with their unconditional love: my wife Cristina and our daughter Irina. When she arrived in America, Irina was only a year and-a-half old. She grew up hearing only about students, professors, due dates, books, exams, and grades, following her parents around in a library stacked with books that had no pictures, and knowing that her daddy was writing stories about angels, while her mommy was writing stories about Plato and Aristotle. Perhaps she will one day leaf through this book to see what the mystery was all about.

I dedicate this work to my dear parents, whose love is always with me, and to my dear grandparents, who taught me the first words of prayer and almost all words in foreign languages.

ABBREVIATIONS

ACW	Ancient Christian Writers
AGJU	Arbeiten zur Geschichte des antiken Judentums und des Urchristentums
AnBib	Analecta Biblica
ANF	The Ante-Nicene Fathers
ANRW	Aufstieg und Niedergang der Römischen Welt
AThR	*Anglican Theological Review*
Aug	*Augustinianum*
Bib	*Biblica*
ByzZ	*Byzantinische Zeitschrift*
BET	Beiträge zur evangelischen Theologie
BETL	Bibliotheca ephemeridum theologicarum lovaniensum
BHT	Beiträge zur historischen Theologie
BJS	Brown Judaic Studies
BSJS	Brill's Series in Jewish Studies
BSIH	Brill's Studies in Intellectual History
CahT	Cahiers Théologiques
CBQ	*Catholic Biblical Quarterly*
CBET	Contributions to Biblical Exegesis and Theology
CCSL	Corpus Christianorum: Series latina
CCSA	Corpus Christianorum: Series apocyrphorum
CH	*Church History*
Colloq	*Colloquium*
ConBOT	Coniectanea biblica: Old Testament Series
CWS	Classics of Western Spirituality
Did	*Didaskalia*
DOP	*Dumbarton Oaks Papers*
ETL	*Ephemerides theologicae lovanienses*
EvQ	*Evangelical Quarterly*
ErJb	*Eranos Jahrbuch*
FC	Fontes christiani
FKDG	Forschungen zur Kirchen- und Dogmengeschichte
GCS	Die griechischen christlichen Schriftsteller der ersten drei Jahrhunderte
GNO	Gregorii Nysseni Opera

GOTR	Greek Orthodox Theological Review
HDR	Harvard Dissertations in Religion
HeyJ	Heythrop Journal
HTR	Harvard Theological Review
ICC	International Critical Commentary
IKZ	Internationale Kirchliche Zeitschrift
IPM	Instrumenta patristica et mediaevalia
JAC	Jahrbuch für Antike und Christentum
JAOS	Journal of the American Oriental Society
JBL	Journal of Biblical Literature
JECS	Journal of Early Christian Studies
JETS	Journal of the Evangelical Theological Society
JJS	Journal of Jewish Studies
JRH	Journal of Religious History
JSJ	Journal for the Study of Judaism
JSJSup	Supplements to the Journal for the Study of Judaism
JR	Journal of Religion
JTS	Journal of Theological Studies
KAV	Kommentar zu den Apostolischen Vätern
LNTS	Library of New Testament Studies
MBT	Münsterische Beiträge zur Theologie
MH	Museum helveticum
Mus	Le Muséon
NHMS	Nag Hammadi and Manichaean Studies
NovT	Novum Testamentum
NovTSup	Supplements to Novum Testamentum
NPNF	The Nicene and Post-Nicene Fathers
NTS	New Testament Studies
OTP	Old Testament Pseudepigrapha
OrChr	Oriens christianus
OrChrAn	Orientalia Christiana Analecta
PG	Patrologiae cursus completus, Series graeca
PL	Patrologiae cursus completus, Series latina
ProEccl	Pro Ecclesia
PS	Patrologia Syriaca
PTS	Patristische Texte und Studien
RB	Revue Biblique
RE	Realencyklopädie für protestantische Theologie und Kirche
RelS	Religious Studies
RHE	Revue d'histoire ecclésiastique

RPh	*Revue de philologie de littérature et d'histoire anciennes*
RSLR	*Rivista di storia e letteratura religiosa*
RSR	*Recherches de science religieuse*
RSPT	*Revue des sciences philosophiques et theologiques*
RTAMSup	Recherches de Theologie ancienne et medievale, Supplementa
SacEr	*Sacris Erudiri: Jaarboek voor Godsdienstwetenschappen*
SANT	Studien zum Alten und Neuen Testament
SBLDS	Society of Biblical Literature Dissertation Series
SBLSCS	Society of Biblical Literature Septuagint and Cognate Studies
SBLSP	*Society of Biblical Literature Seminar Papers*
SC	Sources chrétiennes
Scr	*Scripture*
SecCent	*The Second Century*
SHR	Studies in the History of Religions
SJLA	Studies in Judaism in Late Antiquity
SJT	*Scottish Journal of Theology*
SNTSMS	Society for New Testament Studies Monograph Series
SPhilo	*Studia Philonica*
SROC	*Studi e ricerche sull'Oriente cristiano*
ST	*Studia Theologica*
STDJ	Studies on the Texts of the Desert of Judah
STL	Studia Theologica Lundensia
StPatr	*Studia Patristica*
StudMon	*Studia Monastica*
SVOTS	*Saint Vladimir's Theological Quarterly*
TANZ	Texte und Arbeiten zum neutestamentlichen Zeitalter
TEG	Traditio Exegetica Graeca
ThH	Théologie historique
TQ	*Theologische Quartalschrift*
TR	*Traditio*
TS	*Theological Studies*
TSAJ	Texte und Studien zum antiken Judentum
TU	Texte und Untersuchungen zur Geschichte der altchristlichen Literatur
UaLG	Untersuchungen zur antiken Literatur und Geschichte
VC	*Vigiliae Christianae*
VCSup	Supplements to Vigiliae Christianae

VH   *Vivens homo*
VL   Vetus Latina
WBC   Word Biblical Commentary
WUNT Wissenschaftliche Untersuchungen zum Neuen Testament
ZKG   *Zeitschrift für Kirchengeschichte*
ZNW   *Zeitschrift für die neutestamentliche Wissenschaft*
ZTK   *Zeitschrift für Theologie und Kirche*
ZWT   *Zeitschrift für wissenschaftliche Theologie*

No abbreviations are given for the following:

Analekta Vlatadon
Apocrypha
Catholic Theological Studies of India
Christianismes anciens
Collection des études augustiniennes, Série Antiquité
Die Apostolischen Väter
Estudios trinitarios
Graecitas Christianorum Primaeva
Hermeneia
Modern Theology
Oxford Early Christian Studies
Oxford Theological Monographs
Paradosis
Patristica Sorbonensia
Quaderni di "Vetera Christianorum"
Schriften des Urchristentums
Sileno
Studies in Biblical Literature
Theoforum
Theophaneia: Beiträge zur Religions- und Kirchengeschichte des Altertums
Vivre et Penser

INTRODUCTION

Much of the material in the present monograph has appeared relatively recently in various articles.[1] Writing a book on the basis of those articles has not only allowed me to make all the corrections, additions, and other modifications that I deemed necessary, but has also given me the opportunity to propose a fuller, integrated account of the early Christian tradition of angelomorphic pneumatology.

This study brings together scholarly research in three apparently distinct areas. The first is what has been styled "angelomorphic pneumatology," that is, the use of angelic imagery in early Christian discourse about the Holy Spirit. The second is the pneumatology of Clement of Alexandria, a topic generally acknowledged as ripe for research. The third is Clement's *Eclogae propheticae, Excerpta ex Theodoto*, and *Adumbrationes*—writings that have until now been allowed only a minor role in the reconstruction of this author's theological thought. As will become clear in the course of my exposition, these areas of study are only apparently separate.

In the conclusion of his article entitled "The Angelic Spirit in Early Judaism," John R. Levison invited the scholarly community to use his work as "a suitable foundation for discussion of the angelic spirit" in early Christianity.[2] A few years later, in his study of angelomorphic

---

[1] "Hierarchy, Prophecy, and the Angelomorphic Spirit: A Contribution to the Study of the Book of Revelation's *Wirkungsgeschichte*," *JBL* 127 (2008): 183–204; "The Son of God and the Angelomorphic Holy Spirit: A Rereading of the Shepherd's Christology," *ZNW* 98 (2007): 121–43; "Observations on the Ascetic Doctrine of the *Shepherd of Hermas*," *StudMon* 48 (2006): 7–23; "The Angelic Spirit in Early Christianity: Justin, the Martyr and Philosopher," *JR* 88 (2008): 190–208; "The Other Clement: Cosmic Hierarchy and Interiorized Apocalypticism," *VC* 60 (2006): 251–68; "Revisiting Christian Oeyen: 'The Other Clement' on Father, Son, and the Angelomorphic Spirit," *VC* 61 (2007): 381–413; "Matt. 18:10 in Early Christology and Pneumatology: A Contribution to the Study of Matthean *Wirkungsgeschichte*," *NovT* 49 (2007): 209–31; "Early Christian Angelomorphic Pneumatology: Aphrahat the Persian Sage," *Hugoye: Journal of Syriac Studies* 11 (2008); "The Place of the *Hypotyposeis* in the Clementine Corpus: An Apology for the 'Other Clement of Alexandria'," *JECS* (forthcoming).

[2] "Discussions of the spirit of God in Early Judaism and Christianity...ought to consider...interpretations of the spirit as an angelic presence...The texts included in the present analysis serve...to provide a suitable foundation for discussion of the angelic spirit in the Fourth Gospel, the Shepherd of Hermas, and the Ascension of Isaiah" (Levison, "The Angelic Spirit in Early Judaism," *SBLSP* 34 [1995]: 492). See also idem, *The Spirit in First Century Judaism* (AGJU 29; Leiden: Brill, 1997).

christology, Charles A. Gieschen highlighted the need for similar work
in the field of early pneumatology.[3] His own book, as well as Mehrdad
Fatehi's study of Pauline pneumatology, included dense but necessarily
brief surveys of early Jewish and Christian examples of angelomorphic
pneumatology.[4]

I shall take up the challenge in this monograph, and pursue the occurrence of angelomorphic pneumatology in early Christian literature. As
an entry-point into the tradition of angelomorphic pneumatology I have
chosen, for reasons that I shall explain presently, Clement of Alexandria's *Excerpta ex Theodoto*, *Eclogae propheticae*, and *Adumbrationes*.
This is the centerpiece of my study, and as such, deserves mention in
its subtitle.

Clement of Alexandria provides an ideal entry-point into earlier
Christian traditions. This author has left behind a body of writings vaster
and more varied than that of any Christian writer before Origen. The
Clementine corpus preserves, despite Clement's self-assumed mission
of presenting a bold and intelligent account of the faith, an invaluable
collection of older traditions (whether "orthodox," "heretical," "Jewish,"
"Greek," or "barbarian"). Most importantly, however, this author claims
to furnish a written record of certain oral traditions inherited from
earlier authoritative, even charismatic, teachers, whom he refers to as
"the elders." This is especially true of the *Eclogae* and the *Adumbrationes*, where the voice of these ancient teachers is heard more often
and more clearly than in other Clementine writings. As I shall argue
in a separate section of my study, it is in these surviving fragments of
the *Hypotyposeis*, more than anywhere else in the Clementine corpus,
that the Alexandrian master also sets out certain views of the Spirit
and the angels. Clement reworks early Jewish and Christian traditions
about the seven first-created angels (πρωτόκτιστοι), providing a complex exegesis of specific biblical passages (Zech 4:10; Isa 11:2–3; Matt

---

[3] Gieschen, *Angelomorphic Christology: Antecedents and Early Evidence* (AGJU 42;
Leiden: Brill, 1998), 6: "Ignorance concerning the influence of angelomorphic traditions
has also plagued scholarship on early Pneumatology…the same or similar angelomorphic traditions also influenced teaching about the Holy Spirit."

[4] Gieschen, *Angelomorphic Christology*, 114–19; Fatehi, *The Spirit's Relation to
the Risen Lord in Paul* (WUNT 128; Tübingen: Mohr Siebeck, 2000), 133–37. See
also Jean Daniélou, *The Theology of Jewish Christianity* (French ed. 1958; London:
Darton, Longman & Todd, 1964), 127–31 ("The Spirit and Gabriel"); Gedaliahu
A. G. Stroumsa, "Le couple de l'ange et de l'Esprit: Traditions juives et chrétiennes,"
RB 88 (1981): 42–61.

18:10). The resulting angelomorphic pneumatology occurs in tandem with spirit christology, and within a theological framework still characterized by a binitarian orientation. All of the above constitute the subject of the first part of this study.

In the second and third parts, I argue that far from being an oddity of Clement's, the theological articulation of angelomorphic pneumatology, spirit christology, and binitarianism constitutes a relatively widespread phenomenon in early Christianity. Evidence to support this claim will be presented in the course of separate studies of Revelation, the *Shepherd of Hermas*, Justin Martyr, and Aphrahat.[5]

This book, then, has three parts. The first one deals with Clement of Alexandria, the second one with some of Clement's predecessors—Revelation, *Shepherd of Hermas*, Justin Martyr—and the third one with Aphrahat. I discuss each of these writers in six separate and, to a large extent, independent chapters, addressing specific problems in the primary texts and engaging the relevant scholarly literature. In each case, however, I pursue the three themes announced above: angelomorphic pneumatology, binitarianism, spirit christology.

It may be objected that proceeding in this manner is fundamentally wrong, because these categories may not be equally appropriate for understanding each of the respective texts, and because considering a rather diverse literature through the same lens might create the illusion of conformity and coherence.

I respond by pointing out, first, that this is primarily a study of Clement of Alexandria, and that the coherence of tradition is part of the Clementine vantage-point that this work must follow in order to understand its subject-matter. Clement assumes that there is a coherent angelological and pneumatological discourse, rooted in a religious experience of angels and the Spirit, and shared across the centuries and across geographical boundaries. Therefore, after discussing Clement's

---

[5] Another highly relevant text would have been the apocryphal *Martyrdom and Ascension of Isaiah*, which is notorious for its references to "the angel of the Holy Spirit." However, the older research of Georg Kretschmar and Guy Stroumsa, and a more recent study by Loren T. Stuckenbruck, have already furnished a treatment of this writing's pneumatology, with which I agree entirely and without reserve: Kretschmar, *Studien zur frühchristlichen Trinitätstheologie* (BHT 21; Tübingen: Mohr, 1956), 64–74; Stroumsa, "Le couple de l'ange et de l'Esprit," esp. 42–47; Stuckenbruck, "The Holy Spirit in the Ascension of Isaiah," *The Holy Spirit and Christian Origins: Essays in Honor of James D. G. Dunn* (ed. G. N. Stanton, B. W. Longenecker, and S. C. Barton; Grand Rapids, Mich.: Eerdmans, 2004), 308–20.

pneumatological speculations, it is important to understand how it is that the Alexandrian master, who time and again claimed the authority of the "elders" for these views, was able to see himself as part of, and witness to, the tradition that he viewed as apostolic and mainstream. The coherence with earlier traditions may well be, in some cases more than in others, Clement's own theological construction; but it is crucial to see on what basis such construction would have been possible. In the case of Revelation, for instance, even if reading the text with a little bit of help from Clement is an exercise in tradition-criticism and *Wirkungsgeschichte* rather than strictly textual-based exegesis, this approach is important if it can shed light on second-century pneumatology.

Second, I have tried to reduce the risks outlined above by my choice of non-Clementine authors, in the second and third parts of this work. Revelation, the *Shepherd of Hermas*, and Justin's *Dialogue* and *Apologies* are texts that the Alexandrian master is certain to have read and, as in the case of *Shepherd*, held in particularly high esteem.[6] They are important inasmuch as they may offer insight into some of the teachings that Clement ascribed to the tradition of the "elders". At the very least, as I have said, we shall gain some understanding of the elements in these texts that Clement would have considered to agree with his own pneumatological views.

The relevance of Aphrahat, a fourth century Syriac writer, is of a different kind. There is no literary connection, so far as we know, between him and Clement of Alexandria—and no literary connection, either, between Aphrahat and Justin, *Shepherd*, or Revelation. Nevertheless, Aphrahat displays an exegesis of the biblical verses linking traditions about the highest angelic company with early Christian pneumatology that is strikingly similar to what one finds in Justin and, especially, Clement of Alexandria. Moreover, scholars over the past century have raised concerns about the Persian Sage's theology—e.g., *Geistchristologie*, binitarianism, a certain overlap of angelology and pneumatology—that are similar to those raised by many of Clement's readers. If it can be shown that the conclusions set forth at the end of the studies of Clement and his predecessors are also valid in the case of Aphrahat, then, even though certain details of the demonstration may

---

[6] For precise references, see *Clemens Alexandrinus 4.1: Register* (GCS 39/1; 2nd, rev. ed.; O. Stählin and U. Treu, eds.; Berlin: Akademie-Verlag, 1980).

still call for further investigation, my thesis of an early and relatively widespread Christian tradition of angelomorphic pneumatology will stand on solid ground.

Working Definitions

It is obvious that considering pre-Nicene views of the Spirit through the lens of late fourth-century pneumatology limits our ability to capture important elements. The doctrine of the Spirit is fluid in the second century, and one must adopt a wider perspective, one that takes into consideration the frequent intersection and overlap between pneumatology, christology, and angelology, labeled in scholarship as "spirit christology," "binitarianism," and "angelomorphic pneumatology."

It is necessary at this point to provide some clarification for my use of these concepts. I am, first of all, acutely aware of their limitations. Scholars create concepts in order to grasp and render intelligible their objects of study; sooner or later those concepts are found lacking in explanatory power and are discarded. There are numerous examples of expired and sometimes embarrassing terms, once hailed for their power to illuminate and guide the scholarly quest: "late Judaism," "Frühkatholizismus," "Pharisaic legalism," "Jewish Christianity," "Gnosticism," "semi-Pelagianism," "semi-Arianism," "Messalianism"—the list could certainly continue. The time will come for "Logos-sarx christology" and "Logos-anthropos christology," "Enochic Judaism," "interiorized apocalypticism," "mediatorial polemics," or "consort pneumatology."

I have no doubt that my own terms of choice are also imperfect lenses, which bring into focus certain things while necessarily overlooking others and perhaps distorting the overall picture to a certain degree. Nevertheless, I contend that, at the current state of scholarship, the categories of angelomorphic pneumatology, spirit christology, and binitarianism allow us to discern certain important elements in early Christian literature that one would miss without these lenses.

The term "angelomorphic" was coined by Jean Daniélou in his *Theology of Jewish Christianity*.[7] Even though Daniélou's conceptual

---

[7] Daniélou, *Jewish Christianity*, 146: "These then are the strictly Jewish Christian conceptions of *angelomorphic Christology*, those which have been borrowed from the angelology of later Judaism, and in which Christ and the Holy Spirit are represented

framework has been called into question, the term "angelomorphic" is now widely used by scholars writing on the emergence of christology.[8] I shall follow Crispin Fletcher-Louis' definition, according to which this term is to be used "wherever there are signs that an individual or community possesses specifically angelic characteristics or status, though for whom identity cannot be reduced to that of an angel."[9] The virtue of this definition—and the reason for my substituting the term "angelomorphic pneumatology" for Levison's "angelic Spirit"—is that it signals the use of angelic *characteristics* in descriptions of God or humans, while not necessarily implying that either are angels *stricto sensu*. Neither "angelomorphic christology" nor "angelomorphic pneumatology" implies the identification of Christ or the Holy Spirit with "angels."[10] In the words

---

in their eternal nature, and not simply in their mission, by means of the imagery of various angelic beings" (emphasis added). The respective chapter (*Jewish Christianity*, 117–46) had appeared earlier in article form: Daniélou, "Trinité et angélologie dans la théologie judéo-chrétienne," *RSR* 45 (1957): 5–41.

[8] Richard N. Longenecker, "Some Distinctive Early Christological Motifs," *NTS* 14 (1968): 529–33; Robert Gundry, "Angelomorphic Christology in Revelation," *SBLSP* 33 (1994): 662–78; Stuckenbruck, *Angel Veneration and Christology: A Study in Early Judaism and in the Christology of the Apocalypse of John* (WUNT 2/70; Tübingen: Mohr Siebeck, 1995); Peter R. Carrell, *Jesus and the Angels: Angelology and the Christology of the Apocalypse of John* (SNTSMS 95; Cambridge/New York: Cambridge University Press, 1997); Crispin Fletcher-Louis, *Luke-Acts: Angels, Christology and Soteriology* (WUNT 2/94; Tübingen: Mohr Siebeck, 1997); Gieschen, *Angelomorphic Christology;* Darrell D. Hannah, *Michael and Christ: Michael Traditions and Angel Christology in Early Christianity* (WUNT 2/109; Tübingen: Mohr Siebeck, 1999); Edgar G. Foster, *Angelomorphic Christology and the Exegesis of Psalm 8:5 in Tertullian's Adversus Praxean: An Examination of Tertullian's Reluctance to Attribute Angelic Properties to the Son of God* (Lanham, Md.: University Press of America, 2005); J. A. McGuckin, "Lactantius as Theologian: An Angelic Christology on the Eve of Nicaea," *RSLR* 22 (1986): 492–97. Hannah (*Michael and Christ*, 12–13) prefers to use "angelic christology" as the overarching category, which he then subdivides as follows: "angel christology" designates the identification of Jesus as an angel *stricto sensu* (either as the incarnation of an angel or an exaltation to angelic nature); "angelomorphic christology" refers to visual portrayals of Jesus in the form of an angel; finally, "theophanic angel christology" stands for the patristic identification of Jesus Christ as the "angel of the Lord" in biblical theophanies.

[9] Fletcher-Louis, *Luke-Acts*, 14–15. Similarly Gieschen, *Angelomorphic Christology*, 4, 349.

[10] According to Daniélou (*Jewish Christianity*, 118), "the use of such terms in no way implies that Christ was by nature an angel.... The word angel...connotes a supernatural being manifesting itself. The nature of this supernatural being is not determined by the expression but by the context. 'Angel' is the old-fashioned equivalent of 'person.'" Similarly Eric Francis Osborn, *Justin Martyr* (Tübingen: Mohr Siebeck, 1973), 34; Christopher Rowland, "A Man Clothed in Linen: Daniel 10.6ff. and Jewish Angelology," *JSNT* 24 (1985): 100; Philippe Henne, *La Christologie chez Clément de Rome et dans le Pasteur d'Hermas* (Paradosis 33; Fribourg: Éditions Universitaires, 1992), 225; Jonathan Knight, *Disciples of the Beloved One: The Christology, Social Setting, and Theological*

of Tertullian, who refers here to the designation of Christ as μεγάλης βουλῆς ἄγγελος (Isa 9:5, LXX), *dictus est quidem (Christus) magni consilii angelus, id est nuntius, oficii, non naturae vocabulo.*[11]

"Binitarianism" and "spirit christology (*Geistchristologie*)" are scholarly concepts that go back at least as far as Friedrich Loofs.[12] I consider them useful, although imperfect, tools for research in early Christian thought. In what follows, I shall use the term "spirit christology" to designate the use of "pneuma" language for Christ—whether in reference to his divinity as opposed to his humanity, as a characteristic of his divine identity, or as a personal title. Some scholars, such as Manlio Simonetti, find these distinctions extremely important.[13] I consider them unnecessary for the present investigation, especially since the problems involved in the procedure are quite evident to Simonetti himself: these distinctions did not present themselves as such to patristic authors, so that, *even in cases that appear certain to the modern scholar*, there remains a doubt with respect to the precise meaning that patristic authors ascribe to the term πνεῦμα.[14]

I shall use the term "binitarian" to suggest a bifurcation of the divinity that does not preclude a fundamentally monotheistic conception. Here I follow especially Alan F. Segal's study of Jewish "two-power" theologies, and Daniel Boyarin's more recent work on Jewish precursors of early Logos-Christology.[15] "Binitarian *monotheism*," as exemplified by Philo's

---

Context of the Ascension of Isaiah (JSPSup 18; Sheffield: Sheffield Academic Press, 1996), 18–19, 142; Gieschen, *Angelomorphic Christology*, 28; Matthias Reinhard Hoffmann, *The Destroyer and the Lamb: The Relationship Between Angelomorphic and Lamb Christology in the Book of Revelation* (WUNT 2/203; Tübingen: Mohr Siebeck, 2005), 28.

[11] Tertullian, *Carn. Chr.* 14. Cf. *Origen, Comm. Jo.* 2.23.145–146 (SC 120: 302–304): the biblical names of angelic powers (e.g., "thrones," "principalities," "dominions") do not designate natures but their rank (τὰ ὀνόματα οὐχὶ φύσεων ζῴων ἐστὶν ὀνόματα ἀλλὰ τάξεων); similarly certain passages (e.g., Gen 18:2) refer to angels as "men" not not because of their nature but because of their work (παρὰ τὸ ἔργον...οὐ παρὰ τὴν φύσιν). Cf. Cyril of Alexandria, *In Ioann.* 1.7 (PG 73:105): τὸ ἄγγελος ὄνομα λειτουργίας μᾶλλόν ἐστιν, ἤπερ οὐσίας σημαντικὸν; thus, John the Baptist was called "angel" because of his ministry and message, not by virtue of being one of the heavenly beings (οὐκ αὐτὸ κατὰ φύσιν ἄγγελος ὢν, ἀλλ᾽ ὡς εἰς τὸ ἀγγέλλειν ἀπεσταλμένος, καὶ τὴν ὁδὸν τοῦ Κυρίου ἑτοιμάσατε βοῶν).

[12] Loofs, "Christologie, Kirchenlehre," RE 4 (3rd ed.; ed. A. Hauck; Leipzig: Hinrichs, 1898), 16–56, at 26.

[13] Luis Ladaria, *El Espíritu en Clemente Alejandrino: Estudio teológico antropológico* (Madrid: UPCM, 1980), 47; Manlio Simonetti, "Note di cristologia pneumatica," *Aug* 12 (1972): 201–32, esp. 202–3.

[14] Simonetti, "Note," 209.

[15] Segal, *Two Powers in Heaven: Early Rabbinic Reports about Christianity and Gnosticism* (SJLA 25; Leiden: Brill, 1977). See also Daniel Boyarin, *Border Lines: The*

speculations about the Logos as "second God," by the *memrā*-theology of the targums, by various strands of apocalyptic Judaism emphasizing the heavenly preeminence of exalted patriarchs (e.g., Enoch; cf. *3 En.* 12.5, "lesser YHWH") or quasi-hypostatic divine attributes (e.g., Wisdom, Glory), perhaps even by the Johannine prologue (according to Boyarin), is not dualism. Indeed, "neither the apocalyptic, mystical, nor Christianized Judaism affirmed two separate deities. They understood themselves to be monotheistic... Only radical gnosticism posited two different and opposing deities."[16] Such binitarian monotheism, positing a "second power in heaven," God's vice-regent, is an important part of Christianity's Jewish roots.[17] It is generally accepted that on the way from the use of trinitarian formulas to a mature trinitarian theology, these formulas coexisted with a certain binitarian orientation.[18] Early Christian binitarianism is often the result of an unclear distinction between the Logos and the Spirit; in other words, binitarianism and "spirit christology" are two aspects of the same phenomenon.[19]

Partition of Judaeo-Christianity (Philadelphia, Pa.: University of Pennsylvania Press, 2004), 112–27.

[16] Segal, "Dualism in Judaism, Christianity and Gnosticism: A Definitive Issue," in his *The Other Judaisms of Late Antiquity* (BJS 127; Atlanta, Ga.: Scholars Press, 1987), 13.

[17] A collection of relevant articles is found in *The Jewish Roots of Christological Monotheism: Papers from the St. Andrews Conference on the Historical Origins of the Worship of Jesus* (JSJSup 63; ed. J. R. Davila et al.; Leiden: Brill, 1999). See also Gilles Quispel, "Der Gnostische Anthropos und die Jüdische Tradition," in *Gnostic Studies* I (Istanbul: Nederlands Historisch-Archaeologisch Instituut in het Nabije Oosten, 1974), 173–95; Segal, *Two Powers in Heaven*; Jarl Fossum, "Gen. 1:26 and 2:7 in Judaism, Samaritanism and Gnosticism," *JJS* 16 (1985): 202–39; Paul A. Rainbow, "Jewish Monotheism as the Matrix for New Testament Christology: A Review Article", *NovT* 33 (1991): 78–91; idem, "Monotheism—A Misused Word in Jewish Studies?" *JJS* 42 (1991): 1–15; Margaret Barker, *The Great Angel: A Study of Israel's Second God* (Westminster/John Knox, 1992).

[18] See, in this respect, Friedrich Loofs, *Theophilus von Antiochien Adversus Marcionem und die anderen theologischen Quellen bei Irenaeus* (TU 46; Leipzig: Hinrichs, 1930), 114–205; H. E. W. Turner, *The Pattern of Christian Truth: A Study in the Relations between Orthodoxy and Heresy in the Early Church* (Bampton Lectures 1954; London: Mowbray & Co., 1954), 133–36; Raniero Cantalamessa, *L'omelia in S. Pascha dello Pseudo-Ippolito di Roma: Ricerche sulla teologia dell'Asia Minore nella seconda metà del II secolo* (Milan: Vita e pensiero, 1967), 171–85; Harry A. Wolfson, *The Philosophy of the Church Fathers* (3rd ed., rev.; Cambridge: Harvard University Press, 1970), 177–256; Salvatore Lilla, *Clement of Alexandria: A Study in Christian Platonism and Gnosticism* (Oxford: Oxford University Press, 1971), 26, 53; Simonetti, "Note"; Paul McGuckin, "Spirit Christology: Lactantius and His Sources," *HeyJ* 24 (1983): 141–8; Christopher Stead, *Philosophy in Christian Antiquity* (Cambridge: Cambridge University Press, 1994), 155–56.

[19] Kretschmar, *Trinitätstheologie*, 115–16; Waldemar Macholz, *Spuren binitarischer*

Finally, I shall on rare occasions use the term "Jewish Christian," construed in the broad sense described in Daniélou's *Theology of Jewish Christianity*. As long as the narrative of an early and radical parting of the ways between "Christianity" and "Judaism" remains the normative scholarly paradigm, despite its documented inability to explain a great deal of evidence from the first four centuries, the term "Jewish Christianity" remains useful as a description of "Christianity" itself.[20]

Denkweise im Abendlande seit Tertullian (Diss Halle 1902; Jena: Kämpfe, 1902); Loofs, *Theophilus*, 114–205; Joseph Barbel, *Christos Angelos: Die Anschauung von Christus als Bote und Engel in der gelehrten und volkstümlichen Literatur des christlichen Altertums: Zugleich ein Beitrag zur Geschichte des Ursprungs und der Fortdauer des Arianismus* (Fotomechanischer Nachdruck mit einem Anhang; Bonn: Peter Hannstein, 1964 [1941]), 188–92; Basil Studer, "La sotériologie de Lactance," in *Lactance et son temps: Recherches actuelles*. Actes du IVe Colloque d'Études Historiques et Patristiques, Chantilly 21–23 septembre 1976 (ed. J. Fontaine and M. Perrin; Paris: Beauchesne, 1978), 259–60, 270–71; McGuckin, "Spirit Christology," 142.

[20] For more recent treatments of this problem, see the essays collected in *The Ways that Never Parted* (ed. A. H. Becker and A. Y. Reed; TSAJ 95; Tübingen: Mohr Siebeck, 2003).

PART ONE

ANGELOMORPHIC PNEUMATOLOGY IN
CLEMENT OF ALEXANDRIA

CHAPTER ONE

"THE OTHER CLEMENT" AND
ANGELOMORPHIC PNEUMATOLOGY[1]

Clement of Alexandria's pneumatology is a relatively under-researched area in Patristic studies. Johannes Frangoulis made this remark as early as 1936.[2] Ten years later, Jules Lebreton's fundamental study of Clement's "theology of the Trinity" discusses the Father and the Son, but has absolutely nothing to say about the Spirit.[3] The situation seemed not to have changed much by 1972, when Wolf-Dieter Hauschild made a similar observation in his book on early Christian pneumatology.[4] Aside from Frangoulis' pioneering but very limited study, Clement's pneumatology has been given some attention in works treating broader subjects.[5] To this date, however, I know of only a single work dedicated exclusively to this subject, namely that of Ladaria, published in 1980.[6]

It is all the more regrettable therefore that one of the most thorough and creative studies in the field, Christian Oeyen's *Eine frühchristliche Engelpneumatologie bei Klemens von Alexandrien*, has been almost entirely absent from the scholarly debate. This small but extremely dense work is a slightly revised reprint of a two-part article published in 1965, which is in turn a revision of an excerpt from Oeyen's 1961 dissertation

---

[1] The treatment of Clement's pneumatology is a revised and expanded version of Bogdan G. Bucur, "Revisiting Christian Oeyen: 'The Other Clement' on Father, Son, and the Angelomorphic Spirit," *VC* 61 (2007): 381–413.

[2] Frangoulis, *Der Begriff des Geistes Πνεῦμα bei Clemens Alexandrinus* (Leipzig: Robert Noske, 1936), 1.

[3] Lebreton, "La théologie de la Trinité chez Clément d'Alexandrie," *RSR* 34 (1946): 55–76, 142–79.

[4] Hauschild, *Gottes Geist und der Mensch: Studien zur frühchristlichen Pneumatologie* (BevT 63; Munich: Kaiser, 1972), 13 n. 10.

[5] Hauschild, *Gottes Geist*, 11–85; Henning Ziebritzki, *Heiliger Geist und Weltseele: das Problem der dritten Hypostase bei Origenes, Plotin und ihren Vorläufern* (BHT 84; Tübingen: Mohr Siebeck, 1994), 93–129; Osborn, *Clement of Alexandria* (Cambridge: Cambridge University Press, 2005), 149–53. For the anthropological relevance of πνεῦμα, see Gérard Verbeke, *L'évolution de la doctrine du pneuma, du stoïcisme à s. Augustin: étude philosophique* (Bibliothèque de l'Institut supérieur de philosophie, Université de Louvain; Paris: Desclée de Brouwer/Louvain: Institut supérieur de philosophie, 1945), 429–40.

[6] Ladaria, *Espíritu en Clemente*.

under Antonio Orbe.[7] *Habent sua fata libelli*: Oeyen's study, which was based largely on the *Excerpta, Eclogae*, and *Adumbrationes*, found only marginal appeal, thus confirming the fate of "the other Clement," who, as I have suggested above, remains sorely neglected in scholarship.

With the exception of Osborn—whose thesis that Clement (and Origen) had a "worthy theology of the Holy Spirit" I shall discuss later on—scholars judge that Clement himself had precious little to say about the Holy Spirit.[8] If he did speak about the Spirit, "freely, and with much beauty," it is usually "with reference either to some passage of Holy Scripture or to the experience of Christian life."[9] According to Theodor Zahn and Georg Kretschmar, Clement's all-encompassing Logos-theology completely overshadowed his notion of the Holy Spirit. In W. H. C. Frend's terms, "there would appear to be little real place for Him in his [Clement's] system."[10] Hauschild thinks that Clement "knows the Trinity as an element of Tradition, but does not think in a trinitarian way."[11] More recently, Henning Ziebritzki passed the following verdict:

> Klemens hat explizit den Heiligen Geist weder in seiner individuellen Substanz begriffen, noch seinen metaphysischen Status auch nur ansatzweise bestimmt. Damit fehlen aber auch die entscheidenden Voraussetzungen, die

---

[7] Oeyen, *Eine frühchristliche Engelpneumatologie bei Klemens von Alexandrien* (Erweiterter Separatdruck aus der Internationalen Kirchlichen Zeitschrift; Bern, 1966). The article had been published in *IKZ* 55 (1965): 102–20; 56 (1966): 27–47, as a revision of Oeyen's *Las potencias de Dios en los dos primeros siglos cristianos, I: Acerca de la Pneumatologia de Clemente Alejandrino* (Buenos Aires: s. n., 1963), which was itself based on Oeyen's doctoral dissertation.

[8] A solitary opinion to the contrary is that of Henny Fiskå Hägg, *Clement of Alexandria and the Beginnings of Christian Apophaticism* (Oxford: Oxford University Press, 2006), 201: "Clement even claims co-substantiality for the Spirit, the third person of the Trinity." This, however, is an assertion made without any serious investigation of the subject-matter, in a short paragraph of a book treating of Clement's apophaticism.

[9] Henry Barclay Swete, *The Holy Spirit in the Ancient Church: A Study of Christian Teaching in the Age of the Fathers* (London: Macmillan, 1912), 125. Ladaria concludes his extensive study of Clementine pneumatology by noting that the Holy Spirit seems to possess characteristics of a personal subject only in passages dealing with the inspiration of the Bible, especially of the prophetic writings (Ladaria, *Espíritu en Clemente*, 264).

[10] Frend, *Martyrdom and Persecution in the Early Church: A Study of a Conflict from the Maccabees to Donatus* (Garden City, N.Y.: Doubleday, 1967), 264. Cf. Theodor Zahn, *Forschungen zur Geschichte des neutestamentlichen Kanons und der altkirchlichen Literatur 3: Supplementum Clementinum* (Erlangen: Andreas Deichert, 1884), 98: "[der Geist] den er wie die Alten so oft in seinen Speculationen über das Verhältnis des Logos zu Gott und zur Welt regelmässig übergeht"; Kretschmar, *Trinitätstheologie*, 63: "im allgemeinen denkt er [Klemens] logozentrisch, der Geist tritt zurück."

[11] Hauschild, *Gottes Geist*, 83.

es erlauben würden, im klementinischen Verständnis des Heiligen Geistes den Ansatz zum Begriff einer dritten göttlichen Hypostase zu sehen.[12]

It appears that some important elements are being overlooked in research about Clement's pneumatology. According to his own statements, Clement set out to explain "what the Holy Spirit is" in his treatises "On Prophecy" and "On the Soul."[13] These works were most likely part of the *Hypotyposeis*.[14] It makes sense, therefore, to approach Clement's understanding of the Holy Spirit by focusing mainly on the surviving parts of the *Hypotyposeis*. As I will make clear presently, among these surviving parts we should also count the *Eclogae*, *Excerpta*, and *Adumbrationes*. It is in these writings more than anywhere else that one is likely to learn about Clement's pneumatology. It comes as no surprise, therefore, that the marginalization of these writings in scholarship coincides with the noted disinterest in (and, occasionally, misunderstanding of) Clement's pneumatology.

According particular attention to the *Hypotyposeis*, especially in what concerns Clement's pneumatology, represents a reversal of the scholarly consensus on Clement in general, and on Clement's pneumatology in particular. It is nevertheless not an untrodden path, as I happily follow in the footsteps of Christian Oeyen. His study, however, which I have mentioned earlier, found only marginal reception.

Before moving on to the theological substance of these writings, and a discussion of Clement's pneumatology, it is necessary to explain and justify my use of the *Hypotyposeis* by pointing to their likely role in Clement's corpus of writings. The place of a given text in the Clementine corpus holds crucial importance, because it determines the relative theological

---

[12] Ziebritzki, *Heiliger Geist und Weltseele*, 123.

[13] *Strom.* 5.13.88; cf. *Strom.* 1.24.158; 4.13.93.

[14] André Méhat, *Étude sur les "Stromates" de Clément d'Alexandrie* (Patristica Sorbonensia 7; Paris: Seuil, 1966), 521; Alain Le Boulluec, "Commentaire," in *Clément d'Alexandrie*: Stromate V/2 (SC 279; Paris: Cerf, 1981), 286–88. Le Boulluec states the following: "Le contenu et le style des *Excerpta ex Theodoto* correspondent bien à ce que Clement dit de la section Sur la prophétie. On peut de même supposer que les nombreuses citations de Théodote ou d'autres valentiniens concernant les semences spirituelles ont été amenées par ce problème et que Clément les discutait plus longuement que dans les extraits conservés.... Et Clément répondait probablement, dans les passages que le copiste n'a pas retenus, à la question: qu'est-ce que l'Esprit Saint?" As for *On the Soul*, Le Boulluec concludes: "il est donc tout a fait vraisemblable que les *Eclogae propheticae* contiennent des extraits du Περὶ ψυχῆς annoncés par Clément dans les *Stromates*" (Le Boulluec, "Commentaire" [SC 279:288]).

"weight" of that text. As I explain in what follows, I adopt the conclusions of Pierre Nautin and André Méhat, who demonstrated that the Clement's writings constitute a progressive disclosure of Christian tradition, a mystagogy of sorts, organized according to specific pedagogical principles, and that the *Eclogae, Excerpta,* and *Adumbrationes* represent the pinnacle of Clement's curriculum. Given the received view on Clement, which hardly ever mentions—let alone studies—these writings, I view the following section as an apology of sorts: an apology for "the other Clement."

1. Prolegomena:
The Place of the *Hypotyposeis* in the Clementine Corpus[15]

The current GCS critical edition of Clement of Alexandria's writings includes as fragments from the *Hypotyposeis* several Greek passages—to which a new edition will probably add a new fragment identified by Filippo di Benedetto—and a Latin text entitled *Adumbrationes.* Two other writings, entitled *Excerpta ex Theodoto* and *Eclogae propheticae,* are printed separately from the *Hypotyposeis* fragments.[16] To this day there is no reliable English translation of these writings.[17] The received

---

[15] This section is a revised version of Bucur, "The Place of the *Hypotyposeis* in the Clementine Corpus: An Apology for 'The Other Clement,'" *JECS* 17.3 (2009), forthcoming.

[16] *Clemens Alexandrinus 3: Stromata VII–VIII, Excerpta ex Theodoto, Eclogae propheticae, Quis dives salvetur, Fragmente* (GCS 17; 2nd ed., O. Stählin, L. Früchtel, U. Treu, eds.; Berlin: Akademie-Verlag, 1970); Di Benedetto, "Un nuovo frammento delle Ipotiposi di Clemente Alessandrino," *Sileno* 9 (1983): 75–82. The *Excerpta ex Theodoto* and *Eclogae propheticae* are preserved by a single manuscript, which also contains Clement of Alexandria's *Stromateis*: the 11th century Codex Laurentianus at the Laurentian Library at Florence (Codex Laur. V 3). Another manuscript, Paris. Suppl. Graec. 250, is only a copy of the first, made some time during the sixteenth century. For details see *Clemens Alexandrinus 1: Protrepticus und Paedagogus* (GCS 12; 3rd ed.; O. Stählin, L. Früchtel, U. Treu, eds.; Berlin: Akademie-Verlag, 1972), xxxix–lxi; Carlo Nardi, *Estratti profetici* (Biblioteca patristica 4; Florence: Centro internazionale del libro, 1985), 33–35. The *Adumbrationes* are a Latin translation, commissioned by Cassiodorus (~485–585), of parts of the *Hypotyposeis*—most likely of excerpts from Books 7 and 8 (Christian K. J. von Bunsen, *Analecta Antenicena* [orig. ed. London, 1854; repr. Aalen: Scientia, 1968], 1:164, 325–40; Zahn, *Forschungen* 3:156). The *Adumbrationes* are extant in the ninth-century Codex Laudunensis 96, the thirteenth-century Codex Berolinensis latinus 45, and the sixteenth-century Codex Vaticanus 6154.

[17] The existing English translations are based on a text that differs (at times quite significantly) from the Greek and Latin of the critical editions. The *Adumbrationes*

scholarly view on Clement of Alexandria dismisses these writings as inferior in style, dubious in content, and certainly marginal in importance for Clementine studies. In the words of Ronald E. Heine, "neither [the *Excerpta* nor the *Eclogae*] contribute much to our understanding of Clement."[18] The fragments printed as *Hypotyposeis* are sometimes the subject of historical and philological interest, and some of the passages are of relevance for research on the canon of the New Testament.[19] If the *Excerpta* have generally fared slightly better than the *Eclogae* and *Adumbrationes*, this is due only to scholarly interest in the Valentinian doctrines contained therein.

---

and *Eclogae* are only available in the nineteenth-century translation of William Wilson (*ANF* 2:571–77; 8:39–50); it should be noted that the *Eclogae* appear under the confusing title "Excerpts of Theodotus or, Selections from the Prophetic Scriptures." For the *Excerpta* see Robert P. Casey, ed. and trans., *Excerpta ex Theodoto of Clement of Alexandria* (London: Christophers, 1934). The situation is not much better in continental scholarship. Aside from François Sagnard's 1948 translation of the *Excerpta* (*Clément d'Alexandrie: Extraits de Théodote* [SC 23; Paris: Cerf, 1948]), there exists only Nardi's edition and Italian translation of the *Eclogae*, noted above. An annotated Czech translation of the entire Clementine corpus (including the *Excerpta*, *Eclogae*, and *Adumbrationes*), prepared by Matyáš Havrda, Veronika Černušková, Miroslav Šedina, and Jana Plátová, is currently underway at the University of Olomouc. See also Nardi, *Il battesimo in Clemente Alessandrino: Interpretazione di Eclogae propheticae 1–26* (Rome: Institutum Patristicum "Augustinianum," 1984); idem, "Note di Clemente Alessandrino al Salmo 18: *EP* 51–63," *VH* 6 (1995): 9–42.

[18] Ronald E. Heine, "The Alexandrians," in *The Cambridge History of Early Christian Literature*, ed. F. Young, L. Ayres, and A. Louth (Cambridge; Cambridge University Press, 2004), 121; Hägg, *Beginnings of Christian Apophaticism*, 62. Similarly, Luis Ladaria, the author of the standard work on Clement's pneumatology, thinks that passages from the *Excerpta*, *Adumbrationes* and *Eclogae propheticae* ought to be treated as a secondary witness—"a brief appendix"—to Clement's thought (Ladaria, *El Espíritu en Clemente Alejandrino: Estudio teológico antropológico* [Madrid: UPCM, 1980], 256).

[19] Helmut Merkel, "Clemens Alexandrinus über die Reihenfolge der Evangelien," *ETL* 60 (1984): 382–385; Dénes Farkasfalvy, "The Presbyters' Witness on the Order of the Gospels as Reported by Clement of Alexandria," *CBQ* 54 (1992): 260–270; Stephen C. Carlson, "Clement of Alexandria on the Order of the Gospels," *NTS* 47 (2001): 118–125; Harry A. Echle, "The Baptism of the Apostles: A Fragment of Clement of Alexandria's Lost Work *Hypotyposeis* in the *Pratum Spirituale* of John Moschus," *TR* 3 (1945): 365–68; Utto Riedinger, "Neue Hypotyposenfragmente bei Ps.-Caesarius und Isidor von Pelusium," *ZNW* (1960): 154–96; "Eine Paraphrase des Engel-Traktates von Klemens von Alexandreia in den Erotapokriseis des Pseudo-Kaisarios?," *ZKG* 73 (1962): 253–71; Di Benedetto, "Un nuovo frammento delle *Ipotiposi*"; Colin Duckworth and Eric Osborn, "Clement of Alexandria's Hypotyposeis: A French Eighteenth-Century Sighting," *JTS* n.s. 36 (1985): 67–83; Osborn, "Clement's *Hypotyposeis*: Macarius Revisited," *SecCent* 10 (1990): 233–35; Jana Plátová, "Bemerkungen zu den Hypotyposen-Fragmenten des Clemens Alexandrinus," *StPatr* (forthcoming; I am grateful to the author for sharing with me the manuscript of this study).

To a considerable extent, the received view reflects the victory of one strand of nineteenth-century German scholarship over another. These two strands can be identified, roughly, with Adolf Harnack and Otto Stählin, on the one hand, and Christian K. J. von Bunsen and Theodor Zahn, on the other. Bunsen argued that the *Eclogae*, *Excerpta*, and *Adumbrationes* were in fact surviving portions of the *Hypotyposeis*.[20] B. F. Westcott accepted his judgment. Zahn, however, saw the *Eclogae* and *Excerpta* as distinct from the *Hypotyposeis*, namely as surviving portions of *Strom.* 8, and argued that the current state of the texts could only be explained as the result of "Verstümmelung und Abkürzung" undertaken by a later "epitomator."[21]

Harnack rejected these views. Acknowledging the contribution of two doctoral dissertations,[22] and guided by his firm conviction that Clement must have evolved from more "heretical" to more "orthodox" theological positions, Harnack concluded that the *Hypotyposeis* were composed by the young Clement, who later came to develop a more orthodox theology; that they were not related to the so-called *Strom.* 8, *Excerpta*, and *Eclogae*; that the latter were not excerpts from a book—whether *Strom.* 8 (Zahn) or *Hypotyposeis* (Bunsen)—but excerpts made in view of a book, whose project, however, was interrupted by the Alexandrian's death; and that it was Clement's disciples who started circulating these study notes.[23] The Arnim–Ruben–Harnack hypothesis was endorsed by Stählin, in the introduction to his critical edition of Clement, and became established as the accepted view.[24] The victory of this strand of Clementine scholarship is reflected in the fact that the works of Clement that are edited and translated, researched in books, articles, and dissertations, and taught to students—we might well say "the canonical Clement"—are the *Protreptikos*, *Paidagogos*, and *Stromateis*, rather than that the *Excerpta*, *Eclogae*, and *Adumbrationes*.

---

[20] Christian K. J. Bunsen, *Analecta Antenicena* 1:159, 163–65, 325–40.

[21] B. F. Westcott, "Clement of Alexandria," in *A Dictionary of Christian Biography, Literature, Sects, and Doctrines*, ed. W. Smith and H. Ware (London: Murray, 1877), 1:559–64; Zahn, *Forschungen* 3:117–30; for the "epitomator" thesis, see 118.

[22] Paul Ruben, "Clementis Alexandrini Excerpta ex Theodoto" (Ph.D. diss. University of Bonn; Leipzig: Teubner, 1892); Hans Friedrich August von Arnim, "De octavo Clementis Stromateorum libro" (Ph.D. diss. University of Rostock; Rostock: Adler, 1894). Both of these works are cited approvingly in Harnack, *Geschichte der altchristlichen Literatur bis Eusebius* II/2 (2nd rev. ed.; Hinrichs: Leipzig, 1904), 17–18.

[23] Harnack, *Geschichte der altchristlichen Literatur* II/2:18–20.

[24] Stählin, ed., *Clemens Alexandrinus 1* (GCS 12; Hinrichs: Leipzig, 1905), xlii. For Anglophone scholarship, see Casey, "Introduction," in *Excerpta ex Theodoto*, 4, 14.

The insights of Bunsen and Zahn were vindicated, however. Wilhelm Bousset first conjectured that the fragments were the work of the old Clement, who, once he had left Alexandria, felt free to indulge in the "colorful" speculations he had once heard as a student of Pantaenus, for which he possessed lecture notes.[25] This view was followed by Lebreton and deemed "attractive" by H. E. W. Turner.[26] An important contribution was made in 1966, when André Méhat concluded his study of the sophisticated and purposeful arrangement of the *Stromateis* by stating that the *Hypotyposeis* would have naturally followed after the *Stromateis* and represented the pinnacle of Clement's exposition of doctrine.[27] The major breakthrough came a few years later, with Pierre Nautin's analysis of the 11th century Codex Laurentianus (Codex Laur. V 3 = L), the only manuscript containing the *Stromateis, Excerpta*, and *Eclogae*.[28] Nautin argues that the writings that follow *Strom. 7*—"*Strom.* 8," *Excerpta*, and *Eclogae*—represent a selection *made by the scribe himself* once he realized that the codex would not suffice for the entire text of the *Stromateis* and *Hypotyposeis*.[29] Since, as he notes, the Tura Codex excerpts from Origen's *Against Celsus*, the *Commentary on Romans*, and the *Homily on the Witch of Endor* offer precedent for such scribal practices, this thesis stands on solid ground.[30] In a way, Nautin's contribution

---

[25] Bousset, *Jüdisch-christlicher Schulbetrieb in Alexandria und Rom: Literarische Untersuchungen zu Philo und Clemens von Alexandria, Justin und Irenäus* (Göttingen: Vandenhoeck & Ruprecht, 1915), 248–63. Bousset (*Jüdisch-christlicher Schulbetrieb*, 268) offers the following description of the type of speculations Clement endulged in: "Wir schauen hier in eine bunte, gefährliche, von kirchlicher Kontrolle noch ganz unberührte Gesamtauffassung hinein. Eschatologische Phantasien vom Aufstieg und der Entwicklung der Seele nach dem Tode stehen im Mittelpunkt dieser Gedankenwelt. Damit verbindet sich die Annahme von Stufen innherhalb der Geisterwelt.... Christus erscheint als das Haupt und die Krönung dieser ganzen mannigfachen und wunderbaren Welt." For the hypothesis of lecture notes, see Bousset, *Jüdisch-christlicher Schulbetrieb*, 155–271, esp. 198–204.

[26] Lebreton, "Le désaccord entre la foi populaire et la théologie savante dans l'Église chrétienne du IIe. siècle," *RHE* 19 (1923): 496; Turner, *Pattern of Christian Truth*, 398.

[27] André Méhat, *Étude sur les "Stromates" de Clément d'Alexandrie* (Patristica Sorbonensia 7; Paris: Seuil, 1966), 517–22, 530–33.

[28] Nautin, "La fin des *Stromates* et les *Hypotyposes* de Clément d'Alexandrie," *VS* 30 (1976): 268–302.

[29] Nautin, "La fin des *Stromates*," 269–82.

[30] "[C]e qui est bien attesté à l'époque ancienne, notamment par le papyrus de Toura, c'est que parfois des copistes, renonçant à transcrire intégralement le texte de leur modèle, n'en ont reproduit que des extraits. Si nous cherchons une explication qui ne soit pas oeuvre de pure imagination, mai qui repose sur des exemples précis fournis par l'histoire des textes, c'est celle-là et nulle autre que nous devenons retenir" (Nautin, "La fin des *Stromates*," 282).

represents a return to and vindication of the views about the *Hypo-typoseis* proposed much earlier by Bunsen, and of the "epitomator" hypothesis set forth by Zahn.

There are, of course, scholars who have not been convinced by Nautin's hypothesis.[31] It is significant, however, that these critics dismiss Nautin's proposal as simply a "personal theory" (Annewies van den Hoek), and a "perplexing" one at that (Nardi), while focusing only on his discussion of the Clementine program, without any objection to the first half of his study, which discusses the state of the manuscript, weighs various proposals to explain the situation, and draws the comparison with the Tura Codex II of Origen.

Today Nautin's conclusions are accepted by Alain le Boulluec, the eminent Clement scholar and author of the edition, translation, and extensive commentary of Clement's fifth and seventh *Stromateis* in *Sources chrétiennes*, and by Patrick Descourtieux, to whom we owe the edition and translation of the sixth of the *Stromateis* in the same series.[32]

Nevertheless, to speak, as do Méhat and Nautin, of Clement's *Hypotyposeis* as the pinnacle of a Clementine corpus, organized according to a hierarchic architecture, and offering a progressive disclosure of Christian tradition organized according to specific pedagogical principles—a mystagogy of sorts—is begging the question. Is there a Clementine "master plan" to begin with? If there is, did Clement proceed to write according to such a plan? If he did, what place did the author assign to his various writings?[33]

---

[31] For instance, the noted Clement scholar Annewies van den Hoek, who also edited *Strom.* 4 for *Sources Chrétiennes*, considers it to be the latest in a series of "personal theories" (Annewies van den Hoek, "Introduction," in *Clément d'Alexandrie: Stromate IV* [SC 463; Paris: Cerf, 2001], 13 and n. 7). Similarly Nardi, *Estratti profetici*, 11.

[32] Le Boulluec, "Commentaire" (SC 279: 286–88); idem, *Clément d'Alexandrie: Stromate VII* (SC 428; Paris: Cerf, 1997), 7 n. 1; 11 n. 6; 330 n. 2; idem, "Extraits d'oeuvres de Clément d'Alexandrie: la transmission et le sens de leur titres," in *Titres et articulations du texte dans les oeuvres antiques*. Actes du colloque international de Chantilly 13–15 décembre 1994 (ed. J.-C. Fredouille et al.; Paris: Institut d'Études Augustiniennes, 1997), 287–300, esp. 289, 292, 296, 300; idem, "Pour qui, pourquoi, comment? Les 'Stromates' de Clément d'Alexandrie," in *Entrer en matière: Les prologues* (ed. J.-D. Dubois and B. Roussel; Paris: Cerf, 1998), 23–36, esp. 24 n. 10; Patrick Descourtieux, *Clément d'Alexandrie: Stromate VI* (SC 446; Paris: Cerf, 1999), 399 n. 4.

[33] The problem is similar to the debates among scholars of the Ps.-Areopagitic Corpus. Dionysius also mentions a number of treatises, none of which were ever available to his readers. Scholars have the option of treating them either as a literary fiction, or as unfulfilled intentions, or as lost elements of a grand theological complex. For the latter option, see Hans Urs von Balthasar, *Herrlichkeit: Eine theologische Ästhetik*, vol. 2: *Fächer der Stile* (Einsiedeln: Johannes Verlag, 1962), 157–67.

Scholars do not agree on this subject. Eugène de Faye faults Clement precisely for his alleged inability to organize his writing according to a plan.[34] At the other end of the spectrum, some scholars have proposed elaborate schemes describing not only Clement's actual writings, but also writings that he would have—one is tempted to say "should have"—composed.[35] This approach elicited the reaction of Walther Völker (*contra* Johannes Munck) and Annewies van den Hoek (*contra* Nautin), who both warned against over-interpreting Clement's repeated introductory announcements.[36]

Protreptikos—Paidagogos—Didaskalos

For Clement, there is an organic relation between the oral tradition of the "elders" and his own writing, and more generally, between teaching and writing.[37] As Osborn notes, "[t]he *Stromateis* are not merely

---

[34] De Faye, *Clément d'Alexandrie: étude sur les rapports du christianisme et de la philosophie grecque au IIe siècle* (Paris: Leroux, 1898), 113: "L'idée ne lui vient pas, avant d'écrire, d'analyser sa pensée, d'en ordonner toutes les parties, d'en disposer avec soin les éléments, en un mot de dresser un plan mûri et logique...Ce qui manque à cet ouvrage, ce n'est pas la logique de la pensée; c'est le talent d'en disposer en bon ordre les développements...." This harsh judgment concerns, however, only the *Stromateis*.

[35] Such are the proposals of Carl Heussi ("Die Stromateis des Clemens Alexandrinus und ihr Verhältnis zum Protreptikos und Pädagogos," *ZWT* 45 [1902]: 465–512): *Strom. I–III* was composed before the *Protreptikos*, and followed by the trilogy *Protreptikos—Paidagogos—Strom. IV–VIII*; Johannes Munck (*Untersuchungen über Klemens von Alexandria* [Stuttgart: Kohlhammer, 1933], 9–126, esp. 98, 108–109, 111, 121, 125–26): two trilogies— *Protreptikos—Paidagogos— Didaskalos* and *Strom. I–III—Strom. IV–VIII—Physiologia*, of which Clement would not have finished the *Didaskalos* and *Physiologia*; Giuseppe Lazzati (*Introduzione allo studio di Clemente Alessandrino* [Milan: Vita e pensiero, 1939]): the trilogy *Protreptikos—Paidagogos—Quis Dives*, destined for the exoteric audience, and *Stromateis* and *Hypotyposeis* for the esoteric circle.

[36] According to Völker (*Der wahre Gnostiker nach Clemens Alexandrinus* [TU 57; Berlin: Akademie-Verlag, 1952], 29, 30 n. 3), Munck's hypothesis "leidet...an dem Grundfehler, daß sie Clemens viel zu einheitlich auffaßt, alle Anspielungen und Hinweise ernst nimmt und deshalb ein förmliches System von Plänen aufbaut...Hatte Clemens von seinen Plänen eine so genaue Vorstellung?...Wird damit nicht alles künstlich systematisiert?" Van den Hoek notes ("Introduction," in *Clément d'Alexandrie: Stromate IV*, 13–15) the following: "Le contraste entre les préambules et le corps de l'ouvrage organisé de façon plutot lâche a été cause de confusion. On a utilisé ces exordes pour conforter des théories personnelles sur la cohésion des oeuvres de Clément prises comme un tout." The latest of such hypotheses, as indicated in a footnote (*Clément d'Alexandrie: Stromate IV*, 13 n. 7), is that of Nautin.

[37] *Ecl.* 27.1–7: "Now, the elders would not write, because they did not want to undermine their preoccupation with the teaching of the tradition by another, namely writing (it) down; nor did they want to expend on writing the time dedicated to pondering what was to be said. But, convinced perhaps that getting the composition right, and the substance of the teaching are entirely separate matters, they deferred to

notes which teach. They are also notes which have taught.... The *Stro-mateis* are a record of teaching."[38] Since Clement understood his oral instruction as proceeding in accordance with principles of intellectual and spiritual formation, it is quite likely that he would organize—or at least *intend* to organize—his own writing on the same principle of progressive initiation.[39] The following two passages occur at the beginning and the end of Clement's *Paidagogos*:

> Eagerly desiring, then, to render us perfect by a salvific gradation, the Logos, entirely a lover of mankind, makes use of a beautiful dispensation (τῇ καλῇ...οἰκονομίᾳ) suited for efficacious discipline: first exhorting, then training, finally teaching [προτρέπων...παιδαγωγῶν...ἐκδιδάσκων];
>
> Many things are spoken in enigmas, many in parables...However, it does not behoove me to teach about these things further, says the Instructor [παιδαγωγός]. But we need a Teacher [διδασκάλου] for the interpretation of those sacred words, to whom we must direct our steps. And now, in truth, it is time for me to cease from my pedagogy [παιδαγωγίας], and for you to listen to the Teacher [διδασκάλου].[40]

---

others naturally endowed (as writers)....but that which will be repeatedly consulted by those who have access to it [i.e., the book] is worth even the utmost effort, and is, as it were, the written confirmation of the instruction and of the voice so transmitted to (our) descendents by means of the (written) composition. Speaking in writing, the elders' "circulating deposit" uses the writer for the purpose of a transmission that leads to the salvation of those who are to read. So, just like a magnet, which repels all substance and only attracts iron, on account of affinity, books also attract only those who are capable of understanding them, even though there are many who engage them....As for jealousy—far be it from the Gnostic! This is actually why he seeks (to determine) whether it be worse to give to the unworthy or not to hand down to the worthy; and out of (so) much love he runs the risk of sharing (knowledge) not only with the person fit (for such teaching), but—as it sometimes happens—also with some unworthy person that entreats him slickly."

[38] Osborn, "Teaching and Writing in the First Chapter of the Stromateis of Clement of Alexandria," *JTS* n.s. 10 (1959): 343.

[39] See in this respect Judith Kovacs, "Divine Pedagogy and the Gnostic Teacher According to Clement of Alexandria," *JECS* 9 (2001): 3–25. This point was also emphasized by De Faye, who notes about Clement's planned trilogy: "Ce plan lui a été exclusivement imposé par la forme de son enseignement catéchétique et par la conception toute pédagogique de la tâche qu'il s'est donnée" (De Faye, *Clément d'Alexandrie*, 53). Cf. Christoph Riedweg, *Mysterienterminologie bei Platon, Philon und Klemens von Alexandrien* (UaLG 26; Berlin/New York: de Gruyter, 1986), 138–39: "Bereits die von Klemens ursprünglich intendierte Werktrilogie *Protreptikos—Paidagogos—Didaskal(ik)os* belegt anschaulich, daß für ihn das Konzept eines strukturiert aufsteigenden religiösen Erkenntnisprozesses sehr zentral ist."

[40] *Paed.* 1.1.3; 3.12.97.

Clement describes three stages: *exhortation* (which leads to baptism), continued by ethical *training*, and subsequent doctrinal *instruction*. The text of the *Paidagogos* is presented as a continuation of the *Protreptikos*, and explicitly mentions "listening to the *didaskalos*" as the next stage in the curriculum. But does this necessarily refer to written work?

This question was raised forcefully by Friedrich Quatember, who noted that Clement actually speaks *of the divine Logos* as exhorting, then training, finally teaching, and not about a human teacher. According to Quatember, when Clement points the reader to a treatise he has already composed, or announces that he will expand on a certain problem in the course of a later writing, his references tend to be explicit: "our treatise On Marriage," "our writing On the Resurrection," "this we shall show at another place," and so forth. By contrast, Clement never mentions a writing entitled *Didaskalos*.[41] All of this suggests that the search for *Didaskalos* as part of a curriculum of writings is utterly misguided: Clement refers to "the objective plan of salvation (*Heilsplan*) of the personal Logos," and would never have thought of committing to writing the doctrines that a *Didaskalos* would have required.[42] Quatember's arguments, coming at a moment of general dissatisfaction with the multitude of hypotheses regarding Clement's literary plans, struck the scholarly community as fresh and worthy of serious consideration.[43]

The fact remains, however, that there is an intimate link between the activity of the Logos and that of the Christian teacher.[44] The work of the Logos as προτρέπων and παιδαγωγῶν finds its counterpart in Clement's *Logos Protreptikos* and *Logos Paidagogos*. The question is to determine what corresponds to the divine Logos as ἐκδιδάσκων. It is clear that Clement derives the sequence of catechetical activity from the οἰκονομία of the divine Logos. In the words of Kovacs,

---

[41] Quatember, *Die christliche Lebenshaltung des Klemens nach seinem Pädagogus* (Vienna: Herder, 1946), 34, 36.

[42] Quatember, *Christliche Lebenshaltung*, 38, 41.

[43] E.g., Claude Mondésert, "Introduction," in *Clément d'Alexandrie: Stromate I* (SC 30; Paris: Cerf, 1951), 20; Walter H. Wagner, "Another Look at the Literary Problem in Clement of Alexandria's Major Writings," *CH* 37 (1968): 253; Osborn, *Clement*, 6.

[44] Similarly Ulrich Neymeyr, *Die christlichen Lehrer im zweiten Jahrhundert: Ihre Lehrtätigkeit, ihr Selbstverständnis und ihre Geschichte* (VCSup 4; Leiden: Brill, 1989), 64–65.

[t]he Gnostic teacher follows the Logos in thoughtfully arranging the order of the curriculum, knowing that certain things must be learned before others, just as in secular education the ἐγκύκλια need to be mastered before the student is ready for rhetoric and philosophy. The Logos has provided a model for this…[45]

The unity and coherence of the curriculum is given by the fact that it is the same Logos who exhorts, trains, and teaches. The variety of levels, on the other hand, is a natural result of the different levels occupied by the addressees of the Logos. Progression from one level to the next is a matter of biblical exegesis. As the passage discussed above (*Paed.* 3.12.97) states explicitly: "we need a διδάσκαλος for the interpretation [εἰς τὴν ἐξήγησιν] of those sacred words." This can be exemplified with another passage from the *Paidagogos*. At one point, while pondering whether Christians should crown themselves with flowers, Clement ventures into more mystical territory (adding what he calls "a mystic meaning"), and connects the manifestation of the Logos in the burning bush—"the bush is a thorny plant," he explains—with the crown of thorns worn by the incarnate Logos. He then explains this excursus of mystical exegesis in the following way: "I have departed from the *paedagogic* manner of speech, introducing the *didaskalic* one. I return accordingly to my subject."[46]

The *Protreptikos—Paidagogos—Didaskalos* sequence is problematic, however, insofar as it is not clear which of Clement's writings correspond to the *Didaskalos*. This issue "has vexed scholars for almost a century."[47] The traditional scholarly view was to consider the *Didaskalos* as a written document, and to identify it with the *Stromateis*.[48] The *Didaskalos–Stromateis* identification was challenged vigorously in 1898 by De Faye, who observed that the *Stromateis* kept deferring the

---

[45] Kovacs, "Divine Pedagogy," 7. The Gnostic mimics the pedagogical methods of the Logos. In the words of Kovacs ("Divine Pedagogy," 17, 25), "[h]e organizes the curriculum in an orderly way, so as to facilitate the upward progress of his students"; he "follows the Logos in addressing a wide variety of students and in adapting his teaching to the capabilities and the readiness of each one. Like the divine teacher he designs an orderly progression through the sacred curriculum…In order to protect his less mature students, he mimics the concealment practiced by the Logos." Similarly Hägg, *Clement of Alexandria and the Beginnings of Christian Apophaticism*, 141, 143.

[46] *Paed.* 2.8.76.

[47] The most complete and substantive expositions of the *Didaskalos* debate is Wagner's study "Literary Problem." See also Mondésert, "Introduction," 11–22; Osborn, *Clement*, 5–15; "One Hundred Years of Books on Clement," *VC* 60 (2006): 367–88. The quotation is from Wagner, "Another Look," 251.

[48] Zahn, *Supplementum Clementinum*, 108–14.

exposition of specific doctrines (e.g., creation of the world, treatise on the soul, on prophecy, on the resurrection, on the Holy Spirit), and concluded that it was much rather a *preparatory* work for the *Didaskalos*.[49] The same argument was also made by Gustave Bardy, Salvatore Lilla, and, with important modifications, André Méhat.[50] Other scholars (e.g., Heussi *contra* De Faye) have replied that the *Stromateis* are replete with doctrine, and thus to be identified with the *Didaskalos*.[51] This position is championed by Osborn, who claims that today "[i]t has become increasingly easy to believe that the *Stromateis* are the *Didascalus*." His argument is essentially the following:

> In view of...the explicit use of διδάσκαλος and διδάσκαλία it is right to regard the argument as the justification of teaching through writing.... There is no point whatever in filling the first chapter of the *Stromateis* with intricate argument in favour of written teaching if the *Stromateis* are not going to teach.[52]

The doctrinal exposition of the *Stromateis* is, however, presented "in a literary form appropriate to Clement's understanding of teaching"—namely by means of Clement's special technique of simultaneous disclosure and concealment.[53] E. L. Fortin mentions elliptical and allusive speech, judicious selection of words and symbols, apparent

---

[49] De Faye, *Clément d'Alexandrie*, 81–83. He characterizes the *Stromateis* as a parenthesis between *Paidagogos* and *Didaskalos*, a protracted introduction to the latter, designed to justify his intended use of philosophy in the *Didaskalos*, and to provide a higher level of ethics, more suitable to advanced students than that of the *Paidagogos*. Although Clement had initially set out to write a single volume (*Strom.* 4.1.1), the *Stromateis* soon grew out of proportion, turning into an amorphous body because of the writer's inability to channel the flow of his ideas according to a definite plan (De Faye, *Clément d'Alexandrie*, 106, 108, 113–14). Cf. Méhat, *Étude* 522: "L'idée de cette ouvrage a dû lui venire progressivement à mesure que les Stromates prenaient une ampleur qu'il n'avait pas prévue au départ."

[50] According to Gustave Bardy (*Clément d'Alexandrie* [Paris: Gabalda, 1926], 22), the *Didaskalos* "had to be something else entirely. Would one not have found precisely those explanations on the resurrection, on prophecy, on the soul, on birth, on the devil, on prayer, on the origin of the world, which are promised in various passages of the *Stromateis*...and which one encounters nowhere?" See also Lilla, *Clement of Alexandria: A Study in Christian Platonism and Gnosticism* (Oxford: Oxford University Press, 1971), 189 n. 4. According to Méhat, the *Stromateis* contain the gnosis in the form of veiled and dispersed allusions (*Étude*, 516); it is a work of Gnostic education, which Clement insistently presents as "un livre de *préparation à* la gnose" (*Étude*, 491; emphasis added).

[51] Heussi, "Die Stromateis des Clemens Alexandrinus," 487–90.

[52] Osborn, *Clement*, 15 n. 45; Idem, "Teaching and Writing," 342.

[53] Osborn, "Teaching and Writing," 343.

contradictions, deliberate omissions, and explains that such techniques were designed to make it possible that "the content of the oral teaching or tradition should find its way into the written text, but in such a way that its presence will be missed by the casual or unprepared reader and sniffed, as it were, by the student who has somehow been made aware of the deeper issues (*Strom.* 1.1.15)."[54] These techniques are not accidental; they grow out of Clement's understanding of the pedagogical work of the Logos:

> Clement's practice of concealment is closely connected to his idea of the sacred *oikonomia*, the orderly lesson plan of the divine pedagogy... Clement sees his own practice of concealment as an imitation of the parabolic, enigmatic character of Scripture (6.15.115.5–6, 124.4–125.3, 127.5, 131.3–132.5).[55]

It should be noted, however, that the "disclosure" aspect was equally important. As Méhat observes, the *Stromateis* were destined not only to readers who were already initiated but also—in fact, chiefly—to readers who were in the course of initiation.[56]

The debate over the relation between the *Didaskalos* and the *Stromateis* left out of sight those works that constitute, in De Faye's formulation, "the torment of scholars": the *Eclogae*, the *Excerpta*, and the *Adumbrationes*. Naturally, those scholars who see the *Didaskalos* realized in the *Stromateis* have almost nothing to say about the place of the *Hypotyposeis* in the Clementine corpus. Kovacs, for instance, suggests that Clement avoided writing "a *Didaskalos* that was to contain the highest level of Christian teaching," because "with written works, it is impossible for the teacher to control his audience, or to make a careful selection of the level of teaching appropriate for each student"; he wrote the *Stromateis* instead because their literary genre "allowed him to reveal and conceal at the same time."[57] In this case, whatever doctrine Clement

---

[54] Fortin, "Clement of Alexandria and the Esoteric Tradition," *StPatr* 9 (1966)/TU 94: 41–56.

[55] Kovacs, "Divine Pedagogy," 20, 23. Similarly Hägg, *Beginnings of Christian Apophaticism*, 140–50.

[56] Méhat, *Étude*, 491.

[57] Kovacs, "Divine Pedagogy," 24. Cf. also Hägg, *Clement of Alexandria and the Beginnings of Christian Apophaticism*, 142, 144. A similar view was formulated earlier by Richard B. Tollinton, *Clement of Alexandria: A Study in Christian Liberalism* (2 vols.; London: Williams and Norgate, 1914), 1:14: "the fact that Clement chose to write a series of *Stromateis* in the place of the projected 'Master' must in the main be

was prepared to communicate is found in the *Stromateis*, and there is obviously no room for any consideration of the *Hypotyposeis*. Even more interesting is the case of Osborn, one of the undisputed authorities in the field, whose two monographs preface and bring to a close half a century's worth of research on the Alexandrian. Osborn also spent a great amount of time and energy in an attempt to locate a copy of the *Hypotyposeis* in the Egyptian "St. Macarius" monastery. He knows well "how important they [the *Hypotyposeis*] are and why they deserve our attention": "they provide a unique source for early Christian thought," and especially "examples of the use of scripture in a distinctive way."[58] Yet Osborn, whose interest has always been to find the coherence of Clement's thought, simply does not take into account the *Hypotyposeis*.[59] And even though he insists on the eminently exegetical method of the *Hypotyposeis*, and points out that Clement's secret tradition "was a way of interpreting Scripture, not an additional document," he never discusses the possible relevance of the *Hypotyposeis* for shedding light on the content of Clement's secret tradition.[60]

On the contrary, scholars who deny the identity of *Stromateis* and *Didaskalos* leave open the possibility that the lost *Hypotyposeis* should present a better candidate. Méhat, for instance, concluded that the *Eclogae* and *Excerpta* represent "notes by Clement containing elements of logic and *physics*," thus constituting "indispensable complements" for understanding the Alexandrian's gnosis in the *Stromateis*, and that the latter would have been followed naturally by the *Hypotyposeis*.[61]

The reigning scholarly assumption has been that the *Eclogae* and *Excerpta* are "preparatory notes" or "files" that Clement intended to use for the composition of other works, perhaps the *Didaskalos*.[62] This

---

set down to the character of his public.... In a word, the Stromateis are and yet are not the projected 'Master.' In writing them Clement realised, in part, his purpose of higher teaching."

[58] Duckworth and Osborn, "Eighteenth-Century Sighting," 83; Osborn, "Macarius Revisited," 235.

[59] Osborn, *Clement*, 6–7, 14–15.

[60] Duckworth and Osborn, "French Eighteenth-Century Sighting," 76. Similarly Hägg, *Beginnings of Christian Apophaticism*, 139.

[61] Méhat, *Étude*, 516–17 ("La 'physique' des Stromates"), 517–22 ("La suite des Stromates: les *Hypotyposes*"). Méhat does not clarify the relation between "Strom. 8," *Excerpta*, *Eclogae*, and *Hypotyposeis*, but suggests (*Étude*, 54) that *Strom.* 7 may have been composed in 203, the *Eclogae* in 204, and the *Hypotyposeis* around 204–210.

[62] Paul Collomp, "Une source de Clément d'Alexandrie et des Homélies Pseudo-Clémentines," *RPh* 37 (1913): 20; De Faye, *Clément d'Alexandrie*, 84–85 (following older

assumption has been laid to rest by Nautin. As I mentioned earlier, Nautin's "erudite analysis" and "certain" conclusions have been endorsed more recently by Le Boulluec.[63] Some recent scholars remain, however, strangely unaware of Nautin's groundbreaking contribution.[64]

Ethics—Physics—Epoptics

At the time of Clement, philosophy was understood, on the one hand, as a corpus consisting of various "parts"—for Plato, *ethics, physics,* and *dialectics* (understood as science of the Forms); for Aristotle, *ethics, physics,* and *theology* or *first philosophy*; or, since Plutarch, *ethics, physics,* and *epoptics*—and, on the other hand, as a transformative pedagogy following a curriculum designed to guide the student along a path of ethical, intellectual, and spiritual formation.[65] This second aspect became increasingly prominent after the first century C.E., so that Clement writes "in an environment that has come to definitively identify philosophy with a spiritual exercise."[66]

Porphyry proceeds to arrange Plotinus' *Enneads* according to this tripartite scheme, and is most likely the source for Calcidius' notion that the *Timaeus* represents Plato's *physics,* and the *Parmenides* his *epoptics*.[67] Perhaps more relevant is the case of Origen, who in the prologue to his commentary on the Song of Songs states that the Solomonic writings (Proverbs, Ecclesiastes, and the Song of Songs) illustrate the

---

proposals); Tollinton, *Christian Liberalism,* 202–3; Völker, *Der wahre Gnostiker,* 351; Méhat, *Étude,* 517. I mentioned earlier Bousset's hypothesis, now largely dismissed, of class notes taken by Clement during his own instruction under Pantaenus.

[63] Le Boulluec, "Extraits," 289, 292, 296, 300; "Pour qui, pourquoi, comment?," 24 n. 10.

[64] Heine, "The Alexandrians," 117–21; Neymeyr, *Die christlichen Lehrer,* 84; Rüdiger Feulner, *Clemens von Alexandrien: sein Leben, Werk und philosophisch-theologisches Denken* (Frankfurt am Main/New York: Peter Lang, 2006), 33–36; Hägg, *Beginnings of Christian Apophaticism,* 61, 198. See also Harnack, Harnack, *Geschichte der altchristlichen Literatur* II/2:18. It is noteworthy that even Uwe Swarat's thorough study of Zahn and his contribution to scholarship seems convinced that the Arnim–Ruben–Harnack thesis has definitively triumphed over Zahn's proposal (Swarat, *Alte Kirche und Neues Testament: Theodor Zahn als Patristiker* [Wuppertal: Brockhaus, 1991], 201).

[65] According to Pierre Hadot ("Les divisions des parties de la philosophie dans l'Antiquité," *MH* 36 [1979]: 219–20), "[c]e schéma fondamental: *éthique, physique, époptique,* sera le noyau du programme des études philosophiques de la fin du Ier siècle ap. J.-C. jusqu'à la fin de l'Antiquité." Similarly Laura Rizzerio, *Clemente di Alessandria e la "φυσιολογία veramente gnostica": saggio sulle origini e le implicazioni di un'epistemologia e di un'ontologia "cristiane"* (RTAMSup 6; Leuven: Peeters, 1996), 150–61.

[66] Rizzerio, *φυσιολογία,* 159.

[67] Hadot, "Les divisions," 219.

ethics—physics—epoptics sequence, and argues that the Song of Song
is to be classified in the latter category.[68] In fact, Origen's "mystagogical curriculum" of biblical studies applies the *ethics—physics—epoptics*
sequence both to the Old Testament as a whole (Law—Prophets—beginning of Genesis, Ezekiel's throne-vision, Song of Songs) and to the New
Testament (Matthew and Luke—Mark—John).[69]

Clement of Alexandria is also familiar with the *ethics—physics—epoptics* scheme. At the very end of *Strom.* 6 (*Strom.* 6.18.168), for instance,
Clement looks back on the *ethical* description of the Gnostic ("the
greatness and beauty of his character [ἤθους]"), and announces that
he will later advance to a new level of the description:

> Καθάπερ οὖν ἀνδριάντα ἀποπλασάμενοι τοῦ γνωστικοῦ, ἤδη μὲν
> ἐπεδείξαμεν, οἷός ἐστι, μέγεθός τε καὶ κάλλος ἤθους αὐτοῦ ὡς ἐν
> ὑπογραφῇ δηλώσαντες· ὁποῖος γὰρ κατὰ τὴν θεωρίαν ἐν τοῖς φυσικοῖς
> μετὰ ταῦτα δηλωθήσεται ἐπὰν περὶ γενέσεως κόσμου διαλαμβάνειν
> ἀρξώμεθα.

The standard reading of this text is the following:

> Having as it were fashioned a statue of the Gnostic, we have so far indi-
> cated *how* he is by showing as in a sketch the greatness and beauty of
> his *ethos; what* he is with respect to natural contemplation (θεωρίαν ἐν
> τοῖς φυσικοῖς) will be shown presently, when we begin to treat of the
> making of the world.

---

[68] Origen, *Comm. Cant. prol.* 3.1, 4 (SC 375:128, 130): *Generales disciplinae quibus
ad rerum scientiam pervenitur tres sunt, quas Graeci ethicam, physicam, epopticen
appellarunt....Haec ergo, ut mihi videtur, sapientes quique Graecorum sumpta a
Solomone...tamquam propria inventa protulerunt.* The English translations of both
R. P. Lawson (*Origen: The Song of Songs, Commentary and Homilies* [ACW 26; New York:
Newman, 1956]) and Rowan A. Greer (*Origen* [CWS 11; New York: Paulist, 1979])
mention "enoptics," because they are based on the older GCS edition, which chose
to follow a manuscript that reads *ethicam, physicam, enopticen.* For the correction of
enopticen into *epopticen,* on both linguistic and doctrinal grounds, see J. Kirchmeyer,
"Origène, Commentaire sur le Cantique, prol. (GCS Origenes 8, Baehrens, p. 75, ligne
8)," *StPatr 10* (1970)/TU 107: 230–35.
[69] See in this respect, Ilsetraut Hadot, "Les introductions aux commentaries exégétiques chez les auteurs néoplatoniciens et les auteurs chrétiens," in *Les règles de
l'interprétation* (ed. Michel Tardieu; Paris: Cerf, 1987), 99–119, esp. 115–19. A more
detailed exposition is offered by Michael-Vlad Niculescu, "Spiritual Leavening: The
Communication and Reception of the Good News in Origen's Biblical Exegesis and
Transformative Pedagogy," *JECS* 15 (2007): 447–81; idem, *The Spell of the Logos: Origen's
Exegetic Pedagogy in the Contemporary Debate Regarding Logocentrism* (Piscataway,
NJ: Gorgias, 2009). I am grateful to the author for generously sharing with me the
manuscript of this book before its publication.

An alternative reading, advocated by Méhat, takes ἐν τοῖς φυσικοῖς together with δηλωθήσεται rather than with θεωρίαν, rendering the text even clearer:

> Having as it were fashioned a statue of the Gnostic, we have so far indicated *how* he is by showing as in a sketch the greatness and beauty of his *ethos*; *what* he is with respect to contemplation will be shown presently in the *physics* (ἐν τοῖς φυσικοῖς δηλωθήσεται), when we begin to treat of the making of the world.[70]

Regardless of what reading is preferred, Clement has in mind three stages of advancement. First, *ethics*; second *physics*, which is a matter of *theōria* whether or not one accepts the reading "natural contemplation" (θεωρίαν ἐν τοῖς φυσικοῖς);[71] third, according to *Strom.* 1.1.15, *epoptics*: "the gnosis according to the *epoptic* contemplation" (τῆς κατὰ τὴν ἐποπτικὴν θεωρίαν γνώσεως). As Descourtieux notes, for Clement "the study of nature, θεωρία φυσική, is a preamble to theology, which itself contains the study of creation (cf. *Strom.* 1.15.2, 1.60.4). This reflection, announced several times (cf. *Strom.* 4.3.1), has only reached us in snippets, in the *Eclogae propheticae*."[72] At the end of *Strom.* 7, Clement had not yet fulfilled his promise, as can be seen from his progress report:

> These points, then, having been formerly thoroughly treated, and the department of *ethics* having been sketched summarily in a fragmentary way, as we promised; and having here and there interspersed the dogmas which are the gems of true knowledge, so that the discovery of the sacred traditions may not be easy to any one of the uninitiated, let us proceed to what we promised.... And now, after this seventh *Miscellany* of ours, we shall give the account of what follows in order from a new beginning.[73]

---

[70] Méhat, *Étude*, 443 n. 115. This reading also has the advantage of breaking up the phrase κατὰ τὴν θεωρίαν ἐν τοῖς φυσικοῖς, which Clement would have perhaps expressed as κατὰ τὴν ἐν τοῖς φυσικοῖς θεωρίαν (cf. *Strom.* 1.1.15: κατὰ τὴν ἐποπτικὴν θεωρίαν).

[71] According to *Strom.* 1.1.15, the exposition of the "gnosis according to the *epoptic* contemplation" will start ἀπὸ τῆς τοῦ κόσμου γενέσεως, with considerations of natural contemplation (φυσικῆς θεωρίας). And *Strom.* 4.1.3 even speaks of "physiology, or rather contemplation" (φυσιολογία, μᾶλλον δὲ ἐποπτεία). This phrase should not surprise in an author as philosophically eclectic as Clement. Hadot ("Les divisions," 208) notes that, for Stoics, "Platonic dialectics, as the science of the Forms, being eliminated, all theoretical activity is concentrated in *physics*. It absorbs theology, which corresponds to a widening of the notion of physics, which no longer designates, as in Aristotle, a particular domain, but the totality of the cosmos and the force that animates it."

[72] Descourtieux, *Clément d'Alexandrie: Stromate VI* (SC 446; Paris: Cerf, 1999), 399 n. 4.

[73] *Strom.* 7.18.110.

In other words, even though Clement says explicitly that he has here and there interspersed the dogmas, which are the gems of true knowledge, "at the end of *Strom.* 7, we are still not out of the *ethics*". As for the puzzling reference to a "new beginning," Méhat thinks that it announced the beginning of *Hypotyposeis*, which must have "overflowed" with *physics*.[74] Nautin observed, however, that only a couple of chapters earlier (*Strom.* 7.15.89) Clement had announced his plan to "move on to the next Stroma." It appears, by way of consequence, that at least one more book of the *Stromateis* existed before the *Hypotyposeis*, of which the fragment entitled "Strom. 8" is a remnant.[75]

As I noted above, Nautin broke new ground in scholarship by founding his discussion of Clement's "program" on an analysis of the actual manuscript in which the writings are contained, and a cogent explanation of the text's fragmentary shape on the basis of similarities with the preservation of Origen in the Tura Codex II. This makes much less vulnerable to critique—*pace* van den Hoek and Nardi[76]—Nautin's conclusion that the *Excerpta* and *Eclogae* are excerpts from the *Hypotyposeis*, which, within the program of Clementine works, represent Clement's *physics* and *epoptics*.[77]

Physics to Epoptics: *Ma'asse Bereshīt* to *Ma'asse Merkavah*

But what was *epoptics* about? On the basis of his detailed analysis of Clement's statements about *gnosis*, Méhat came to the conclusion that the so-called secret doctrine consisted essentially in an exposition of the Johannine "God is love," shedding light on the reason for creation, the angels, *apokatastasis*.[78] Indeed, like Origen later on, Clement viewed

---

[74] Méhat, *Étude*, 516: "à la fin du *VIIᵉ Stromate*, nous ne sommes toujours pas sortis de l'éthique"; Méhat, *Étude*, 521–22: "si la gnose est essentiellement du domaine de la 'physique,' les *Hypotyposes* devaient en regorger, en quoi elles tenaient en grande partie les promesses des *Stromates*."

[75] Nautin, "La fin des *Stromates*," 295–96.

[76] See my earlier note.

[77] Nautin, "La fin des *Stromates*," 297–98.

[78] Méhat, "Θεὸς Ἀγάπη: Une hypothèse sur l'objet de la gnose orthodoxe," *StPatr* 9 (1966)/TU 94): 82–86; idem, *Étude*, 488: "une doctrine ayant pour fondement le primat de la charité, se développant en une théologie du Logos, de la création, et de la fin du monde, des anges, enfin de l'homme, servant de fondement à une morale d'assimilation progressive à Dieu à travers l'obéissance et la contemplation."

the Gospel of John as a "spiritual Gospel."[79] Before entering into a more detailed discussion about Clement, it is useful to consider briefly Origen's views of this topic.

I noted earlier that Origen classified the Song of Songs as an "epoptic" writing. In the same prologue to the commentary on the Song of Songs, however, he had also spoken (with obvious approval) of Jewish traditions that placed the Song of Songs, together with the beginning of Genesis, and the throne-vision and Temple-vision in Ezekiel, among the so-called δευτερώσεις—writings that "should be reserved for study till the last," because they concern the highest mysteries of the divinity. The biblical passages under discussion would have been the beginning of Genesis, the beginning and end of Ezekiel (the throne-vision and the eschatological temple), and the entire Song of Songs.[80]

Origen's fusion of Greek ἐποπτεία and Jewish δευτερώσεις may have been anticipated by Clement. Relevant in this respect are texts such as *Strom.* 1.28.176, where Clement characteristically reconciles "the fourfold division of Moses's philosophy" with the threefold scheme of *ethics, physics,* and *epoptics*,[81] and *Strom.* 4.1.3, where, according to

---

[79] In a passage attributed to the *Hypotyposeis*, quoted by Eusebius (*Hist. eccl.* 6.14.5–7 [SC 41:107]), Clement writes: "But, last of all, John, perceiving that the corporeal aspects (τὰ σωματικὰ) had been made plain in the Gospel, being urged by his friends [and] inspired by the Spirit, composed a spiritual Gospel (πνευματικὸν…εὐαγγέλιον)."

[80] Origen, *Comm. Cant. prol.* 1.7. The relevance of Origen's reference to Jewish δευτερώσεις for Jewish mystical exegesis has been argued by Gershom Scholem, *Jewish Gnosticism, Merkabah Mysticism, and Talmudic Tradition* (New York: Jewish Theological Seminary of America, 1965), 38–40. Scholem noted (*Jewish Gnosticism*, 38) that the Song of Songs was "a favorite subject for the public aggadic teachings of the rabbis in the second and third centuries." Among certain strands of Judaism, however, the Song's "detailed description of the limbs of the lover" suggested a connection with the anthropomorphic depiction of the enthroned deity in Ezekiel's vision. As a result certain Jewish teachers, "instead of interpreting the Song of Songs as an allegory within the framework of the generally accepted midrashic interpretations, saw it as a strictly esoteric text containing sublime and tremendous mysteries regarding God in his appearance upon the throne of the Merkabah" (*Jewish Gnosticism*, 39). This interpretation of Origen's reference to δευτερώσεις is accepted by Marguerite Harl ("Les prologue des commentaries sur le Cantique des Cantiques," in *Texte und Textkritik: Eine Aufsatzsammlung* [ed. J. Dummer et al.; TU 133; Berlin: Akademie-Verlag, 1987], 253). For a discussion of the parallels between Origen's and his rabbinic contemporaries' interpretation of the Song of Songs and of Ezekiel's throne-vision, see Reuven Kimelman, "Rabbi Yohanan and Origen on the Song of Songs: A Third-Century Jewish-Christian Disputation," *HTR* 73 (1980): 567–95; David J. Halperin, "Origen, Ezekiel's Merkabah, and the *Ascension of Moses*," *CH* 50 (1981): 261–75.

[81] *Strom.* 1.28.176: Ἡ μὲν οὖν κατὰ Μωυσέα φιλοσοφία τετραχῇ τέμνεται, εἴς τε τὸ ἱστορικὸν καὶ τὸ κυρίως λεγόμενον νομοθετικόν, ἅπερ ἂν εἴη τῆς ἠθικῆς πραγματείας ἴδια, τὸ τρίτον δὲ εἰς τὸ ἱερουργικόν, ὅ ἐστιν ἤδη τῆς φυσικῆς θεωρίας· καὶ τέταρτον

Gedaliahu Guy Stroumsa, he lays out something similar to the "secret tradition" of rabbinic circles (*m. Hag.* 2.1): an initiation into "the things pertaining to creation" (*ma'asse bereshīt*) and the mysteries of the divine chariot-throne (*ma'asse merkavah*), on the basis of mystical exegesis of key texts in Genesis and Ezekiel.[82]

Stroumsa's brief note is worth exploring in greater detail. According to Clement, "the gnostic tradition according to the canon of the truth" comprises, first, an account of the world's coming into being (περὶ κοσμογονίας), beginning with "the prophetically-uttered Genesis" (ἀπὸ τῆς προφητευθείσης... γενέσεως), followed by an ascent to "the subject-matter of theology" (ἐπὶ τὸ θεολογικὸν εἶδος).[83] This is not the only time that Clement states that his "physiology" begins with a discussion of Genesis. After discussing the relevant passages Méhat concludes that they "announce, as clearly as one can expect from Clement, a commentary on the beginning of Genesis, "which must have been part of the first book of the *Hypotyposeis*.[84]

As for the θεολογικὸν εἶδος, *Strom.* 1.28.176 (quoted above) explains it as a matter of visionary contemplation, ἐποπτεία, the highest part

---

ἐπὶ πᾶσι τὸ θεολογικὸν εἶδος, ἡ ἐποπτεία, ἥν φησιν ὁ Πλάτων τῶν μεγάλων ὄντως εἶναι μυστηρίων, Ἀριστοτέλης δὲ τὸ εἶδος τοῦτο μετὰ τὰ φυσικὰ καλεῖ ("Now, Moses's philosophy is divided into four parts: the historical part and the part properly called legislative (these would properly belong to the study of *ethics*); the third part, sacred rites, which belongs to natural contemplation; and fourth, above all, there is the subject-matter of theology, the vision, so Plato says, of the truly great mysteries...").

[82] Stroumsa, "'*Paradosis*': Esoteric Traditions in Early Christianity," in *Hidden Wisdom: Esoteric Traditions and the Roots of Christian Mysticism*, SHR 70 (Leiden/New York/Cologne: Brill, 1996), 42–43. See also his article "Clement, Origen, and Jewish Esoteric Traditions," in *Hidden Wisdom*, 109–31. It should be noted, however, that Clement, unlike Origen, "does not reflect living contacts with Jewish scholars" (Van den Hoek, "The 'Catechetical' School of Early Christian Alexandria and Its Philonic Heritage," *HTR* 90 [1997]: 59–87, at 80).

[83] *Strom.* 4.1.3: ἡ γοῦν κατὰ τὸν τῆς ἀληθείας κανόνα γνωστικῆς παραδόσεως φυσιολογία, μᾶλλον δὲ ἐποπτεία, ἐκ τοῦ περὶ κοσμογονίας ἤρτηται λόγου, ἐνθένδε ἀναβαίνουσα ἐπὶ τὸ θεολογικὸν εἶδος. ὅθεν εἰκότως τὴν ἀρχὴν τῆς παραδόσεως ἀπὸ τῆς προφητευθείσης ποιησόμεθα γενέσεως ("The science of nature, then—or rather vision—as contained in the gnostic tradition according to the rule of the truth, depends on the account of the world's coming into being [or, following Méhat, *Étude*, 442–3: "starts with the treatise 'On the creation of world'"], ascending from there to the subject-matter of theology. Whence, then, we shall begin our account of what is handed down with the prophetically-uttered Genesis").

[84] Méhat, *Étude*, 442–3 and 443 n. 117. "Commentary" is not the right term, as the work was most likely a *capitulus* rather than a large work. Eusebius, who claims to know the *Hypotyposeis*, also notes that in the *Stromateis* Clement "promises to write a commentary on Genesis," but never identifies the latter with a section of the *Hypotyposeis*. See *Hist. eccl.* 6.13.9.

of philosophy according to Plato and Aristotle. Indeed, ἐποπτεία, a term whose roots lie in the language of the Eleusinian mysteries, had come to designate, since Plutarch, the highest part of both Platonic and Aristotelian philosophy.[85] Clement does the same, by equating it with Plato's "dialectics" and Aristotle's "metaphysics." Rizzerio is certainly correct to conclude that "ἐποπτεία represents for Clement the highest knowledge that a human being can obtain, corresponding to that very vision of God, accessible only to a few, without thereby growing into a non-rational (*arazionale*) mystical knowledge."[86]

Yet εἶδος also happens to be a term used in several LXX renderings of visionary texts. In Gen 32:31–32 εἶδος θεοῦ is used in connection with God's anthropomorphic appearance as the warrior who wrestled Jacob; in Num 12:8 Moses sees the glory of God ἐν εἴδει; finally, in Ezek 1:26 the anthropomorphic "glory of God" on the chariot-throne is referred to as ὁμοίωμα ὡς εἶδος ἀνθρώπου. Moreover, we know that Jews and Christians of the Greek diaspora were fond of drawing a connection between Ezek 1:26 and the Platonic theory of forms (e.g., εἶδος ἀνθρώπου in Parm. 130C).[87] Perhaps Clement intended to suggest, in the subtle manner characteristic of the *Stromateis*, that "the subject-matter of theology" is both Plato's "vision of truly great mysteries" and the biblical notion of God's anthropomorphic appearance on the divine chariot-throne.[88] This must remain only a hypothesis.

---

[85] Hadot, "Les divisions," 218. See *Is. Os.* 77 (*Plutarch's de Iside et Osiride* [ed. and trans. J. Gwyn Griffith; Cambridge: University of Wales Press, 1970], 242): "For this reason both Plato (*Symp.*, 210A) and Aristotle call this branch of philosophy that concerned with the highest mysteries (ἐποπτικὸν), in that those who have passed beyond these conjectural, confused and widely varied matters spring by force of reason to that primal, simple and immaterial element; and having directly grasped the pure truth attached to it, they believe that they hold the ultimate end of philosophy in the manner of a mystic revelation." Plutarch has in mind *Symp.* 210 A, where Diotima refers to the highest goal of instruction (by anticipation of her subsequent exposition on the upward flight of the soul) as τὰ τέλεα καὶ ἐποπτικά.

[86] Rizzerio, *Physiologia*, 49. Similarly Riedweg, *Mysterienterminologie*, 145–47.

[87] Jarl Fossum, "Colossians 1.15–18a in the Light of Jewish Mysticism and Gnosticism," *NTS* 35 (1989): 183–201, at 188; Alan Segal, *Paul the Convert: The Apostolate and Apostasy of Saul the Pharisee* (New Haven/London: Yale University Press, 1990), 42.

[88] For Clement's style of concealment through veiled allusions, see Fortin, "Clement and the Esoteric Tradition," 52.

The Hypotyposeis and Later Orthodoxy[89]

The *Hypotyposeis* were judged as heretical by later guardians of Orthodoxy. The fatal element was undoubtedly the growing association with Origen and later Origenism. Ironically enough, it is none other than Rufinus who bears part of the responsibility for this association. In defending Origen of the charge of occasionally calling the Son a creature, Rufinus argued that similar statements occur in some Clementine writings, and that this can only be due to interpolations: how else could anyone believe that a man so catholic in all respects and so erudite as Clement would have written such dreadful impieties?[90] Even though writers such as Cyril of Alexandria and Maximus the Confessor praised him for his towering learning as "philosopher of philosophers," and even though Epiphanius of Salamis and Jerome saw in him a learned defender against heresies, Rufinus' ultimately unsuccessful defense of Origen also planted the seed of future accusations against Clement.[91] By the ninth century, this seed had come to fruition: according to George the Monk, writing some time between 843 and 847, God had revealed the truth about Clement to one of the fathers: Clement had been an "Origenist"![92]

Most notorious and of lasting influence is the harsh criticism of Clement by Photius of Constantinople. The Byzantine patriarch is

---

[89] For the reception of Clement, see Zahn, *Forschungen* 3:140–43; Adolf Knauber, "Die patrologische Schätzung des Clemens von Alexandrien bis zu seinem neuerlichen Bekanntwerden durch die ersten Druckeditionen des 16. Jahrhunderts," in *Kyriakon: FS Johannes Quasten* (ed. P. Granfield and J. A. Jungmann; Münster: Aschendorff, 1970), 289–308; Wagner, "A Father's Fate: Attitudes Toward and Interpretations of Clement of Alexandria," *JRH* 6 (1971): 209–31.

[90] Ruf. *Apol. adv. Hier.*, 4 (SC 464:294): *Numquid credibile est de tanto viro, tam in omnibus catholico, tam erudito ut uel sibi contraria senserit uel ea quae de Deo, non dicam credere se uel audire quidem impium est, scripta reliquerit?*

[91] See the references reviewed by Descourtieux, "Introduction," 8–9.

[92] Georgius Monachus (Hamartolos), *Chronicon Breve* 26 (PG 110:84): Κλήμης δὲ ὁ Στρωματεὺς, Ὠριγενιαστὴς ὤν, ὥς τινι τῶν πατέρων ἀπεκαλύφθη. It is interesting that this reference occurs in a section that deals with the transmission of wisdom and letters from the Hebrews to the pagans. George the Monk simply indicates his sources, adding some offhand remarks: on the one hand, there is Josephus, a "blind" Jew (ἐν τῷ Ἰουδαϊσμῷ μείνας τυφλώττων); on the other, there is Clement, who is not a Jew (μὴ ἐν κολάσει Ἰουδαῖος ὤν), but an "Origenist" heretic. In the section dedicated to the reign of Commodus (*Chronicon Breve* 140 [PG 110:532]), Clement of Alexandria is once again linked to Origen—"Origen was his pupil"—and listed among the heretics who flourished during that period: Paul of Samosata, Theodotion, and Montanus. For the dating of Georgius Monachus, see Dmitry Afinogenov, "The Date of Georgios Monachos Reconsidered," *ByzZ* 92 (1999): 437–47.

scandalized by the heresies he finds in the *Hypotyposeis*: distinguishing between the Father's Logos and the Logos that took flesh, reducing
Christ to a mere creature, the doctrine of "metempsychosis," the idea
that there existed "many worlds before Adam."[93] The Photian evaluation
of Clement's theology has been much discussed in scholarship.[94] It is
now clear that "the embattled patriarch judged the work in the light of
an orthodoxy hammered out on anti-Origenist and anti-Arian anvils,"[95]
and that his accusations were without ground, based on misreadings,
misunderstandings, or misinterpretations of the text.[96] The question is
further complicated by the fact that the Clementine authenticity of the
text quoted by Photius (now "fragment 23") is still open to debate.[97]

My concern here is not with the substance of Photius's critique of
Clement, or with the authenticity of the texts attributed to the Alex-
andrian, but with what this critique suggests about the structure of the
Clementine corpus. Photius claims that the *Hypotyposeis* were replete
with "impieties," "fables," and "blasphemous nonsense". He finds the
Stromateis much more acceptable, although "unsound" in some parts.
Finally, he notes that the *Paidagogos* has nothing in common with the
Hypotyposeis, and is entirely free from idle and blasphemous opinions.
This is an important insight into the hierarchical organization of the
Clementine writings. Even though Photius reverses the value of the
Clementine hierarchy, such that the summit of theology becomes
the abyss of heresy, his evaluation provides confirmation of the fact
that Clement had intended for the *Hypotyposeis* to initiate his students
into the highest level of "gnosis."

---

[93] Phot., *Cod.* 109 (Photius, *Bibliothèque* [ed. and trans. René Henry; 9 vols. Paris: Société d'édition les Belles lettres, 1960], 2:80).

[94] Knauber, "Patrologische Schätzung des Clemens," 297–304; Casey, "Clement and the Two Divine Logoi," *JTS* 25 (1923): 43–56; Lilla, *Clement of Alexandria* 199–212; Raoul Mortley, Carsten Colpe, "Gnosis I (Erkenntnislehre)," *RAC* 11 (1981): 446–537, at 479–80; Osborn, "French Eighteenth-Century Sighting," 77–83; M. J. Edwards, "Clement of Alexandria and His Doctrine of the Logos," *VC* 54 (2000): 159–77, at 168–71; Christoph Markschies, "Die wunderliche Mär von zwei Logoi": Clemens Alexandrinus, Fragment 23—Zeugnis eines *Arius ante Arium* oder des arianischen Streits selbst?, in *Logos: FS Luise Abramowski* (BZNW 67; Berlin/New York: De Gruyter, 1993), 193–219. The text was republished in Markschies, *Alta Trinità Beata: Gesammelte Studien zur altkirchlichen Trinitätstheologie* (Tübingen: Mohr Siebeck, 2000), 70–98. For a detailed overviewof scholarly positions, see Oleh Kindiy, *Christos Didaskalos: The Christology of Clement of Alexandria* (Saarbrücken: VDM Verlag Dr. Müller, 2008), 57–117.

[95] Wagner, "A Father's Fate," 213.

[96] See especially the above-mentioned studies of Knauber, Osborn, and Edwards.

[97] Markschies' painstaking analysis has shown that there are good reasons to at least label Fragment 23 as "pseudo-(?) Clement," thus indicating strong doubts as to its authenticity.

Conclusions

Like most teachers of wisdom in his time—whether Platonists, Stoics, Jews or Christians—Clement paid foremost attention to the pedagogical element in producing his works. His Logos-doctrine offered the hermeneutical basis for a curriculum designed to meet the students at their lowest level—paganism—, exhort them "to the laver, to salvation, to illumination" (*Protr.* 10.94), then train them in virtue, and instruct them into increasingly higher levels of the revelation by means of gradual descent into the depths of Scripture.

This pedagogical method, however, did not make use of a fixed nomenclature for the various stages of instruction. Clement speaks of *Protreptikos—Paidagogos—Didaskalos*, but he also uses the *Ethics—Physics—Epoptics* sequence, and seems to be aware of the special place held by the opening verses of Genesis and the account of Ezekiel's throne-vision, a tradition which surfaces explicitly with Origen and the Tannaim. Eclecticism and fluidity are, after all, the characteristic features of Clement's thought.[98]

The *Stromateis* fulfill Clement's projected doctrinal exposition only in part: "having here and there interspersed the dogmas which are the gems of true knowledge." A still higher and clearer exposition of Christian doctrine would have followed, using Scripture in such a way—selection of certain themes and passages, use of allegory—as to move from *ethics* to *physics* and *epoptics* and offer students the possibility to "listen to the *Didaskalos*."

For several reasons, the most likely candidate for this next stage is the work known as the *Hypotyposeis*. According to unanimous patristic verdict, the *Hypotyposeis* were exegetical in method and doctrinal in character.[99] Some ideas that are discussed in both the *Stromateis* and the *Hypotyposeis* (e.g., the angelic hierarchy, pneumatology) are presented "mostly in a dispersed, allusive form" in the former, and more explicitly in the latter.[100] Finally, the doctrines contained in the *Hypotyposeis* were judged as heretical by later guardians of Orthodoxy.

---

[98] Méhat, *Étude*, 426–27: "Par une habitude constante de sa langue, Clément use selon les circonstances d'un grand nombre de synonymes pour exprimer la même idée. Ainsi pour la gnose.... Il faut donc se fier moins au vocabulaire qu'au contexte."

[99] Eusebius (*Hist. eccl.* 6.13.2, 6.14.1 [SC 41:104, 106]), Cassiodorus (*Div. litt., praef.* 4 [FC 39/1:98]), and Photius (*Cod.* 109 [*Bibliothèque*, 2:79]) all state that the *Hypotyposeis* were concise expositions of biblical passages. For a reconstruction of their content, see Zahn, *Forschungen* 3:156; Swarat, *Theodor Zahn als Patristiker*, 198.

[100] Méhat, *Étude*, 516, 519; Le Boulluec, "Introduction," 185 n. 7.

I now return to the subject of my study—Clement's pneumatology—
which will be carried out by paying special attention to the speculations
in the *Excerpta, Eclogae,* and *Adumbrationes*. In the following pages,
I shall reaffirm Oeyen's thesis that Clement's pneumatology is best
understood within the framework of traditional speculation on the
"first created" angelic spirits (πρωτόκτιστοι), which Clement inherited from revered teachers (the so-called elders). On the other hand,
I shall advance the discussion by attempting to provide a context for
Clement's *Engelpneumatologie*. This phenomenon (which, I shall argue,
would be better termed "angelomorphic pneumatology") is understood
adequately only in conjunction with Clement's spirit christology and
overall binitarian orientation. Finally, I submit that all of the above
place Clement in a larger company of early Christian writers.

At this point it is necessary to discuss Clement's hierarchical cosmology and complex articulation between the unity of the godhead and
the multiplicity of the cosmos. I shall show that these two elements
provide the basis for a specific theory of prophetic inspiration, which
is best accounted for by Oeyen's thesis of "Engelpneumatologie" in
Clement of Alexandria.

2. CLEMENT ON DIVINE UNITY AND THE COSMIC MULTIPLICITY

Unity and Multiplicity in the Logos

Clement speaks of the utterly transcendent God and the Logos as his
agent in *Strom.* 4.25.156, which Osborn calls "the decisive passage
for the doctrine of the trinity in Clement."[101] The difference between
Father and Son is very similar to Numenius' distinction between the
first and the second god: God cannot be the object of any epistemology
(ἀναπόδεικτος; οὐκ ἔστιν ἐπιστημονικός), while the exact opposite is
true of the Son (σοφία τέ ἐστι καὶ ἐπιστήμη; ἀπόδειξιν ἔχει).[102] This
difference on the epistemological level corresponds to a different relation
to the cosmos, where it is the Son who founds multiplicity: "The Son is

---

[101] Osborn, *Clement,* 151.
[102] See the discussion in Hägg, *Beginnings of Christian Apophaticism,* 163, 175–77, 262.

neither simply one thing as one thing (ἓν ὡς ἕν), nor many things as parts (πολλὰ ὡς μέρη), but one thing as all things (ὡς πάντα ἕν)."[103]

In this statement, Clement surveys the following theoretical possibilities: (a) absolute unity, in no way connected to multiplicity (ἓν ὡς ἕν); (b) absolute multiplicity, in no way connected to unity (πολλὰ ὡς μέρη); (c) unity *qua* multiplicity (ὡς πάντα ἕν). Clement embraces the third option as the most appropriate account of the Son's activity: the Son founds the multiplicity of creation, but this multiplicity, being founded by the same one principle, can be eventually reduced to Logos. It is in this sense that "the Word is called the Alpha and the Omega, of whom alone the end becomes beginning, and ends again at the original beginning."[104]

All of this seems fairly clear in light of the philosophical tradition. As Hägg explains, "Clement distinguishes between God as τὸ ἕν, as simple unity, and the Son as πάντα ἕν, the unity of all things…. Just as the interpretation of the first hypothesis of the *Parmenides* was applied to the Christian God, so the second hypothesis of the *Parmenides* was interpreted in relation to the Son of God."[105] Salvatore Lilla thinks that Clement may have come across speculations about unity and diversity in Neopythagorean interpretations of the *Parmenides*.[106] Osborn notes that "[a]ccording to Posidonius and Philo, the cosmos was governed by a system of powers, which took the place of the forms of Plato and the immanent logos of the earlier Stoics." Granted, however, that "Clement found already formed in Philo the doctrine of the Logos as the totality of powers which are identical with the ideas,"[107] what are we to make of the following affirmation?

> all the powers of the spirit, taken together as one thing, find their perfection in the same, that is, in the Son…He [the Son] is the circle of all powers rolled and united into one.[108]

---

[103] *Strom.* 4.25.156.
[104] *Strom.* 4.25.157.
[105] Hägg, *Beginnings of Christian Apophaticism*, 214–15.
[106] Osborn, *Clement*, 152; Lilla, *Clement*, 205.
[107] Lilla, *Clement*, 204. For relevant passages in Philo, see Lilla, *Clement*, 205.
[108] πᾶσαι δὲ αἱ δυνάμεις τοῦ πνεύματος συλλήβδην μὲν ἕν τι πρᾶγμα γενόμεναι συντελοῦσιν εἰς τὸ αὐτό, τὸν υἱόν…κύκλος γὰρ ὁ αὐτὸς πασῶν τῶν δυνάμεων εἰς ἓν εἰλουμένων καὶ ἑνουμένων (*Strom.* 4.25.156).

To say, with Hägg, that the "powers" are "the thoughts and actions of God," or with Osborn, in an earlier work, that Clement "explained the existence and nature of things by 'powers' just as Plato had done by 'forms' and the earlier Stoics had done by immanent reason or divine fire," does not account for the complexity of this text.[109] Both Lilla and Osborn (in his latest book) suggest in passing that the biblical doctrine of angelic powers may also have influenced Clement.[110] Following Oeyen, one can say confidently that Clement is fusing the Logos-speculation with an established teaching on the "powers of the spirit" that originated in Jewish or Jewish Christian speculation about angelic "powers." It is significant in this respect that Clement immediately quotes Revelation: "the Word is called the Alpha and the Omega..." (Rev 1:8; 21:6; 22:13). What he has in mind is surely the throne-visions of Revelation, depicting the seven spirits or angels in attendance before the throne (Rev 1:4; 8:2).[111]

Following Oeyen, I contend that Clement's phrase "powers of the Spirit" alludes to the seven spirits in Revelation, which Clement subjects to the spiritualizing interpretation and the Logos-theology inherited from Philo. It seems clear, in light of this overlapping of doctrinal frameworks, that "powers" *do* hold an important place in Clement's account of reality.[112] In the following section I shall present evidence for this assertion.

Unity and Multiplicity in the Spirit

In *Strom.* 5.6, Clement provides an allegorical interpretation of the Temple and its furnishings, an enterprise in which he is by no means unique, since Barnabas before him, and Origen and Cyril of Alexandria afterwards, are engaged in the very same project. I shall confine myself to the menorah, the cherubim, and the twelve stones.

---

[109] Osborn, *The Philosophy of Clement of Alexandria* (Cambridge: Cambridge University Press, 1957), 41; Hägg, *Beginnings of Christian Apophaticism*, 232.

[110] Lilla, *Clement*, 204 n. 3: "Clement may have believed in the identity between angels, the ideas, and the powers of God"; Osborn, *Clement*, 152: "A still stronger influence on Clement was the concept of the manifold powers of the spirit in the Old Testament and especially in Paul (1 Cor 12)."

[111] In fact, Clement is reported by Oecumenius and Arethas of Caesarea to have viewed the seven spirits of Revelation as the seven highest angels. For the passage from Arethas' commentary on Revelation see fragment 59 (*Clemens Alexandrinus 3*, 227).

[112] David T. Runia ("Clement of Alexandria and the Philonic Doctrine of the Divine Power[s]," *VC* 58 [2004]: 256–76) holds that "Clement transfers the full weight of the cosmic powers onto Christ the Logos," so that "the role of these powers in Clement's thought is very limited" (268–69).

Clement's exegesis follows a recognizable pattern. He introduces the object of interpretation, offers a first level of explanation, then a second one. The first level of explanation is astrological: the lamp signifies "the motions of the seven planets that perform their revolutions towards the south," the cherubim signify the two bears, or the two hemispheres, and the twelve wings and twelve stones describe for us the circle of the zodiac.[113] The second interpretation is christological: the lamp conveys a "symbol of Christ," the twelve stones are discussed in reference to the Lord, the Word, the Holy Spirit, etc. The "eighth region" mentioned in the interpretation of the cherubim refers to the place above the seven heavens, and we can assume that this is where Clement would picture the enthroned Christ.

The interpretations of the lamp, the cherubim, and the stones are very similar in that they all deal with the relation between unity and multiplicity. In the symbolic description of the lamp, Christ represents "what is one," while "the seven eyes of the Lord" and "the seven spirits" stand for "what is many." In the description of the cherubim, "the eighth region," "the world of thought," and "God," represent "what is one," while the zodiac, time, and the world of sense represent "what is many."[114] Finally, in the interpretation of the twelve stones, "the one and the self-same Holy Spirit," "the Lord," "the Savior," "the Word" stand for "what is one," while "the whole world," and "all things" represent "what is many."

The cosmological scheme at work here seems to consist of "the invisible God" (who is only alluded to, because he is beyond the dialectic of one/many), the Son/Word/Savior as principle of all things, and the multiplicity of things:

> The golden lamp conveys another enigma as a symbol of Christ...in his casting light, "at sundry times and diverse manners," on those who believe in him and hope and see by means of the ministry of the *protoctists* (διὰ τῆς τῶν πρωτοκτίστων διακονίας). And they say that the seven eyes of

---

[113] This interpretation is not Clement's own creation, and his allusion to "some" others who interpret the cherubim as images of the zodiac may be extrapolated to the other two elements. Philo has a very similar interpretation of the cherubim (*Cherubim* 7.21–24). For a comprehensive survey of Clement's debt to Philo in his exegesis of the Temple, the vestments and the high priest, see Annewies van den Hoek, *Clement of Alexandria and His Use of Philo in the Stromateis: An Early Christian Reshaping of a Jewish Model* (VCSup 3; Leiden/New York: Brill, 1988), 116–47.

[114] To indicate "what is many" in the case of the cherubim, I had to introduce elements from the first level of interpretation, because the interpretation switches from the cherubim to the ark, and the idea of multiplicity remains to be conveyed by the twelve wings.

the Lord are the seven spirits resting on the rod that springs from the root of Jesse.[115]

Clement draws here on a series of biblical passages (Isa 11:1–2; Zech 4:2.10; Rev 1:4; 5:6; 8:2) that might have already been combined by earlier tradition.[116]

Isaiah's seven gifts of the Holy Spirit are Zechariah's seven spirits (eyes of the Lord), understood as the seven "first born" angels, the *protoctists*. These are presumably the seven "first-born princes of the angels (οἱ πρωτόγονοι ἀγγέλων ἄρχοντες) who have the greatest power."[117] Consistent with the christological framework in which he places the Old Testament prophecies and theophanies throughout his writings, Clement sees the seven angelic spirits as exercising a certain διακονία by which the Logos is imparted to the world.[118]

The cosmological aspect of this activity consists in the move from unity to multiplicity, by which the Logos establishes "what is many" in creation: the one "Spirit" (the Logos) relates to "seven spirits" in the same way that Logos relates to the "powers" in *Strom.* 4.25.156. Equally important is the theo-gnoseological aspect of the discussion. The Logos, who intrinsically possesses the perfect vision of God, passes this vision on to creation by the ministry of the *protoctists* (*Strom.* 5.6.35).

Clement seems to suppose the sequence Father—Son—*protoctists*. Confirmation of this idea, and a fairly detailed description of the multi-layered cosmos, is provided by the *Excerpta*.

3. Clement's "Celestial Hierarchy"[119]

The title of this section is deliberately anachronistic, borrowing from the vocabulary of the much later Ps.-Dionysius Areopagite. Even if

---

[115] *Strom.* 5.6.35. I shall have more to say about the *protoctists* in the next section.
[116] Karl Schlütz, *Isaias 11:2 (Die sieben Gaben des Heiligen Geistes) in den ersten vier christlichen Jahrhunderten* (Münster: Aschendorff, 1932).
[117] *Strom.* 6.16.142–143.
[118] It is noteworthy that the brief quotation from Heb 1:1 ("at sundry times and diverse manners") is also subtly molded into an explicitly christological affirmation: the one speaking "at sundry times and diverse manners" to the patriarchs and prophets is, originally, "God"; Clement, however, speaks about *Christ* casting his light "at sundry times and diverse manners."
[119] This section is a revision of Bucur, "The Other Clement: Cosmic Hierarchy and Interiorized Apocalypticism," *VC* 60 (2006): 251–68.

the term "hierarchy" was coined by this anonymous late fifth-century author, whose writings mark the confluence of Christian theology and late Neoplatonism, it is perfectly legitimate to use it in a discussion of a second-century Christian author who makes heavy use of Middle Platonism. Obviously, I do not use "hierarchy" for the relation between Father and Son. As Osborn has noted, Clement's view of the Father-Son relation, derived from the Fourth Gospel, and expressed with the help of Middle Platonic duality between God and Intellect, is different from the later Plotinian "hierarchy" in which the One utterly transcends Mind.[120] "Hierarchy" and "hierarchical" are instead appropriate designations for the multi-storied cosmos characteristic of apocalyptic writings such as the *Ascension of Isaiah, 2 Enoch* or the *Epistula Apostolorum*. In the case of Ps.-Dionysius, the hierarchy is not one among other features of his worldview: the hierarchy *is* the world.[121] Clement of Alexandria seems to view reality in a similar way:

> Christ has turned the world into an ocean of blessings.... The whole of the new creation is a saving *activity*. Every part does something to carry the world forward and to lift it higher. It is saving and being saved. Its *hierarchy* expands the Platonic world of forms. It is powerful as the *energeia* of God. The world culminates in the ever-present word whose light penetrates everywhere and casts no shadow.[122]

Aside from the use of "hierarchy," Osborn's beautiful description is unmistakably "Dionysian." It was, after all, the Ps.-Areopagite that defined the hierarchy as "a sacred order, and knowledge, and activity (ἐνέργεια)"![123] And it is none other than the sixth-century scholiast of the *Corpus Dionysiacum*, John of Scythopolis, who tried to bring into harmony the Dionysian and the Clementine angelic hierarchies.[124]

---

[120] Osborn, *Clement*, 107, 115, 117, 118, 122, 131.

[121] Cf. René Roques, *L'univers dionysien: structure hiérarchique du monde selon le Pseudo-Denys* (Paris: Cerf, 1983), 131.

[122] Osborn, *Clement*, 158 (emphasis added).

[123] Ps.-Dionysius, *CH* 3.1 (PTS 36:17).

[124] In a scholion to *DN* 2.9, where the text had mentioned "the premier among the oldest angels" (τῷ πρωτίστῳ τῶν πρεσβυτάτων ἀγγέλων), John of Scythopolis writes: "Note how he says that certain angels are oldest (πρεσβυτάτους ἀγγέλους εἶναι τινας) and that one of them is premier (πρῶτον αὐτῶν). The divine John speaks of elder angels in the Apocalypse, and we read in Tobit as well as in the fifth book of Clement's *Hypotyposeis* that the premier angels are seven (ἑπτὰ εἶναι τοὺς πρώτους). He [Dionysius] was wont to call the three highest orders 'the oldest angels' (πρεσβυτάτους ἀγγέλους)—Thrones, Seraphim, and Cherubim—as he often signifies in his treatise *The Celestial Hierarchy*" (PG 4:225, 228). The English translation, with slight modifications,

It is a fact, however, that the similarity between the Clementine and Dionysian "hierarchies" is only seldom addressed in scholarship. The exceptions therefore deserve special mention. While considering the possible connections between Clement's "celestial hierarchy" (*Zusammenhänge der himmlischen Hierarchie*) and later developments, Bousset points to the "line" uniting the latter to the Ps.-Dionysian system.[125] There is, then, Riedinger's demonstration that the Clementine treatise "On Angels," contained in the *Hypotyposeis*, was paraphrased in a section of Ps.-Caesarius' *Erotapokriseis*, a little-known writing stemming from the same monastic environment that is likely to have produced the *Corpus Dionysiacum*.[126] Finally, Alexander Golitzin has argued that a correct understanding of the Ps.-Dionysian writings requires careful consideration of its patristic background, of which Clement is an important part. As a case in point, Clement's angelic hierarchy, in particular, is "remarkably reminiscent" of the *Corpus Dionysiacum*.[127]

It should be noted, finally, that the centrality of the hierarchically ordered universe and its denizens was an important "archaizing" feature of the Ps.-Dionysian work, subordinated to one of the likely goals of this "New Testament pseudepigraphon"—namely, the subversion of similar apocalyptic imagery (and associated doctrines) among competing

---

is that of Paul Rorem and John C. Lamoreaux, *John of Scythopolis and the Dionysian Corpus: Annotating the Areopagite* (Oxford: Clarendon, 1998), 198.

[125] Bousset, *Jüdisch-christlicher Schulbetrieb*, 179 n. 1.

[126] Riedinger, "Paraphrase": "Wenn er [Clement] auch in der kirchlichen Hierarchie ein Abbild der himmlischen erblickt (Strom. VI, 107, 2; II 485, 24–32) und die einen Engel von anderen 'gerettet' denkt, selber wiederum andere 'rettend' (Strom. VII 9, 3; III 8, 17–21), dann bleibt es rätselhaft, daß man bisher diese Lehre nicht als Quelle für die Engel-Hierarchien und deren Tätigkeit bei Pseudo-Dionysius erkannt hat. Bei R. Roques: L'Univers Dionysien, Aubier 1954, finde ich nichts davon" (262); "Unter der Voraussetzung daß wir in Petros dem Walker den Verfasser der pseudo-dionysischen Schriften sehen dürfen und in dem Kompilator der Erotapokriseis des Pseudo-Kaisarios einen Akoimeten aus der Mitte des 6. Jahrhunderts, ist dann die Feststellung überaus characteristisch, daß wir den Akoimeten die Überlieferung bzw. Entstehung der einzigen beiden Monographien über die Engel verdanken, die uns aus der christlichen Antike erhalten sind. Die Mönche des 5.–6. Jahrhunderts sahen in ihrer Liturgie eben ein Spiegelbild der himmlischen Liturgie der Engel…" (260). See also Riedinger, "Pseudo-Dionysius Areopagites, Pseudo-Kaisarios und die Akoimeten," *ByzZ* 52 (1959): 276–96.

[127] Golitzin, *Et introibo ad altare Dei: The Mystagogy of Dionysius Areopagita, with Special Reference to Its Predecessors in the Eastern Christian Tradition* (Analekta Vlatadon 59; Thessalonica: Patriarchal Institute of Patristic Studies, 1994), 261–69, esp. 265.

groups in Christianity.[128] Given all of the above, it is perfectly justified to speak of "hierarchy" in the case of Clement.

I now return to Clement of Alexandria's "celestial hierarchy." This worldview, which *Strom.* 7.2.9 presents in a somewhat veiled and less explicit manner, is described in great detail in *Exc.* 10, 11, and 27, and *Ecl.* 56–57.[129] This is a theological tradition that goes back not only to Pantaenus, but to an older generation of Jewish-Christian "elders."[130] According to Daniélou, it represented "the continuation within Christianity of a Jewish esotericism that existed at the time of the apostles," it consisted of oral instruction going back to the apostles themselves, and was aimed primarily at relating the mystery of Christ's death and resurrection to the mysteries of the heavenly world.[131]

---

[128] The argument has been made by Golitzin, "Dionysius Areopagita: A Christian Mysticism?," *ProEccl* 12 (2003): 161–212, esp. 178.

[129] In his notes to the *Strom.* 7, Le Boulluec often refers the reader to the *Eclogae* or *Excerpta*, noting at one point that the latter offer "a more precise description of these angelic hierarchies in relation to the Son" (SC 428:185 n. 7).

[130] That Clement's strictly hierarchical universe goes back to earlier tradition has been demonstrated by older research: Collomp, "Une source"; Bousset, *Jüdisch-christlicher Schulbetrieb*, 263–64; Kretschmar, *Trinitätstheologie*, 68. Despite the pertinent critique of some of Bousset's conclusions (Munck, *Untersuchungen*, 127–204), the thesis of a Jewish and Jewish-Christian literary source behind Clement remains solidly established: Kretschmar, *Trinitätstheologie*, 68 n. 3; Daniélou, "Les traditions secrètes des Apôtres," *ErJb* 31 [1962]: 199–215. On the place of Pantaenus in the development of Alexandrian catechetical tradition, see Pierre Nautin, "Pantène," in *Tome commémoratif du millénaire de la bibliothèque patriarchale d'Alexandrie* (T. D. Mosconas, ed.; Alexandria: Publications de l'Institut d'études orientales de la bibliothèque patriarchale d'Alexandrie, 1953), 145–52; Martiniano Pellegrino Roncaglia, "Pantène et le didascalée d'Alexandrie: Du Judéo-Christianisme au Christianisme Hellénistique," in *A Tribute to Arthur Vööbus: Studies in Early Christian Literature and Its Environment, Primarily in the Christian East* (ed. R. Fisher; Chicago: The Lutheran School of Theology, 1977), 211–23. Many scholars judge the evidence about Pantaenus insufficient for an assessment of his theology: Attila Jakab, *Ecclesia Alexandrina: Evolution sociale et institutionnelle du christianisme alexandrin (II⁴ et III⁴ siècles)* (Christianismes anciens 1; Bern: Peter Lang, 2004), 111, 115; Van den Hoek, "The 'Catechetical' School," 61; Osborn, *Clement*, 102.

[131] "Le contenu de cette tradition secrète concerne les secrets du monde céleste, qui était déja dans le judaïsme l'objet d'un savoir réservé. Cette tradition secrète n'est donc à aucun degré relative à l'essence du message apostolique, qui est le Christ mort et ressuscité. Mais elle correspond à une explicitation de ce mystère dans sa relation avec le monde céleste. Les Apôtres pensaient que cette explicitation ne relevait pas de l'enseignement commun, mais d'une initiation plus poussée, de caractère oral" (Daniélou, "Les traditions secrètes," 214). See also Daniélou, *Gospel Message and Hellenistic Culture* (London: Darton, Longman & Todd/Philadelphia: Westminster Press, 1973), 453–64.

The Principles of the Hierarchy

Having at its pinnacle the Logos, the spiritual universe features, in descending order, the seven *protoctists*, the archangels, and the angels.[132] This "celestial hierarchy" seems to be continued by an ecclesiastical hierarchy, since Clement affirms that "the advancements (προκοπαί) pertaining to the Church here below, namely those of bishops, presbyters and deacons, are imitations (μιμήματα) of the angelic glory."[133]

The orienting principle (ἀρχή) of the hierarchy is the "Face of God," a theme whose prominence in the apocalyptic literature of Second Temple Judaism was only amplified with the emergence of Christianity.[134] For Clement, the Face of God is more than "the radiant façade of God's anthropomorphic extent," more than a code-expression for "a vision

---

[132] Since God is neither an accident (συμβεβηκός), nor described by anything accidental (*Strom.* 5.12.81), he is beyond the hierarchy, and should not be counted as the first of five hierarchical levels (*pace* Collomp, "Une source," 24; Oeyen, *Engelpneumatologie*, 20). Rizzerio, φυσιολογία, 265: "da questa classificatione gerarchica...il Principio è escluso...resta superiore alla gerarchia e la transcende....il Principio di tutte le cose è aldillà della οὐσία." Indeed, to designate the Father, Clement repeatedly alludes to the famous Platonic phrase ἐπέκεινα τῆς οὐσίας (Rep 509B), which had been already appropriated by Justin (ἐπέκεινα πάσης οὐσίας, *Dial.* 4.1). God is one and *beyond* the one and the monad (*Paed.* 1.8.71), and *beyond* cause (τὸ ἐπέκεινα αἴτιον, *Strom.* 7.2.2). See John Whittaker, "ΕΠΕΚΕΙΝΑ ΝΩΥ ΚΑΙ ΟΥΣΙΑΣ," *VC* 23 (1969): 93–94; Hägg, *Beginnings of Christian Apophaticism*, 154–79; Ziebritzki, *Geist und Weltseele*, 96–99; Raoul Mortley, *Connaissance religieuse et herméneutique chez Clément d'Alexandrie* (Leiden: Brill, 1973), 68–70.

[133] *Strom.* 6.13.107.

[134] According to Andrei Orlov (*The Enoch–Metatron Tradition* [TSAJ 107; Tübingen: Mohr Siebeck, 2005], 153; 279), early Enochic texts made little use of "face" imagery; however, in the context of a continued polemic against other Jewish traditions of divine mediatorship, later Enochic booklets—2 Enoch, 3 Enoch—produced extensive reflections on the Face. For a presentation of Jewish traditions centering on the vision of God's "Face," their Mesopotamian roots and later development from the Second Temple to later rabbinic Judaism, see Friedrich Nötscher, *"Das Angesicht Gottes schauen" nach biblischer und babilonischer Auffassung* (Darmstadt: Wissenschaftliche Buchgesellschaft, 1969 [1924]); C. L. Seow, "Face," in *Dictionary of Deities and Demons in the Bible* (ed. K. van der Toorn et al.; Leiden/Boston: Brill; Grand Rapids, Mich.: Eerdmans, 1999), 322–25; Orlov, "Exodus 33 on God's Face: A Lesson From the Enochic Tradition," and "The Face as the Heavenly Counterpart of the Visionary in the Slavonic *Ladder of Jacob*," republished in Orlov, *From Apocalypticism to Merkabah Mysticism: Studies in the Slavonic Pseudepigrapha* (JSJSup 114; Leiden: Brill, 2006), 311–25, 399–419; Orlov, *Enoch-Metatron Tradition*, 227–29, 254–303; April D. DeConick, "Heavenly Temple Traditions and Valentinian Worship: A Case for First-Century Christology in the Second Century," in *The Jewish Roots of Christological Monotheism* (ed. C. C. Newman et al.; JSJSup 63; Leiden: Brill, 1999], 327–29.

of the enthroned Glory."[135] It is, as for some later Hekhalot traditions, a hypostatic "Face."[136] For Clement, "the Face of God is the Son."[137]

To describe the continual propagation of light from the Face down to the lowest level of existence, Clement uses the adverb προσεχῶς ("proximately"), suggesting immediacy, the lack of any interval between the levels. Each rank of spiritual entities is "moved" by the one above it, and will in turn "move" the immediately lower level.[138]

The purpose of hierarchy consists in the spiritual "advancement" (προκοπή) of each of the orders or levels (τάξεις).[139] The first level

---

[135] Orlov, *Enoch–Metatron Tradition*, 282: "It is evident that all four accounts, Exodus 33:18–23, Psalm 17:15, 1 Enoch 14, and 2 Enoch 39:3–6, represent a single tradition in which the divine Face serves as the *terminus technicus* for the designation of the Lord's anthropomorphic extent."

[136] According to Nathaniel Deutsch (*Guardians of the Gate: Angelic Vice Regency in Late Antiquity* [BSJS 22; Leiden/Boston: Brill, 1999], 43), at least one Merkabah passage (§§ 396–397) "explicitly identifies Metatron as the hypostatic face of God," so that "the title *sar ha-panim*...is better understood as 'prince who is the face [of God]." The reference is to sections in Peter Schäfer's *Synopse zur Hekhalot-Literatur* (TSAJ 2; Tübingen: Mohr Siebeck, 1981). Since an English translation of the treatise *Hekhalot Zutarti* (which contains §§ 396–397) has not yet been produced, I quote the relevant lines in the authoritative German rendering of Schäfer (*Übersetzung der Hekhalot-Literatur III: §§ 335–597* [TSAJ 22; Tübingen: Mohr Siebeck, 1989], 120–23): "Mose sprach vor dem Herrn aller Welten: Wenn dein Angesicht nicht (voran)geht, laß mich nicht vorn hier hinaufsteigen. Und der Herr aller Welten warnte Mose, er soll sich vor ihm hüten, wie es heißt: Hüte dich vor ihm!...Mit heiligen Buchstaben nennt man ihn Metatron...Er ist der Fürst, der Fürst des Angesichts, und alle Dienstengel erheben sich vor ihm." See also Orlov, *Enoch–Metatron Tradition*, 124–25.

[137] *Exc.* 10.6; 12.1. De Conick ("Heavenly Temple Traditions," 325) states that "the image of the Son as the Father's Face may have played a significant role in Valentinian theologies." The repeated occurrence of the same designation in Clement of Alexandria (*Paed.* 1.57; 1.124.4; *Strom.* 7.10.58), as well as in Tertullian (*Prax.* 14), suggests that "Face" as a christological title was at least as popular in mainstream Christianity as it was in Valentinian tradition. In fact, "the idea that the Glory of God is beheld in the very 'face of Christ' is already present in 2 Cor 4:6" (Gieschen, *Angelomophic Christology*, 334).

[138] Cf. the veiled description in *Strom.* 6.16.148; 7.2.9: "the operative power (ἡ δραστικὴ ἐνέργεια) is imparted by descent through those that are being moved in strictest succession (διὰ τῶν προσεχέστερον κινουμένων)"; "For on one original first principle, which acts according to the [Father's] will, the first, and the second, and the third depend; then at the highest extremity of the visible world is the blessed abode of the angels (μακαρία ἀγγελοθεσία); and coming down to us there are ranged, one [level] under the other (ἄλλοι ὑπ' ἄλλοις), those who, from One and by One, both are saved and save (σῳζόμενοί τε καὶ σῴζοντες)." The resemblance with Ps.-Dionysius, *CH* 13.4 (PTS 36:48) is evident.

[139] According to François Sagnard, προσεχῶς "indique la continuité dans l'espace, sans intermédiaire. La dynamis (ou: le logos) du Père passe continuellement dans le Monogène pour l'engendrer. On peut dire aussi que le Monogène *est* cette dynamis du Père" (Sagnard, *Extraits*, 79 n. 2; emphasis added); "l'ὑπεροχή est la différence entre

of celestial entities contemplating the Face consists of the seven πρωτόκτιστοι, celestial beings "first created." On the one hand, these *protoctists* are numbered with the angels and archangels, their subordinates.[140] On the other hand, they are bearers of the divine Name, and as such they are called "gods."[141] Clement equates them with "the seven eyes of the Lord" (Zech 3:9; 4:10; Rev 5:6), the "thrones" (Col 1:16), and the "angels ever contemplating the Face of God" (Matt 18:10).[142] The *protoctists* are seven, but they are simultaneously characterized by unity and multiplicity. Although distinct in number, Clement writes, "their liturgy is common and undivided":

> As for the *protoctists*, even while they are distinct in number, and individually defined and circumscribed, the similarity of [their] deeds nevertheless points to [their] unity, equality and being alike. Among the seven, there has not been given more to the one and less to the other; nor is any of them lacking in advancement; [they] have received perfection from the beginning, at the first [moment of their] coming into being, from God through the Son.[143]

---

deux échelons de la προκοπή" (77 n. 3). Pointing to *Strom.* 7.2.10, Oeyen notes: "Die verschiedenen Stufen des Fortschrittes heissen…τάξεις, das Fortschreiten von einer zur anderen προκοπή" (*Engelpneumatologie*, 9).

[140] *Hae namque primitivae virtutes ac primo creatae* (rendering πρωτόγονοι καὶ πρωτόκτιστοι δυνάμεις), *inmobiles exsistentes secundum substantiam, cum subiectis angelis et archangelis* (*Adumbr.* 1 John 2:1). Stählin's critical edition introduces a comma between *inmobiles* and *exsistentes*. I prefer to revert to Zahn's text (*Forschungen* 3:88), which has no comma. Thus, I take *inmobiles exsistentes secundum substantiam* to mean that their substance is immovable according to substance, i.e., does not undergo change. I shall discuss the identification of these "powers" at a later point.

[141] "Now, in the Gospel according to Mark, when the Lord was interrogated by the high priest if he was 'the Christ, the Son of the blessed God,' he answered saying, 'I am; and you shall see the Son of man seated at the right hand of power (*a dextris virtutis*).' But 'powers' indicates the holy angels. Further, when he says 'at the right hand of God,' he means the same ones, on account of the equality and likeness of the angelic and holy powers, which are called by the one name of God (*quae uno nominabantur nomine dei*)" (*Adumbr.* Jude 5:24). Clement equates here "power" in the Gospel text with "angels"; in an earlier sentence, he had equated "glory" with "angels": "*In the presence of his glory*: he means before the angels…" (*Adumbr.* Jude 5:24).

[142] *Exc.* 10; *Ecl.* 57.1. For a synthetic presentation of the *protoctists*, see Le Boulluec, "Commentaire" (SC 279:143).

[143] *Exc.* 10.3–4: οἱ δὲ Πρωτόκτιστοι, εἰ καὶ ἀριθμῷ διάφοροι καὶ ὁ καθ' ἕκαστον περιώρισται καὶ περιγέγραπται, ἀλλ' ἡ ὁμοιότης τῶν πραγμάτων ἑνότητα καὶ ἰσότητα καὶ ὁμοιότητα ἐνδείκνυται. Οὐ γὰρ τῷδε μὲν πλέον, τῷδε δὲ ἧττον παρέσχηται τῶν Ἑπτά, οὐδ' ὑπολείπεταί τις αὐτοῖς προκοπή· ἐξ ἀρχῆς ἀπειληφότων τὸ τέλειον ἅμα τῇ πρώτῃ γενέσει παρὰ τοῦ Θεοῦ διὰ τοῦ Υἱοῦ. I have used two different English words for ὁμοιότης ("similarity" and "being alike"), because our post-Nicene theological bias would automatically weaken the bearing of this word in Clement. The second time he uses ὁμοιότης, Clement has in mind "being like" as opposed to "being unlike," not to "being the same as."

And each of the spiritual beings has, on the one hand, both its proper power and its individual dispensation; but, on the other hand, given that the *protoctists* have come to be and have received [their] perfection at the same time, their service is common and undivided.[144]

The *protoctists* fulfill multiple functions: in relation to Christ, they present the prayers ascending from below (*Exc.* 27.2); on the other hand, they function as "high priests" with regard to the archangels, just as the archangels are "high priests" to the angels (*Exc.* 27.2). In their unceasing contemplation of the Face of God, they represent the model (προκέντημα) of perfected souls (*Exc.* 10.6; 11.1).

Clement's *protoctists* echo Jewish and Christian traditions about the sevenfold highest angelic company.[145] Among Christian texts, for

---

[144] *Exc.* 11.4: καὶ δύναμιν μὲν ἰδίαν ἔχει ἕκαστον τῶν πνευματικῶν καὶ ἰδίαν οἰκονομίαν· καθὸ δὲ ὁμοῦ τε ἐγένοντο καὶ τὸ ἐντελὲς ἀπειλήφασιν οἱ Πρωτόκτιστοι, κοινὴν τὴν λειτουργίαν καὶ ἀμέριστον. Cf. Cyprian, *Fort.* 11 (CC 3/1:205): "Now, what about the seven brothers in Maccabees, alike in their lot of birth and virtues (*et natalium pariter et uirtutum sorte consimiles*), filling up the number seven in the sacrament of a perfected completion?... As the first seven days in the divine arrangement containing seven thousand of years, as the seven spirits and seven angels which stand and go in and out before the face of God (*adsistunt et conuersantur ante faciem dei*), and the seven-branched lamp in the tabernacle of witness."

[145] Passages featuring the group of seven heavenly beings are Ezek 9:2–3 (seven angelic beings, of which the seventh is more important than the other six); Tob 12:15 (seven "holy angels" who have access before the Glory, where they present the prayers of "the saints"); *1 En.* (ch. 20, seven archangels; ch. 90.21, "the seven first snow-white ones"); *Test. Levi* 7.4–8.3 (seven men in white clothing, vesting Levi with the [sevenfold] priestly apparel); *2 En.* 19.6 (seven phoenixes, seven cherubim, and seven seraphim, all singing in unison). The notion of "first created" is important to the author of *Jubilees*: the angels of the presence are said to be circumcised from their creation on the second day, thus possessing a certain perfection and functioning as heavenly models and final destination of the people of Israel (*Jub.* 2.2; 15.27). According to the *Prayer of Joseph*, dated to the first century C.E., Israel is a heavenly being—called indistinctly both ἄγγελος θεοῦ and πνεῦμα ἀρχικόν—who ranks higher than the seven archangels, as chief captain and first minister before the face of God. See also the discussion of heptadic traditions in Second Temple Judaism in Willem F. Smelik, "On Mystical Transformation of the Righteous into Light in Judaism," *JSJ* 26 (1995): 131–41; Rachel Elior, *The Three Temples: On the Emergence of Jewish Mysticism* (Oxford/Portland: The Littman Library of Jewish Civilization, 2005), 77–81. Note also the alternative tradition of four archangels (e.g., *1 En.* 10.1–9); for the relation between the seven-based pattern and the fourfold/twelvefold pattern (four archangels, four faces of the sacred creatures, twelve heavenly gates, months, signs of the zodiac, tribes, etc., see Elior, *Three Temples*, 57–58). Among later Jewish writings, *3 En.* 10.2–6 mentions that Metatron is exalted above the "eight great princes" who bear the divine Name. *Pirkê de Rabbi Eliezer*, a work composed around 750 C.E. but incorporating material going back to the Pseudepigrapha, speaks about "the *seven angels which were created first*," who are said to minister before God within the Pargod (*The Chapters of Rabbi Eliezer the Great According to the Text of the Manuscript Belonging to Abraham Epstein of Vienna* [tr. G. Friedländer; New York: Hermon 1965], iv, 23).

instance, Revelation mentions seven spirits/angels before the divine throne (Rev 1:4; 3:1; 4:5; 5:6; 8:2), and the *Shepherd of Hermas* knows of a group of seven consisting of the six "first created ones" (πρῶτοι κτισθέντες) who accompany the Son of God as their seventh (Herm. *Vis.* 3.4.1; Herm. *Sim.* 5.5.3).[146] It is clear, however, that Clement subjects this apocalyptic material to the spiritualizing interpretation and the Logos-theology inherited from Philo. The *protoctists* are both "angelic powers" and "powers of the Logos" that mark the passing of divine unity into multiplicity, and, conversely, the reassembly of cosmic multiplicity into the unity of the Godhead.[147]

The entire hierarchy is characterized by relative corporality. On the presupposition that anything that exists is an οὐσία, and is implicitly characterized by form, Clement states that "neither the spiritual and intelligible beings, nor the archangels, nor the *protoctists*, not even [Christ] himself, are without form, without shape, without frame, and bodiless; rather they do have both individual form and body..."[148] However, Clement immediately notes, this type of "form" is entirely different from any earthly forms.[149] Indeed, the corporality of the spiritual beings is characterized by progressive subtlety, in proportion to their position in the hierarchy.[150] This type of subtle corporality is

---

[146] See also the sermon *De centesima, sexagesima, tricesima* (whose dating ranges, among scholars, from late second to the fourth century) states that God first created seven angelic princes out of fire, and later made one of the seven into his Son. For the text, see Richard Reitzenstein, "Eine frühchristliche Schrift von den dreierlei Früchten des christlichen Lebens," *ZNW* 15 (1914): 82. The idea of angels being made out of fire is widespread: 4Q403 20–21–22 10; *1 En.* 14.11; Heb 1:7 (= Ps 103/104:4); *2 Bar.* 21.6; *Apoc. Abr.* 19.6; *2 En.* 29.1–3; 39.5; Tertullian, *Marc.* 3.9; Evagrius, *Gnost.* 1.11; *b. Hag.* 13b–14a; *Gen. Rab.* 78.1; *Deut. Rab.* 11.4; *Pirq. R. El* 22; *Tg. Job* 25.2. Jean Pépin has shown (*Théologie cosmique et théologie chrétienne* [Paris: PUF, 1964], 221–47, 314–19) that Jewish and Christian speculation on the nature of angels also owes to the theory of the "fifth element," ascribed to Aristotle's now lost *De philosophia*. On the latter, see Abraham P. Bos, *Cosmic and Meta-Cosmic Theology in Aristotle's Lost Dialogues* (BSIH 16; Leiden/New York: Brill, 1989), 89–94.

[147] See the analysis of *Strom.* 4.25.156 above.

[148] *Exc.* 10.1: Ἀλλ' οὐδὲ τὰ πνευματικὰ καὶ νοερά, οὐδὲ οἱ Ἀρχάγγελοι, <οὐδὲ> οἱ Πρωτόκτιστοι, οὐδὲ μὴν οὐδ' αὐτός, ἄμορφος καὶ ἀνείδεος καὶ ἀσχημάτιστος καὶ ἀσώματός ἐστιν. According to Collomp ("Une source," 34, 39), here Clement seems to be reworking a source either identical or similar to what has been preserved in the Ps.-Clementine *Homilies* (17.7), featuring much cruder descriptions.

[149] *Exc.* 10.2–3: Ὅλως γὰρ τὸ γενητὸν οὐκ ἀνούσιον μέν, οὐχ ὅμοιον δὲ μορφὴν καὶ σῶμα ἔχουσι τοῖς ἐν τῷδε τῷ κόσμῳ σώμασιν ("On the one hand, anything that has come to be is not without *ousia*; on the other, they [referring back to the spiritual beings] do not have a form and a body like the bodies [to be found] in this world").

[150] Each of the celestial entities posssesses its specific shape and a body that corre-

entirely relative: the beings on any given level can be described at the same time as "bodiless," from the perspective of inferior ranks, and "bodily," from the perspective of superior levels of being.[151] A more extensive and rigorous discussion of this type of incorporality and of the "luminous," "ethereal," and "astral" or "angelic," bodies in the afterlife occurs in Origen.[152] In fact, there is an evident link between the relative incorporality of the angelic hierarchy, as expressed in Clement's *Eclogae*, and Origen's theory, condemned at the fifth ecumenical council, that the protological fall of the spiritual intelligences (νόες) caused their diversification into angelic, human, and demonic realms, each characterized by a specific degree of corporality.[153]

The Function of the Hierarchy

The advancement on the cosmic ladder leads to the progressive transformation of one level into the next, an idea concerning which Clement offers a highly complex account.[154] In his view the believers are being instructed by the angels, and their horizon is one of angelification: at the end of a millennial cycle, they will be translated into the rank of angels,[155] while their instructors will become archangels, replacing their

---

sponds to its rank among spiritual beings: καὶ μορφὴν ἔχει ἰδίαν καὶ σῶμα ἀνὰ λόγον τῆς ὑπεροχῆς τῶν πνευματικῶν ἁπάντων (*Exc.* 10.1). Cf. Sagnard, *Extraits*, 77 n. 3: "Ὑπεροχή est la différence entre deux échelons de la προκοπή."

[151] *Exc.* 11.3: Ὡς πρὸς τὴν σύγκρισιν τῶν τῇδε σωμάτων (οἷον ἄστρων) ἀσώματα καὶ ἀνείδεα, <ἀλλ'> ὡς πρὸς τὴν σύγκρισιν τοῦ Υἱοῦ σώματα μεμετρημένα καὶ αἰσθητά· οὕτως καὶ ὁ Υἱὸς πρὸς τὸν Πατέρα παραβαλλόμενος ("Thus, compared to the bodies here, such as the stars, they are bodiless and shapeless; yet, compared to the Son, they are measured and sensible bodies. Likewise is the Son in regards to the Father").

[152] See Henri Crouzel, "Le thème platonicien du 'véhicule de l'âme' chez Origène," *Did* 7 (1977): 225–38; Lawrence R. Hennessey, "A Philosophical Issue in Origen's Eschatology: The Three Senses of Incorporeality," in *Origeniana Quinta: Papers of the 5th International Origen Congress, Boston College, 14–18 August 1989* (ed. Robert J. Daly; BETL 105; Leuven: Leuven University Press, 1992), 373–80; Hermann S. Schibli, "Origen, Didymus, and the Vehicle of the Soul," in *Origeniana Quinta*, 381–91. The notion of the soul's pneumatic vehicle has been traced back to Aristotle: Abraham P. Bos, *The Soul and its Instrumental Body: A Reinterpretation of Aristotle's Philosophy of Living Nature* (BSIH 112; Leiden/Boston: Brill, 2003), 281–90.

[153] See the relevant passages and the discussion in Pépin, *Théologie cosmique*, 324–25.

[154] See Collomp, "Une source," 23–24; Oeyen, *Engelpneumatologie*, 8–9, 12; Nardi, "Note," 14–15, 19.

[155] Daniélou, "Doctrines secrètes," 207: "The different degrees of the hierarchy are not immutable natures, but rather degrees of a spiritual ascent, so that it is possible to pass from one order to the next." As Nardi ("Note," 19) notes, Clement does not see an essential difference between humans, angel, and protoctists.

own instructors, who will in turn be promoted to a higher level. All levels of the hierarchy move one step higher evey one thousand years:

> For those among humans who start being transformed into angels are instructed by the angels for a thousand years, in order to be promoted to perfection (εἰς τελειότητα ἀποκαθιστάμενοι). Then the instructors are translated into archangelic authority, while those who have received instruction will in turn instruct those among humans who are transformed into angels; thereupon they are, at the specified period, reestablished into the proper angelic state of the body.[156]

This periodic "upgrading" also applies to the *protoctists*, who are "set" higher,

> so that they may no longer exercise a definite ministry, according to providence, but may abide in rest and solely in the contemplation of God alone. But those closest to them will advance to the level that they themselves have left. And the same occurs by analogy with those on an inferior level.[157]

Clement on the Interior Ascent

As Oeyen has rightly noted, Clement's account raises numerous problems. Have the *protoctists* been created perfect and immutable (*Exc.* 10.3; 11.4), or have they *acquired* perfection? (*Ecl.* 57)? How can the *protoctists* be a group of no more and no less than seven, given that no limitation on the number of those "promoted" in their stead has been mentioned? If the *protoctists* are "the highest level of disposition" (*Ecl.* 57.1), to what "higher" level can they be translated?[158]

---

[156] *Ecl.* 57.5. Note the expression εἰς τελειότητα ἀποκαθιστάμενοι in reference to the promotion of archangels to the status of *protoctists*. Cf. *Ecl.* 57.1: οἱ ἐν τῇ ἄκρᾳ ἀποκαταστάσει πρωτόκτιστοι. In both cases Clement speaks of ἀποκατάστασις in the sense of promotion to eschatological perfection rather than restoration to a protological state. As André Mehat explains ("'Apocatastase': Origène, Clément d'Alexandrie, Act. 3, 21," *VC* 10 [1956]: 196–214), "l'apocatastase est une échelle et nullment un retour. L'expression est à rapprocher d'autres similaires: le sommet de l'héritage, de l'adoption, du Repos, etc. (*Strom.* 2.22.134; 2.22.136; 4.22.145). Les Protoctistes, qui ont recu des le principe l aperfection (*Exc. ex Theod.* 10, 1–12) n'apparaissent nulle part comme en ayant eter dechus a quelque moment que ce soit. L'apocatastase n'est donc pas un retour, mais elle est l'état définitif où Dieu a rangé le monde des Esprits qui sont les plus proches de lui. Le préfixe ἀπο—n'exprime rien d'autre ici que l'idée d'achévement."

[157] *Ecl.* 56.5.

[158] Oeyen, *Engelpneumatologie*, 12. It should be mentioned that the vast majority of scholars are in agreement that all of these passages belong to Clement. Lilla instead (*Clement*, 176–83), attributes them to a Gnostic source (179: "perhaps to Theodotus

To answer the questions just raised, it is necessary to determine to what extent the Alexandrian master is in agreement with the Jewish and Jewish Christian traditions that he is drawing on. I assume, *pace* Nardi, that Clement is drawing on such traditions from the "elders."[159] I submit that the so-called "noetic exegesis," which Clement, following Philo, routinely applies to authoritative (biblical and "Greek") texts,[160] has as its result the internalization of the cosmic ladder and of the associated experience of ascent and transformation.

In *Strom.* 4.25.158, Clement discusses the necessity of the seven-day purification required for the priest who has touched a corpse (Ezek 44:26). Since the entire text is a prophetic vision about the eschatological temple and its ministers, Clement can easily allude to an interpretation of the seven days of purification and subsequent entry into the temple as a purification from *moral* corruption.[161] This purification is followed by the ascent through the seven heavens.[162] But Clement moves beyond the traditional seven-storied cosmology:

> Whether, then, the time be that which through the seven periods enumerated returns to the chiefest rest, or the seven heavens, which some reckon one above the other; or whether also the fixed sphere which borders on the intellectual world be called the eighth, the expression denotes that the Gnostic ought to rise out of the sphere of creation and of sin.[163]

---

himself"), arguing that the type of *Himmelsreise* present in these passages "plunges directly into Gnosticism" (181, cf. 183). The underlying understanding of "Gnosticism" has in the meantime become untenable. But even if one were to concede the Gnostic character of *Exc.* 10–15 and 27, the problem remains no less acute, because *Ecl.* 57 would then also be labeled as "Gnostic" (see Lilla, *Clement*, 185, 179 n. 6). In short, whether Clementine, "Jewish Christian," or Gnostic, these passages incorporate a contradiction.

[159] Discussing Clement's speculations about the millennial cycle, Nardi ("Note," 30–31) sets up an opposition, questionable in my opinion, between Jewish-Christian (chiliastic) traditions, on the one hand, and Platonic myths (*Phaed.* 248E–249A; *Rep.* 615A) on the other, and judges that the latter is a more likely background to Clement.

[160] Osborn, "Philo and Clement: Quiet Conversion and Noetic Exegesis," *SPhilo* 10 (1998): 108–24.

[161] Nevertheless, Clement emphatically rejects anti-somatic ideas: "not that the body was polluted, but that sin and disobedience were incarnate, and embodied, and dead, and therefore abominable."

[162] For the origin of the seven-heaven cosmology in Second Temple Judaism and Christianity, see Ioan-Petru Culianu, *Psychanodia: A Survey of the Evidence Concerning the Ascension of the Soul and its Relevance* (Leiden: Brill, 1983), and Adela Yarbro-Collins, "The Seven Heavens in Jewish and Christian Apocalypses," in *Death, Ecstasy, and Other Worldly Journeys* (ed. J. J. Collins and M. Fishbane; New York: SUNY, 1995), 59–93.

[163] *Strom.* 4.25.159.

It seems that all imagistic details, such as specific intervals of space or time are emptied of the literal meaning they had had in the apocalyptic cosmology of the "elders." Whether "seven days," or "one thousand years," or "seven heavens," or "archangels," or "*protoctists*," the details of the cosmic-ladder imagery become images of interior transformation. This is why the inconsistencies in Clement's account about the *protoctists* are only apparent. At times, Clement refers to the data he has received from tradition. Thus, in the *Stromateis*, he shows himself familiar with the idea that "the whole world of creatures...revolves in sevens" and that "the first-born princes of the angels (πρωτόγονοι ἀγγέλων ἄρχοντες), who have the greatest power, are seven" (*Strom.* 6.16.142–143), and in the *Excerpta* he offers a detailed description of the entire hierarchy. At other times, however, Clement suggests that these data require further interpretation. For instance, he speaks of

> ...gnostic souls that surpass in the greatness of contemplation the mode of life of each of the holy ranks (τῇ μεγαλοπρεπείᾳ τῆς θεωρίας ὑπερβαινούσας ἑκάστης ἁγίας τάξεως τὴν πολιτείαν)...ever moving to higher and yet higher places [lit. "reaching places better than the better places," ἀμείνους ἀμεινόνων τόπων τόπους], embracing the divine vision (θεωρίαν) not in mirrors or by means of mirrors. This is the vision attainable by "the pure in heart"; this is the function (ἐνέργεια) of the Gnostic, who has been perfected, to have converse with God through the great High Priest...The Gnostic even forms and creates himself (ναὶ μὴν ἑαυτὸν κτίζει καὶ δημιουργεῖ), and, what is more, he adorns those who hear him, becoming similar to God (ἐξομοιούμενος θεῷ);
> ...Then become pure in heart, and close (κατὰ τὸ προσεχὲς) to the Lord, there awaits them promotion (ἀποκατάστασις) to everlasting contemplation.[164] And they are called by the appellation of "gods," to be co-enthroned (σύνθρονοι) with the other "gods" that have been set in first place (πρώτων τεταγμένων) by the Savior;
> ..."This is the generation of them that seek the Lord, that seek the Face of the God of Jacob" (Ps 24:3–6). The prophet has, in my opinion, concisely indicated the Gnostic. David, as appears, has cursorily demonstrated the Savior to be God, by calling him "the Face of the God of Jacob"...[165]

In these passages, the "Gnostic soul" is described as possessing unmediated, perfect access to the vision of the Face, taking its stand in

---

[164] See my earlier note about the absence of protological speculations associated with Clement's use of ἀποκατάστασις.

[165] *Strom.* 7.3.13; 7.10.56–57; 7.10.58.

his immediate proximity, κατὰ τὸ προσεχὲς (cf. the repeated use of προσεχῶς in the *Excerpta* to express the immediacy, the lack of any interval between the levels of the hierarchy!). The true Gnostic has been brought "*in the presence of his glory*: he means before the angels, *faultless in joyousness*, having become angels."[166] The Gnostic "has pitched his tent in *El*, that is, in God."[167] Clement arrives at this conclusion after a creative exegesis of Ps 18:5 ("he pitched his tent in the sun").[168] First, he moves from ἐν τῷ ἡλίῳ to ἐν τῷ ἤλ, on the basis of similarity of sound.[169] Then, he moves from ἐν τῷ ἤλ to ἐν τῷ θεῷ, on the basis of Mark 15:34 ("*Eli, Eli*, that is, *my God, my God*").[170] Moreover, when Clement says that "the function (ἐνέργεια) of the Gnostic who has been perfected" is such that "he even forms and creates himself" (ναὶ μὴν ἑαυτὸν κτίζει καὶ δημιουργεῖ) (*Strom.* 7.3.13), the verbs (κτίζει and δημιουργεῖ) are a transparent allusion to Gen 1:26, and signal the transfer of divine functions to the Gnostic.[171] One could well say that the Gnostics actually become *protoctists*, since Clement states that "they are called by the appellation of "gods," to be co-enthroned (σύνθρονοι) with the other "gods" that have been set in first place (πρώτων τεταγμένων) by the Savior."[172] It is in light of this conception, inherited from earlier tradition, that one should be reading Clement's numerous passages in which he quotes Ps 81:6, LXX ("you are gods and all of you sons of

---

[166] *Adumbr.* Jude 5:24.

[167] *Ecl.* 57.3.

[168] The procedure is typical of Clement; see Ursula Treu, "Etymologie und Allegorie bei Klemens," *StPatr* 4 (1961)/TU 79: 190–211.

[169] It appears that "aspiration had ceased in Athens already before the end of the classical period. When observed in script, it was as an old relic, not as a living item of language" (Chris Caragounis, *The Development of Greek and the New Testament* [WUNT 167; Tübingen: Mohr Siebeck, 2004], 391). According to the rhetorician Tryphon, living in the first century B.C.E., aspiration was "a rule of the ancients, which the moderns set aside" (Caragounis, *Development*, 391 n. 166). Nardi ("Note," 27) notes Clement's "suggestive paretymology," but does not address the issue of pronunciation.

[170] *Ecl.* 57.3: καὶ μή τι τὸ "ἐν τῷ ἡλίῳ ἔθετο τὸ σκήνωμα αὐτοῦ" οὕτως ἐξακούεται ἐν τῷ ἡλίῳ ἔθετο, τουτέστιν ἐν τῷ ἤλ ἤγουν θεῷ, ὡς ἐν τῷ εὐαγγελίῳ "ἠλὶ ἠλὶ" ἀντὶ τοῦ "θεέ μου, θεέ μου" ("And is not *he set his tabernacle in the sun* to be understood as follows: *he set in the* "sun," that is "in El," or "God," just as in the Gospel: *Eli, Eli* instead of *my God, my God*?").

[171] Le Boulluec draws attention to the verbs (*Clément d'Alexandrie, Stromate VII* [SC 428 Paris: Cerf, 1997], 70 n. 2).

[172] *Strom.* 7.10.56–57. The preeminent position of the "other gods" can also indicate that they are the earliest to have been placed in their position of highest ranking celestial beings ("gods") by the Savior. Cf. *Exc.* 10.4, on the *protoctists*: ἐξ ἀρχῆς ἀπειληφότων τὸ τέλειον ἅμα τῇ πρώτῃ γενέσει παρὰ τοῦ Θεοῦ διὰ τοῦ Υἱοῦ.

the Most High"), a foundational passage for the patristic doctrine of
deification.[173]

There can be no doubt that these texts by Clement of Alexandria
preserve an ancient biblical and extra-biblical tradition—namely that of
a transformation from human into angelic—which will be eliminated
in mainstream Christian theology, but retained by certain strands of
Judaism (e.g., *1 En.* 71.11; *2 En.* 28.11; cf. *3 En.* 15.48C).[174] *T. Levi* 4.2,
for instance, is explicit about the possibility of becoming a "prince of the
presence" (cf. 4QSb 4.25). Similarly, in *2 En.*, for instance, the patriarch
is not merely a visitor to the heavenly realms, but "a servant permanently

---

[173] For Clement's use of Ps 81:6, LXX, see van den Hoek, "'I Said, You Are Gods…':
The Significance of Psalm 82 for Some Early Christian Authors," in *The Use of Sacred
Books in the Ancient World* (ed. Leonard Victor Rutgers et al.; CBET 22; Peeters, 1998),
203–19, esp. 213–18; Norman Russell, *The Doctrine of Deification in the Greek Patristic
Tradition* (Oxford: Oxford University Press, 2004), 128–34.

[174] See the discussion and extensive list of primary sources in W. D. Davies, Dale
C. Allison, Jr., *A Critical and Exegetical Commentary on the Gospel According to Saint
Matthew* (ICC 1; London: T&T Clark, 1989), 3:227–8; James H. Charlesworth, "The
Portrayal of the Righteous as an Angel," in *Ideal Figures in Ancient Judaism; Profiles
and Paradigms* (ed. J. J. Collins and G. W. E. Nickelsburg; SBLSCS 12; Chico, CA:
Scholars, 1980), 135–51; Michael Mach, *Entwicklungsstadien des jüdischen Engelglaubens
in vorrabbinischer Zeit* (TSAJ 34; Tübingen: Mohr Siebeck, 1992), 163–73. According to
Fletcher-Louis, "the Lukan angelomorphic Christ brings an angelic identity and status to
his followers" (*Luke-Acts*, 254); the relation between Jesus-followers and angels is one of
"substantive continuity of identity" and "ontological affinity" (78). Deutsch (*Guardians
of the Gate*, 32–34; emphasis added) writes that "Metatron's… transformation from
a human being into an angel reflects an *ontological* process which may be repeated
by mystics…" For a different opinion, see Kevin P. Sullivan, *Wrestling with Angels: A
Study of the Relationship Between Angels and Humans in Ancient Jewish Literature and
the New Testament* (AGJU 55; Leiden, Brill 2004): "Despite the similarity in *appearance*
and the closeness of *interaction*, there does not seem to be any reason to suppose that
there was any blurring of categories between angels and humans. When there was an
apparent transformation from the human to the angelic (Enoch = Metatron or Jacob
= Israel), it was a one-time transformation that occurred beyond the earthly sphere"
(229); the boundary between humans and angels is "fix, but not absolute" (230): "fix"
because these remain "very different beings," yet "not absolute" because the boundary
between the human and angelic realms can be crossed. Regardless of the manner in
which one understands the angelic or simili-angelic status of humanity, it is important
to observe that the depiction of *eschatological* humanity as angelic or angelomorphic
corresponds to the depiction of *protological* humanity as angelic or angelomorphic
(e.g., *2 En.* 30.11, where Adam is said to have been created as "a second angel, honored
and great and glorious"); thus, angelification signals the return to Paradise. See in this
respect Mach, *Entwicklungsstadien*, 168–69; Orlov, "Resurrection of Adam's Body: The
Redeeming Role of Enoch-Metatron in *2 (Slavonic) Enoch*," in Orlov, *Apocalypticism
to Merkabah Mysticism*, 231–36; "The Pillar of the World: The Eschatological Role of
the Seventh Antediluvian Hero in *2 (Slavonic) Enoch*," *Hen* 30 (2008): 119–34, esp.
129, 132, 133.

installed in the office of the *sar happanim*."[175] According to Rachel Elior, the Qumranites "expressed profound identification with the angels...they envisaged a heavenly cult of angelic priests," and saw themselves as "partners and counterparts of the angels." For them, "[a]dherence to the solar calendar...was construed as *imitatio angelorum*, imitation of the angelic sacred service in sacred heavenly space"; indeed, "[t]hose who fulfill the covenantal terms, including the observance of the commandments, maintenance of strict purity, and the proper sequence of time, indicate that they have joined the ranks of the angels."[176] The Sages, by contrast, were at best ambivalent about—and usually critical of—such transformational mysticism; however, "rejected traditions often went underground only to emerge again as soon as the circumstances changed."[177] Indeed, Hekhalot literature speaks about becoming superior, more glorious than the "eight great princes" (*3 En.* 10.2–6), even becoming "the lesser YHWH" (*3 En.* 12).

The description of eschatological humanity as having undergone a transformation towards an angelic (or simili-angelic) status is also affirmed in early Christianity: ἰδοὺ μυστήριον ὑμῖν λέγω· πάντες οὐ κοιμηθησόμεθα πάντες δὲ ἀλλαγησόμεθα (1 Cor 15:51); ὡς ἄγγελοι ἐν τῷ οὐρανῷ εἰσιν (Matt 22:30); ἰσάγγελοι γάρ εἰσιν καὶ υἱοί εἰσιν θεοῦ (Luke 20:36). Some two hundred years later, Tertullian still interprets these statements as indicating a process of real "angelification."[178] Nevertheless, the notion of an angelic transformation at the end time is recontextualized and made dependent on the Christian *kerygma*. For instance, according to Phil 3:20–21, the transformation of the believer is effected by Christ upon his end-time return (σωτῆρα ἀπεκδεχόμεθα κύριον Ἰησοῦν Χριστόν, ὃς μετασχηματίσει τὸ σῶμα τῆς ταπεινώσεως ἡμῶν), and consists of a change that results in a "christomorphic"

---

[175] Orlov, *Enoch–Metatron Tradition*, 156.

[176] Elior, *Three Temples*, 58, 171, 99, 93.

[177] C. R. A. Morray-Jones, "Transformational Mysticism in the Apocalyptic-Merkabah Tradition," *JJS* 43 (1992): 11; Smelik, "Transformation of the Righteous into Light," 127.

[178] Tertullian, *Marc.* 3.9.4, 7: "And, really, if your god promises to men some time or other the true nature of angels (*veram substantiam angelorum*)—for he says, "They shall be like the angels"—why should not my God also have fitted on to angels the true substance of men (*veram substantiam hominum*), from whatever source derived?...Since the Creator 'makes his angels spirits, and his ministers a flame of fire'...he [God] will one day form men into angels, who once formed angels into men (*homines in angelos reformandi quandoque qui angelos in homines formarit aliquando*)."

humanity ([Χριστός]) (σύμμορφον τῷ σώματι τῆς δόξης αὐτοῦ).[179] It is no wonder, therefore, that some early Christians express the conviction that, at the eschaton, humanity will even surpass the angels.[180]

In later Christian tradition, the idea of a real "angelification" was eventually discarded. Despite extensive talk about the ascetical holy man living as an "angel in the body," and despite the depiction of an angelic life in heaven, the transformed holy man of monastic literature is "angelomorphic" rather than "angelic." This evolution had, most probably, something to do with the concern for the Incarnation as a "confirmation" of human existence, and with an awareness of the difficulties that a worldview such as Clement's would raise for eschatology.[181]

In light of these considerations, it becomes obvious that Clement interprets the millennial cycles and the ascent on the cosmic ladder as descriptions of an interior phenomenon. The archaic theory of the elders, postulating the celestial hierarchy as the locus of a real transformation from archangels into *protoctists*, from angels into archangels, and from humans into angels, sheds light on Clement's affirmation that the Christian "studies to be a god" (*Strom.* 6.14.113, μελετᾷ εἶναι θεός); or his statement about the perfected human "living as an angel on earth, but already luminous, and resplendent like the sun" (*Strom.* 7.10.57, ἰσάγγελος μὲν ἐνταῦθα· φωτεινὸς δὲ ἤδη καὶ ὡς ὁ ἥλιος λάμπων), even "a god going about in the flesh" (*Strom.* 7.16.101, ἐν σαρκὶ περιπολῶν θεός); or the affirmation that "the name 'gods' is

---

[179] Cf. Mark 9:1–2, where the eschatological reality of "the Kingdom of God come into power" is represented by the transfigured Jesus.

[180] The best known proponent of this view is Irenaeus of Lyon (*Haer* 5.36.3): after the *parousia*, humankind will contain the Word, and ascend to Him, passing beyond the angels (*supergrediens angelos*). Cf. *2 Bar.* 51.12, "And the excellence of the righteous will be greater than that of the angels." In the *Shepherd of Hermas*, the eschatological reward is described successively as "being numbered with us [the angels]" (Herm. *Sim.* 9.24.4), or "being granted entry (πάροδος) with the angels" (Herm. *Sim.* 9.25.2; Herm. *Vis.* 2.6.7). However, becoming "coheir with the son" (Herm. *Sim.* 5.2.7–8) is, logically, a status superior to that of the angelic counselors; this would suggest (although Hermas never says it explicitly) that the exalted Christian will be placed *above* the angels, even above the first-created angels. See the discussion in Ysabel de Andia, *Homo Vivens: Incorruptibilité et divinisation de l'homme chez Irénée de Lyon* (Paris: Études Augustiniennes, 1986), 327–28.

[181] In his concise but very dense treatment of Clement's eschatology, Brian Daley notes that Clement's dynamic conception of "a painstaking development rather than…eschatological crisis" is consonant with his view of the punishments after death as "a medicinal and therefore temporary measure" (*The Hope of the Early Church: A Handbook of Patristic Eschatology* [1991; reprint, Peabody, Mass.: Hendrickson, 2003], 46). Similarly Nardi, "Note," 35.

given to those that will be enthroned with the other 'gods,' who were first assigned (πρῶτων τεταγμένων) beneath the Savior" (*Strom.* 7.10.56). Such views are not unrelated to the later notion of the ascetical *bios angelikos*. Indeed, the interiorized ascent to heaven and transformation before the divine Face is what Christian tradition calls, in shorthand, θέωσις, "deification."[182]

Clement's interiorization of the cosmic ladder is consistent with his view of church hierarchy. I have noted earlier his conviction that "the advancements (προκοπαί) pertaining to the Church here below, namely those of bishops, presbyters and deacons, are imitations (μιμήματα) of the angelic glory."[183] This would yield a model of "church hierarchy," composed of bishops, priests, and deacons, quite similar to that advocated by Ignatius of Antioch. However, Clement undermines this edifice by offering the following exegesis:

> Such one is in reality a presbyter of the Church, and a true minister (deacon) of the will of God, if he do and teach what is the Lord's; not as being ordained by men, nor regarded righteous because a presbyter, but enrolled in the presbyterate because righteous. And although here upon earth he be not honored with the chief seat, he will sit down on the four-and-twenty thrones, judging the people, as John says in the Apocalypse.[184]

Quite clearly, Clement takes "bishop," "priest," or "deacon" not as designations of ecclesiastical office-holders—he appears, in fact, quite unhappy with those "ordained by men" and "honored with the chief seat"—but rather as functional designations of the stages of spiritual advancement.[185] For Clement (and later for Origen), function trumps rank; or, to be more accurate, the inner quality creates the function,

---

[182] For the deification of the perfected Christian, Clement uses mostly θεοποιέω and ἐκθεόω. Evem though he does not use the term θέωσις, he is a great proponent of the notion of deification. See, for instance, *Protr.* 1.8 (ὁ λόγος ὁ τοῦ θεοῦ ἄνθρωπος γενόμενος, ἵνα δὴ καὶ σὺ παρὰ ἀνθρώπου μάθῃς, πῇ ποτε ἄρα ἄνθρωπος γένηται θεός); *Protr.* 11.114 (οὐρανίῳ διδασκαλίᾳ θεοποιῶν τὸν ἄνθρωπον). For a study of deification in Clement, see G. W. Butterworth, "The Deification of Man in Clement of Alexandria," *JTS* 17 (1916): 157–69; Norman Russell, *Doctrine of Deification*, 121–40. Unfortunately, Russell does not discuss the *Eclogae and Adumbrationes*.

[183] *Strom.* 6.13.107. Cf. *Strom.* 7.1.3: the presbyters and deacons are "images" of the (angelic) models of superordinate and subordinate activities (κατὰ τὴν ἐκκλησίαν τὴν μὲν βελτιωτικὴν οἱ πρεσβύτεροι σῴζουσιν εἰκόνα, τὴν ὑπηρετικὴν δὲ οἱ διάκονοι).

[184] *Strom.* 6.13.106.

[185] Evidently, Clement's assertions about Church hierarchy imply the real existence of ecclesiastical office holders in Alexandria (Jakab, *Ecclesia Alexandrina*, 183).

which is then reflected in the ecclesiastical rank.[186] The "promotion" from one level of the hierarchy to the next corresponds to one's spiritual progress:

> …those who, following the footsteps of the apostles, have lived in perfection of righteousness according to the Gospel…[are] taken up in the clouds, the apostle writes, will first minister [as deacons], then be classed in the presbyterate, by promotion in glory (for glory differs from glory) till they grow into "a perfect man."[187]

If the affirmation that the church hierarchy is an imitation of the celestial hierarchy is given full weight, it would seem logical for Clement to posit the same sort of "promotion" and transformation on the cosmic ladder—from "angels" to "archangels" to *protoctists*—as dependent solely upon the degree of spiritual progress. Obviously, the number twenty-four in the case of the elders from Revelation is not taken any more literally than the number seven in the case of the *protoctists*.

A fitting formula to describe Clement of Alexandria's treatment of the inherited apocalyptic cosmology of the elders would be Golitzin's "interiorized apocalyptic." This term—which, in keeping with the established definitions, I would change to "interiorized apocalypticism"—has been proposed for the use of apocalyptic motifs in Byzantine monastic literature, and its definition seems perfectly applicable to Clement: "the transposition of the cosmic setting of apocalyptic literature, and in particular of the 'out of body' experience of heavenly ascent and transformation, to the inner theater of the soul."[188] Golitzin has furnished

---

[186] This point is argued emphatically and supported by quotations from Origen and Cyprian of Carthage, by Roncaglia, *Histoire de l'église copte* (Beirut: Dar al-Kalima, 1971), 3:187–89, 192–94. Jakab (*Ecclesia Alexandrina*, 183) offers the same interpretation. Clement's hierarchy has, on this point, great affinities with that of Ps.-Dionysius. However, in order to uphold the perfect mirroring between the celestial and the ecclesiastical hierarchies in spite of a disappointing historical reality, they adopt divergent strategies: while Clement approaches the issue from the perspective of "function" and thus challenges the authenticity of any "degree" that does not fully mirror the "function," Ps.-Dionysius writes from the perspective of "degree" and is forced to paint a "supremely idealistic—to say the least—portrait of the Christian clergy" (Golitzin, *Et Introibo*, 134). For the continuing tension between hierarchy and personal holiness in ascetic literature (reaching back to Origen), see Golitzin, "Hierarchy Versus Anarchy? Dionysius Areopagita, Symeon the New Theologian, Nicetas Stethatos, and Their Common Roots in Ascetical Tradition," *SVTQ* 38 (1994): 131–79.

[187] *Strom.* 6.13.107.

[188] Golitzin, "Earthly Angels and Heavenly Men: the Old Testament Pseudepigrapha, Nicetas Stethatos, and the Tradition of Interiorized Apocalyptic in Eastern Christian

proof of this transposition as early as the fourth and early fifth-century Eastern monastic literature; Stroumsa, on the other hand, argues that the shift was completed, at least in the Christian West, with Augustine of Hippo.[189] I believe that we may safely affirm that Clement of Alexandria offers one of the earliest examples of "interiorized apocalypticism."

Clement's celestial hierarchy is paradigmatic for the widespread hierarchical cosmology in the early centuries of the common era, as well as for the type of difficulties faced by the emerging Christian theology. The most acute problem was the necessity of adapting the hierarchical framework to a theology of the Trinity; more precisely, the difficulty of including the Holy Spirit in the hierarchy.

In the case of Clement, the cosmic ladder described above seems to reserve no place to the Holy Spirit: in descending order, one reads about the Father, the Son/Logos as principle of all things, and the *protoctists,* the level where multiplicity sets in. One may wonder what place this account leaves for the Holy Spirit. Le Boulluec synthesizes what we know about this group of seven superior angelic beings.[190] He does not, however, discuss the relation between the seven *protoctists* and the Holy Spirit. This problem constitutes, instead, the heart of Oeyen's contribution. In what follows I shall revisit his thesis of an *Engelpneumatologie* in Clement, and discuss the conjunction of hierarchy, prophecy, and the angelic spirit.

Ascetical and Mystical Literature," DOP 55 (2001): 141. For the generally accepted distinction between "apocalypticism" as a worldview and "apocalypse" as a literary form, see Paul D. Hanson, "Apocalypses and Apocalypticism," ABD 1 (1992): 279–92; John J. Collins, *The Apocalyptic Imagination: An Introduction to Jewish Apocalyptic Literature* (2nd ed.; Grand Rapids, Mich.: Eerdmans, 1998), 2–14. Collins defines apocalypticism as "a worldview in which supernatural revelation, the heavenly world, and eschatological judgment play an essential role" (*Apocalyptic Imagination*, 13).

[189] "For him [Augustine], the real secrets are no longer those of God, but those of the individual, hidden in the depth of his or her heart, or soul. With him, we witness more clearly than elsewhere, perhaps, the link between the end of esotericism and the development of a new interiorization. This process of interiorization is *ipso facto* a process of demotization: there remains no place for esoteric doctrine in such an approach" (Stroumsa, *Hidden Wisdom*, 7).

[190] Le Boulluec, "Commentaire," SC 279:143. Oeyen identifies the *protoctists* with the particular angelic rank called "powers," in Justin Martyr, Clement, and Origen (Oeyen, *Engelpneumatologie*, 28–30; idem, "Die Lehre von den göttlichen Kräften bei Justin," *StPatr* 11 (1972)/TU 108: 214–21).

4. CLEMENT'S THEORY OF PROPHETIC INSPIRATION

Clement is aware of the two major functions usually ascribed to the Holy Spirit, namely the inspiration of Old Testament prophets and the indwelling of Christian believers.[191] On the other hand, he often ascribes the same functions to the Logos, even while maintaining some role for the Holy Spirit. He affirms, for instance, that the Logos "tunes" the world—the great cosmos, as well as the human microcosm—by the Holy Spirit, ἁγίῳ πνεύματι (*Protr.* 1.5.3). Osborn finds that inasmuch as Clement (and Origen) articulate a robust doctrine of divine presence in the world, they possess a "worthy theology of the Holy Spirit."

> The activity of the spirit in the created world, as it has been renewed by Christ's recapitulation, is more direct than in other accounts;
> [Clement and Origen] had...a real doctrine of the continuity and energy of God's working in the world—that is a worthy theology of the Holy Spirit. Clement may have assigned to the Logos the functions of the Spirit; Origen may have failed to discriminate between the functions of the second and third Persons of the Trinity: but both of them had the root of the matter in their lives and in their thought. For them the constant vitalizing activity of God at work in his world was the essential element of their teaching.[192]

There is nothing to disagree with in this statement. However, what exactly Clement understood by "the Logos through the Spirit" becomes clear only in his account of prophecy in the *Eclogae* and *Adumbrationes*—that is, precisely in those texts that Osborn (and Clementine scholarship, generally) treats with less attention.

> *The heavens proclaim the glory of God* (Ps 18:2). By "heavens" are designated in manifold ways both "the heavens" pertaining to distance and cycle [= the sky; my note], and the proximate operation (ἐνέργεια προσεχής) of the first-created angels, which pertains to covenant. For the covenants were wrought (ἐνηργήθησαν) by the visitation of angels, namely those upon Adam, Noah, Abraham, and Moses. For, moved by the Lord, the first-created angels worked in (ἐνήργουν εἰς) the angels that

---

[191] "The Holy Spirit, by Isaiah, denounces…" (*Paed* 2.1.8); "the Holy Spirit, uttering his voice by Amos" (*Paed.* 2.2.30); "the Spirit prophesies by Zephaniah" (*Paed.* 2.12.126); "the Spirit [says] by Solomon" (*Paed.* 2.12.129). In *Exc.* 24.2, Clement affirms the perfect identity (i.e., an identity of οὐσία and δύναμις) between the paraclete that is working (ἐνεργῶν) in the Church, and the paraclete who was active (ἐνεργήσαντι) in the prophets. See my analysis above.

[192] Osborn, *Clement*, 152–53.

are close to the prophets, as they are telling the "glory of God," [namely] the covenants. But the works accomplished by the angels on earth also came about for "the glory of God," through the first-created angels. So, [the following] are called "heavens": in a primary sense, the Lord; but then also the first-created [angels]; and with them also the holy persons [that lived] before the Law, as well as the patriarchs, and Moses and the prophets, and finally the apostles.[193]

It is clear that the explanations above presuppose the hierarchical worldview presented in *Exc.* 10, 11, and 27. Prophecy occurs when the Logos moves the first rank of the *protoctists,* and this movement is transmitted from one level of the angelic hierarchy down to the next. The lowest angelic rank, which is the one closest to the human world, transmits the "movement" to the prophet.[194] Through a sort of telescoping effect, the first mover—the Logos—is simultaneously far removed from the effect of prophecy and immediately present. This principle of "mediated immediacy" becomes evident when Clement says that Jude refers the action of a lower angel ("an angel near us") to a superior angelic entity, the archangel Michael;[195] or when "Moses calls on the power of the angel Michael through an angel near to himself and of the lowest degree (*vicinum sibi et infimum*)."[196] Ultimately, the action of inspiration must be referred to the original mover, the Logos, since Clement also applies the outlined theory of angelic mediation to the prophetic call of Samuel (1 Samuel 3), where the text repeatedly mentions the Lord or the voice of the Lord.[197]

---

[193] *Ecl.* 51–52.

[194] Following the logic of the text, one could say that the prophet represents the highest level in the human hierarchy. A few centuries later, the Ps.-Areopagite will assign this position to the bishop. Clement, instead, seems much closer on this issue to the *Shepherd of Hermas* (Herm. *Mand.* 11.9), for whom the point of contact between the inspiring angel and the community of believers is the prophet, or to the *Book of Revelation.* I shall discuss both writings at a later point.

[195] "'When the archangel Michael, disputing with the devil, was arguing over the body of Moses.' This confirms the *Assumption of Moses.* 'Michael' here designates the one who argued with the devil through an angel close to us" (*Adumbr.* Jude 9).

[196] *Adumbr.* 1 John 2:1. Clement's explanation of biblical passages reporting an interaction between humans and a higher angelic being (e.g., the archangel Michael), rather than an angel of "lower" degree, is strikingly similar to the Ps.-Dionysian explanation of Isa 6:1, which states that Isaiah was "initiated" by a seraph rather than an angel (*CH* 13.1 [PTS 36:43–49]).

[197] *Adumbr.* 1 John 2:1. It is significant that the same idea is alluded to in the *Stromateis,* yet in a much more veiled manner. Speaking about the Sinai theophany, Clement says the following: "But there being a cloud and a lofty mountain, how is it not possible to hear a different sound, *the πνεῦμα being moved by the active cause*

In this light, it is possible to see how Clement understands the traditional statements about the Logos speaking in the prophets ἁγίῳ πνεύματι: the prophet experienced the presence and message of the Logos by receiving the "energy" of the proximate angel.[198] It appears, overall, that "the constant vitalizing activity of God at work in his world" was, indeed, as Osborn noted, an essential element of Clement's thought. What must be added, however, is that when it came to such deeply traditional elements as prophecy, Clement also had recourse to the traditional angelic imagery inherited from the "elders."

5. Clement's Understanding of "Spirit of Christ" and "Paraclete"

The *Adumbrationes, Excerpta* and *Eclogae* provide an interesting interpretation of fundamental pneumatological concepts: "Spirit of Christ" and "paraclete."

"Spirit of Christ"

It is thereby made clear that the prophets conversed with Wisdom, and that there was in them the "Spirit of Christ," in the sense of "possession by Christ," and "subjection to Christ" (*secundum possessionem et subiectionem Christi*). For the Lord works through archangels and through angels that are close (*per…propinquos angelos*), who are called "the Spirit of Christ" (*qui Christi vocantur spiritus*);[199]…He says, "Blessed are you, because there rests upon you that which is of his glory, and of

---

(πνεύματος κινουμένου διὰ τῆς ἐνεργούσης αἰτίας)?…You see how the Lord's voice, the Word without shape, the power of the Word, the luminous Word of the Lord, the Truth from heaven, from above, coming to the assembly of the Church, *worked* by the luminous *immediate ministry* (διὰ φωτεινῆς τῆς προσεχοῦς διακονίας ἐνήργει)" (*Strom.* 6.3.34). To anyone not previously familiar with the doctrine of inspiration presented above, several important elements can easily go unnoticed: Christ ("the luminous Word" cf. SC 446: 130 n. 3) is the active cause of the theophany; he *works* through the immediate ministry; conversely, the "wind" is "moved" by him. Since he is using "ministry" and "immediate," Clement probably interprets what he calls "the descent of God," and "manifestation of the divine Power" (*Strom.* 6.3.32) in light of Acts 7:35, 38, 53, as an *angelic* manifestation, and an *angelic* giving of the law. Thus πνεῦμα here signals the presence of the *angelic* spirit.

[198] In *Strom.* 7.2.12, divine providence is said to lead souls to repentance "by means of the proximate angels" (διά τε τῶν προσεχῶν ἀγγέλων). The same phenomenon applies to the gift of philosophy to the pagans: the Logos "gave philosophy to the Greeks by means of the inferior angels," διὰ τῶν ὑποδεεστέρων ἀγγέλων (*Strom.* 7.2.6).

[199] *Spiritus Christi* could, in theory, be translated as a plural ("spirits of Christ"); but Clement is here expanding on 1 Pet 4:14, ὁ τοῦ Θεοῦ πνεῦμα ἐφ᾽ ἡμᾶς ἀναπαύεται.

God's honor and power, and who is his Spirit. This "his" is possessive, and designates the angelic spirit (*Hic possessivum est eius et angelicum spiritum significat*).[200]

Once again, the "telescopic" view of the hierarchy is presupposed so as to convey the presence of Christ through (*per*, presumably rendering διά) the work of the lowest angelic level.[201] *Adumbr.* 1 Pet 4:14 presents three entities: first, God; second, God's Glory/Honor/Power (= "He"); third, the Spirit of God's Glory/Honor/Power (= "His Spirit").[202] Yet the Spirit of Christ is treated, in a way that could hardly be more explicit, as a designation for angelic beings.

For a comparison with the way in which Clement approached this problem in the *Stromateis*, it is instructive to look at the exegesis of Gen 18:5–6 (Abraham meeting the three heavenly visitors) in the following text:

> ...on looking up to heaven, whether it was that he saw the Son in the spirit, as some explain, or a glorious angel, or in any other way recognized God to be superior to the creation...he receives in addition the Alpha, the knowledge of the one and only God, and is called Abraham, having, instead of a natural philosopher, become wise, and a lover of God.[203]

The text suggests Clement's disagreement with other exegetes, who posit a direct manifestation of the Logos. In light of the theory of prophecy discussed above, the choice between Abraham seeing the Logos, and Abraham conversing with an angel represents, indeed, a false alternative. What Abraham saw was neither the Logos as such, nor a glorious angel, but rather the Logos in the *angelic* spirit.[204]

---

[200] *Adumbr.* 1 Pet 2:3; *Adumbr.* 1 Pet 4:14.

[201] Oeyen (*Engelpneumatologie*, 27–28) and Hauschild (*Gottes Geist*, 79) identify the *angeli propinqui* with the *protoctists*. In light of the principle of mediated immediacy, outlined above, this interpretation appears to miss half of Clement's intention. The prophetic inspiration is, indeed, worked out through the *protoctists*, who are "close" to the Son; yet the movement is further transmitted in the same way to the archangels, who are "close" to the *protoctists*, and the angels, who are "close" to the archangels. Finally, the lowest angelic rank is the last element in the chain of prophetic inspiration: this is, for Clement, the "spirit" that rests upon the prophets.

[202] For a discussion of the variant reading of 1 Pet 4:14, see Zahn, *Forschungen* 3:95 n. 11; Oeyen, *Engelpneumatologie*, 28 n. 24; Michael Mees, *Die Zitate aus dem Neuen Testament bei Clemens von Alexandrien* (Quaderni di "Vetera Christianorum" 2; Bari: Instituto di letteratura cristiana antica, 1970), 1:179–80, 2:242.

[203] *Strom.* 5.1.8.

[204] Oeyen discusses this passage in *Engelpneumatologie*, 18–19.

"Paraclete"

As noted earlier, "paraclete" was implicitly identified with the Logos in *Exc.* 24.2, where Clement affirms the perfect identity between the paraclete that is working (ἐνεργῶν) in the Church, and the paraclete who was active (ἐνεργήσαντι) in the prophets. The *Adumbrationes* provide further details about the paraclete:

> The things of old (*vetera*) that were wrought through the prophets, and are concealed from most, are now revealed to you through the evangelists. "For to you," it says, "have these things been revealed (*manifestata sunt*) through the Holy Spirit who was sent," that is, the paraclete, of whom the Lord said, "Unless I depart, he will not come"; "unto whom," it is said, "the angels desire to look"—not the fallen angels, as most suspect; rather, as is true and godly, the angels who desire to attain to the sight of his perfection (*prospectum perfectionis illius*).[205]

This passage reinforces Clement's identification of the Church's Paraclete Spirit with the Spirit already manifested in Old Testament prophetic inspiration. The paraclete sent to the Church is at the same time an object of contemplation for the angels. This evokes the hierarchical universe described in the *Excerpta*. There, however, the angels are contemplating the *protoctists*, who are mediating to them the light of the divine Face. To make things even more ambiguous, the passage above follows immediately after Clement's affirmation that the spirit of Christ in the prophets must be understood in the sense of "possession by Christ," which later on is explained as "Christ working through archangels and angels who are close to us." The exact relation between Christ, the paraclete, and the *protoctists* becomes clearer in light of the discussion of "paraclete" references in the *Adumbr.* 1 John 2:1 ("But if anyone does sin, we have a *paraclete* with the Father, namely Jesus Christ"):

> Just as the Lord is a *paraclete* for us with the Father, so also is he a *paraclete* whom he [scil. the Lord] has deigned to send after his ascension. For these primitive and first-created powers, unchangeable according to substance, effect divine operations together with the subordinate angels and archangels whose names they share (*hae namque primitivae virtutes ac primo creatae, inmobiles exsistentes secundum substantiam, cum subiectis angelis et archangelis, cum quibus vocantur equivoce, diversas operationes efficiunt*).[206]

---

[205] *Adumbr.* 1 Pet 1:10–12.
[206] *Adumbr.* 1 John 2:1.

The reference to the "primitive and first-created powers" (rendering πρωτόγονοι καὶ πρωτόκτιστοι δυνάμεις) in the first passage is a subject of marked disagreement among scholars. The first interpretation, going back at least as far as Zahn's annotated edition of the text, sees the "primitive powers" as none other than the two paracletes, the Son and the Spirit.[207] A second position, argued by Westcott (prior to Zahn), and by Wilhelm Lueken (in direct polemic with Zahn), was adopted by Sagnard, and more recently by Ziebritzki. Its most extensive exposition, however, was furnished by Oeyen.[208] According to this reading, the "powers" under discussion are the seven *protoctists*, situated below the Son/Logos, and either identified with the sevenfold Spirit (Oeyen), or juxtaposed to the Spirit (Ziebritzki).[209]

At first sight, the two-paraclete scheme, discussed by Kretschmar with reference to early Christian trinitarian speculation on the basis of Isa 6:1–3,[210] seems perfectly applicable to the passage. Christ is the Church's *paraclete* before the Father, the Spirit is the *paraclete* sent to the Church: hence, the two paracletes, Christ and the Holy Spirit. According to Zahn and Kretschmar, here as well as in other passages (*Strom.* 6.16.143; *Exc.* 10.4.20; *Ecl.* 56–57), Clement applies the designation and characteristics of angels or *protoctists* to Christ and the Spirit, without thereby numbering the latter two among the angels. Yet unlike "mere" angelic beings, Christ and the Spirit would be *inmobiles exsistentes secundum substantiam*, that is, according to Zahn, characterized by "an ethical immutability rooted in their essence." These scholars also argue that the equation between the Holy Spirit and the angelic spirits in *Adumbr.* 1 Pet 4:14 should not be taken literally.[211]

---

[207] Zahn, *Forschungen* 3:79–103, esp. 98–99. Zahn's opinions carry on to this day: Frangoulis (Πνεῦμα *bei Clemens*, 16–17); Barbel (*Christos Angelos*, 202–3); Kretschmar (*Trinitätstheologie*, 71 n. 2); Ladaria (*Espíritu en Clemente*, 255); Hauschild (*Gottes Geist*, 80 and n. 13).

[208] Westcott, "Clement of Alexandria," 1:564; Wilhelm Lueken, *Michael: Eine Darstellung und Vergleich der jüdischen und morgenländisch-christlichen Tradition vom Erzengel Michael* (Göttingen: Vandenhoeck & Ruprecht, 1898), 113 n. 1; Sagnard, *Extraits*, 77 n. 2; Ziebritzki, *Geist und Weltseele*, 122 n. 148; Oeyen, *Engelpneumatologie*, 31–33.

[209] Ziebritzki's contention that the identification between the Spirit and the *protoctists* is "unlikely" because Christian tradition originally conceived of the Holy Spirit as a singular entity (*Geist und Weltseele*, 122) is unfounded. The combination of the seven gifts of the Spirit (Isa 11:1–2) and the seven angelic spirits of the Lord (Zech 4:2.10; Rev 1:4; 5:6; 8:2), which we have seen in Clement's exegesis of the sevenfold candlestick, is well-established in early Christianity. See Schlütz, *Die sieben Gaben*, passim.

[210] Kretschmar, *Trinitätstheologie*, 64–67, 73; Daniélou, *Jewish Christianity*, 134–40.

[211] Zahn, *Forschungen* 3:98; Frangoulis, Πνεῦμα *bei Clemens*, 17; Kretschmar,

Westcott and Lueken have pointed to a textual problem in the *Adumbrationes*. The entire passage beginning with *hae namque virtutes* and continuing with a discussion of the now familiar principle of mediated immediacy, illustrated by the cases of the archangel Michael, Samuel, and Elisha, seems oddly out of place in an exegesis of 1 John 2:1. This material might have been displaced from the *Adumbr.* Jude 9, where Clement discusses precisely the alleged presence of the archangel Michael at the scene of Moses' death; the digression on Moses, Samuel, and Elisha, and Michael working through subordinate angels, would be perfectly justified.[212] However, Westcott's displacement hypothesis finds no support in the meager text tradition of the *Adumbrationes*, and must therefore remain a mere conjecture.

For some, accepting the preeminence of the text tradition implies accepting the Zahn–Kretschmar exegesis.[213] Yet the equation of the *virtutes* with the seven *protoctists* is not dependent on the displacement hypothesis. For Oeyen (who is, of course, sympathetic to this theory), making sense of the reference to "the primitive powers" requires the larger theological context provided by the *Adumbrationes*, *Excerpta*, and *Eclogae*. In this perspective, for instance, the "paraclete" working in the Church is by no means an unambiguous referent: a few passages earlier in the *Adumbr.* 1 Pet, Clement discloses to his readers that the "Spirit of Christ" resting upon the faithful is, in fact, Christ working through the "angelic spirit," through archangels and inferior angels. Secondly, the description of the "powers" matches other Clementine references to the *protoctists*. Their being "first-created" (πρωτόκτιστοι), "primitive" (πρωτόγονοι), and "immutable," perfectly matches the description in *Exc.* 10; *aequivoce* (ὁμονύμως) can be better explained as referring to the personal name (e.g., "Michael"), which is ascribed, as a condescension to human weakness, to an angel of the lowest rank; the "diverse operations" effected by these powers fit well Clement's detailed account of prophetic inspiration.

Trinitätstheologie, 71 n. 2. Barbel, *Christos Angelos*, 203 n. 106: "Man kann sich fragen, ob der Ausdruck [the Logos as *protoctist*, "first born"] in seinem wörtlichen Sinn zu nehmen ist."

[212] Westcott, "Clement," 564; Lueken, *Michael*, 113 n. 8. Lueken rejected Zahn's statement about "ethical immutability," and proposed "local immutability." As Barbel (*Christos Angelos*, 203) notes, however, substantial immutability implies both.

[213] Barbel (*Christos Angelos*, 202) notes: "Doch wird man dem Zeugnis des Überlieferung das Vorrecht lassen müssen"; he then embraces the identification of the *primitivae virtutes* with Christ and the Spirit.

The divergence in the interpretation of the *Adumbr.* 1 John 2:1 is not as radical as it may seem. It is possible to move beyond the divergence by considering the *primitivae virtutes* in light of a new descriptive category: "angelomorphic pneumatology."

6. ANGELIC OR ANGELOMORPHIC PNEUMATOLOGY?

Oeyen contends that the *protoctists* simply *are* the Spirit, a plural designation of the sevenfold Holy Spirit.[214] Ladaria refuses this identification on the grounds that the indwelling work of the Spirit finds no counterpart in the action of the *protoctists*, and that there is a clear distinction between the paradigmatic status of the *protoctists* with respect to the vision of God, and work of Holy Spirit who enables one to see God.[215] These objections are easily overcome as soon as it is understood that the *protoctists* serve as "high priests" of the deifying and theophanic action ultimately performed by the Logos, and therefore mediators of the *visio dei*. Ziebritzki agrees with Oeyen that the Spirit is, indeed, subordinated to the Logos and abides in unchanging contemplation of the latter. He asserts, however, without offering any proof, that the Spirit is assigned the same hierarchical rank as the *protoctists*, although he remains a distinct entity.[216] Hauschild's cautious observations seem extremely apt at this point: interpreting Clement's pneumatology depends to a great extent on determining the extent to which Clement is in agreement with the traditions that he is reworking. Given that Clement nowhere identifies them explicitly, he *could* be equating the *protoctists* with the Spirit, but he could also be resorting to a traditional view that simply does not speak of a "Holy Spirit," and *not* have the capacity to bend the inherited framework so as to accommodate the hypostasis of the Spirit.[217] The following text may provide more clarity:

---

[214] Oeyen, *Engelpneumatologie*, 20, 25, 31, 33, 40. For a presentation of the functional identity between the Holy Spirit and the *protoctists*, see Oeyen, *Engelpneumatologie*, 22–23.

[215] "Mientras que El Espíritu Santo es comunicado al hombre y en él habita, es decir, se convierte en un principio interno de actuación del creyente, nada de esto se dice en relación con los 'protoctistos'" (Ladaria, *Espíritu en Clemente*, 252); "hay diferencia entre 'ser ejemplo' y 'hacer capaz de'" (Ladaria, *Espíritu en Clemente*, 252 n. 17).

[216] *Geist und Weltseele*, 122–23.

[217] Hauschild, *Gottes Geist*, 79 n. 10. The close association between "possessing the Spirit" and the process of angelification might originally have been part of a tradition featuring an angelic "Holy Spirit" (cf. Hauschild, *Gottes Geist*, 78–79).

And by one God are many treasures dispensed; some are disclosed through the Law, others through the prophets; some by the divine mouth, another by the heptad of the spirit (τοῦ πνεύματος τῇ ἑπτάδι) singing in accompaniment. And the Lord being one, is the same Instructor in all of these.[218]

According to Schlütz this text describes the revelation of the Instructor Logos as both unitary and progressive: the Logos works in the law, later in the prophets, then in the Incarnation ("the divine mouth"), and, finally, in the descent of the Spirit at Pentecost. Oeyen prefers a direct equation of "the divine mouth" with the Spirit, on the basis of *Protr.* 9.82 (where the Spirit is precisely the mouth of the Lord).[219] On either view (and I would argue that Clement's spirit christology annuls their distinction), the expression "heptad of the spirit" refers to the Holy Spirit. The question is to decide whether "holy spirit" is a designation for the seven angels of the Face, or "seven protoctists" is a designation for the Holy Spirit. In other words, "angel" pneumatology or "pneuma" angelology?[220]

Ladaria prefers to interpret "angels" as references to the Holy Spirit.[221] Similarly, Oeyen notes, commenting on the passage discussing the *spiritus angelicus* (*Adumbr.* 1 Pet 4:14): "nicht nur werden Engel Geist genannt; auch der Geist wird als *engelhaft* bezeichnet," and concludes "dass es sich ohne Zweifel um den Heiligen Geist handelt, und nicht um einen niedrigeren Engel, der *Geist* im abgeschwächten Sinne genannt würde."[222]

These observations amount to a distinction between "angelic" and "angelomorphic" pneumatology. It would, indeed, be preferable to use the newer descriptive category of "angelomorphic pneumatology,"

---

[218] *Paed.* 3.12.87.

[219] Schlütz, *Die sieben Gaben*, 77; Oeyen, *Engelpneumatologie*, 27 n. 22.

[220] Far from being a Christian invention, much less a peculiarity of Clement's, the use of πνεῦμα to designate an angelic being is widespread in pre- and post-exilic Judaism, witnessed by the LXX and authors of the diaspora, and prominent at Qumran. In the Old Testament, the *locus classicus*, as Gieschen shows (*Angelomorphic Christology*, 117–18) is Isa 63:9–10, where the agent of Exodus is referred to neither as "angel" nor as "pillar of cloud," but as "holy spirit"; in the New Testament, aside from the designation of *evil* angels as (impure) "spirits," the equivalence of "spirit" and "angel" is implicit in Heb 12:9 ("Father of spirits"), and Acts 8:26.29.39, where Philip's guide is successively described as "angel of the Lord," "spirit," and, "spirit of the Lord." See Levison, "The Angelic Spirit," passim; idem, *Spirit in First-Century Judaism*; Arthur E. Sekki, *The Meaning of Ruach at Qumran* (SBLDS 110; Atlanta, Ga.: Scholars Press, 1989), 145–71.

[221] Ladaria, *Espíritu en Clemente*, 254.

[222] Oeyen, *Engelpneumatologie*, 28.

following Fletcher-Louis' definition of "angelomorphic" noted in my Introduction.[223]

This new lens can help us overcome the two divergent readings of the passage about the *primitivae virtutes* in the *Adumbr.* 1 John 2:1. Granting the basic divergence between the number of the powers involved (two, for Zahn and Kretschmar; seven, for Lueken and Oeyen), there is much in the two exegeses that is only apparently in conflict. Zahn and his followers affirm that Clement is speaking about Christ and the Holy Spirit. As we have seen, Oeyen does not deny the pneumatological content of passage: the seven first-created angels *are* the sevenfold Holy Spirit in archaic angelomorphic "disguise."

Clement equates the seven *protoctists* with the seven gifts of the Spirit and interprets them as the "heptad of the Spirit" (*Paed.* 3.12.87). One is therefore justified in speaking of pneumatology. It is important to note that the apocalyptic imagery of the seven *protoctists* is subjected to a process of spiritualization. Spiritual exegesis helps Clement understand the seven *protoctists* as the sevenfold Spirit, just as it helps equate Ps.-Plato's "third" with the third article of the Christian rule of faith (*Strom.* 5.14.103).[224]

Excursus: Matt 18:10 and Clement's Protoctists[225]

In his attempt to isolate a pre-Clementine source, Collomp pointed to the peculiar exegesis ("exégèse insolite") of Matt 18:10, and its relation with the Ps.-Clementine *Hom.* 17.[226] Several decades later, Gilles Quispel, one of the very few scholars to take into account Oeyen's *Engelpneumatologie*, also highlighted the pneumatological use of this verse in Clement and, as we shall see, in Aphrahat the Persian Sage.[227]

---

[223] According to Fletcher-Louis (*Luke-Acts*, 14–15), the term ought to be used "wherever there are signs that an individual or community possesses specifically angelic characteristics or status, though for whom identity cannot be reduced to that of an angel."

[224] For detailed discussion and relevant secondary literature, Franz Dünzl, *Pneuma: Funktionen des theologischen Begriffs in frühchristlicher Literatur* (JAC Ergänzungsband 30; Münster, Westfalen: Aschendorffsche Verlagsbuchhandlung, 2000), 143–44.

[225] For a more detailed treatment, see Bucur, "Matt. 18:10 in Early Christology and Pneumatology: A Contribution to the Study of Matthean *Wirkungsgeschichte*," *NovT* 49 (2007): 209–31.

[226] Collomp, "Une source," 21, 34.

[227] Quispel, "Genius and Spirit," in *Essays on the Nag Hammadi Texts in Honour of Pahor Lahib* (ed. M. Krause; Leiden: Brill, 1975), 155–69. Quispel agrees with Oeyen's thesis of "angel Pneumatology" in Clement ("Genius and Spirit," 158, 164, 168).

In what follows I shall document the early Christian use of Matt 18:10 in greater detail.

I have shown earlier, in the section describing the celestial hierarchy, that Clement equates the "seven eyes of the Lord" (Zech 3:9; 4:10; Rev 5:6) with the "thrones" (Col 1:16) and "angels ever contemplating the face of God" (Matt 18:10). Whether one has in mind the mainstream of patristic interpretations of this verse or the sensibilities of today's readers, Clement's use of Matt 18:10 is unusual. Much of patristic exegesis seized upon the obvious ethical implications of the passage. For most modern exegetes as well, Matt 18:10 is primarily an exhortation to take care of those despised as socially inferior, spiritually distraught, recently baptized, etc. In fact, highlighting "God's special concern for...the humble and despised" is, according to leading contemporary exegetes, the only interpretation by which Matt. 18:10 retains some relevance for today's world.[228]

It is also true that Matt 18:10 is "a *locus classicus* of Christian angelology."[229] But Clement's speculation on the identity of the "angels" and the "face" mentioned in Matt 18:10—specifically the idea that Matthew is speaking about the seven highest-ranking members of the celestial hierarchy, who are gazing upon Christ, the face of God—is surprising.

---

[228] See, for instance, John Chrysostom, whose exegesis will be adopted by countless other interpreters: "He calls 'little ones' not them that are really little... (for how should he be little who is equal in value to the whole world; how should he be little, who is dear to God?); but them who in the imagination of the multitude are so esteemed.... Then in another way also He makes them objects of reverence, saying, that 'their angels do always behold the face of my Father which is in Heaven.' If then God thus rejoices over the little one that is found, how dost thou despise them that are the objects of God's earnest care, when one ought to give up even one's very life for one of these little ones?...Let us not then be careless about such souls as these. For all these things are said for this object" (*Hom. Matt.* 59.4–5; PG 57:578; *NPNF* translation). Among modern exegetes, see Claude G. Montefiore, *The Synoptic Gospels* (New York: Ktav, 1968 [1927]), 2:248; Wilhelm Pesch, *Matthäus der Seelsorger* (SBS 2; Stuttgart: Verlag Katholisches Bibelwerk, 1966), 28–29; W. G. Thomson, *Matthew's Advice to A Divided Community* (AnBib 44; Rome: Biblical Institute, 1970), 153; Simon Légasse, "μικρός," *EDNT* 2:427; Rowland, "Apocalyptic, The Poor, and the Gospel of Matthew," *JTS* 45 (1994) 504–18; Ulrich Luz, *Matthew 8–20: A Commentary* (Hermeneia; Minneapolis, Minn.: Augsburg Fortress, 2001), 443.

[229] Ulrich Luz, *Matthew*, 441. Aside from providing proof of the existence of angels (guardian angels, in particular), this verse was also used in later controversies about the baptism of children. See in this respect Jean Héring, "Un texte oublié: Mt 18, 10: À propos des controverses récentes sur le pédobaptisme," in *Aux sources de la tradition chrétienne: FS Maurice Goguel* (ed. O. Cullmann et al.; Neuchâtel; Paris: Delachaux & Niestlé, 1950), 95–102.

These bold exegetical moves suggest that the Alexandrian is here drawing upon older material.

There are five occurrences of Matt 18:10 in Clement of Alexandria's
surviving writings: *Strom.* 5.14.91; *Exc.* 10.6; 11:1; 23:4; *Quis div.* 31.1.[230]
The first of these passages displays an interesting formal variation. The
text reads:

> But indicating "the angels," as the Scripture says, "of the little ones, and of
> the least, which see God" (τῶν μικρῶν δὲ κατὰ τὴν γραφὴν καὶ ἐλαχίστων
> τοὺς ἀγγέλους τοὺς ὁρῶντας τὸν θεόν) and also the oversight reaching to
> us exercised by the tutelary angels, he shrinks not from writing: "When
> all the souls have selected their several lives, according as it has fallen
> to their lot, they advance in order to Lachesis; and she sends along with
> each one, as his guide in life, and the joint accomplisher of his purposes,
> the demon which he has chosen." Perhaps also the demon of Socrates
> suggested to him something similar.[231]

Leaving aside Clement's characteristic fusion of biblical sources with
texts and writers authoritative for the Greek philosophical tradition,
it is noteworthy that Clement supplements τῶν μικρῶν in Matt 18:10
with ἐλαχίστων, the term used in Matt 25:40, 45 for those whom the
Son of Man calls his "brethren" (τῶν ἀδελφῶν τῶν ἐλαχίστων).[232] This
connection between τῶν μικρῶν (Matt 18:10) and τῶν ἐλαχίστων (Matt
25:40, 45) is reminiscent of a passage in the *Ps.-Clem. Hom.* 17:

> Of his commandments this is the first and great one, to fear the Lord
> God, and to serve him only. But he meant us to fear that God whose
> angels they are who are *the angels of the least of the faithful amongst us,*
> *and who stand in heaven continually beholding the face of the Father.* For
> he has shape (μορφήν), and he has every limb primarily and solely for
> beauty's sake, and not for use.… But he has the most beautiful shape
> (καλλίστην μορφήν) on account of man, that the pure in heart may be
> able to see him.… What affection ought therefore to arise within us if we
> gaze with our mind on his beautiful shape (εὐμορφίαν)! But otherwise it

---

[230] For Clement's use of Scripture, see Mees, *Zitate*; Percy Mordaunt Barnard, *The
Biblical Text of Clement of Alexandria: In the Four Gospels and the Acts of the Apostles*
(Cambridge: Cambridge University Press, 1899); Van den Hoek, "Divergent Traditions in Clement of Alexandria,' and other Authors of the 2nd century," *Apocrypha* 7
(1996): 43–62; Carl. P. Cosaert, "The Text of the Gospels in the Writings of Clement
of Alexandria" (Ph.D. diss., University of North Carolina at Chapel Hill, 2005).

[231] *Strom.* 5.14.91.

[232] For a discussion of Clement's exegetical techniques and of his overall hermeneu-
tic strategy, see David Dawson, *Allegorical Readers and Cultural Revision in Ancient
Alexandria* (Berkeley: University of California Press, 1992), 183–234, 287–95.

is absurd to speak of beauty. For beauty cannot exist apart from shape (ἄνευ μορφῆς); nor can one be attracted to the love of God (πρὸς τὸν αὐτοῦ ἔρωτα ἐπισπᾶσθαί τινα), nor even deem that he can see him, if God has no form (εἶδος).[233]

This passage in the Ps.-Clementina was apparently not part of the so-called Basic Writing (now lost), but was introduced by the author of the *Homilies*, who reworked it around 300–320 C.E.[234] The homilist introduced a number of Jewish and Jewish-Christian traditions. As Collomp argued almost a century ago, Clement of Alexandria was most likely aware of one of the sources used by the homilist in his reworking the Ps.-Clementine material.[235] Whether or not the term "source" is accurate—since a direct literary link with Clement cannot be established—the passage in question is important in that it makes evident the archaism of Clement's exegesis of Matt 18:10.

To better understand the doctrine of this fragment and its use of Matt 18:10, it is necessary to sketch out the polemical context of *Ps.-Clem. Hom.* 17.7–10. The apostle Peter and Simon Magus disagree sharply over who, or what, constitutes the "true God." To Simon's taste, the biblical divinity appears crude and unsatisfactory, because it does not meet certain standards of perfection derived from metaphysical speculation.[236] Peter rejects Simon's higher God as mere fancy, the

---

[233] *Ps.-Clem. Hom.* 17.7.1–4; 17.10.5 (GCS 42: 232–33).

[234] Georg Strecker, *Das Judenchristentum in den Pseudoklementinen* (2d rev. and enl. ed.; TU 70; Berlin: Akademie Verlag, 1981), 62–65, 267–68, 271. This conclusion is supported by scholarship before and after Strecker. For a detailed review of the history of Pseudo-Clementine scholarship, see F. Stanley Jones, "The Pseudo-Clementines: A History of Research," *SecCent* 2 (1982): 1–33, 63–96.

[235] Collomp, "Une source."

[236] See, for instance, Simon's statements in *Ps.-Clem. Hom.* 5.49, 53, 61. The descriptions of this lofty divinity appear related to the Middle Platonic definition of the divinity set forth, for instance, in Alcinous, *Didaskalikos* 10, or Apuleius, *De Platone et eius dogmate* 190–91. Roelof van den Broek ("Eugnostus and Aristides on the Ineffable God," in his *Studies in Gnosticism and Alexandrian Christianity* [NHMS 39; Leiden/New York: Brill, 1996], 22–41) has demonstrated the existence of a common Middle Platonic source behind the similar "definitions of God" present in *Eugnostus the Blessed, The Tripartite Tractate*, and Aristides' Apology. Bentley Layton (*The Gnostic Scriptures* [New York/London/Toronto/Sydney/Auckland: Doubleday, 1995], 14 n. 2) has singled out the obvious parallels between the discourse on "the parent of entirety" in the *Apocryphon Johannis* and a passage in Alcinous. Thus, the fact that Gnostic speculation on the higher divinity is markedly Middle-Platonic in character seems hardly disputable. See Birger Pearson, "Gnosticism as Platonism," in *Gnosticism, Judaism, and Egyptian Christianity* (Minneapolis: Fortress, 1990), 164; Ioan P. Culianu, *The Tree of Gnosis* (San Francisco: Harper Collins, 1992); Gerard P. Luttikhuizen, "The Thought Patterns of Gnostic Mythologizers and Their Use of Biblical Traditions," in *The Nag Hammadi Library after*

result of an imagination harassed by demons,[237] and affirms forcefully his attachment to the biblical God who made heaven and earth.[238] The passage from *Ps.-Clem. Hom.* 17 identifies this "true God"; not Simon's abstract "great power," distinct from the Creator, but precisely the Creator and Lawgiver, the biblical God whose luminous and beautiful form is enthroned and worshiped by angels. This anthropomorphic appearance, which includes "all the limbs," such as eyes and ears, is, however, only for our sake: God himself does not need eyes, ears, or any form; yet, unless he showed himself in this most beautiful form, how could anyone long for him, and gaze on him?[239]

It is now possible to take a closer look at the use of Matt 18:10 in *Hom.* 17. The verse is crucial for Peter's argument, since it serves as a means of identifying "the true God." This "true God" is, for Peter, the one who is attended by "the angels of the least of the faithful...who stand in heaven continually beholding the face of the Father." Implied in this description is the image of an enthroned deity, and, as Peter adds immediately, the throne-imagery implies that God has a form: "for he has shape and he has every limb."

The wording in Peter's statements suggests that Matt 18:10 is here combined with Matt 25:40.[240] The first and most obvious element to suggest this is the replacement of τῶν μικρῶν (from Matt 18:30) by τῶν ἐλαχίστων, the term used for those whom the Son of Man calls his "brethren" in Matt 25:40 (τῶν ἀδελφῶν τῶν ἐλαχίστων). Secondly, *Hom.* 17.7.4–6 also evokes Matt 25:40, 45.[241] By way of consequence, there is

---

Fifty Years: Proceedings of the 1995 Society of Biblical Literature Commemoration (ed. J. D. Turner and A. McGuire; Leiden/New York/Cologne: Brill, 1997), 89–101. For a detailed examination of the interaction between Gnosticism, especially the so-called Sethian texts, and the Platonic tradition, see the essays collected in *Neoplatonism and Gnosticism* (ed. R. T. Wallis and J. Bregman; Albany, N.Y.: SUNY, 1992), and John D. Turner's monograph, *Sethian Gnosticism and the Platonic Tradition* (Québec: Presses de l'Université Laval; Louvain: Peeters, 2001).

[237] *Ps.-Clem. Hom.* 5.62–65. Cf. *Ps.-Clem. Recogn.* 56–58.

[238] E.g., *Ps.-Clem. Hom.* 18.22.

[239] Peter's insistence on the "beauty" of God's body, the mentioning of various limbs, and the general "erotic" language (e.g., πρὸς τὸν αὐτοῦ ἔρωτα ἐπισπᾶσθαί τινα) suggest a certain relation between the passage in *Ps.-Clem. Hom.* 17 and the mystical exegesis of the Song of Songs in Jewish Shiur Qomah literature. This has already been noted in scholarship: Scholem, *Jewish Gnosticism*, 41; Quispel, "The Discussion of Judaic Christianity," in his *Gnostic Studies* II (Istanbul: Nederlands Historisch-Archaeologisch Instituut in het Nabije Oosten, 1974), 148; Stroumsa, "Form(s) of God: Some Notes on Metatron and Christ," *HTR* 76 (1983): 287 n. 85.

[240] This has been duly noted in the critical edition (GCS 42:233).

[241] The argument in *Hom.* 17.7.4–6 runs as follows: honoring the invisible God is

an overlap between the "face of God" in Matt 18:10, the enthroned Son
of Man in Matt 25:31–46, and God's "form" or "body" which constitutes
the heavenly "model" of the human being.[242]

There is a second source that must be brought into the discussion
at this juncture, namely Irenaeus of Lyon's report on Marcosian ritual
practices.[243] According to Irenaeus, Marcus the Magician claimed to have
received a supreme and all-encompassing revelation.[244] At the center
of this revelation lies the figure of the Logos: he is the manifestation of
the ineffable God, the "primal Anthropos," or "Body of Truth," and is
composed of thirty letters in four distinct enunciations.[245] As a crown-
ing of the revelation, Marcus is granted the auditory manifestation of
this celestial reality: "Christ Jesus." Marcus must have reacted with a
certain disappointment, for he is immediately scolded and instructed
as follows:

> You regard as contemptible (ὡς εὐκαταφρόνητον) the word that you have
> heard from the mouth of Truth? What you know and appear to possess
> is not the ancient Name. For the mere sound of it is what you possess;
> but you do not know its power. Now, "Jesus" is a symbolic (ἐπίσημον)
> six-letter name known by all who are of the "calling." But [the Name]
> that exists among the Aeons of the Pleroma consists of many parts, and
> has a different form and shape (ἄλλης ἐστιν μορφῆς καὶ ἑτέρου τύπου),
> being known by those who are joined in affinity (συγγενῶν) with him,
> and whose greatnesses are always (διὰ παντός) present with him.[246]

---

possible by honoring his "visible image (εἰκόνα)"; but since this image is quite simply
the human being, honoring God ultimately requires feeding the hungry, clothing the
naked, etc., as stated in Matt 25:40, 45. The homilist understands creation "in the
image" to mean that God "molded (διετυπώσατο) man in his own shape (μορφῇ)," i.e.,
he used as a pattern the beautiful, radiant, divine extent mentioned earlier; what results
from this process—the human being—is the "image"; "likeness" refers to the spiritual
growth of the image. The same connection between Gen 1:26 and Matt 25:36–45 occurs
in *Hom.* 11.4. The use of "image" is markedly different from that of Col 1:15 and the
later theology of Irenaeus (*Epid.* 22; *Adv. haer.* 4.33.4), where Christ is the image, while
humans are patterned after and oriented towards the image, i.e., Christ.

[242] Similarly Fossum, "Jewish-Christian Christology and Jewish Mysticism," *VC* 37
(1983): 265; Gieschen, *Angelomorphic Christology*, 205.

[243] For the Marcosians, see Niclas Förster, *Marcus Magus: Kult, Lehre und Gemeinde-
leben einer valentinianischen Gnostikergruppe. Sammlung der Quellen und Kommentar*
(WUNT 2/114; Tübingen: Mohr Siebeck, 1999).

[244] For a detailed presentation and analysis of the passage, see Sagnard, *La gnose
valentinienne*, 358–69; Förster, *Marcus*, 229–92. Marcus' entire tractate (which Irenaeus
would have used in his refutation) had the form of revelatory discourses pronounced
by a host of celestial entities (Förster, *Marcus*, 391).

[245] See *Haer.* 1.14.3.

[246] *Haer.* 1.14.4.

This passage introduces the following teaching: the six-letter name "Jesus" represents merely the "sound" of the celestial Name, which is all that those of the "calling" (certainly the "psychic" Church) are able to comprehend; the Marcosian initiates, instead, have access to the celestial Name, by virtue of their (presumably "pneumatic") co-naturality; finally, the "greatnesses" of these initiates continually abide with the Name/Anthropos.[247]

Here, as in other Marcosian passages, "greatness" is a term for angelic beings.[248] Consequently, the passage under discussion (*Adv. haer.* 1.14.4) can be read as an exegesis of Matt 18:10. The Matthean admonishment is applied to those who would show contempt for the revelation disclosed to Marcus (namely the celestial "Logos"/"Anthropos"/"Body of Truth"). The "little ones" are understood to designate the Marcosian elite, who will be joined to their angels ("greatnesses") and thus participate in the contemplation of the heavenly Anthropos. A few paragraphs later, Marcus refers to "the seven powers who praise the Logos."[249]

Returning now to the use of Matt 18:10 in the *Ps.-Clementine Homilies*, it is quite clear that the exegesis of this passage is not very different from that of Irenaeus' Marcosians. Even though the theological frameworks of the texts are very different (one is dualistic, the other rejects dualism, hence terms such as "God" or "Christ" mean different things), both view the "Face of God" in Matt 18:10 as the enthroned "form" or "body" of God, which they identify with Christ. The fact that the same exegesis of Matt 18:10 occurs in Clement of Alexandria

---

[247] For the identification of "those of the calling" with the "psychic" Church, and the "pneumatic" co-naturality between the Marcosian initiates and the true divinity, see Förster, *Marcus*, 232–33.

[248] Irenaeus reports on the following invocation of Sophia in certain rites of the Marcosians: "O, companion of God and of the mystical Silence from before the aeons, through whom the greatnesses that continually behold the face of the Father draw up their forms (ἀνασπῶσιν ἄνω τὰς αὐτῶν μορφάς), taking you as guide and leader..." (*Adv. haer.* 1.13.6). Sophia is here asked to help the initiated to ascend invisibly and to enter the bridal chamber of their angelic counterpart. Matthew 18:10 is used in a somewhat altered form: it is "the greatnesses" that continually behold the face of the Father. Obviously, "greatnesses" here designates certain angelic entities. These angels behold the face of God and function as the heavenly counterpart of the Marcosian initiates on earth. Being "images" of the angels who behold the face of God (εἰκόνας αὐτῶν, as the text goes on to explain), the initiates will reach their authentic being only when united with their celestial models in the wedding chamber. For the Valentinian rite of the bridal chamber, see De Conick, "The Great Mystery of Marriage: Sex and Conception in Ancient Valentinian Traditions," *VC* 57 (2003): 307–42.

[249] *Haer.* 1.14.8; discussion in Förster, *Marcus*, 284–85.

is very significant, because Clement has read all the material discussed so far: Irenaeus' account of the Marcosians, the writings of the Oriental branch of Valentinianism, as well as the source used by the *Ps.-Clem. Hom.* 17.[250]

Clement of Alexandria identifies the Face of God mentioned in Matt 18:10 with Christ, the Logos; quite naturally, then, he identifies the πρόσωπον of Matt 18:10 with the χαρακτήρ of Heb 1:3 and the εἰκών of Col 1:15.[251] As for the "angels ever contemplating the Face of God" in Matt 18:10, they are the "thrones" of Col 1:16, and "the seven eyes of the Lord" of Rev 5:6 and Zech 3:9; 4:10.[252] All of these passages become, for Clement, descriptions of the seven πρωτόκτιστοι, or seven "first-born princes of the angels (πρωτόγονοι ἀγγέλων ἄρχοντες), who have the greatest power."[253] The seven *protoctists*, however, also carry a definite pneumatological content, since Clement identifies them not only with the first created angels, but also with the "seven spirits resting on the rod that springs from the root of Jesse" (Isa 11:1–3, LXX) and "the heptad of the Spirit."[254]

Clement's angelomorphic pneumatology and the underlying use of Matt 18:10 became the subject of severe polemics during the debates on the divinity of the Holy Spirit that followed the Arian controversy. Here are two excerpts from Gregory of Nyssa and Basil of Caesareea, summarizing much of the argument:

> Who...would not agree, that every intellectual nature is governed by the ordering of the Holy Spirit? For since it is said *the angels do always behold the Face of my Father which is in heaven* [Matt 18:10] and it is not possible to behold the person (ὑπόστασιν) of the Father otherwise than by fixing the sight upon it through His image (διὰ τοῦ χαρακτῆρος); but the image (χαρακτήρ) of the person (ὑποστάσεως) of the Father is the Only-begotten, and to Him again no man can draw near whose mind has not been illumined by the Holy Spirit, what else is shown from this but that the Holy Spirit is not separated from any operation which is wrought (ἐνεργείας ἐνεργουμένης) by the Father and the Son? Thus the identity of

---

[250] According to Colin Roberts (*Manuscript, Society, and Belief in Early Christian Egypt* [London/New York: Oxford University Press, 1979], 53), *Adversus Haereses* was circulating in Egypt "not long after the ink was dry on the author's manuscript." For the source behind Clement and the *Hom.* 17, see Collomp, "Une source de Clément d'Alexandrie."

[251] *Strom.* 7.58.3–6; *Exc.* 19.4.

[252] *Strom.* 5.6.35; *Ecl.* 57.1; *Exc.* 10.

[253] *Strom.* 6.16.142–143.

[254] *Strom.* 5.6.35; *Paed.* 3.12.87.

operation (ἐνεργείας) in Father, Son, and Holy Spirit shows plainly the undistinguishable character of their substance (φύσεως);

The pure, intelligent, and super-mundane powers (ὑπερκόσμιοι δυνάμεις) are and are styled holy, because they have their holiness of the grace given by the Holy Spirit.... The powers of the heavens are not holy by nature; were it so there would in this respect be no difference between them and the Holy Spirit.... And how could "thrones, dominions, principalities and powers" live their blessed life, did they not "behold the face of the Father which is in heaven" [Matt 18:10]? But to behold it is impossible without the Spirit!...in the order of the intellectual world it is impossible for the high life of Law to abide without the Spirit. For it so to abide were as likely as that an army should maintain its discipline in the absence of its commander, or a chorus its harmony without the guidance of the choirmaster (τοῦ κορυφαίου μὴ συναρμόζοντος).... Thus with those beings who are not gradually perfected by advancement (οὐκ ἐκ προκοπῆς τελειουμένοις) but are perfect from the moment of the creation (ἀπ᾽ αὐτῆς τῆς κτίσεως εὐθὺς τελείοις), there is in creation the presence of the Holy Spirit, who confers on them the grace that flows from Him for the completion and perfection of their essence.[255]

According to Gregory of Nyssa, the "face" mentioned in Matt 18:10 is none other than the Son, because πρόσωπον in Matt 18:10 is the same as χαρακτήρ in Heb 1:3. Even though Matthew does not state it explicitly, the angels do not have direct access to the Face: they are rather enabled to see, guided and illumined by the Holy Spirit. In fact, for Gregory, this is what reveals the "identity of operation" between Father, Son, and Holy Spirit, from which one is bound to infer the identity of substance.[256] Basil mentions the "supermundane powers," angelic beings that "are not gradually perfected by increase and advance, but are perfect from the moment of the creation," only to insist that the Spirit is to the angels as an army commander to his troops, or a choirmaster to a choir.

At first sight, the use of Matt 18:10 in an apology for the divinity of the Spirit seems peculiar—especially since elsewhere (*Eun.* 3.1 [SC 305:148]) Basil also uses the verse to support the teaching about guardian angels. In light of earlier uses of Matt. 18:10, however, such as those echoed by Clement and Aphrahat, it can be conjectured that

---

[255] Gregory of Nyssa, *Trin.* (GNO 3/1:13); Basil of Caesarea, *Spir.* 16.38 (SC 17bis: 376, 380, 382).
[256] For a description of the argument, together with extensive presentation of its philosophical and exegetical background, see Michel R. Barnes, *The Power of God: Δύναμις in Gregory of Nyssa's Trinitarian Theology* (Washington, D.C.: CUA Press, 2001).

the verse carried some weight in the Pneumatomachian argument. It is noteworthy that Basil still accepts the identification of the angels in Matt. 18:10 with the "thrones, dominions, principalities and powers" of Col 1:16, while Gregory still equates πρόσωπον (Matt 18:10) with χαρακτήρ (Heb 1:3). Basil's description of the Spirit as a "choirmaster" who ensures the order and harmony of the celestial liturgy, also has unmistakable angelic overtones, stemming perhaps from the high angelology of the opponents.[257] Moreover, Basil's reference to "those beings who are not gradually perfected by increase and advance, but are perfect from the moment of the creation," seems a clear enough evocation of the *protoctists* about whom Clement had said that they are not lacking in advancement (προκοπή), but have received perfection from the beginning, at the first [moment of their] creation.[258]

It seems, then, that just as Arianism was articulating an archaic doctrine of *Christos Angelos,* so also were the Pneumatomachians using a theology of the Holy Spirit that may be traced back to angelological speculations in Second Temple Judaism. Even while they offer one of the last echoes of the Face christology, the passages from Basil and Nyssen illustrate the demise of angelomorphic Pneumatotology.

To conclude, it appears that in Clement's interpretation of Matt 18:10, "the face of God" is a christological title, while the angels contemplating the Face occupy a theological area of confluence of angelology and pneumatology. On this latter point Clement's exegesis met the decided

---

[257] "Commander of the heavenly hosts" is a title commonly associated with the archangel Michael. Enoch in *2 En.* and Enoch-Metatron in the Rabbinic Hekhalot tradition, take on the role of "celestial choirmaster" in charge of directing the angelic liturgy before the Throne of Glory. In later Rabbinic literature, Enoch-Metatron's role in the angelic liturgy is more elaborate: while leading the choir, he also pronounces the divine Name ("invoke the deity's name in seven voices"); but he is also kind enough to protect his angelic chanters from its divinely devastating effects by "go[ing] beneath the Throne of Glory,...and bring[ing] out the deafening fire"—only so can the angels safely participate in the awesome liturgy of the heavens (*3 En.* 15B; cf. *Synopse* 390:164). For extensive discussion of these traditions, see A. Orlov, "Celestial Choirmaster: the Liturgical Role of Enoch-Metatron in 2 Enoch and the Merkabah Tradition," *JSP* 14 (2004): 3–29.

[258] *Exc.* 10.4; see discussion above. The roots of this idea might in fact lie far back. According to the *Book of Jubilees*—a very popular work of "rewritten Bible"—"the nature of all the angels of the presence and of the angels of sanctification was *circumcized* from the day of their creation," and these supreme angels are the heavenly model and destination of the people Israel. Circumcision in *Jubilees* expresses the same perfection that Clement or Basil would have expressed in ontological terms; and we note a similar preoccupation to link the highest angelic company and the perfected believers.

rebuttal of Gregory of Nyssa and Basil the Great, who were engaged in battle against the Pneumatomachians. As I shall show in a separate section, the use of Matt 18:10 as a proof-text for pneumatology finds a surprising confirmation in the writings of the famous early Syriac author Aphrahat.

CHAPTER TWO

THE LARGER THEOLOGICAL FRAMEWORK
FOR CLEMENT'S ANGELOMORPHIC PNEUMATOLOGY

The discussion so far has largely confirmed the conclusions advanced by Christian Oeyen. His thesis of *Engelpneumatologie* in Clement of Alexandria seems to stand on solid ground. It will be further strengthened by a study of other Christian authors, writing before and after Clement, which will show that angelomorphic pneumatology was not a peculiarity of Clement's but rather the continuation, in Christian thought, of the phenomenon that Levison termed "angelic spirit."

At this point it is important to inquire about the place of angelomorphic pneumatology in the larger framework of Clementine theology. I shall argue that angelomorphic pneumatology occurs in tandem with spirit christology, as part of a binitarian theological framework.

1. BINITARIAN MONOTHEISM IN CLEMENT OF ALEXANDRIA

> Clement's theology was really binitarian...[although] he mentions the Spirit as the agent of Faith in the believer, there would appear to be little real place for Him in his system.[1]

This blunt statement by W. H. C. Frend calls for some refinement. According to Osborn, even though "the centre of Clement's understanding of God is the reciprocity of father and son," which is similar "to the Platonic simple and complex unity," Clement "sees the reciprocity of father and son proliferated in spirit."[2] In other words, Clement's starting-point is a "binitarian" structure, or, in Osborn's language, the "reciprocity of father and son." This divine reciprocity is made to "overflow" or "proliferate," so as to account for divine economy, and especially God's spiritual presence in the believers.[3] Osborn highlights

---

[1] Frend, *Martyrdom and Persecution*, 264.
[2] Osborn, *Clement*, 107, 117, 128, 150. Osborn uses lower case for "father" and "son."
[3] Osborn, *Clement*, 150. The Father–Son reciprocity "overflows to the salvation of the world"; this proliferation is "from father and son to spirit and then to the ultimate union of believers in God" (Osborn, *Clement*, 141, 152).

the second element, and states, on its basis, that Clement has a "worthy
theology of the Holy Spirit." Yet if due consideration is given to the
first element, the divine reciprocity of Father and Spirit, which Osborn
himself regards as the "center" of Clementine theology, the conclusion
can also be different. Clement's theological intention is certainly trinitarian, and can be documented by his use of trinitarian formulas. The
corresponding theological account, however, has not reached the concept of a triadic Father—Son—Spirit "reciprocity." Clement's thought
remains determined in large measure by a binitarian framework.[4]

How do we recognize whether a monotheistic text is unitarian,
binitarian, or trinitarian? I find it helpful to apply a principle developed
by Larry Hurtado, which can be reduced to the following formula: that
which is considered "God" is necessarily the object of worship, and that
which is the object of worship is considered "God."[5] It is noteworthy,
in this light, that Clement seems reluctant to include the Spirit as a
recipient of worship. In the closing chapter of the *Instructor* (*Paed.*
3.12.101), the text invokes God as υἱὲ καὶ πατήρ, ἓν ἄμφω, κύριε;
praise, glory, and worship are given "to the only Father and Son, the
Son and Father, the Son—Instructor and Teacher—together with the
Holy Spirit."[6] It may be true that in Clement's thought the Father-Son
reciprocity "proliferates from father and son to spirit and then to the

---

[4] According to Osborn (*Clement*, 150), Clement's trinitarian theology is "well-
grounded in the Johannine account of the reciprocity of father with spirit and son with
spirit (John 14:15–20, 16:7–15)," and uses whatever it finds helpful in Middle Platonism
(e.g., Ep. 2, 312 E). These "building blocks," however, are quite problematic. Ziebritzki
(*Geist und Weltseele*) has demonstrated that the Platonic tradition could not contribute to the articulation of the pneumatology of Clement and Origen. With respect to
Clement's use of Ep 2 in *Strom.* 5.14.89 as a proof text for the Trinity, Ziebritzki (*Geist
und Weltseele*, 126) observes that Clement "dem Heiligen Geist...keine besondere Rolle
zuweist," even while to the Son he ascribes John 1:3 ("by whom all things are made"),
implying that the Father made all things through the Logos. As for the Johannine sayings about the "other paraclete," the relation between the two paracletes—the exalted
Christ and the Holy Spirit—poses major exegetical and theological problems. I shall
discuss Clement's views in a separate section.

[5] Hurtado, *At the Origins of Christian Worship* (Grand Rapids, Mich.: Eerdmans,
1999), and *Lord Jesus Christ: Devotion to Jesus in Earliest Christianity* (Grand Rapids,
Mich.: Eerdmans, 2003), esp. 11–53. For an older formulation of the argument, see
Richard J. Bauckham, "The Worship of Jesus in Apocalyptic Christianity," *NTS* 27
(1981): 322–41.

[6] τῷ μόνῳ πατρὶ καὶ υἱῷ, υἱῷ καὶ πατρί, παιδαγωγῷ καὶ διδασκάλῳ υἱῷ, σὺν καὶ
τῷ ἁγίῳ πνεύματι (*Paed.* 3.12.101).

ultimate union of believers in God."[7] The reference to the Holy Spirit in this text seems nevertheless simply a formulaic afterthought.[8]

Clement sometimes presents the Father alone receiving praise *through* the Son and the Holy Spirit.[9] More significant are the passages in which Clement suggests a subordination of the Holy Spirit to both the Father and the Son. For instance, he calls only the Father and the Son "God": "they know not what a 'treasure in an earthen vessel' we bear, protected as it is by the power of God the Father, and the blood of God the Son, and the dew of the Holy Spirit."[10]

It has often been remarked that such early Christian binitarianism is often the result of unclear, and sometimes even non-existent, distinctions between the Son and the Spirit; in other words, that binitarianism and "spirit christology" are two aspects of the same phenomenon. Clement of Alexandria's theology is representative in this regard.

2. SPIRIT CHRISTOLOGY IN CLEMENT OF ALEXANDRIA

Clement illustrates a widespread phenomenon in early Christian thought, namely the lack of careful distinction between "Logos" and "Spirit."[11] Whenever he offers his own theological reflection (as opposed to simply passing on traditional formulas of faith), Clement feels free to use "Logos" and "Pneuma" as synonyms by shifting between them repeatedly and without much explanation.[12]

---

[7] Osborn, *Clement*, 152.

[8] As noted by Ziebritzki, *Geist und Weltseele*, 124. Pace Kindiy (*Christos Didaskalos*, 87–88) who thinks that with this trinitarian formula "Clement eulogizes the Father, the Son, and the Holy Spirit...emphasizing their trinitarian unity and eternal glory."

[9] "To whom [to the Father], by (διά) his Son Jesus Christ, the Lord of the living and dead, and by (διά) the Holy Spirit, be glory, honor, power, eternal majesty..." (*Quis div.* 42.20).

[10] *Quis div.* 34.1. See the discussion in Hauschild, *Gottes Geist*, 84; Ziebritzki, *Geist und Weltseele*, 124.

[11] See Stead, *Philosophy in Christian Antiquity*, ch. 13: "Logos and Spirit" (148–59).

[12] *Paed.* 1.6.43: "the Lord Jesus, the Word of God, that is, the Spirit made flesh." Commenting on the fourth commandment of the Decalogue, Clement writes: "The seventh day, therefore, is proclaimed a rest...preparing for the primal day, our true rest; which, in truth, is the first creation of light, in which all things are viewed and possessed.... For the light of truth, a light true, casting no shadow, is the Spirit of God indivisibly divided to all.... By following him, therefore, through our whole life, we become impassible; and this is to rest" (*Strom.* 6.16.138). "Day" and "true Light" are quite transparently referring to Christ (cf. John 1:4–8; 8:56), as becomes clear immediately afterwards, when the text speaks about following Christ. However, the latter's identity is, in this passage, "Spirit of God." Clement is obviously drawing on an archaic

In *Strom.* 5.6, Clement ascribes the divine acts of creation, preservation, and revelation to the "Name," "Son," "Savior," or "Logos."
Nevertheless, the latter's role in organizing the cosmos and in prophetic revelation is documented with a quotation from 1 Cor 12:11
("the self-same Holy Spirit works in all"). Moreover, this verse is soon
afterwards reworked in a christological key: "God the Savior works... it
is the same Logos which prophesies, and judges, and discerns all
things." There seems to be a perfect parallel between the reference to
the Spirit and the reference to the Logos: both are introduced as the
agent of prophetic inspiration ("the apostles were at once prophets and
righteous"; "the oracle exhibits the prophecy which by the Word cries
and preaches... since it is the same Word which prophesies."); both
use ἐνεργέω; both designate "what is one," and each at the same time
becomes "what is many." It seems that Clement offers a translation
sui generis of 1 Cor 12:11 into his own theological idiom: the "Spirit"
mentioned by the Apostle is identified as the Logos.

In *Exc.* 24.2, a text directed against the dualist views of the Valentinians, Clement affirms the perfect identity (i.e., an identity of οὐσία and
δύναμις) between the paraclete who is at work (ἐνεργῶν) in the Church
and the paraclete who was active (ἐνεργήσαντι) in the prophets. Implicit
here is the identification of this paraclete with the Logos, because (a)
Clement had previously affirmed that it was the Logos who worked
in the prophets (ἐνεργήσας, *Exc.* 19.2); (b) the adverb "proximately"
(προσεχῶς), qualifying the action of the paraclete, functions as a technical term in Clement's description of how the Logos transforms the
perfect souls towards godlikeness.[13]

The same exegetical procedure occurs in *Exc.* 17, where Clement
discusses the work of the δύναμις in the world. This is significant,
because here and elsewhere in Clement δύναμις is a christological
term.[14] The biblical proof texts, however, are, once again, references to

---

christology designating the preexistent Christ as πνεῦμα interchangeably with λόγος. See
the article by Simonetti, quoted above; Wolfson, *Philosophy*, 177–256; Cantalamessa,
L'omelia in S. Pascha, 181–83. This seems to be a widespread phenomenon, present
in Syria-Palestine, Asia Minor, Alexandria, Carthage, and Rome, in authors speaking
Latin, Greek and Syriac.

[13] *Exc.* 27.3.6. See my earlier remarks on προσεχῶς.
[14] E.g., *Strom.* 7.2.7, 9; *Exc.* 4.2; 12.3. See also Sagnard's remarks on δύναμις in
Extraits, 79 n. 2. A beautiful passage in the homily "On the Rich Man's Salvation"
distinguishes between God in his ineffability and God in loving self-manifestation to
the world, calling the former "father" and the latter "mother": ἔστι δὲ καὶ αὐτὸς ὁ
θεὸς ἀγάπη καὶ δι' ἀγάπην ἡμῖν ἐθεάθη. καὶ τὸ μὲν ἄρρητον αὐτοῦ πατήρ, τὸ δὲ εἰς

πνεῦμα: John 4:24 ("God is πνεῦμα") and John 3:8 ("the πνεῦμα blows where it wills").

Clement ends *Strom.* 4.26.172 with the following words: "I shall pray the Spirit of Christ to wing me (εὐξαίμην τὸ πνεῦμα τοῦ Χριστοῦ πτερῶσαί με) to my Jerusalem." A very similar invocation occurs in the hymn to Christ (*Paed.* 3.12.101): Christ is called upon as the "wing (πτερόν) of unwandering birds," and "heavenly wing (πτερὸν οὐράνιον) of the all-holy flock." The evident parallelism between the invocations in *Strom.* 4.26.172 and *Paed.* 3.12.101 suggests that "Spirit of Christ" is simply Christ in his function as heavenly guide.

At least three factors determining the attributions above can be pointed out. First, similar to earlier writers, Clement deploys an all-encompassing theory of the Logos, and thereby inevitably claims for the Logos certain areas of activity traditionally associated with the Holy Spirit, namely the inspiration of Scripture and the charismatic empowerment of the believer.[15] Second, Clement follows the Philonic model of "translating" Scriptural terms and images into philosophical concepts, and "explains" the biblical πνεῦμα in light of the philosophical "Logos."[16] Finally, the term δύναμις seems to facilitate this tendency, insofar as Clement uses it alternatively for the Logos and the Spirit.[17]

ἡμᾶς συμπαθὲς γέγονε μήτηρ. ἀγαπήσας ὁ πατὴρ ἐθηλύνθη (*Quis dives?* 37.1–2). The metaphor of the ineffable God ("father") becoming manifest God ("feminine") out of love (ἀγαπήσας ὁ πατὴρ ἐθηλύνθη) is transparently christological: Clement first echoes the revelatory *logos*-language of John 1:18 (τότε ἐποπτεύσεις τὸν κόλπον τοῦ πατρός, ὃν ὁ μονογενὴς θεὸς μόνος ἐξηγήσατο); he then moves to the Incarnation ("he came down...he put on humanity...he voluntarily subjected himself to human experience"); finally, he appeals to δύναμις-language to describe the reverse of the incarnation: he will "bring us to the measure of his own δύναμις" (*Quis dives?* 37.3).

[15] Cf. Zahn, *Forschungen* 3:98; Kretschmar, *Trinitätstheologie*, 63. Ladaria (*Espíritu en Clemente*, 25) notes that the Spirit's "efficient causality" in the phenomenon of inspiration is equally applied to the Logos or Kyrios, especially in the *Instructor*, but he does not believe that these coincidences amount to an identification of the Word with the Spirit.

[16] Simonetti ("Note," 209) and Cantalamessa (*L'omelia in S. Pascha*, 184) attribute this primarily to Stoic influence. Others view it rather as a Stoic-influenced Middle Platonism: Whittaker, "ΕΠΕΚΕΙΝΑ ΝΩΥ ΚΑΙ ΟΥΣΙΑΣ," 99; Osborn, *Clement*, 142–43; Jan H. Waszink, "Bemerkungen zum Einfluss des Platonismus im frühen Christentum," *VC* 19 (1965): 146, 150, 155; Hägg, *Beginnings of Christian Apophaticism*, 215.

[17] Frangoulis (*Πνεῦμα bei Clemens*, 16) also makes a brief note to this effect: "[es] findet sich bei Clemens auch eine enge Verbindung von Pneuma und Sohn in dem übergeordneten Begriff des δύναμις." As part of the inherited philosophical tradition, the concept of δύναμις, in conjunction with οὐσία is extremely helpful for a discourse on the interplay between divine transcendence and immanence ("God is remote in essence, but very near in power, πόρρω μὲν κατ' οὐσίαν...ἐγγυτάτω δὲ δυνάμει" [*Strom.*

To sum up: Clement refers often to the "Holy Spirit," but he also uses πνεῦμα to designate the second hypostasis. Similarly to what one finds in other early Christian writers, the distinction between the Logos and the Holy Spirit is blurred.[18] But how does Clement himself relate Logos and Spirit? He is clearly not advocating an ontological identification. In a text from the *Paidagogos* he states that "the Spirit is the power of the Word":

> And the blood of the Lord is twofold. For there is the blood of his flesh, by which we are redeemed from corruption; and the spiritual, that by which we are anointed. And to drink the blood of Jesus is to become partaker of the Lord's immortality; for the Spirit is the power of the Word (ἰσχὺς δὲ τοῦ λόγου τὸ πνεῦμα), as blood is of flesh.[19]

As Ladaria has rightly observed, the Spirit here is "the power, the dynamic character of the Logos."[20] This is certainly true. Yet Clement's own explanations, which I surveyed earlier, offer a more detailed and

---

2.2.5]); "For human speech is by nature feeble, and incapable of uttering God. . . . not his essence [τὴν οὐσίαν], for this is impossible, but the power [τὴν δύναμιν] and the works [τὰ ἔργα] of God" [*Strom.* 6.18.166]). This use of δύναμις is well established in Philo and Clement. See in this respect Pépin, *Théologie cosmique*, 378–79; Cristina Termini, *Le Potenze di Dio: Studio su δύναμις in Filon di Alessandria* (Rome: Institutum Patristicum Augustinianum, 2000) and Hägg, *Beginnings of Christian Apophaticism*, 239–40 (Philo), 246–51, 260–7 (Clement). But δύναμις also has a venerable history in Jewish and Jewish-Christian angelology and demonology. Both Philo and Clement know about "power" as an angelic being (e.g., Philo, *Leg. All.* 3.177; Clement, *Strom.* 1.29.181; 2.2.3, both in reference to the "power" that spoke to Hermas). As already discussed, Clement is also aware of the specifically christological use of the term. Philo, Justin, Theophilus, and Clement, are some of the writers who are exploiting the double affiliation of the concept (philosophical, and Jewish-Christian) in order to ascertain their credibility in both areas. Since both "types" of δύναμις imply the idea of mediation and agency, it was only natural for Christians to "explain" what they meant by "Logos" and "Spirit" in terms of δύναμις. For a larger discussion of the use of δύναμις in the Early Common Era—which, however, devotes only a footnote to Clement—see Barnes, *Power of God*, 94–124; references to Clement are at 96 n. 4.

[18] Cf. Justin Martyr, *Apol.* 1.33.6: "It is wrong, therefore, to understand 'the Spirit and the power of God' [in Luke 1:35] as anything else than the Word, who is also the first-born of God, as the foresaid prophet Moses declared; and it was this which, when it came upon the virgin and overshadowed her, caused her to conceive." Aside from Justin (discussed at length below), this interpretation of Luke 1:35 also occurs in the *Protevangelium of James*, Origen, the *Epistula Apostolorum*, Tertullian, and Lactantius. See Cantalamessa, "La primitiva esegesi cristologica di 'Romani' I, 3–4 e 'Luca' I, 35," *RSLR* 2 (1966): 75–76; José Antonio de Aldama, "El Espíritu Santo y el Verbo en la exégesis de Lc 1, 35," in idem, *María en la patrística de los siglos I y II* (Madrid, 1970), 140–66; Aloys Grillmeier, *Christ in Christian Tradition* (2nd, rev. ed. Atlanta, Ga: John Knox, 1975), 198–9; McGuckin, "Spirit Christology," 144–5.

[19] *Paed.* 2.2.19–20.

[20] Ladaria, *Espíritu en Clemente*, 50, 266.

remarkably clear explanation: the dynamic aspect of the Logos, the πνεῦμα, manifests itself in the work of angelic spirits.

3. A FINAL LOOK AT CLEMENT'S SPECULATIONS ON UNITY AND DIVERSITY

The case for Clement's spirit christology has direct bearing on the interpretation of certain crucial texts and ideas discussed earlier. How, for instance, is the equation of the paraclete with the *protoctists* compatible with the identification between the paraclete and the Logos? And what is the relation between the πνεῦμα as Logos and the first created angelic πνεύματα? The solution resides, I think, in Clement's view on the relation between unity and multiplicity: the one "Spirit," the Logos, becomes multiform in the angelic "seven spirits." Clement's speculation on the interplay between the "Spirit" (the Logos) and the first created "spirits" has been discussed above. To the passage *Strom.* 5.6.35, quoted earlier, it is now useful to add a fragment from *Adumbrationes*:

> The golden lamp conveys another enigma as a symbol of Christ…in his casting light, "at sundry times and diverse manners," on those who believe in him and hope and see by means of the ministry of the *protoctists* (διὰ τῆς τῶν πρωτοκτίστων διακονίας). And they say that the seven eyes of the Lord are the seven spirits resting on the rod that springs from the root of Jesse;
> For the eyes of the Lord, he says, are *upon the righteous, and his ears on their prayers*: he means the manifold inspection (*multiformem speculationem*) of the Holy Spirit.[21]

At first sight, it would seem that the passage turns an anthropomorphism in the Psalms (Ps 33:16 [LXX], quoted in 1 Pet 3:12) into a reference to the Holy Spirit. Yet the "inspection" of the Spirit is described as "manifold," suggesting that Clement understands "the eyes of the Lord" to be not the two eyes of an anthropomorphic God, but rather the same seven "eyes of the Lord" discussed in *Strom.* 5.6.35, the *protoctists*. On this reading, the use of Heb 1:1 ("God—more specifically, Christ, according to *Strom.* 5.6—spoke to the prophets and patriarchs *at sundry times and diverse manners*) in both texts, and later in the *Adumbrationes*, makes excellent sense: the inspiring Spirit of Old Testament revelation is identified with the Logos working through the

---

[21] *Strom.* 5.6.35; *Adumbr.* 1 Pet 2:3.

protoctists and the entire angelic hierarchy. Clement's texts allow us to restate this idea by using πνεῦμα as the reference point. Given that the theory of the one Logos as multiplicity perfectly parallels the relation between one Spirit and seven powers of the Spirit, and the repeated identification between Logos and Spirit discussed earlier, it is legitimate to conclude that πνεῦμα is simultaneously one (*qua* Logos) and many (*qua protoctists*).

CONCLUSIONS

It is possible at this point to summarize the results of both chapters in Part One. I began by positing what seems to be the fundamental aspect of Clement's cosmological and theological view, namely the hierarchically ordered cosmos, featuring several angelic ranks. This is a worldview inherited from older tradition (e.g., *Mart. Ascen. Isa., 2 En., Ep. Apos.*), and strikingly anticipates the *Corpus Dionysiacum*.

Clement refers to the utterly transcendent God whose "Face" is the Logos, and who manifests himself, in descending order, to the seven *protoctists*, the archangels, the angels, and finally the prophets, as highest representatives of the Church. There is little or no explicit mention of the Holy Spirit in this hierarchy. Moreover, a sophisticated and technical exegesis explains πνεῦμα in such traditional expressions as "Spirit of Christ" as designations for the angelic spirits. The interplay between the Logos as πνεῦμα and the angelic πνεύματα (or, for that matter, Logos as δύναμις and the angelic δυνάμεις) reflects Clement's understanding of the interplay between unity and multiplicity, more precisely, his understanding unity *as* multiplicity (ὡς πάντα ἕν, *Strom.* 4.25.156).

The question is whether we can still speak about pneumatology at all in Clement. The problem depends on what one expects of second-century pneumatology. If "pneumatology" is a matter of metaphysics—conceiving of the Spirit "in his individual substance" alongside the Father and the Logos—then Ziebritzki is right to fault Clement for not yet thinking of a distinct hypostasis.[22] If, however, what we expect is "a real doctrine of the continuity and energy of God's working in the world," then Clement truly offers, as Osborn thinks, "a worthy

---

[22] Ziebritzki, *Geist und Weltseele*, 123 (quoted in full above).

theology of the Holy Spirit."[23] It should be noted, in fact, that many of the passages illustrating Clement's angelomorphic pneumatology center around the phenomenon of prophecy; the starting-point is the claimed religious experience and the *functional identity* of Christ, the Holy Spirit, and the angel, as grasped by this experience.

Second, as already noted, despite his abundant use of apocalyptic imagery inherited from older tradition (the Face of God, the seven highest angels performing their liturgy before the Face, the various levels of the angelic hierarchy, etc.), Clement's project in fact "sabotages" these very elements by a sustained process of internalization and spiritualization. In the words of Bousset, "[e]r spiritualisiert...bis zur Unverständlichkeit und zum leeren Spiel mit Worten."[24] Just like Greek or barbarian wisdom, the apocalyptic worldview of the predecessors conveys the truth only if subjected to what Osborn calls "noetic exegesis." A literal reading of the passages illustrating Clement's *Engelpneumatologie* would therefore be profoundly erroneous, because the same imagery is true differently for Clement than for his predecessors. For him, understanding the seven *protoctists* as the sevenfold Spirit is no less a matter of spiritual exegesis than understanding Ps.-Plato's "third" as the third article of the Christian rule of faith (*Strom.* 5.14.103). Clement equates the seven *protoctists* with the seven gifts of the Spirit and interprets them as the "heptad of the Spirit" (*Paed.* 3.12.87). One is therefore justified in speaking of pneumatology.

A generation later, Origen was clearly aware of, although not satisfied with, this theological tradition.[25] In his *Commentary on John*, for instance, while contrasting the deceitful inspiration coming from "lying spirits" (3 Rgns [1 Kgs] 22:19–22; 2 Chron 18:18–21) with the genuine inspiration by the Holy Spirit, Origen quotes John 16:13–14 ("when the Spirit of truth comes...he will not speak on his own, but

---

[23] Osborn, *Clement*, 152–53 (quoted in full above).

[24] Bousset, *Jüdisch-christlicher Schulbetrieb*, 269.

[25] As Kretschmar noted (*Trinitätstheologie*, 7–8), Origen's soteriology and cosmology have a trinitarian structure. In comparison to Justin Martyr, the *Shepherd*, and Clement, Origen has overcome both their binitarian orientation and the ambiguous relation between the Holy Spirit and the angelic spirits. In this respect, the clearest refutation of Hauschild's assertations to the contrary (*Gottes Geist*, 13 n. 10, 136, 138) is that of Markschies, "Der Heilige Geist im Johanneskommentar des Origenes: Einige vorläufige Bemerkungen," in his *Origenes und sein Erbe: Gesammelte Studien* (TU 160; Berlin/New York: De Gruyter, 2007), 107–26. See also Ziebritzki, *Heiliger Geist und Weltseele*, 240–43; George C. Berthold, "Origen and the Holy Spirit," *Origeniana Quinta*, 444–48.

will speak whatever he hears, and he will declare to you the things that are to come") and offers an explanation reminiscent of the *Shepherd*: "whenever the Holy Spirit or an angelic spirit speaks (τὸ μὲν οὖν ἅγιον πνεῦμα ἢ ἀγγελικὸν πνεῦμα ὅταν λαλῇ), he does not speak of his own but from the Word of Truth and of Wisdom."[26] In the seventh book of his *Commentary on Romans*, for instance, while discussing at length the possible meanings of πνεῦμα, Origen stated that the Holy Spirit was termed ἡγεμονικόν, *principalis* in Ps 50:14 (ἀπόδος μοι τὴν ἀγαλλίασιν τοῦ σωτηρίου σου καὶ πνεύματι ἡγεμονικῷ στήρισόν με) because "he holds dominion and sovereignty among the many holy spirits" (7.1). Indeed, the Holy Spirit is "the firstfruits of many spirits" by analogy with Christ, who is "the first born of all creation" (7.5).[27] Origen's understanding of the Holy Spirit in relation to the angelic spirits is perhaps the following:

> All spirits...are a part of the School of God's Spirit. The Holy Spirit is the head Teacher, who oversees the spiritual growth and education of every human being. However, like schools in Origen's day, the teachers are different from and inferior to the divine Spirit, but they assist in aspects of the Spirit's work.[28]

Certainly, the *Shepherd of Hermas* and the *Testament of Reuben* illustrate the tradition behind Origen's statements here.[29] The more important element, however, is to be located in the surviving fragments from Clement's *Hypotyposeis*, where an elaborated angelomorphic pneuma-

---

[26] Origen, *Comm. Jo.* 20.29.263 (SC 290: 286).

[27] Origen, *Comm. Rom.* 7.1 [554]: *quemque principalem spiritum propterea arbitror nominatum ut ostenderetur esse quidem multos spiritus sed in his principatum et dominationem hunc Spiritum Sanctum qui et principalis appellatur tenere*; 7.5 (574): *ut ille primogenitus dicitur omnis creaturae tali quadam ratione etiam multorum spirituum primitiae dicatur Spiritus Sanctus*. Numbers in parantheses refer to C. P. Hammond Bammel, ed. and trans., *Der Römerbriefkommentar des Origenes: Kritische Ausgabe der Übersetzung Rufins* (Vetus Latina 34; Freiburg: Herder, 1998). For a detailed analysis of Origen's pneumatology in the Romans commentary, see Maureen Beyer Moser, *Teacher of Holiness: The Holy Spirit in Origen's Commentary on the Epistle to the Romans* (Piscataway, NJ: Gorgias, 2005). See also the discussion of the same passages in Philip L. Tite, "The Holy Spirit's Role in Origen's Trinitarian System: A Comparison with Valentinian Pneumatology," *Theoforum* 32 (2001): 149–51.

[28] Moser, *Teacher of Holiness*, 51.

[29] This is argued by Moser, *Teacher of Holiness*, 37–41. "It should be noted that Origen is not convinced by these received traditions about the Holy Spirit. His own interpretation of the same verses in Ps 50 (51), as it occurs, for instance, in his homilies on Jeremiah (*Hom.* 8.2), is strikingly different: "with a governing spirit uphold me" indicates the Father, the "right spirit within me" refers to the Son, and "take not your holy spirit from me" to the Holy Spirit.

tology is embedded in the tradition of Bible exegesis to which Origen is the direct heir.[30]

Whether one chooses to say that for Clement the Holy Spirit is a plural entity consisting of the seven highest angels, or that the hypostasis of the Spirit is functionally absorbed and replaced by the *protoctists*, or, as I am inclined to think, that Clement simultaneously transmits and "sabotages" the apocalyptic imagery of his predecessors, by interpreting the *protoctists* as an angelomorphic representation of Spirit, there is abundant proof to confirm the thesis proposed by Christian Oeyen in 1966. I have argued that the theological phenomenon under discussion would be more accurately described as "angelomorphic pneumatology," and that it occurs in tandem with spirit christology, within a theological framework still determined by binitarianism.

The pages to follow will demonstrate that, from a religio-historical perspective, angelomorphic pneumatology constitutes a significant phase in Christian reflection on the Holy Spirit.

---

[30] Cf. Méhat, *Étude*, 521 n. 159: "les commentaires d'Origène, qui ont sans doutes utilisé les *Hypotyposeis*, ont dû contribuer à les éclipser." One should recall, however, that the *Hypotyposeis* also enjoyed a Byzantine afterlife: not only as occasional scholia to the Ps.-Dionysian Corpus, but more importantly, by being taken apart and paraphrased independently in Ps.-Caesarius' *Erotapokriseis* and Isidor of Pelusium's *Epistles*.

PART TWO

ANGELOMORPHIC PNEUMATOLOGY IN
CLEMENT'S PREDECESSORS

INTRODUCTION

So far I have argued the case for angelomorphic pneumatology in Clement of Alexandria. I have shown that it is not Clement's own creation, but rather an already existing tradition, inherited from the so-called elders, which Clement reworked and integrated into his account of Christian thought. Who these "elders" were is nearly impossible to tell, because these teachers were not given to writing, but were rather interested in passing on a certain way of life. Clement, on the other hand, saw his own writings as a medium through which the wisdom of the "elders" was to reach subsequent generations.[1]

If we have no direct access to the thought of the "elders," it is nevertheless possible to gain some insight into their teachings by considering early Christian writings that Clement would have read and regarded as authoritative. To prove my overall thesis concerning the tradition of angelomorphic pneumatology in early Christianity, and provide some insight into the pneumatological traditions inherited and reworked by Clement of Alexandria, I shall discuss the Book of Revelation, the *Shepherd of Hermas*, Justin Martyr's *Apologies* and *Dialogue*, and the *Demonstrations* of Aphrahat "the Persian Sage." The first three writings Clement would have known very well. Aphrahat is relevant, as I shall argue, because he provides access to early Syriac exegetical and doctrinal traditions very similar to those echoed by Clement.

---

[1] *Ecl.* 27.1–2, 4–7. I have quoted these texts earlier.

CHAPTER THREE

ANGELOMORPHIC PNEUMATOLOGY IN THE BOOK OF REVELATION[1]

INTRODUCTION

In this chapter I shall argue that the Book of Revelation exemplifies an archaic angelomorphic pneumatology similar to the one discerned in Clement of Alexandria. Moreover, I shall show that, just as in Clement, such depictions of the Holy Spirit occur in tandem with spirit christology, within a theological framework still marked by binitarianism.

The earliest surviving commentary on Revelation is that of Victorinus of Poetovio, composed around 258–260.[2] The exegetical works by Melito and Hippolytus have not survived, and the few scholia ascribed to Origen are probably not authentic.[3] The text of one of these scholia is recognizable as *Strom.* 4.25.156;[4] we are thus back to Clement of Alexandria.

Judging from the overall structure of the *Hypotyposeis* as a commentary on the entire Bible, Clement 's notes on Revelation (as well as

---

[1] This chapter is a revised version of Bucur, "Hierarchy, Prophecy, and the Angelomorphic Spirit: A Contribution to the Study of the Book of Revelation's *Wirkungsgeschichte*," *JBL* 127 (2008): 183–204.

[2] M. Dulaey, ed. and trans, *Victorin de Poetovio: Sur L'Apocalypse et autres écrits* (SC 423; Paris: Cerf, 1997), 15.

[3] C. I. Dyobouniotes and A. von Harnack, *Der Scholien-Kommentar des Origenes zur Apokalypse Johannis* (TU 38.3; Leipzig: Hinrichs, 1911): 21–44; C. H. Turner, "The Text of the Newly Discovered Scholia of Origen on the Apocalypse," *JTS* 13 (1912): 386–97; idem, "Document: Origen, Scholia in Apocalypsin," *JTS* 25 (1924): 1–15. The scholia have been translated into French by Solange Bouquet and published in the volume *L'Apocalypse expliquée par Césaire d'Arles: Scholies attribuées à Origène* (Paris: Desclée de Brouwer, 1989), 167–203. Éric Junod's detailed and sober analysis of the fragments yields the following conclusion: "Résignons-nous donc à parler de citations patristiques rattachées à des passages de l'Apocalypse par un (ou plusieurs) lecteur(s) byzantin(s); en effet, on ne peut même pas dire que ce soient des citations patristiques *sur* l'Apocalypse puisque les citations de Clément et d'Irénée ne sont pas extraites d'ouvrages consacrés à l'Apocalypse" (Junod, "À propos des soi-disants scolies sur l'Apocalypse d'Origène," *RSLR* 20 [1984]: 121).

[4] Origen, *Schol. Apoc.* 5 (*Scholien–Kommentar des Origenes*, 22) = *Strom.* 4.25.156.

on the Apocalypse of Peter) should have been part of the eighth book.[5] However, the Latin translation of this work, titled *Adumbrationes*, and commissioned by Cassiodorus, only consists of scholia to 1 Pet, 1–2 John, and Jude. This corresponds with the information that Cassiodorus provides in the *Divine Institutions*, which specifically mentions Clement as a commentator on the catholic epistles. Elsewhere in the same work, however, Cassiodorus clearly shows that Clement commented on a broader range of biblical texts.[6] Zahn is convinced that he knew of Clement's reputation as a biblical exegete, but only possessed the text of *Hypotyposeis* to 1 Pet, 1–2 John, and Jude.[7] Less probable, but not to be ruled out, is the possibility that Cassiodorus left out some of the Clementine texts available to him if he judged them doctrinally unsound; the scholia to Revelation could have suffered this fate. In support of this hypothesis would be the odd error in Cassiodorus' description of the content of the *Adumbrationes* (he mentions a commentary on James that is not part of the current text, but fails to mention the commentary

---

[5] Bunsen, *Analecta Antenicena* 1:164; Zahn, *Forschungen* 3:156. An objection can be raised on the basis of a passage that occurs in the scholia to Ps-Dionysius (PG 4:225, 228): "The divine John speaks of elder angels in the Apocalypse, and we read in Tobit as well as in the fifth book of Clement's *Hypotyposeis* that the premier angels are seven (ἑπτὰ εἶναι τοὺς πρώτους)." Nevertheless, a repetitious and quite disorderly manner of writing—in this case, an excursus on the angels of Revelation placed in book five, before the actual scholia on Revelation—is characteristic of Clement in general, and perhaps especially, as Photius noted, of the *Hypotyposeis*; in any case, it is common occurrence in the *Adumbrationes*. A passage can be ascribed with certainty to a specific book of the *Hypotyposeis* only when Clement's commentary is preserved together with the biblical text to which it refers. When this is not the case, it is impossible to know whether Clement's exegetical statement on a biblical passage belongs to his commentary of the respective biblical book, or represents an excursus occurring in Clement's commentary of a different biblical book: "Selbst bei den Fragmenten, welche als Citate aus einem bestimmten Buch der Hypotyposen angeführt sind und auf ein bestimmtes biblisches Buch hinzuweisen scheinen, ist manchmal noch fraglich, ob das betreffende Buch in dem bezeichneten Buch der Hypotyposen commentirt war" (Zahn, *Forschungen* 3:147).

[6] *Div. litt.*, Praef. 4 (FC 39/1:98, 100): *Ferunt itaque scripturas divinas veteris novique Testamenti ab ipso principio usque ad finem Graeco sermone declarasse Clementem Alexandrinum cognomento Stromateum et Cyrillum eiusdem civitatis episcopum et Iohannem Chrysostomum, Gregorium et Basilium, necnon et alios studiosissimos viros quos Graecia facunda concelebrat.* Leaving aside the striking absence of Origen, this passage surprises by its mentioning of Clement among the exegetical heavyweights of the Greek East. According to Zahn (*Forschungen*, 3:137), this indicates that Cassiodorus, like Eusebius before him and Photius centuries later, was aware of the Stromatist's major exegetical accomplishment: to have produced the *Hypotyposeis*, that is, scholia to all or much of Scripture.

[7] This is Zahn's conviction: "aber nur gehört hat er davon" (*Forschungen* 3:137).

on Jude),[8] and the fact that he candidly admits to have "purged" these Clementinian passages of certain doctrinal *offendicula*, just as he says to have purged other "subtle" but "poisonous" writings.[9]

We simply cannot know whether Cassiodorus had direct knowledge of Clement's *Hypotyposeis* to Revelation. His own notes on Revelation, however, contained in the *Complexiones*, do seem to echo, on occasion, theological views that go back to Clement and the "elders." Such is the case with the interpretation of Revelation's "seven spirits."

1. The "Seven Spirits" in Revelation and Clement's *Protoctists*

Revelation refers several times to a mysterious group of "seven spirits" (Rev 1:4; 3:1; 4:5; 5:6). The first of these occurrences is also the most important one, because it places the seven spirits in the initial greeting: "grace and peace" are said to come from God, and from the seven spirits, and from Jesus Christ.

Revelation takes the form of a large epistle, in which are embedded seven letters, introduced and ended as such (Rev 1:4–5; 22:16).[10] Revelation 1:4, in which "grace and peace" from God are invoked upon the recipient, illustrates one of the formal components of the apostolic letter: the greeting.[11] The structure of the phrase (καὶ...καὶ...καὶ)

---

[8] Zahn (*Forschungen* 3:137) suspects simple forgetfulness of the exact content of the *Adumbrationes*, due to the fact that the translation was not Cassiodorus' own.

[9] *In epistolis autem canonicis Clemens Alexandrinus presbyter, qui et Stromatheus vocatur...quaedam Attico sermone declaravit; ubi multa quidem subtiliter, sed aliqua incaute locutus est. Quae nos ita transferri fecimus in Latinum, ut exclusis quibusdam offendiculis, purificata doctrina eius securior potuisset auriri* (*Div. litt.* 1.8.4 [FC 39/1:160]). Cassiodorus also reports on his "purging" of Origen's works and of a Pelagian commentary on Romans, whose "poisonous" words he also views as "most subtle" (*subtilissimas...dictiones*) (*Div. litt.* 1.8.4 [FC 39/1:158–60, 170]).

[10] Revelation opens with a direct self-characterization as "apocalypse" (Rev 1:1–3), it then introduces an epistolary greeting (Rev 1:4–6), and it closes with a standard epistle ending (Rev 22:21).

[11] Numerous opinions have been voiced as to the formal characteristics of these letters. One of the most complex proposals is that of David E. Aune (*Revelation* [3 vols.; Dallas, Tex.: Word Books, 1997], 1:119–24), who maintains that the seven letters are an original fusion of two literary models: the imperial edicts and the prophetic proclamations of judgment and salvation. Other solutions are listed by Pierre Prigent (*Commentary on the Apocalypse of St. John* [Tübingen: Mohr Siebeck, 2001], 57). Prigent believes that "the biblical realm offers interesting and, in the final analysis, satisfying parallels" (57). Similarly Robert Muse, "Revelation 2–3: A Critical Analysis of Seven Prophetic Messages," *JETS* 29 (1986): 147–61.

suggests that "the seven spirits before his [God's] throne" are one among three coordinated entities. The blessing with "grace and peace" is suggestive of a divine origin.[12] The three must, then, in some way stand for the divinity (cf. 2 Cor 13:14, *The grace of the Lord Jesus Christ, and the love of God, and the communion of the Holy Spirit, be with you all*; 1 Cor 12:4–6, which mentions *the same Spirit, the same Lord, the same God*).[13]

It seems most likely, therefore, that the mentioning of the "seven spirits" corresponds to the expected reference to the Holy Spirit. In other words, the author's expression "seven spirits" would designate what the early Church usually referred to as "Holy Spirit." This makes perfect sense, according to Edmondo F. Lupieri, of the dualism between the sevenfold Spirit and the sevenfold demonic power (Rev 12:3; 13:1).[14] Moreover, the "Satanic triad" composed of the dragon, the beast, and the false prophet (Rev 16:13; cf. Revelation 13), suggests the existence of a similar triadic structure in the opposite, divine world.[15] In the cautious words of Lupieri, with the greeting in Revelation "John is developing some kind of (pre-) Trinitarian thinking."[16] Whether one chooses to term this a "grotesque conception" of the Trinity or one that is "quite orthodox," depends on whether or not one considers this theology in its proper context, which is that of Jewish apocalyptic traditions appropriated by early Christians.[17]

---

[12] *Pace* Joseph Michl, *Die Engelvorstellungen in der Apokalypse des hl. Johannes* (Munich: Max Hueber, 1937), 155–56. Michl tries to escape the difficulty by interpreting the blessing with "grace and peace" coming from the angels as "eine Spendung im uneigentlichen Sinne" (156). On the other hand, he adduces a number of Jewish and Christian texts in which angels appear to hold a certain exalted status in their relations with humans. The difficulty of Rev 1:4, however, is due to the fact that angels appear to be placed on the same level with the Father and the Son.

[13] See also the list of passages illustrating Paul's "soteriological trinitarianism" in Gordon D. Fee, *God's Empowering Presence: The Holy Spirit in the Letters of Paul* (Peabody, Mass.: Hendrickson, 1994), 839–42.

[14] Edmondo F. Lupieri, *A Commentary on the Apocalypse of John* (Grand Rapids, Mich.: Eerdmans, 2006), 136: "We are to understand that whenever the Spirit comes forth in human history…it must be sevenfold, in contrast to the Satanic dominion. That this dominion is in fact sevenfold is shown by the fact that the various demonic beasts always have seven heads, which in its turn probably reflects Satan's dominion over the seven periods into which the duration of this world seems to be divided… The sevenfold pattern of the Spirit's interventions thus probably indicates the constant presence of the Spirit throughout the duration of human history."

[15] Lupieri, *A Commentary on the Apocalypse*, 103.

[16] Lupieri, *Commentary on the Apocalypse*, 102.

[17] These are the terms used by R. H. Charles (*A Critical And Exegetical Commentary on The Revelation of St. John* [2 vols.; Edinburgh: T&T Clark International, 1920],

On the other hand, the angelic traits of the seven spirits are quite obvious. Revelation explicitly says that "the seven stars" represent "the seven angels" (Rev 1:20), and brings together "the seven spirits before his throne" (Rev 1:4) and "the seven angels before the throne" (Rev 8:2) in Rev 3:1, where we read of the one who "has" (ὁ ἔχων) "the seven spirits and the seven stars."

Pierre Prigent argues that the seven spirits are different from the seven stars because they are mentioned separately in Rev 3:1.[18] We must bear in mind, however, that "star," like "spirit," is routinely used for angelic beings. On the basis of overwhelming evidence drawn from Jewish, Christian, and "pagan" sources, Dale Allison has demonstrated that ancient readers identified the star of the magi (Matthew 2) with an angelic apparition. In other words, early Christians would have had in mind not a star in the astronomical sense, but rather "an angel in the form of that star," "a starry likeness," "a watcher," "an invisible power," "a certain holy power in the form of a star," "a divine and angelic power that appeared in the form of a star."[19] According to Allison, "the star that goes before the magi is like the pillar and cloud that went before Israel as the people fled Pharaoh's armies (and which Philo, *Mos.* 1.166, identified with an angel)."[20] The link between the magi's star and the pillar of cloud (Exod 13:21; 14:19; 23:20; 40:38; Neh 9:19; Ps 78:14; 105:39) also makes possible a connection with "spirit."

1:lii; cf. 1:12) and Gregory Dix ("The Seven Archangels and the Seven Spirits: A Study in the Origin, Development, and Messianic Associations of the Two Themes," *JTS* 28 [1927]: 248).

[18] Prigent, *Commentary*, 117.

[19] Dale Allison, "The Magi's Angel (Matt. 2:2, 9–10)," in his *Studies in Matthew: Interpretation Past and Present* (Grand Rapids, Mich.: Baker Academic, 2005), 17–41. For precise references, the reader is referred to the article, since it is impossible to reproduce here the avalanche of proof-texts in the footnotes, supplemented by a six-page Appendix. Allison shows that even after the Church's condemnation of the equation of heavenly bodies with angels, prominent in Origenistic circles, the interpretation of the "star" of Bethlehem as an angelic apparition remained in force. It was bound to succumb, however, once the animated cosmos was replaced by the scientific astronomy of the post-Renaissance era. This paradigm shift brought with itself the unfortunate but stubborn attempts to consider Matt 2:2 in light of what modern astronomy knows of stars, comets, supernovas, and so forth. Speculations of this sort are as widespread and recurrent as they are misguided, being rooted in the exegetical *peccatum originale* of "reading ancient text with modern minds" (Allison, *Studies in Matthew*, 35).

[20] Allison, *Studies in Matthew*, 28–29. The connection is made explicitly by John Chrysostom, *Hom. Matt.* 6.3 (PG 57:578): [The star] "did not even have a certain course of its own; rather, when they had to move, it moved, when they had to stand, it stood, regulating everything according to what was necessary, just as the pillar of cloud that now halted and now roused up the camp of the Jews when it was needful."

In Isaiah 63:9–10, 14 (LXX), for instance, "angel" (cf. Exod 14:19) is used interchangeably with God's "holy spirit" in order to designate the saving action of "the Lord himself."[21] It is noteworthy, too, that Origen points to the similarity between the "star" that descended and abided over the infant and the Holy Spirit who descended and abided over Jesus at the Jordan baptism.[22]

The simplest solution, then, also adopted by patristic exegetes, is to admit that we have, in Revelation, symbolic references to the same reality—the seven stars are the seven spirits—which the author conveyed by recourse to the language of angelic worship before the divine throne.[23] The well-defined group of *the* seven stars, *the* seven angels, *the* seven spirits, is intimately linked with, and clearly subordinated to, Christ: seven eyes of the Lord, seven stars in his hand, seven horns of the Lamb, and seven thunders of the "mighty angel" (Rev. 10:3).[24]

---

[21] In the case of MT, the equation also includes "presence" (cf. Exod 33:14–15; Deut 4:37). For the connection of "spirit" and "presence" see also Ps 138 (139):7; Ps 50 (51):13.

[22] Origen, *Hom. Num.* 18.4 (SC 442:330).

[23] See Lupieri, *Commentary on the Apocalypse*, 102–3, 136; David E. Aune, *Revelation* (3 vols.; Dallas, Tex.: Word Books, 1997), 1:33; Allison, "The Magi's Angel," in Allison, *Studies in Matthew*, 39. Among patristic commentators, see Oecumenius, *Comm. Apoc.* 2.11 (TEG 8:94); Andrew of Caesarea, *Comm. Apoc.* 3.7 (Schmid, 36); Arethas, *Comm. Apoc.* 2 (PG 106:520D–521B, 525B). For Oecumenius and Andrew of Caesarea, the references are to the critical editions: Marc de Groote, ed., *Oecumenii Commentarius in Apocalypsin* (TEG 8; Leuven: Peeters, 1999); Josef Schmid, *Studien zur Geschichte des griechischen Apokalypse-Textes. Vol. 1: Der Apokalypse-Kommentar des Andreas von Kaisareia* (Munich: Zink, 1955).

[24] The vision in Revelation 10 suggests a close link between the "mighty angel" and the "seven thunders." Revelation 10:3 (καὶ ἔκραξεν φωνῇ μεγάλῃ ὥσπερ λέων μυκᾶται. καὶ ὅτε ἔκραξεν ἐλάλησαν αἱ ἑπτὰ βρονταὶ τὰς ἑαυτῶν φωνάς) suggests the simultaneity of—even identity between—the angel's shout "with a mighty voice" (φωνὴ μεγάλη) and the voices (τὰς φωνάς) of the seven thunders. Similarly Lupieri, *Commentary on the Apocalypse*, 169. For the identity of the seven thunders, "[t]he closest connection we can make is with the 'seven spirits' that John has named four times" (Lupieri, *Commentary on the Apocalypse*, 169). According to both Oecumenius (*Comm. Apoc.* 6 [TEG 8:157]) and Victorinus (*Comm. Apoc.* 10.2; 1.1; 1.6 [SC423:90, 46, 52]), the seven thunders are the same "seven spirits" of Rev 1:4; however, Oecumenius understands the thunders as angelic powers, while Victorinus interprets them, on the basis of Isa 11:1-2, as "the Spirit of sevenfold power" (*spiritus septiformis virtutis*). Andrew of Caesarea (*Comm. Apoc.* 28 [Schmid, 107]) and Arethas (*Comm. Apoc.* 28 [106:640C]) agree that the seven thunders can be interpreted as "angelic powers," but do not draw an explicit connection to the seven spirits. The identity of the mighty angel is even more disputed: Victorinus (*Comm. Apoc.* 10.1 [SC423:88]) identifies the angel with Christ, via Isa 9:11 (LXX), μεγάλης βουλῆς ἄγγελος. Oecumenius, Andrew of Caesarea, and Arethas, by contrast, see in this figure nothing more than an angelic minister. Some scholars agree with Victorinus (whom they all invoke), and identify the angels with Christ (Gundry, "Angelomorphic Christology," 664; Stuckenbruck, *Angel*

Placed before the divine throne, the seven are envisaged as offering up
the prayers mounting from below and passing on the illumination that
descends from above. These are characteristic elements in the depiction
of angelic intercession, contemplation and service.

To make sense of all of the above, patristic as well as modern-day
commentators have outlined the following alternative: (a) Revelation
connects the seven spirits/eyes/lamps of the Lord (Zech 3:9; 4:10)
with the rest/tabernacling of the seven spiritual gifts (Isa 11:2; Prov
8:12–16);[25] (b) Revelation connects the seven spirits/eyes/lamps of the
Lord (Zech 3:9; 4:10) with the seven angels of the presence (Tob 12:15;
1 En. 90.20–21).[26]

The exegetical impasse is evident. Even patristic authors who affirm
or accept the angelic interpretation of the seven spirits do so with
great caution, anxious to eliminate any misunderstanding that could

---

Veneration, 229–32; Gieschen, *Angelomophic Christology*, 256–60). Others disagree
(e.g., Carrell, *Jesus and the Angels*, 131–37; Lupieri, *Commentary on the Apocalypse*,
166–67; Matthias Reinhard Hoffmann, *The Destroyer and the Lamb: The Relationship
Between Angelomorphic and Lamb Christology in the Book of Revelation* [WUNT 2/203;
Tübingen: Mohr Siebeck, 2005], 72–76), pointing out that despite the lofty, Christ-like
appearance of the angel, a number of details preclude its identification with Christ. The
"mighty angel" is sometimes identified with "the angel of Jesus Christ" (Rev 1:1; 22:16),
who delivers the prophetic message to the visionary (Aune, *Revelation*, 2:557; Richard
Baukham, *The Climax of Prophecy: Studies on the Book of Revelation* [Edinburgh: T&T
Clark, 1993], 253–57; Lupieri, *Commentary on the Apocalypse*, 168). Finally, a fresh
and singular proposal is that of Robby Waddell (*The Spirit in the Book of Revelation*
[JPTS 30; Dorset, UK: Deo, 2006], 158–60): the angel of Rev 10:1, who is "exceptionally
remarkable, possessing divine characteristics" (155), "serves as a symbol for the Spirit
rather than Christ" (158). This is, as the author concedes, a "possible but conjectural"
interpretation (160), whose appeal is primarily theological (Waddell's study seeks "to
integrate the text of Revelation...and my [the author's] own context of Pentecostalism"
[*Spirit in the Book of Revelation*, 4]).

[25] This position is held by the majority of scholars, patristic and modern. Schlütz
(*Isaias* 11:2, 34) has shown that a connection between Isa 11:2 (the seven gifts of the
Spirit) and Zech 4:10 (the seven lamps) was an established *topos* in patristic exegesis.

[26] Scholars who maintain this position include Charles, *Revelation*, 1:11; Aune
(*Revelation* 1:33–35), Gieschen (*Angelomorphic Christology*, 264–5), Gottfried Schimanowski (*Die himmlische Liturgie in der Apokalypse des Johannes* [WUNT 2/154;
Tübingen: Mohr Siebeck, 2002], 118), and Hoffmann, *Destroyer and the Lamb*, 150–52.
Among patristic writers, this explanation is implied by Cyprian (*Fort.* 11), affirmed
by Oecumenius (*Comm. Apoc.* 1.9; 3.7 [TEG 8:70, 108]) and accepted as one of two
possible solutions by Andrew of Caesarea (*Comm. Apoc.* 1.1; 3.7; 4.10 [Schmid, 13–14,
36, 50]), and Arethas, *Comm. Apoc.* 1; 10 (PG 106:505B, 569C). Many of the relevant
passages are presented and discussed in Swete, *The Apocalypse of St. John: The Greek
Text with Introduction, Notes and Indices* (3rd ed.; London: Macmillan, 1909), 5–6;
Albin Škrinjar, "Les sept esprits: Apoc. 1, 4; 3, 1; 4, 5; 5, 6," *Bib* 16 (1935): 2–24; Michl,
Engelvorstellungen, 113–34.

jeopardize doctrinal orthodoxy. Andrew of Caesarea and Arethas, for instance, seem somewhat hesitant in setting forth the angelic interpretation (both write, νοεῖν δυνατὸν), and, unlike Oecumenius, also present the alternative exegesis of Rev 1:4, which views the seven spirits as seven operations of the Spirit. Moreover, all three writers find it important to stress the fact that the seven spirits before the throne (Rev 1:4) are in no way to be numbered with the Trinity.[27] Finally, all three reverse course in their exegesis of Rev 5:6, where they interpret the seven spirits in reference to Isaiah 11.[28]

Modern exegetes tend to juxtapose the two solutions, rarely daring to eliminate either possibility.[29] Both solutions have significant strengths and weaknesses: the first one accounts for the number seven, and the position in the greeting; the second accounts for the undeniable angelic traits of these seven spirits. However, neither is able to integrate the advantages of the alternative interpretation, and so both are still open to criticism.[30]

---

[27] Oecumenius, *Comm. Apoc.* 1.9 (TEG 8:70): τὰ δὲ ἑπτὰ πνεύματα εἰσὶν ἄγγελοι ἑπτά· οὐχ ὡς ἰσότιμα δέ, ἢ συναΐδια, συμπαρελήφθη τῇ Ἁγίᾳ Τριάδι—ἄπαγε—ἀλλ' ὡς θεράποντες γνήσιοι καὶ δοῦλοι πιστοί; Andrew of Caesarea, *Comm. Apoc.* 1.1 (Schmid, 13–14): ἑπτὰ δὲ πνεύματα τοὺς ἑπτὰ ἀγγέλους νοεῖν δυνατὸν τοὺς τῶν ἐκκλησιῶν λαχόντας τὴν κυβέρνησιν· οὐ συναριθμούμενος τῇ θεαρχικωτάτῃ καὶ βασιλίδι τριάδι, ἀλλ' ὡς δούλους σὺν αὐτῇ μνημονευομένους. Similarly Arethas (*Comm. Apoc.* 1 [PG 106:505B]). Interestingly, immediately after the statements just quoted, all three writers appeal to 1 Tim 5:21—a text that might raise similar problems!—to establish the subordinate status of the seven.

[28] Oecumenius, *Comm. Apoc.* 3.14 (TEG 8:116); Andrew of Caesarea, *Comm. Apoc.* 4.12 (Schmid, 56); Arethas, *Comm. Apoc.* 12 (PG 106:580D).

[29] Eduard R. Schweizer (*Spirit of God* [Bible Key Words from Gerhard Kittel's *Theologisches Wörterbuch zum Neuen Testament*; London: Adam & Charles Black, 1960], 105–6) simply juxtaposes the religio-historical perspective ("from the point of view of the history of religion, they are simply the seven archangels"), and the traditional theological point of view, according to which the seven spirits "represent the Spirit of God in its fullness and completeness." Aune (*Revelation*, 1:34) is exhaustive in his references, but very reserved in advocating the identification between the seven spirits and the principal angels.

[30] Equating the seven spirits with the seven gifts of the Holy Spirit of Isa 11:2 does not explain the resulting "double blessing" (why is the Holy Spirit dispensing grace and peace if he is *already* designated by his *gifts*?), or the awkward conflation of personal traits (being in service before the throne, blessing the Church), and impersonal traits (the Spirit as spiritual gifts), or the fact that, despite being "seven" and "before the throne," the seven spirits and the seven angels are not the same. Moreover, critics point out that the overwhelming majority of greetings in apostolic epistles mention "grace and peace" from the Father and the Son (Michl, *Engelvorstellungen*, 151; for a list of greetings in the NT, see Aune, *Revelation* 1:26–27), and that a trinitarian interpretation of the greeting in Revelation is derived from a "later conceptualization of God" (Aune, *Revelation* 1:34). On the other hand, we have 2 Cor 13:13 ("The grace of the

Could the exegesis of Clement of Alexandria be of some help? Even though we possess no direct reference to Rev 1:4 (and related verses), several passages in Clement suggest that he did hold a specific view about the passages in Revelation dealing with the seven spirits. The following elements are certain: (a) ancient and modern exegetes agree that Rev 1:4 is intended as a reference to the seven spirits/eyes/lamps of the Lord in Zech 3:9; 4:10. Clement also connects his *protoctists* with Zech 3:9 and Isa 11:2-3 (LXX);[31] (b) Oecumenius (shortly after 500),[32] Andrew of Crete (ca. 660-740), and Arethas of Caesarea (ca. 860-940)—who uses both—point to Clement of Alexandria as an ancient authority for the view that the seven spirits of Revelation are the seven archangels.[33] Moreover, a passage from John of Scythopolis' scholia to Ps.-Dionysius, quoted earlier, links the seven supreme angels of Revelation and those of Clement's *Hypotyposeis*.[34]

Some have tended to dismiss these witnesses by pointing out that they only tell us that Irenaeus and Clement *knew* of a group of seven principal angels, without connecting this theological opinion with the exegesis of Revelation.[35] Let us note, first, that the reference to Irenaeus finds a counterpart in *Epid.* 9.[36] As far as Clement is concerned,

---

Lord Jesus Christ, the love of God, and the communion of the Holy Spirit be with all of you") and the trinitarian baptismal formula, both of which suggest that a reference to the Holy Spirit could very well have been intended in Rev 1:4.

[31] *Exc.* 10; *Ecl.* 57.1; *Strom.* 5.6.35.

[32] For the dating of Oecumenius, see John C. Lamoreaux, "The Provenance of Ecumenius' Commentary on the Apocalypse," *VC* 52 (1998): 88-108. For a later dating (second half of the sixth century), convincingly rejected by Lamoreaux, see Marc De Groote, "Die *Quaestio Oecumeniana*," *SacEr* 36 (1996): 67-105.

[33] Oecumenius appeals to *Strom.* 6.16.143, which mentions the seven "first-born princes of the angels," and presupposes that Clement meant the seven spirits of Revelation (3.5); Arethas (*Comm. Apoc.* 10 [PG 106:569C]) invokes his reading of Irenaeus and Clement of Alexandria: Τὰς ἑπτὰ λαμπάδας αὐτὸς [John the Seer] ἡρμήνευσεν ἑπτὰ πνεύματα, ἄτινα ἤτοι, ὡς Ἠσαΐας, τὰ θεῖα τοῦ πνεύματος χαρίσματα σοφίας, ἰσχύος, βουλῆς καὶ τὰ τούτοις ἑξῆς δεῖ νοεῖν, ἢ ὡς Εἰρηναῖος καὶ Κλήμης ὁ Στρωματεὺς τὰ λειτουργικὰ καὶ τῶν ἄλλων ἐξέχοντα ταγμάτων.

[34] Λέγει δὲ πρεσβυτέρους ἀγγέλους ὁ θεῖος Ἰωάννης ἐν τῇ Ἀποκαλύψει, καὶ ἑπτὰ εἶναι τοὺς πρώτους ἐν τῷ Τωβίᾳ ἀνέγνωμεν καὶ παρὰ Κλήμεντι βιβλίῳ ε΄ τῶν Ὑποτυπώσεων (PG 4:225, 228).

[35] See Škrinjar, "Les sept esprits," 4-6, 14, 21; Michl, *Engelvorstellungen*, 113-14.

[36] *Epid.* 9 (St Irenaeus of Lyons, *On the Apostolic Preaching* [trans. John Behr; Crestwood, NY: Saint Vladimir's Seminary Press, 1997], 45-46): "But this world is encompassed by seven heavens, in which dwell <innumerable> powers and angels and archangels... Thus the Spirit of God is <active [in] manifold [ways]> (πολύεργος), and seven forms of service were counted by Isaias the prophet resting upon the Son of God... for he says, 'The Spirit shall rest upon him... [quotation from Isa 11:2-3]. Hence, the first heaven... is that of wisdom; and the second, after it, [that] <of>

both Oecumenius and Arethas think that he derived his statements about the seven archangels from a reading of Rev 1:4. It is noteworthy that Cassiodorus' commentary on Revelation seems indebted to the *Adumbrationes* on precisely the point under discussion: the blessing "from the seven spirits" (Rev 1:4) is said to come from the seven archangels mentioned in Tob 12:15.[37] The fact is that, given Clement's familiarity with the idea that "the whole world of creatures…revolves in sevens," and that "the first-born princes of the angels (πρωτόγονοι ἀγγέλων ἄρχοντες), who have the greatest power, are seven" (*Strom.* 6.16.142–143), and given that he goes so far as to interpret the "angels of the little ones" in Matt 18:10 as a proof-text for the seven *protoctists*, it would be quite awkward for him to neglect the explicit groups of seven spirits and angels in Revelation.

Who are the "Seven Spirits"?

The angelic traits of the seven spirits in Rev 1:4 are undeniable. It appears that Revelation illustrates the same use of πνεῦμα language to designate angelic beings that scholars like Levison have shown to be widespread in the Hebrew Bible, the LXX and various authors of the Alexandrian diaspora, at Qumran, as well as in early Christian writings. In Revelation, πνεῦμα is used twice for evil angels (Rev 16:13–14; 18:2). Nevertheless, as can be seen in this table, πνεῦμα can also designate a good angel.

---

understanding…." Irenaeus continues to list the seven "spirits" and concludes as follows: "From this pattern Moses received the seven-branched candlestick, since he received the service as a pattern of heaven." Irenaeus' tenuous connection between the seven heavens and the seven spirits is echoed with greater clarity in Victorinus' treatise *De fabrica mundi* 7–8, where "the seven heavens" corresponds to "the seven spirits," and, among many other things, to "the seven angels": "To those days [the seven days of creation] correspond also seven spirits…Their names are those spirits that rested upon the Christ of God, as is given assurance in the prophet Isaiah…Therefore, the highest heaven [is that] of wisdom, the second [is that] of understanding…Behold! the seven horns of the lamb, seven eyes of God, seven spirits,…seven golden lamps,…seven angels,…seven weeks completed in Pentecost,…the lamp with seven orifices, the seven columns in the house of Solomon…" (translation mine, on the basis of the Latin text in SC 423:145–46).

[37] *a septem angelis qui…sicut in libro Tobiae Rafael angelus dixit, unus sum ex septem angelis* (*Complexiones* 2 [113]); *ante quem erant septem spiritus, id est angeli dei* (*Complexiones* 8 [117]). Text in Roger Gryson, ed., *Variorum auctorum commentaria minora in Apocalypsin Johannis* (CCSL 107; Turnhout: Brepols, 2003), 113–29. The numbers in brackets indicate the page numbers in this volume.

Rev 14:13	Rev 19:9
καὶ ἤκουσα φωνῆς ἐκ τοῦ οὐρανοῦ λεγούσης, Γράψον·	καὶ λέγει μοι, Γράψον·
μακάριοι οἱ νεκροὶ οἱ ἐν κυρίῳ ἀποθνῄσκοντες ἀπ' ἄρτι	μακάριοι οἱ εἰς τὸ δεῖπνον τοῦ γάμου τοῦ ἀρνίου κεκλημένοι.
ναί λέγει τὸ πνεῦμα [the initial locutor, the voice]	καὶ λέγει μοι, [the initial locutor, the angel]
ἵνα ἀναπαήσονται ἐκ τῶν κόπων αὐτῶν τὰ γὰρ ἔργα αὐτῶν ἀκολουθεῖ μετ'αὐτῶν	οὗτοι οἱ λόγοι ἀληθινοὶ τοῦ θεοῦ εἰσιν

Both passages in this table are examples of the so-called promise-to-the-victor, a type of statement that occurs fairly often in Revelation. In both passages, an initial declaration is repeated and confirmed by the same heavenly locutor. The difference consists only in the fact that we read "spirit" in Rev 14:13, and, respectively, "angel" in Rev 19:9. Yet in light of the similarities of structure and content, and given the interchangeability of the terms "angel" and "spirit" in early Jewish and Christian texts, I judge this to be another example of πνεῦμα language in the service of angelology.[38]

It is equally clear, however, that passages displaying angelic imagery (Rev 1:4 and parallels) convey a pneumatological content. As in Clement, where the *protoctists* are both angelic (equated with the "thrones" of Col 1:16 and "the angels of the little ones" of Matt 18:10), *and* the "heptad of the spirit" (*Paed.* 3.12.87), the seven angelic spirits of Revelation occupy an area of confluence between angelology and pneumatology. I have argued earlier that these two realities—angelic imagery and pneumatological content—need not be viewed as mutually exclusive; rather, they can be fused by appealing to the category of "angelomorphic pneumatology," as defined by Fletcher-Louis.[39]

---

[38] Similarly Gieschen, *Angelomorphic Christology*, 266–68.
[39] See also the remark of Lupieri: "perhaps the fact that there are seven spirits is the result of John's reflection on *the angelic nature of the Spirit*" (*Commentary on the Apocalypse*, 103, emphasis added).

2. Binitarianism and Spirit Christology in Revelation

Despite what seems to be a trinitarian opening (Rev 1:4–5), Revelation remains determined by a binitarian framework, concerned to present the divinity as a binitarian reality: God and his Son. I appeal once more to Hurtado's principle, already discussed in my analysis of Clement. Who, then, is "God" in Revelation? The specific Jewish-Christian indicators of a belief in God are abundantly present in this text: the divine Name, the divine throne, the fact of receiving worship. All three indicators point to the same divine identity: God and the Son, Lamb, Christ, or Son of Man. The bearer of the divine name is the Father (Rev 1:4, 8; 4:8, 11, 17; 15:3; 16:7, 14; 19:6, 15; 21:22).[40] Yet as Gieschen has extensively shown, Revelation also attributes the divine Name to the Son.[41] This is especially noteworthy in Rev 1:8 ("'I am the Alpha and the Omega,' says the Lord God, who is and who was and who is to come, the Almighty").[42] The divine throne is occupied jointly by the Father and the Lamb (Rev 5:6), and the Lamb is closely associated with God.[43] There is no indication of a third enthroned entity being

---

[40] The fact that "He–Who–Is" functions as a stand-in for YHWH explains why the writer refuses to subject the Name to the rules of declination in Rev 1:4. According to Prigent (*Commentary*, 15), "it is impossible to suppose that...it was not deliberate, especially since the same expression is repeated later (1:8; 4:8; 11:17; 16:5) with the same persistence in making a noun out of the imperfect form of the verb 'to be.'...the titles of the eternal God cannot be subjected to temporal vicissitudes, and consequently to the laws of noun declension. The God in question is one who can only act as subject."

[41] Gieschen, "The Divine Name in Ante-Nicene Christology," *VC* 57 (2003): 115–57, esp. 131–34. See also Gieschen, *Angelomorphic Christology*, 253–55.

[42] Sean McDonough (*YHWH at Patmos* [WUNT 2/107; Tübingen: Mohr Siebeck, 1999], esp. 195–231), has provided erudite proof that "the designations in Rev 1:8 are...derived from three variations of the name YHWH" (200), namely Iaô/ YHWH Elohim and YHWH Sabaoth (218). Aune (*Revelation* 1:55–59) suggests connections with both Hellenistic revelatory magic and Jewish alphabet symbolism. Martin McNamara found that the passage "is perfectly paralleled in TJI Dt 32, 39 and in this text alone of those available to us.... It is not to be excluded that the Apocalypse is directly dependent on TJI Dt 32, 39 in its use of it, although it is possible that both texts are dependent on the same early liturgical tradition" (*The New Testament and the Palestinian Targum to the Pentateuch* [AnBib 27; Rome: Pontifical Biblical Institute, 1966], 112). In any case, whether the author of Revelation draws on Jewish or Greek traditions, or perhaps on a Jewish Hellenistic fusion of both, he is also subjecting preexisting formulas to his own theological views. His eschatological perspective dictates an original modification of the third member of the *Dreizeitenformel* from "who will be" to "who will come" (so Ben Witherington III, *Revelation* [Cambridge: Cambridge University Press, 2003], 75).

[43] Rev 5:13–14 ("blessing, honor and glory" is given to God and to the Lamb); 7:10 (God and the Lamb receive the acclamation of the martyrs); 14:4 (God and the Lamb receive the self-offering of the martyrs as "first fruits" of humankind); 20:6 (God and

associated with the Father and the Son as bearer of the divine Name, or as recipient of worship. Within this binitarian framework, the Spirit appears at the same time indissolubly linked to the worshiped second person ("seven horns of the Lamb," "seven eyes of the Lord," "seven stars in the Lord's hand"), and strictly subordinated to it ("the seven holy spirits before the throne").

Revelation never uses the expression "holy spirit." The instances in which the author uses πνεῦμα can be divided into the following categories: (1) πνεῦμα as "breath" of life (Rev 11:11; 13:15); (2) πνεῦμα for evil angels (Rev 16:13, 14; 18:2); (3) ἐν πνεύματι as an indicator of the visionary ecstatic state (Rev 1:10; 4:2; 17:3; 21:10); (4) πνεῦμα at the closing of the seven letters: "listen to what the Spirit says to the churches" (Rev 2:7); (5) the seven πνεύματα (Rev 1:4; 3:1; 4:5; 5:6); (6) "the spirit of prophecy" (Rev 19:10); (7) "the God of the spirits of the prophets (Rev 22:6); (8) πνεῦμα in association with the heavenly Church, "the bride" (Rev 22:17).

I have already discussed the category of the seven spirits. Of the remaining categories, the first three are irrelevant for a discussion about the pneumatology of Revelation.[44] At this point it is necessary to explore (4) the use of πνεῦμα in the closing section of the seven letters (Revelation 2–3). I shall discuss the remaining categories in the section on prophecy.

Christ receive priestly service from those who are worthy, and reign together with them); 21:22–23; 22:5 (the Lamb is, or embodies, the divine glory and light). See the summary of Stuckenbruck, *Angel Veneration*, 261–63. Hoffmann (*Destroyer and the Lamb*, 166–67) also draws attention to the fact that the *Ewigkeitsformel* ("unto the ages of ages") is ascribed to both God and the lamb (Rev 5:13; 11:15; 22:5), implying their "similar significance" or "equal status."

[44] I take "breath of life" to simply mean the vital force that characterizes that which is biologically alive, as opposed to dead matter. The designation of evil angelic beings as evil "spirits" implicitly eliminates any reference to the Holy Spirit. For the expression "in the spirit," see Richard Bauckham, "The Role of the Spirit in the Apocalypse," *EvQ* 52 (1980): 66–73. The phrase seems to have functioned in early Christian literature as a technical designation of the inspired state of prophets. In such cases (e.g., *Did.* 11.7–9), "the primary reference is...not the source of inspiration, but the phenomenon of ecstatic speech" (Bauckham, *Climax*, 151). In the case of Revelation, Bauckham believes that "γενέσθαι ἐν πνεύματι...is probably to be taken as both phenomenological and theological, denoting both the visionary as such and the Spirit's authorship of it" (*Climax*, 152). Aune's dense excursus dedicated to the formula "in the spirit" concludes that "ἐγενόμην ἐν πνεύματι is best rendered as 'I fell into a trance'" (Aune, *Revelation* 1:83). George Bradford Caird (*A Commentary on the Revelation of St. John the Divine* [New York: Harper & Row, 1966], 19) and Prigent (*Commentary*, 128) hold the same position.

There is a precise parallelism between the function of Christ and that of the "spirit" as described in the introductory and final parts of the seven letters. The letters are framed by an opening announcement of what Christ proclaims (τάδε λέγει ὁ... [completed with descriptions of Christ drawn from the Revelation 1]), and a final exhortation to hear what the Spirit says (τὸ πνεῦμα λέγει). It is clear that the parallelism is intentional, and that the author consciously and consistently introduces a functional overlapping between "Christ" and "Spirit." [45] Unfortunately, commentators sometimes evade the difficulty of this parallelism by restating the obvious, or they resort to convenient dogmatic "shortcuts," simply bypassing the exegetical trouble zone and stating that "Christ speaks through the Spirit."[46]

Given the prophetic-visionary character of Revelation 2–3, "spirit" is most likely connected to the reality of prophetic experience.[47] From this point on, scholarly opinions begin to diverge. Some take "Spirit" as a christological title, derived from the act of Christ's inspiring the prophet: "the Spirit is none other than...the Ascended Christ in his role of speaking to the Church."[48] Others hold the opposite position:

> it is not that the Spirit is identical to the exalted Lord, but that the exalted Lord speaks to the Churches by...the Spirit of prophecy...When the spirit of prophecy comes upon him, John speaks of himself as being, or becoming, 'in the Spirit' (ἐν πνεύματι).[49]

---

[45] Rev 2:1–2:7; 2:8–2:11; 2:12–2:17; 2:18–2:29; 3:1–3:6; 3:7–3:13; 3:14–3:22.

[46] E.g., "the seven messages are...equated with the words of the exalted Christ" (Bauckham, "Role of the Spirit," 73); "the author is emphasizing the close relation of the Spirit with the exalted Christ" (Aune, *Revelation* 1:123); "the Spirit speaks as Christ and Christ as the Spirit" (Gieschen, *Angelomorphic Christology*, 269); "the Spirit and Christ speak in tandem"; "the Spirit speaks the words of Christ...the Spirit serves as Christ's representative of power and knowledge symbolized as the seven horns and the seven eyes of the Lamb [5:6]" (Waddell, *Spirit in the Book of Revelation*, 178, 189).

[47] Cf. 1 John 4:1–3. According to R. W. L. Moberly ("'Test the Spirits': God, Love, and Critical Discernment in 1 John 4," in *Holy Spirit and Christian Origins*, 298–99), "John's concern is here with the discernment of that which purports to belong to the realm of God, that is 'spirit(s)'. So his basic injunction is clear: 'Do not believe every spirit,' that is, do not be gullible, credulous, or unthinking in the spiritual realm, but rather 'test the spirits' to see whether claims to be from God are indeed justified."

[48] Schweizer, *Spirit of God*, 105.

[49] F. F. Bruce, "The Spirit in the Apocalypse," in *Christ and Spirit in the New Testament: In Honour of C. F. D. Moule* (ed. B. Lindars and S. Smalley; Cambridge: Cambridge University Press, 1973), 340, 339. Similarly Bauckham, *Climax*, 160–61.

According to this interpretation, "listen to what the Spirit says" would be shorthand for "listen to what Christ says through *the one who was in the spirit.*"

The divergence of the opinions I have presented can be reduced to the issue of whether "spirit" should be relegated to Christ or to the seer. Whatever the case, it is obvious that πνεῦμα here is not unambiguously "the Holy Spirit."[50] The first position, advocating a christological use of "Spirit," seems more plausible. It better accounts for the Christ—Spirit parallelism, noted above, and offers a solution simpler than the exegetical acrobatics required to transform τὸ πνεῦμα λέγει into ἐν πνεύματι λέγει. Revelation thus offers an example of spirit christology in the first century of the common era. Similarly to Pauline literature, Revelation

> indicates by the word "spirit" the mode in which the Lord exists...the power in which he encounters his Church....When Christ is seen in terms of his role for the Church and of his works of power within the Church, he can be identified with the Spirit; but insofar as Christ is also Lord over his own power, he can be distinguished from that power, just as "I" can always be distinguished from the power which goes out from me.[51]

Scholars have described in various ways the intimate relation between Christ and the Spirit in early Christian thought, especially in the Pauline corpus and the Fourth Gospel.[52] The identity between the experience of Christ and the experience of the Spirit has been termed "dynamic," "functional," "experiential," "existential," or "immanent"—meaning that, from the perspective of the Christian, the experience of the Spirit *is* the experience of Christ, which *is* the experience of God the Father. Disagreement occurs only when this type of experiential identity is pushed further to describe the theological relation between Christ and Spirit. Some scholars conclude that the terms are fully interchangeable, and implicitly question the trinitarian referent to the three terms

---

[50] *Contra* Charles Brütsch (*La clarté de l'Apocalypse* [Geneva: Labor et Fides, 1966], 58), who does not even debate the matter: "l'Esprit: *indubitablement*, le Saint-Esprit" (emphasis added).

[51] Schweizer, *Spirit of God*, 60.

[52] Fatehi, *Relation*. For the Gospel of John, see Gary M. Burge, *The Anointed Community: the Holy Spirit in the Johannine Tradition* (Grand Rapids, Mich.: Eerdmans, 1987), 137–49.

"God," "Christ," and "Spirit," while others forcefully argue against this identification.[53]

The use of "spirit christology" to designate the first of these two positions can be misleading. It is crucial to keep in mind that, by using this term, we are affirming something about the author's theological language (in this case, the use of the term "spirit" to designate Christ), not about the theological reality signified by the language. With this theological disclaimer, I return to the phrase τὸ πνεῦμα λέγει. My judgment is the following: (a) the hypothesis of spirit christology in Revelation has the advantage of accounting for the functional and experiential overlap between the "Christ" and "Spirit"; (b) this hypothesis does not allow us to speculate about personal identity between Christ and the Spirit; (c) this hypothesis seems verified by the similar phenomenon in the Pauline corpus and in other early Christian texts, most notably—as I shall show later—the *Shepherd of Hermas*; (d) finally, I agree fully with Fatehi's overall thesis that the identification between the concept of "Spirit of God" in the Old Testament and the "Spirit of Christ" in the New Testament is ultimately christologically motivated, since it identifies Christ as divine.[54]

As noted earlier, scholars often speak about the "functional" or "experiential" overlap between the Christ and Spirit in early Christian literature. In what follows I shall offer a more detailed examination of this topic in Revelation, by discussing the phenomenon of prophecy. I shall argue that, similar to Clement's "elders," Revelation views the Spirit-experience as a direct influx of the Logos mediated by the seven spirits and ultimately reaching the prophet as a mystagogical revelation from the *angelic* spirit.

3. The Phenomenon of Prophecy in Revelation

Then he [the angel] said to me, Write: "Blessed [are] those who are called to the marriage supper of the Lamb!" And he said to me, These are the

---

[53] Fatehi (*Relation*, 23–43) provides an overview of scholarly opinions on the subject, ranging from Hermann Gunkel and Adolf Deissmann, to J. D. G. Dunn and Gordon Fee, and many others.

[54] Indeed, as Fatehi repeatedly affirms, no mediatorial figure among the so-called exalted, angelomorphic patriarchs is ever presented as having the same relation to the Spirit that the Old Testament affirms of God and his Spirit. An older formulation of this thesis can be found in Max Turner, "The Spirit of Christ and 'Divine' Christology," in *Jesus of Nazareth: Lord and Christ*, 413–36.

true sayings of God. And I fell at his feet to worship him. But he said to me, See [that you do] not [do that!] I am your fellow servant, and of your brethren who have the testimony of Jesus. Worship God! For the testimony of Jesus is the spirit of prophecy, ἡ γὰρ μαρτυρία Ἰησοῦ ἐστιν τὸ πνεῦμα τῆς προφητείας. (Rev 19:9–10)

Scholarly interpretations of Rev 19:10 vary, most notably on the issue of whether the genitive Ἰησοῦ is objective or subjective.[55] In my opinion, the more probable meaning of μαρτυρία Ἰησοῦ is "the witness borne by Jesus Christ." This is suggested by the fact that one of Christ's fundamental designations in Revelation is "witness" (Rev 1:5; 3:14), and especially by the correspondence between the first mention of "testimony of Jesus" in Rev 19:10 and "the words of this book" in Rev 22:9:

Rev 19:10	Rev 22:8–9
καὶ ἔπεσα ἔμπροσθεν τῶν ποδῶν αὐτοῦ προσκυνῆσαι αὐτῷ	ἔπεσα προσκυνῆσαι ἔμπροσθεν τῶν ποδῶν τοῦ ἀγγέλου
καὶ λέγει μοι ὅρα μὴ συνδουλός σού εἰμι καὶ τῶν ἀδελφῶν σου τῶν ἐχόντων	καὶ λέγει μοι ὅρα μὴ σύνδουλος σού εἰμι καὶ τῶν ἀδελφῶν σου τῶν προφητῶν καὶ τῶν τηρούντων
τὴν μαρτυρίαν Ἰησοῦ	τοὺς λόγους τοῦ βιβλίου τούτου
τῷ θεῷ προσκύνησον.	τῷ θεῷ προσκύνησον
ἡ γὰρ μαρτυρία Ἰησοῦ ἐστιν τὸ πνεῦμα τῆς προφητείας	

---

[55] For a survey of positions, see Aune, *Revelation* 3:1038–39. Cf. the similar debate over the phrase πίστις Χριστοῦ in Rom 3:22, 26; Gal 2:16, 20; 3:22; Phil 3:9; Eph 3:12. For a survey of the relevant literature, followed by an argument in favor of πίστις Χριστοῦ as objective genitive, see J. D. G. Dunn ("Once More, ΠΙΣΤΙΣ ΧΡΙΣΤΟΥ," *SBLSP* 30 [1991]: 730–42). The option for subjective genitive is a significant minority position: Morna D. Hooker, "Πίστις Χριστοῦ," *NTS* 35 (1989): 321–42; Richard B. Hays, *The Faith of Jesus Christ: The Narrative Substructure of Galatians 3:1–4:11* (2nd ed.; Grand Rapids, Mich.: Eerdmans/Dearborn, Mich.: Dove, 2002). Revelation's μαρτυρία Ἰησοῦ and the Pauline πίστις Χριστοῦ are both treated in Ian G. Wallis, *The Faith of Jesus Christ in Early Christian Traditions* (SNTSMS 84; Cambridge/New York: Cambridge University Press, 1995), 65–127, 169–72. In his survey of patristic treatments of the topic (*Faith of Jesus Christ*, 175–212), Wallis shows that after figuring prominently in pre-Nicene literature, "the paradigmatic significance of Jesus' faith…was a casualty of the movement towards establishing Christ's divinity" (*Faith of Jesus Christ*, 212).

The meaning of Rev 19:10 must bear some relation to the visionary's error of worshiping the *angelus interpres*. It may well be that the phrase "I am a fellow servant" functioned as a corrective in the polemic against angel-worship.[56] Yet it must be noted that the attempt to worship the angel occurs after an emphatic declaration about the authority of the "true sayings"—very likely the book of Revelation itself. Thus, as some scholars have argued, the theme of angelic worship and its correction are only secondary, and subservient to a more important theme: "John's purpose was...perhaps, to claim for his brothers a certain primacy in the affairs of churches."[57]

Read in this way, the passage makes perfect sense in the context of early Church debates about the status and authority of prophets, or the polemics concerning the criteria of true versus false prophecy. Moreover, in the context of a widespread interest in ascents to heaven and descriptions of celestial sights, the writer of Revelation performs a significant "bending" of the apocalyptic framework, even a radical restructuring of the symbolic universe.[58] This writing

---

[56] This mirror-reading is confirmed by texts showing that the veneration of angels was not uncommon in Second Temple Judaism and early Christianity (e.g., Tob 12:16–22; Col 2:18; *Mart. Asc. Isa.* 7.21–23; 8.4–5; *Apoc. Zeph.* 6.13–15). For a masterful treatment of the general problematic and the relevant texts, see Stuckenbruck, *Angel Veneration*, 249–56 and passim. Clement of Alexandria (*Strom.* 6.5.41) and Origen (*Comm. Jo.* 13.17) quote the following from the *Pre. Pet.*: "Neither worship as the Jews; for they, thinking that they only know God, do not know him, adoring as they do angels and archangels..." With respect to this fragment, see Stuckenbruck, *Angel Veneration*, 140–46; Michel Cambe, "Critique de la θεοσέβεια juive," in *Kerygma Petri: Textus et commentaries* (CCSA 15; ed. Michel Cambe; Turnhout: Brepols, 2003), 237–47.

[57] Martin Kiddle, *The Revelation of St. John* (London: Hodder and Stoughton, 1963 [1940]), 449; Hanna Roose, *"Das Zeugnis Jesu": Seine Bedeutung für die Christologie, Eschatologie und Prophetie in der Offenbarung des Johannes* (TANZ 32; Tübingen: Francke, 2000), 202–8; Prigent, *Commentary*, 529–33. Similarly, Stuckenbruck, *Angel Veneration*, 250, 256, who notes, however, that Revelation does not intend here to affirm the angelic status, i.e., the divine commission and legitimacy of prophets alone (254). The fact that the divine authority of the book is a crucial theological theme for Revelation becomes evident when Rev 19:10 is read in conjunction with 1:1 and 22:6. For the importance of Christian prophetic circles in Revelation, see Jan Fekkes III, *Isaiah and the Prophetic Traditions in the Book of Revelation: Visionary Antecedents and Their Development* [JSNTSupp. 93; Sheffield: JSOT Press, 1994], 40–41, 49–58; Aune, "The Prophetic Circle of John of Patmos and the Exegesis of Revelation 22.16," *JSNT* 37 (1989): 103–16, esp. 108–11.

[58] "The Christian apocalypticist writes at a different point on the eschatological timetable from his Jewish counterpart. The messiah has already come. The life of the messiah, and especially his suffering and death, are available to the Christian visionary as a source of inspiration and example" (Collins, *Apocalyptic Imagination*, 278).

is a revelation that is prophetic in nature and not apocalyptic. That is why it is necessary for our author to put back into its proper context...the apocalyptic material which he has used so continuously....he has not intended to write a book of revelations, but rather to bring to his brothers and sisters the revelation of Jesus, the revelation that allows them to live as of now as conquerors, those who are associated with the victory, the salvation, the reign, and the wedding of Christ.[59]

It seems, then, that "the spirit of prophecy" in Rev 19:10 refers not to the person of the Holy Spirit, or a heavenly agent ("spirit" as angelic being), but to the charisma of the prophets. Additional proof can be gleaned from Rev 22:6. It is interesting to consider the various readings of this verse:

The Lord God...			
(a)...of the spirits	of the	prophets	sent his angel
(a')...of the spirits	of the holy	prophets	sent his angel
(b)...	of the holy	prophets	sent his angel
(c)...of the spirits	and of the	prophets	sent his angel

Obviously, the textual variation reflects a process of interpretation: (a) and (b) agree in that they both refer not to the Holy Spirit but to the receptive faculty of the prophets.[60] The (b) version, lacking πνεῦμα, makes the very same point. As for (a'), it seems to combine elements of both: "spirits" from (a) and "holy" from (b). Overall, these versions represent, fundamentally, the same understanding of the text, as opposed to a different one witnessed by (c). The latter understands πνεύματα as distinct entities, separate from the prophets.[61] Bearing in mind the

---

[59] Prigent, *Commentary*, 532.

[60] Prigent notes (*Commentary*, 635) that "the expression is also used by Paul (1 Cor 12:10, 14:32) to designate the prophetic gift, the ability to prophesy." Cf. Swete (*Apocalypse*, 303): "they are the natural faculties of the Prophets, raised and quickened by the Holy Spirit, but still under human control, and standing in creaturely relation to God"; Isbon Beckwith: "the divinely illumined spirits of the prophets are meant" (*The Apocalypse of John: Studies in Introduction with a Critical and Exegetical Commentary* [New York: Macmillan, 1919; repr. Grand Rapids, Mich.: Baker, 1967], 772); Witherington (*Revelation*, 279): "John...has in mind not the Holy Spirit but human spirits of the prophets." According to Aune (*Revelation* 3:1182), the expression refers to "the psychic faculty of individual prophets rather than to the Spirit of God."

[61] This manuscript variation recalls Num 16:22, where the MT has *YHWH 'Elohe haruhot le-kol-basar* ("LORD God of the spirits of all flesh), thus presenting God as master over all life-endowed creatures, while the LXX reads Θεὸς τῶν πνευμάτων καὶ πάσης σαρκός ("God of all spirits and of all flesh"). It seems evident that the LXX turns the text into a statement about God as master of two categories of beings—"spirits," on the one hand, and humans, on the other. There is overwhelming evidence that this

established tradition of designating God's sovereignty over the celestial realm by the formula "Lord of spirits" (*1 En.* 37.2; 39.12) or "Father of spirits" (Heb 12:9), I believe it is legitimate to conclude that version (c) of Rev 22:6, witnessed by few codices, understands "spirits" as angelic beings subjected, together with the prophets, to the Lord God.

In conclusion, πνεύματα in Rev 22:6 seems to suggest an interpretive choice between an anthropological reality (a, a') and that of angelic beings (c). This sort of disjunction is perhaps too stringent to do justice to first-century religious sensitivities, for which the line between the perceptive capacity of the visionary and the influence exerted by representatives of the heavenly realm may be difficult to trace with precision.[62] In any case, the following question remains open: in the absence of an unambiguous reference to the Holy Spirit, what is the understanding of prophecy in this verse? I shall address this question shortly after considering one last passage (Rev 22:16–17):

> "I, Jesus, have sent my angel to testify to you these things in the churches. I am the Root and the Offspring of David, the Bright and Morning Star." And the Spirit and the bride say, "Come!" And let him who hears say, "Come!" And let him who thirsts come. Whoever desires, let him take the water of life freely.

So far no use of the singular πνεῦμα has proven to refer unambiguously to the Holy Spirit. It is therefore questionable that the writer would have suddenly included such a reference in the final chapter of his book.[63]

The dialogical setting of the passage, possibly bearing liturgical echoes, places "spirit" and "church" on the same side—namely, the earth—and Christ on the opposite side, in heaven. Christ makes the statement to which, on earth, the Spirit and the Church give their response.[64] In this

---

reworking is in accordance with a semantic evolution of *ruah* towards what has been called "the angelic spirit" (see Levison, "The Angelic Spirit," 475).

[62] Waddell (*Spirit in the Book of Revelation*, 190) suggests that "the verse contains a double-entendre, implying that the hearts and minds of the prophets are thoroughly satiated with the Spirit of prophecy."

[63] I insist on "singular," because I take the seven spirits as an angelomorphic reference to the Holy Spirit.

[64] Prigent notes that "one can hardly avoid describing [this dialog] as liturgical" (*Commentary*, 645). It is commonly accepted that "the influence of early Christian worship on John's thought is evident throughout his book...his visions are set within the context of the heavenly sanctuary, complete with temple imagery and a divine service" (Fekkes, *Prophetic Traditions*, 42, with abundant references). See also Prigent, *Apocalypse et liturgie* (CahT 52; Neuchâtel: Delachaux et Niestlé, 1964).

case, it does make good sense to consider that πνεῦμα and "bride" are collective terms for "prophets" and "saints":

> pneuma is... the Spirit of prophecy, the Spirit of the prophetic order; 'the Spirit and the Bride' is thus practically equivalent to 'the Prophets and the Saints' (16:6; 18:24). The Christian prophets, inspired by the Spirit of Jesus, and the whole Church... respond as with one voice to the Lord's great announcement.[65]

It would be wrong, however, to assume a strict division between the realms of the Church, on earth, and Christ, because any response or appeal to Christ, whether private or corporate, is made under divine influence. "Spirit" is a perfect metonymy for "prophets" precisely because the prophet is never a prophet by his own power.

I return, therefore, to the question raised above: in the absence of an unambiguous reference to the Holy Spirit, what is the understanding of prophecy in Revelation? The answer to this question lies, I suggest, in the formulas used in the opening and closing chapters of Revelation:

> The revelation... sent and signified by his angel to his servant John; I, Jesus, have sent my angel to testify to you these things for the churches.[66]

Commenting on διὰ τοῦ ἀγγέλου αὐτοῦ (Rev 1:1), Lupieri notes the following:

> That the first manifestation of God toward humanity is of an angelic nature superior to all others makes plain that there is a pyramidal angelic hierarchy... Revelation originates with God, is passed on by Jesus Christ who acts by means of his angel, and finally reaches John.[67]

If this type of inspiration is what characterizes prophecy (and the writer clearly considers himself not only a fellow-minister of the angels, but also one among his brothers, the prophets—Rev 22:9), and if "spirit" is also used in Revelation to designate angelic beings, then the following hypothesis can be put forth: prophecy is Christ's illumining and revelatory action upon the prophet, performed through the mediation of the angel.[68] In this interpretation, the angelic imagery of Revelation's

---

[65] Swete, *Apocalypse*, 310; Kiddle, *Revelation*, 456.
[66] Rev 1:1; 22:16.
[67] Lupieri, *Commentary on the Apocalypse*, 98, 168.
[68] Cf. Oecumenius (*Comm. Apoc.* 1 [TEG 8:68]), who speaks about the mystagogic function of the angel mentioned in Rev 1:1: οὐκ αὐτὸς [Χριστὸς] ἐπιφανεὶς ἀλλὰ διὰ τοῦ ἀγγέλου αὐτοῦ μυσταγωγήσας με.

"chain of command," noted by Lupieri, does not preclude the affirmation of a pneumatological content.[69] This is so, in my opinion, because the first level of the angelic hierarchy—the seven spirits—offers not only an example of "pneuma" angelology, but also an instance of early Christian angelomorphic pneumatology.

This conclusion should not be surprising, because a similar understanding of prophecy occurs in another major apocalyptic work of early Christianity, the *Shepherd of Hermas* (Herm. *Mand.* 11), and in Clement of Alexandria's *Eclogae* and *Adumbrationes*. As I have shown, according to *Ecl.* 51–52 prophecy occurs when the Logos moves the first rank of the *protoctists*, and this movement is transmitted from one level of the angelic hierarchy down to the next, until the "operation" (ἐνέργεια) of the lowest angels will "move" the prophet. Clement understands the traditional statements about the Logos speaking to the prophets "through the Spirit" in the sense that Christ inspires the prophets through the ministry of the *protoctists* (διὰ τῆς τῶν πρωτοκτίστων διακονίας, *Strom.* 5.6.35). Obviously, Clement's view, probably inherited from Pantaenus and the elders, fits well with the notion of prophecy in Revelation outlined above.

CONCLUSIONS

In understanding how Revelation was read in the early Christian circles, such as that of Clement of Alexandria's "elders," it is necessary to consider the following three elements present in Revelation: (a) a multi-level cosmos populated by an angelic hierarchy, dominated by the seven angels "first created"; (b) a theological framework that is fundamentally binitarian, even though certain "(pre)-trinitarian" elements are undeniably present; (c) a theory of angelic interaction, according to which communication between the divine and the human world is passed on—"channeled," as it were—from Christ to the *protoctists* and

---

[69] As noted earlier, Waddell agrees that the figure in Revelation 10 is the same as the revealing agent in Rev 1:1; 22:16, but argues that "John personifies the Spirit via the symbol of the divine angel" (Waddell, *Spirit in the Book of Revelation*, 160). See also Gieschen, *Angelomorphic Christology*, 265 n. 66, 266–67: the *angelus interpres*, as well as the "voice" of Rev 1:10, and the seven angels before the throne, are ways of speaking about the Holy Spirit. It is noteworthy, however, that for Oecumenius, Andrew of Caesarea, and Arethas, the angel of Jesus (Rev 1:1; 22:16), as well as the "mighty angel" (Rev 10:1), are no more than angelic ministers.

further down along the angelic hierarchy until it reaches the highest representative of the Christian community: not the bishop, as some centuries later in Ps.-Dionysius' *Hierarchies*, but the prophet—as in the *Shepherd of Hermas*, the *Ascension of Isaiah*, and Clement's *Hypotyposeis*.

There can be no question that Revelation's group of seven spirits/angels before the divine throne (Rev 1:4; 3:1; 4:5; 5:6; 8:2) echoes angelological speculations common in Second Temple Judaism. It is equally true, however, that the traditions about the highest angelic company underwent considerable modifications. One example in this regard is the subordination of the *protoctists* to the Son of God: Zechariah's "eyes of the Lord" (Zech 4:10) are reinterpreted as the seven horns and eyes of the Lamb (Rev 5:6), and, "since the lesson of the vision is 'not by might nor by power but by the Spirit' (Zech 4:6), the lamps of the lampstand, the eyes of the Lord, are his Spirit."[70] Together with Clement's "elders," Revelation is part of an early Christian tradition that reworked the Second Temple tradition of the seven principal angels in the service of pneumatology.[71]

Whether certain details of the interpretation I have proposed in this chapter correspond to the intentions of Revelation's author is irrelevant to the discussion at hand. For the purpose of my argument, it is sufficient to have demonstrated the high degree of compatibility between Clement's views in the *Hypotyposeis* and earlier Christian writings that he would have regarded as authoritative.

---

[70] Bauckham, "Role of the Spirit," 76.
[71] Bauckham ("Role of the Spirit," 66) goes as far as to say that "the prominence of the Spirit is one of the characteristics which mark the Apocalypse out from the category of apocalyptic works in which its literary genre places it."

CHAPTER FOUR

ANGELOMORPHIC PNEUMATOLOGY IN
THE *SHEPHERD OF HERMAS*[1]

INTRODUCTION

In the previous chapter I argued that the book of Revelation witnesses to an archaic "angelomorphic" pneumatology similar to the one discerned in Clement's *Hypotyposeis*. I also showed that, just as in Clement, such depictions of the Spirit occur in a larger theological articulation, namely in tandem with spirit christology, (i.e., the use of "spirit" language to designate Christ), and within a binitarian theological framework. It is now time to consider another early Christian apocalypse which enjoyed huge popularity in the early centuries, and which Clement read with evident affection and reverence: the *Shepherd of Hermas*. The thesis of the pages to follow is that this writing illustrates a complex interaction between the phenomenon discussed by Levison ("spirit" designating angelic/demonic beings), spirit christology, and an "angelomorphic" representation of the Holy Spirit.

The *Shepherd of Hermas* is by all accounts "one of the most enigmatic writings to have come down to us from Christian antiquity," which "bristles with problems, both literary and theological." In the words of Robert J. Hauck, "[t]here are many puzzles in this puzzling little book."[2] Even more puzzling, however, is the fact that this text never

---

[1] This section expands upon Bucur, "The Son of God and the Angelomorphic Holy Spirit: A Rereading of the *Shepherd's* Christology," *ZNW* 98 (2007): 121–43. I shall be using the latest critical edition of the *Shepherd*: Ulrich Körtner and Martin Leutzsch, *Papiasfragmente. Hirt des Hermas* (Schriften des Urchristentums 3; Darmstadt: Wissenschaftliche Buchgesellschaft, 1998). For a detailed presentation of its merits in comparison to the older editions of Joly and Whittaker, see Gianfrancesco Lusini, "Nouvelles recherches sur le texte du Pasteur d'Hermas," *Apocrypha* 12 (2001): 79–97. The English translation is taken from Carolyn Osiek, *Shepherd of Hermas* (Hermeneia; Minneapolis, Minn.: Augsburg Fortress, 1999). References to the text of the *Shepherd* follow the old three-number system of citation, which allows the reader to know whether the quoted passage belongs to the visions, mandates or similitudes.

[2] Leslie W. Barnard, "The Shepherd of Hermas in Recent Study," *HeytJ* 9 (1968): 29. Similarly W. Coleborne, "A Linguistic Approach to the Problem of Structure and

scandalized its contemporaries or later orthodoxy.[3] Indeed, if the christology of this writing "is what most interpreters say it is...it is strange
that this immensely popular document of the early church was never
condemned for christological heresy."[4] The same can be said about
the *Shepherd*'s notion of πνεῦμα: it is significant that certain elements
of the *Shepherd*'s pneumatology were taken over by none other than
Tertullian—otherwise a harsh critic of the *Shepherd*.[5]

In the pages to follow I shall discuss, first, the *Shepherd*'s use of
πνεῦμα for angelic entities, then its use of πνεῦμα for the Son of God,
and finally propose a rereading of the Fifth Similitude, the ultimate test-
case for any theory on the *Shepherd*'s views on angels and spirits. Aside
from my general indebtedness to the studies of Segal, Hurtado, Levison,
Gieschen, and Fletcher-Louis, which I have acknowledged and set out
earlier, my reading of the *Shepherd* owes very much, as I shall note at
the appropriate time, to the studies of Philippe Henne.[6] In submitting to
the current scholarly consensus, I assume that the *Shepherd of Hermas*
is a unitary text from the early decades of the second century.[7]

Composition of the Shepherd of Hermas," *Colloq* 3 (1969): 133; Hauck, "The Great
Fast: Christology in the Shepherd of Hermas," *AThR* 75 (1993): 187.

[3] For a list of mostly positive references to the *Shepherd*, ranging from the second
century to the late middle ages, see Harnack, *Geschichte der altchristlichen Literatur
bis Eusebius* I/1 (Hinrichs: Leipzig, 1958 [1893]), 51–58, and Norbert Brox, *Der Hirt
des Hermas* (KAV 7; Göttingen: Vandenhoek & Ruprecht, 1991), 55–71.

[4] Osiek, *Shepherd Commentary*, 180a. Similarly Brox (*Der Hirt*, 328): "Wie H. solche
Äusserungen in Rom publizieren konnte...bleibt ein Geheimnis."

[5] Karl Adam, "Die Lehre von dem hg Geiste bei Hermas und Tertullian," *TQ* 88
(1906): 36–61; J. E. Morgan-Wynne, "The 'Delicacy' of the Spirit in the Shepherd of
Hermas and in Tertullian," *StPatr* 21 (1989): 154–57. It is noteworthy that while Tertullian finds fault with "the Shepherd of depraved people," he never raises questions
about the theology of this writing.

[6] Henne, *Christologie*; "À propos de la christologie du *Pasteur* d'Hermas. La cohérence des niveaux d'explication dans la *Cinquième Similitude*," *RSPT* 72 (1988):
569–78; "La polysémie allégorique dans le *Pasteur* d'Hermas," *ETL* 65 (1989): 131–5;
"La véritable christologie de la *Cinquième Similitude* du *Pasteur* d'Hermas," *RSPT* 74
(1990): 182–204.

[7] Robert Joly seems to have provided a decisive refutation of the most compelling
thesis of multiple authorship. See Stanislas Giet, *Hermas et les Pasteurs: les trois auteurs
du Pasteur d'Hermas* (Paris: Presses Universitaires de France, 1963), and, in response,
Joly, "Hermas et le Pasteur," *VC* 21 (1967): 201–18; "Le milieu complexe du Pasteur
d'Hermas," *ANRW* II/ 27.1 (1993): 524–51. The thesis of multiple authorship, epitomized
in Coleborne's proposal to distinguish seven sections of the work, and six authors,
all writing before the end of the first century ("The Shepherd of Hermas: A Case for
Multiple Authorship and Some Implications," *StPatr* 10 (1970)/ TU 107: 65–70) has
been discarded today in favor of more attentive consideration of the *Shepherd*'s stylis-
tic peculiarities. One of the recent commentators, Brox, concludes: "Nach der Studie

1. Πνεῦμα as an Angelic Being

Nadia Ibrahim Fredrikson has noted that "Hermas' Pneumatology is inscribed in a dynamic of the Spirit's indwelling—or departure from—the habitation he occupies."[8] This is undoubtedly true; what is less clear, however, is the precise meaning of πνεῦμα. In what follows I shall present cumulative evidence that the *Shepherd*'s use of πνεῦμα is somewhat ambiguous, situated at the confluence of pneumatology and angelology.

(a) The πνεῦμα inhabits the believer (τὸ πνεῦμα τὸ ἅγιον τὸ ἐν σοὶ κατοικοῦν, Herm. *Mand.* 10.2.5) and, under normal circumstances, intercedes *on behalf* of that person. Yet the *Shepherd* warns that the intercessor is easily grieved and driven away by sadness, λύπη (Herm. *Mand.* 10.1.3; 10.2.1).[9] Hermas must therefore drive out sadness, lest the

---

von Coleborne möchte man grundsätzlich davon abraten, die literarischen Probleme des PH weiterhin durch die Annahme mehrfacher Verfasserschaft lösen zu wollen.... Unterscheidend besser lässt sich der problematische Zustand des Buches durch die ungewöhnliche Schriftstellerpersönlichkeit des H. erklären" (*Der Hirt*, 32–33). Most recently, Osiek (*Shepherd Commentary*, 13a; 15b) has argued convincingly that "this loose structure is best explained as the result of underlying oral patterns present in the original use of the text: as a basis for oral proclamation...One consequence of this process of interaction between written text and oral proclamation is that after the author's first draft, there never was an original text, because the text went through many changes in the hand of its author as he and perhaps his assistants or colleagues added more and more material as it developed in the interpretative process in which he and others were engaged on the basis of the text." This new approach to the text has immediate implications for the problem of dating. While the scholarly consensus seems to have settled around the year 140, with a tendency towards the earlier part of the second century (Osiek, *Shepherd Commentary*, 2 n. 13; Joly, "Le milieu complexe," 529; for a survey of opinions, see Brox, *Der Hirt*, 22–25), Osiek concludes on "an expanded duration of time beginning perhaps from the very last years of the first century, but stretching through most of the first half of the second century" (Osiek, *Shepherd Commentary*, 20b). Leutzsch (*Einleitung*, 137) proposes the interval 90–130. A late first-century date of 80–100 is hypothesized by J. Christian Wilson, *Toward a Reassessment of the Shepherd of Hermas: Its Date and Pneumatology* (Lewiston, N.Y.: Mellen, 1993), 60. However, this proposal stands on shaky ground, since the considerations on which it is based are themselves debated issues: the early development of monarchic episcopate in Rome, the *Shepherd*'s relationship to Hebrews (and, implicitly, the dating of Hebrews), the possible echoes of persecutions in the text. It comes as no surprise to find a similar early dating of the *Shepherd* (85 A.D.) in John A. T. Robinson's *Redating the New Testament* (Philadelphia: Westminster, 1976), 322.

[8] Fredrikson, "L'Esprit Saint et les esprits mauvais dans le pasteur d'Hermas: Sources et prolongements," *VC* 55 (2001): 273.

[9] Hermas comes close to the Pauline statement about the Holy Spirit interceding "for us, with sighs too deep for words"/ "for the saints, according to the will of God" (Rom 8:26; the same verb is used as in Herm. *Mand.* 10.41.5, ἐντυγχάνω). According to Hermas, one is not to grieve or "oppress" the indwelling spirit: λυπεῖ τὸ πνεῦμα,

holy spirit intercede to God against him and depart: μήποτε ἐντεύξηται τῷ θεῷ καὶ ἀποστῇ ἀπὸ σοῦ (Herm. *Mand.* 10.41.5).[10]

In Herm. *Sim.* 8.2.5, the archangel Michael tells the angelic "shepherd" left in charge of receiving and inspecting the branches brought by the believers (i.e., their good deeds), that he will personally test every soul again, at the altar (ἐγὼ αὐτοὺς ἐπὶ τὸ θυσιαστήριον δοκιμάσω).

These texts use the traditional imagery of angels carrying the prayer of the humans up to the heavenly altar.[11] The exegetical question is whether the meaning of πνεῦμα is determined by this Jewish apocalyptic framework—in which case the *Shepherd* refers to an angelic presence—or whether the angelomorphism of the descriptions can be allowed to signify something more than an angelic presence.

(b) Herm. *Mand.* 11 discusses at length the action of the inspiring agent upon the Christian prophet, the complex relationship between the prophet and his audience, and the distinction between true and false prophets. Up to Herm. *Mand.* 11.9, the text uses only "spirit" language, giving advice about how to discriminate between the divine

---

Herm. *Mand.* 10.2.2; μὴ θλῖβε τὸ πνεῦμα, Herm. *Mand.* 10.2.5. Cf. μὴ λυπεῖτε τὸ πνεῦμα (Eph 4:30); τὸ πνεῦμα μὴ σβέννυτε (1 Thess 5:19).

[10] Cf. Isa 63:9–10: "he himself redeemed them, and took them up, and lifted them up all the days of old. But they disobeyed, and provoked his Holy Spirit (παρώξυναν τὸ πνεῦμα τὸ ἅγιον αὐτοῦ): so he turned to be an enemy, he himself contended against them."

[11] For a long list of relevant texts and detailed discussion, see Stuckenbruck, *Angel Veneration and Christology* (WUNT 70; Tübingen: Mohr Siebeck, 1994), 173–80; Cornelis Haas, "Die Pneumatologie des 'Hirten des Hermas'," *ANRW* II/ 27.1 (1993): 560, 567 n. 49. Note that the offering on the heavenly altar is mirrored by an interior phenomenon: Mand 5.1.2 describes the proper mission of the indwelling spirit as an act of worship, a "liturgy": λειτουργήσει τῷ θεῷ ἐν ἱλαρότητι. For Hermas, the religious acts of individual ascesis are a "liturgy," emulating the angelic worship before the divine throne. This is the sense in which the verb λειτουργέω is used elsewhere in the *Shepherd* (e.g., Sim 7.6, Sim 9.27.3, Sim 5.3.8). In the LXX, λειτουργέω translates the Hebrew *sharet* and *'abodah* ("to serve," "to work" in a cultic setting, or, more generally, to perform an assigned duty). It occurs for instance in passages dealing with temple service (Exod 30:22; Num 18:6; 1 Chron 9:13). In the NT uses the word family of λειτουργέω is used both for temple worship (Luke 1:23; Heb 9:21; 10:11) and for the ascetic and mystical life of individuals (Acts 13:2), although it may also designate the general idea of service, assistance, help (e.g., Rom. 15:7; Heb 1:14). For a detailed history of usage, see Sibel Ayse Tuzlak, "Service and Performance: 'Leitourgia' and the Study of Early Christian Ritual" (Ph.D. diss. Syracuse University, 2001), 1–49. For prayer as interiorized temple sacrifice, see Irenaeus, *Epid.* 96: a Christian "keeps the Sabbath constantly, that is, celebrating the service (λειτουργέω) of God in the temple of God, which is man's body." The theme is central to Origen. See Theo Hernans, *Origène: Théologie sacrificielle du sacerdoce des chrétiens* (ThH 88; Paris: Beauchesne, 1996), esp. 102–92.

spirit and the earthly spirit, and describing their respective activities in the authentic and the false prophet. Then, in Herm. *Mand.* 11.9, the text uses "angel" for the very same reality that it had described as an indwelling "spirit."[12] Needless to say, in light of the prior discussion of Revelation and Clement of Alexandria, the interchangeability of "spirit" and "angel" is hardly surprising. In any case, reading the *Shepherd of Hermas* in light of Jewish traditions about the "angelic spirit" makes good sense of the text and eliminates the need for interpretative acrobatics.[13]

As for the "angel of the prophetic spirit," a fruitful comparison can be made with "the angel of the Holy Spirit" in *Mart. Ascen. Isa* and, by analogy with the "angel of penitence" in Herm. *Vis.* 5.7, with "the angel presiding over genuine visions" in *2 Bar.* and *3 Bar.*[14] All these texts refer to an angelic being: *Mart.Ascen.Isa.* (9.36; 11.4) identifies the angel of the Holy Spirit with Matthew's "angel of the Lord" (Matt 1:20; 24), *2 Bar.* refers to Ramiel, and *3 Bar.* to Phamael. The phrase

---

[12] "So when the person who has the spirit of God enters the assembly of just men…then the angel of the prophetic spirit that rests upon that person (ὁ κείμενος ἐπ᾽ αὐτῷ) fills the person, who, being filled with the holy spirit speaks to the whole crowd as the Lord wishes" (Herm. *Mand.* 11.9). The phrase ὁ κείμενος ἐπ᾽ αὐτῷ has been translated in various other ways: "qui est près de lui" (Joly), "in charge of him" (Reiling, Gieschen), "der bei ihm ist" (Brox). See the very helpful survey and discussion in Wilson, *Reassessment*, 97.

[13] Helmut Opitz (*Ursprünge Frühkatholischer Pneumatologie* [Berlin: Evangelische Verlagsanstalt Berlin, 1960], 113), followed by Brox (*Der Hirt*, 257 n. 10), proposes the following interpretation: the "abstract fact of prophecy" is personified as "prophetic spirit"; when the phenomenon of prophecy occurs (described as coming of the prophetic spirit), the angel "fills" the prophet. Wilson (*Reassessment*, 98–101) discards the possibility of an appositional genitive ("the angel who is the prophetic spirit") and interprets "angel" and "spirit" as two real and separate beings: "there is one prophetic spirit, but many angels under his charge…The function of the angel of the prophetic spirit…is to fill the man who has the divine spirit with the Holy Spirit so that he may prophesy" (Wilson, *Reassessment*, 98–99). This reading leads Wilson to speculate about the possibility that the *Shepherd* could be fusing the concepts of "momentary possession" and "constant possession."

[14] *Mart. Ascen. Isa.* 7.23; 8.12; 9.36, 39, 40; 11.4; *2 Bar.* 55.3; *3 Bar* 11.7. Note the expression to "the angel of the holy spirit who is upon you" in *Mart. Ascen. Isa.* 9.36, and the use of μετά in Herm. *Mand.* 6.2.1, ἐν in Herm. *Mand.* 6.2.5, and ἐπί in Herm. *Mand.* 11.9 to designate the action of the angelic spirit. Jannes Reiling (*Hermas and Christian Prophecy: A Study of the Eleventh Mandate* [NovTSup 37; Leiden: Brill, 1973], 106) rejects this equation, arguing that the *Shepherd* does not mention an angel "of prophecy" but rather "of the prophetic spirit."

"angel of the prophetic spirit" may, therefore, be included in Levison's category "angelic spirit."[15]

(c) There exists a structural similarity between Herm. *Mand.* 5 and Herm. *Mand.* 6: both make certain statements of spiritual and psychological dualism, continue with a rather detailed symptomatology and prognosis for each alternative, and conclude with an exhortation to choose the good. At the level of vocabulary, however, Herm. *Mand.* 5 uses "spirit" while Herm. *Mand.* 6 has "angel."[16] Thus each person is attended by two spirits (Herm. *Mand.* 5.1.4) or angels (Herm. *Mand.* 6.2.1). The criterion for distinguishing the influence of the good angel or spirit from that of the evil one is the experience and subsequent conduct of the indwelt person (Herm. *Mand.* 5.2.1–3; 6.2.3–4). One is to trust the good spirit (Herm. *Mand.* 11.17; 21) or angel (Herm. *Mand.* 6.2.3) and depart from the evil spirit or angel (Herm. *Mand.* 6.2.7; 5.2; 11.17). The parallelism is particularly notable between "the spirit of righteousness" in Herm. *Mand.* 5.2.7, and "the angel of righteousness" in several verses of Herm. *Mand.* 6.2. Moreover, "delicate" (τρυφερός), "meek"/"meekness" (πραός/πραότης), and "tranquil"/"tranquility" (ἡσύχιος/ἡσυχία) are used of both the angel (Herm. *Mand.* 6.2.3) and the spirit (Herm. *Mand.* 5.2.6).[17]

Wilson discusses this case is some detail, and concludes that, despite the noted similarities, "[a]ngels are different from spirits."[18] In support of this assertion, he mentions that angels have bodies, are visible (at least to Hermas), and have names, while spirits are bodiless, do not have names, and remain invisible to Hermas. I find this argumentation unconvincing. The passage invoked as proof of the alleged visibility of angels, namely Herm. *Sim.* 9.1.2, cannot be questioned on the visibil-

---

[15] Gieschen is right in affirming that "this angel is much more than another angel with a specific function," and that he is "closely linked with 'the Spirit'" (*Angelomorphic Christology*, 218). His solution, however (the "angel of the prophetic spirit" as an angelomorphic manifestation of the Spirit), does not take into account the *Shepherd of Hermas'* use of "spirit" for both angels and the supreme angel, Christ. I shall return to this problem later.

[16] This is mentioned in passing by Haas ("Die Pneumatologie des Hirten," 576).

[17] I mentioned earlier that the theme of the Spirit's "delicacy" was adopted by Tertullian. See in this respect Morgan-Wynne, "The 'Delicacy' of the Spirit in the Shepherd of Hermas and in Tertullian." Opitz (*Ursprünge*, 140–141) traces the "delicacy of the Spirit" to Jewish-Christian exegesis of 1 Sam 16:14–15 (LXX). The fact that the *Shepherd of Hermas* is aware of an old tradition of dualist pneumatology rooted in the exegesis of 1 Sam 16:14 has been proven by recourse to similar passages in Aphrahat. See Fredrikson, "L'Esprit Saint et les esprits mauvais," esp. 273–75.

[18] Wilson, *Reassessment*, 79.

ity or invisibility of angels, because the issue there is rather Hermas'
spiritual development, by which he obtains the ability to perceive
celestial realities. As for the alleged "physical description" of angels
that Hermas would be able to give in Herm. *Sim.* 8.1.2, the fact that
angelic beings are said to be "tall" is not a physical description but an
indication of their celestial status. It is evident, for instance, that the
preeminence of Christ over the angels is expressed symbolically by his
extreme height (Herm. *Sim.* 9.6.1), as in *Gos. Pet.* 10.39–40.[19] On the
other hand, when Hermas spends a night in the joyous company of the
virgins (Herm. *Sim.* 9.11), who are "holy spirits" (Herm. *Sim.* 9.13.2),
he "sees" them, and even describes their "splendidly girded" linen garments and uncovered shoulders (Herm. *Sim.* 9.2.4)! It should be noted,
however, that the concepts of "bodily" versus "bodiless," and "visible"
versus "invisible," have an entirely different meaning for pre-Origenian
authors than they do for us.[20]

So far, it appears that the "spirits" have undeniably angelic traits. It is
just as true, however, that the angel of righteousness in Herm. *Mand.* 6
conveys a pneumatological content. The *Shepherd*'s reference to the
"delicacy" of the good angel or spirit (Herm. *Mand.* 5.2.6; 6.2.3), noted
above, is significant in this respect. Another crucial indicator are the
terms ἡσύχιος and ἡσυχία, whose quasi-technical status in describing the abiding presence of the Holy Spirit has been demonstrated by
Gabriele Winkler.[21]

The question, then, is whether the *Shepherd of Hermas* uses "holy
spirit" as a designation for the angelic beings, or whether it uses angelic
imagery to speak of the Holy Spirit. For the time being it is enough to
recall Daniélou's warning against an anachronistic understanding of the
terms "angel" or "spirit," and Fletcher-Louis' category of "angelomorphism." A full discussion will only become possible after investigating
other uses of πνεῦμα in the *Shepherd of Hermas.*

---

[19] See Grillmeier, *Christ in Christian Tradition* (2nd, rev. ed.; tr. J. Bowden; Atlanta,
Ga.: John Knox, 1975), 50.
[20] See, in this respect, my earlier discussion about the relative visibility and corporality of the entire spiritual universe in Clement of Alexandria's *Exc.* 10.
[21] For ample documentation and a very detailed analysis, see Winkler, "Ein bedeutsamer Zusammenhang zwischen der Erkenntnis und Ruhe in Mt 11, 27–29 und dem
Ruhen des Geistes auf Jesus am Jordan: Eine Analyse zur Geist-Christologie in Syrischen
und Armenischen Quellen," *Mus* 96 (1983): 267–326.

2. Πνεῦμα as the Son of God

In a number of other passages, πνεῦμα takes on a different meaning. Before proceeding to the discussion of those passages, however, I propose to draw a distinction between real and symbolic identity, and a second distinction between revealing agent and object of revelation. Such a distinction is assumed by the text. For instance, in Herm. *Sim.* 9.1.1 (τὸ πνεῦμα τὸ ἅγιον τὸ λαλῆσαν...ἐν μορφῇ τῆς ἐκκλησίας), the real entity is τὸ πνεῦμα τὸ ἅγιον, while the symbolic identity, the "form," is that of the church (ἐν μορφῇ τῆς ἐκκλησίας). On the other hand, "the church" can be spoken of as a revealing agent ("you were shown the building of the tower *through the church*"), or as the object of a vision (the tower-vision as a vision about the Church).

In this section I shall discuss the following themes: (a) the additional information provided by Herm. *Sim.* 9 about the mediator "church"; (b) the relation between "the preexistent holy spirit" and the Son of God; (c) the virgins as "holy spirits."

(a) The introduction to Herm. *Sim.* 9 provides a reinterpretation of the previous visions. Referring back to the first tower-vision, the mediator of that vision, which had been termed "church," is now called "angel" and "spirit." The same tower-vision is said to occur διὰ τῆς πρεσβυτέρας (Herm. *Vis.* 3.1.2), διὰ τῆς ἐκκλησίας, διὰ τοῦ πνεύματος, or δι'ἀγγέλου (all three passages in Herm. *Sim.* 9.1.1–2). The "old woman"/"church" is only the symbolic manifestation of the revealing agent. Who, then, is this agent? The successive identification as "angel" and "spirit" can be united safely under Levison's category "angelic spirit." But the text adds more ambiguity. Hermas learns that the one who spoke to him was the Holy Spirit, and that this Spirit was the Son of God (ἐκεῖνο γὰρ τὸ πνεῦμα ὁ υἱὸς τοῦ Θεοῦ ἐστιν, Herm. *Sim.* 9.1.1). Indeed, given Hermas' request for revelation (Herm. *Vis.* 3.1.2: "when I had fasted a great deal and asked *the Lord* to show me the revelation he had promised to show me..."), one would expect the response to come from "the Lord" as well. The reader is to understand that the "angelic spirit" is not just any celestial entity: the angelic appearance conceals the Son, the Glory, the Name (Herm. *Vis.* 3.1.9–10.1), the Lord of the people.[22]

---

[22] The titles "Son" and "Glory" can be derived from the following two solemn declarations, whose crucial importance is highlighted by the fact that they appear at the

(b) In Herm. *Sim.* 5 the *Shepherd* speaks about God sending τὸ πνεῦμα τὸ ἅγιον τὸ προόν τὸ κτίσαν πᾶσαν τὴν κτίσιν (Herm. *Sim.* 5.6.5). And it is again Herm. *Sim.* 9 that offers a clarifying parallel: ὁ μὲν υἱὸς τοῦ Θεοῦ πασῆς τῆς κτίσεως αὐτοῦ προγενέστερός ἐστιν ὥστε συμβούλον αὐτὸν γενέσθαι τῷ πατρί (Herm. *Sim.* 9.12.2). Moreover, both expressions recall the description of the "church" as πάντων πρώτη ἐκτίσθη (Herm. *Vis.* 2.4.1). All these descriptions have only one referent: the Son of God. There are two elements that lead to this conclusion.

First, the most likely background of the identification of the old rock with the Son of God (Herm. *Sim.* 9.12.1–2) is christological: 1 Cor 10:4 (Christ as the rock), and Col 1:15 (Christ as πρωτότοκος πάσης κτίσεως).[23] Second, "Church" in Herm. *Vis.* 2.4.1 is only the μορφή, i.e., the symbolic identity of the Son.[24] The three elements ("church," Spirit, Son) are thus reduced to only two (the Son and the Spirit),

---

climax of the so-called heavenly letter, prepared by a fifteen-day long fast: ὤμοσεν γὰρ κύριος κατὰ τοῦ υἱοῦ αὐτοῦ...(Herm. *Vis.* 2.2.8); ὤμοσεν γὰρ ὁ δεσπότης κατὰ τῆς δόξης αὐτοῦ (Herm. *Vis.* 2.2.5). Given the parallelism of these declarations, with κύριος corresponding to δεσπότης, and κατὰ τοῦ υἱοῦ αὐτοῦ to κατὰ τῆς δόξης αὐτοῦ, Osiek's translation, "the master has sworn upon his honor," does not convey the entire weight of the term δόξα; the *Shepherd* is here talking about the Son of God as the Glory. In Herm. *Vis.* 2.2.8, the full text of declaration is the following: ὤμοσεν γὰρ κύριος κατὰ τοῦ υἱοῦ αὐτοῦ τοὺς ἀρνησαμένους τὸν κύριον αὐτῶν ἀπεγνωρίσθαι ἀπὸ τῆς ζωῆς αὐτῶν. While the first κύριος refers to God, the second one obviously designates the Son. This is also the idea underlying several text witnesses (L1 and E have *filium*, while S* reads χριστόν; see SC 53, 92, 93 n. 5). The reference to "their Lord" is significant, as it parallels Herm. *Sim.* 5.5.3 and Herm. *Sim.* 5.6.4, where the Son of God is proclaimed as "Lord of the people." A theology of Jewish extraction advocating "two Lords" can be rightly termed "binitarian monotheism." As for "Name," the famous passage in Herm. *Sim.* 9.14.5 clearly implies a christological sense. See in this respect Daniélou, *Jewish Christianity*, 152; Grillmeier, *Christ in Christian Tradition*, 42. For a survey of "Name" christology in the early Church, see Gieschen, "The Divine Name in Ante-Nicene Christology," *VC* 57 (2003): 115–58.

[23] Ultimately, as noted by Lage Pernveden (*The Concept of The Church in the Shepherd of Hermas* [STL 27; Lund: Gleerup, 1966], 65), the roots go back to Jewish speculation about Wisdom as πρότερα πάντων ἔκτισα (Sir 1:4). Pernveden and Brox (*Der Hirt*, 525) have in mind the pre-existence of the Church. But "church" in Herm. *Vis.* 2.4.1 is only the symbolic identity of the Son. It is noteworthy that Philo sees the rock as a symbol of Wisdom (*Leg. All.* 2:86), while Paul equates both "rock" and "wisdom" with Christ (1 Cor 1:24, 10:4). Although "sophia" pneumatology is not unknown in some patristic authors, such as Theophilus of Antioch and Irenaeus, the most common application of Wisdom-speculation in early Christianity is christological.

[24] Brox (*Der Hirt*, 525) hypothesizes that early Jewish Sophia-speculations might have been reworked in the *Shepherd* to construct a "Sophia-ecclesiology," an idea rejected earlier by Daniélou (*Jewish Christianity*, 312). As I have shown, however, "church" here is a symbolic designation of the supreme spirit, i.e., the Son, which is consonant with early Christian use of Sophia in the service of christology and (more seldom), pneumatology.

whose identical descriptions are perfectly coherent with the statement in Herm. *Sim.* 9.1.1: the Spirit is the Son of God. This statement does not posit two entities—God's "natural son" (the Holy Spirit) and his "adopted son" (the Son of God)—whose intimate relationship would only be "thought of" as identity.[25] There is only one subject, namely the highest "angelic spirit," the Son of God, and the one subject is not the polymorphic Holy Spirit, *pace* Gieschen and Barnes, but rather the Son of God.[26]

Scholars have increasingly come to realize that the comparisons of the statement in Herm. *Sim.* 9.1.1 (ἐκεῖνο γὰρ τὸ πνεῦμα ὁ υἱὸς τοῦ Θεοῦ ἐστιν) with 2 Cor 3:17 (ὁ δὲ κύριος τὸ πνεῦμά ἐστιν), and with the phrase in Herm. *Sim.* 5.5.2 (*filius autem spiritus sanctus est*) are as convenient as they are deceiving.[27] The identification between Son and Spirit remains a puzzle. Among the astonishingly divergent interpretations proposed so far, it is sufficient to note three of the more recent.

Henne thinks of πνεῦμα as the trinitarian person of the Holy Spirit, and rejects any ontological identification with the Son of God; he blames the confusion on a certain "maladresse de l'expression" in the text. For Brox the puzzling relation between some of the major characters in the

---

[25] *Pace* Wilson, *Reassessment*, 138: "…the Son of God lived in such complete commonality with the Holy Spirit that they could now be thought of as one. They did not begin as one…But the perfect life of the son of God made them one."

[26] According to Gieschen, all revelational characters (including the Son/slave/flesh) are "a manifestation of the Spirit," in the context of "a very fluid angelomorphic Pneumatology" (*Angelomorphic Christology*, 222, 225). The idea of a second-century version of binitarian monotheism featuring not the Son, but the Spirit as God's vice-regent has been pursued further by Barnes ("Early Christian Binitarianism: The Father and the Holy Spirit," paper presented at the 2001 Annual Meeting of the North American Patristics Society; online at www.mu.edu/maqom). Barnes ("Early Christian Binitarianism," 5) considers Herm. *Sim.* 5.6.5 to offer "a classic articulation of the great church's understanding of Spirit in-hominization."

[27] The latter appears only in the L1, the so-called Latin Vulgate, but virtually all commentators (including Brox and Osiek) consider it original; see Wilson, *Reassessment*, 107–9; Osiek, *Shepherd Commentary*, 177b; Henne, *Christologie*, 189. Read in its proper context, which is a Pauline midrash on Exod 34:29–35, 2 Cor 3:17 proclaims Christ as the content of, and full access to, the glory of divine presence. Moreover, Henne (*La Christologie*, 224) notes that "in 2 Cor 3:17 it is the Lord who is identified with the Spirit, whereas in Herm. *Sim.* 9.1.1 the reverse is true: the Spirit is identified with the Son of God." As for Herm. *Sim.* 5.5.2, this text operates a symbolic identification (one of the terms is an actor in a parable, namely the "son," the second one is its symbolized counterpart, the Holy Spirit); in Herm. *Sim.* 9.1.1, on the other hand, "that spirit," i.e., the revealing entity, is the Son (not the "son" in a parable, but the Son of God). Similarly Osiek, *Shepherd Commentary*, 177–78 n. 18. Similarly, for Brox (*Der Hirt*, 492; cf. 316) the identification in Herm. *Sim.* 5 means nothing more than that the son in the parable represents the Holy Spirit.

Shepherd can only be resolved by positing their identity. One would be well advised, however, not to read any theology into such statements, and instead only take note of the "uncontrollable style" of the *Shepherd*. On the opposite end of the interpretative spectrum, Wilson is adamant that the author "knew exactly what he was doing when he wrote Herm. *Sim.* IX:1:1," and "had a definite theological point to make," albeit one whose explanation "is left to the reader."[28] According to Wilson, this theological message was the following: God, who had a "natural son," the Holy Spirit, later transformed a high celestial entity into a second, "adoptive," son. This celestial entity was "preexistent and served as counselor to God at the beginning of creation," but it "was not at that time related to God as son to father (as was the Holy Spirit)"; it became incarnate and after exemplary service in communion with the Spirit, was exalted to the status of "adopted son." The christology of the *Shepherd* would consequently develop over the three stages of angelic pre-existence, incarnation and indwelling, and adoption.[29]

It is also possible to find a simpler solution. At the risk of repeating myself, I invoke once again the Jewish and Jewish Christian practice of designating angelic beings by the term "spirit." In light of this tradition, the Son of God is, technically, a "holy spirit." To this supreme holy spirit are subordinated all other "(holy) spirits."

(c) Moving on to the interaction of christology, pneumatology and angelomorphism in the collective character of the virgins, it is noteworthy that the virgins are termed "holy spirits," ἅγια πνεύματα, and "powers of the Son of God," δυνάμεις τοῦ υἱοῦ τοῦ Θεοῦ (Herm. *Sim.* 9.13.2). To be clothed with these "powers" means to bear the "power" of the Son of God (Herm. *Sim.* 9.13.2). It would seem that these "holy spirits" are an angelomorphic representation of the activity of the Son.[30]

At the same time, the use of clothing and baptismal language suggests that the virgins can be seen as a plural designation of the Holy Spirit. In describing the eschatological state of those who have the Spirit, the *Shepherd* uses the following expressions: "always clothed with the holy spirit of these young women" (Herm. *Sim.* 9.24.2); "you have

---

[28] Henne, *Christologie*, 225; Brox, *Der Hirt*, 531; Wilson, *Reassessment*, 137.

[29] Wilson, *Reassessment*, 132–34.

[30] Cf. Levison ("The Angelic Spirit," 469), who argues that the metaphor of clothing in Judg 6:34 "is consistent with the interpretation of the spirit as an angelic or demonic being."

received something of his [the Lord's] spirit" (Herm. *Sim.* 9.24.4); "they received the Holy Spirit" (Herm. *Sim.* 9.25.2). Earlier in Herm. *Sim.* 9 the believers are exhorted to "clothe themselves with these spirits" in order to enter the church and the kingdom (Herm. *Sim.* 9.13.2). As a result, they become "one body, *one spirit*, and one color of garment" (Herm. *Sim.* 9.13.5). The white color of the garment finds its symbolic counterpart in the white color of the tower: "So stones of many different colors were brought...And when the variegated stones were put into the building, all alike became white and changed their many colors" (Herm. *Sim.* 9.4.5–6). The tower built on water, the white garment, and the transformation into "one spirit" are obvious references to Baptism and the reception of the Holy Spirit. Indeed, the *Shepherd of Hermas* collapses the spirits and the Spirit in its exhortation to repentance and holiness: "give back the spirit (*reddite spiritum*, L1) as whole as you have received it!...what do you think the Lord will do to you, who gave you the spirit (*spiritum dedit*) whole, but you gave it back useless?" (Herm. *Sim.* 9.32.2,4).[31] Being "clothed with these spirits" (Herm. *Sim.* 9.13.2), which are the "powers" of the Son, means, then, to receive the white garment of Baptism.[32]

I conclude, in agreement with Wilson, that "the term [ἅγια πνεύματα] does signify a plural concept of the Holy Spirit."[33] The angelomorphic character of the virgins, and the fact, noted by Wilson, that the anarthrous noun should perhaps be rendered "spirits that are holy," only strengthens the case for angelomorphic pneumatology in the *Shepherd*.

---

[31] Leutzsch prefers to include L2 in the text: *habebitis spiritum*, "you shall have the spirit," instead of L1, "give back the spirit." However, L1 makes better sense in connection with "you gave it back" in Herm. *Sim.* 9.32.4.

[32] The *Shepherd*'s affirmation that entrance into the kingdom is only possible if one has been clothed with the garment provided by the virgins (Herm. *Sim.* 9.13.2) is very similar to Irenaeus' notion of the paradisiac, baptismal, and eschatological garment as gift of the Holy Spirit (*Adv. haer.* 3.23.5; 4.36.6). See de Andia, *Homo Vivens*: "Si la nudité d'Adam, avant la chute, est une <robe de sainteté reçue de l'Esprit (*ab Spiritu sanctitatis stolam*)>, alors l'Esprit est présent dans le régime de vie paradisiaque et enveloppe Adam de sa sainteté" (97); "Comme les invités ne pourront entrer au repas sans l'habit de noces, de même l'homme qui était revêtu au paradis de la <robe de sainteté> de l'Esprit ne pourra entrer au Royaume des cieux et prendre part au <festin de l'incorruptibilité> que s'il est revêtu de l'Esprit incorruptible. La triple mention, dans l'*Adversus haereses*, de la *stola sanctitatis* d'Adam au paradis, de la *prima stola*, dans la parabole de l'Enfant prodigue, et de l'*indumentum nuptiarum*, dans la parabole des invités aux noces du Fils du Roi, permet donc de définir, chez Irénée, une <théologie du vêtement> paradisiaque, baptismal et eschatologique, en référence à l'Esprit Saint" (99).

[33] Wilson, *Reassessment*, 154 n. 129.

Research into connections with the expression "Lord of the powers," κύριος τῶν δυνάμεων (3 Rgns [= 1 Kgs, MT] 18:15; 4 Rgns [= 2 Kgs, MT] 3:14; Ps 23:10; 45:8,12; Zeph 2:9; Jer 40:12), or the expressions "Father of spirits" (Heb 12:9) and "Lord of the spirits" (1 En.) may shed light on the *Shepherd's* background.[34]

The preceding two sections have shown that the *Shepherd of Hermas* uses πνεῦμα to designate both angelic beings and the Son of God. What then is the relation between the Son of God as "holy spirit," the angelic "spirits," and the believer, with respect to the divine indwelling? The *Shepherd* is somewhat ambiguous on this matter. His favorite ways of expressing the effect of the indwelling are "clothing" (Herm. *Sim.* 9.13.5: one has to be *clothed* with the holy spirits/powers/virtues of the Son of God in order to enter the kingdom), "renewal" (Herm. *Vis.* 3.16.9), "purification" (Herm. *Vis.* 3.16.11; 3.17.8), "rejuvenation" (Herm. *Vis.* 3.21.2), and "strengthening" (Herm. *Vis.* 3.20.3).[35] These expressions mark a transition from past spiritual weakness to present strength (see the use "then" and "now" in Herm. *Vis.* 3.12.3 and Herm. *Sim.* 9.1.2), and correspond to the repeated exhortation to "be a man" that Hermas receives from the angel (ἀνδρίζομαι, used in Herm. *Vis.* 1.4.3; 3.16.4; 3.20.2). It is notable that the text ascribes this indwelling to "the angel," "the spirit," or "the Lord," without the slightest indication of perceiving any overlap or contradiction.[36] In fact, there is no contradiction in these

---

[34] For a brief but very dense overview, see Gieschen, *Angelomorphic Christology*, 119–23 ("Power as designation for an Angel"). Among the relevant passages are Philo, *Conf.* 168–182; Rom 8:38; 1 Cor 15:24; Eph 1:21; 1 Pet 3:22.

[35] For a more detailed treatment, see Bucur, "Observations on the Ascetic Doctrine of the *Shepherd of Hermas*," StudMon 48 (2006): 7–23.

[36] The theme of the spirit dwelling in the faithful recurs again and again in Herm. *Sim.* 5. But at one point, the angel offers the following ideal portrait of the believer: ὃς ἂν δοῦλος ἦν, φησίν, τοῦ θεοῦ καὶ ἔχῃ τὸν κύριον αὐτοῦ ἐν τῇ καρδίᾳ (Herm. *Sim.* 5.4.3). Herm. *Mand.* 3.28.1 speaks about the *spirit* that God made to dwell in the believer (τὸ πνεῦμα ὃ ὁ θεὸς κατῴκισεν ἐν τῇ σαρκὶ ταύτῃ); in a way, however, it is the *Lord* himself who dwells in the believer (ὁ κύριος ὁ ἐν σοὶ κατοικῶν). Then, in Herm. *Mand.* 5.33.1, it is τὸ πνεῦμα τὸ ἅγιον τὸ κατοικοῦν ἐν σοί. I have already discussed the passage in Herm. *Mand.* 11.9 where the *Shepherd* switches from "spirit" to "angel" ("So when the person who has the spirit of God enters the assembly of just men…then the angel of the prophetic spirit that rests upon that person [ὁ κείμενος ἐπ᾽ αὐτῷ] fills the person, who, being filled with the holy spirit speaks to the whole crowd as the Lord wishes"). In Herm. *Sim.* 9.1.2, Hermas' capacity to "bear" divine showings is explained as the result of his "being strengthened" by the "spirit," namely "that" particular spirit identified in the previous verse as the Son of God. In Herm. *Vis.* 3.22.3, the strengthening in faith and rejuvenation of the spirit come from the Lord. However, this "strengthening" seems to be carried out by the Lord through the agency of the angels: in Herm. *Sim.* 5.1.3 and 5.6.2, the angels are appointed by the

affirmations if we consider the *Shepherd*'s view of the heavenly world:
Father, Son and holy spirits/angels. The Son is active in the believers
and is available to them through his angels/spirits. He "strengthens"
the believer either directly (Herm. *Vis.* 1.3.2; 3.12.3; Herm. *Sim.* 7.4), or
through the angels (Herm. *Sim.* 6.1.2; Herm. *Mand.* 12.6.4). As Halvor
Moxnes observed, "the function of the angel...is to such a degree
identical with God's own that the process in Herm. *Sim.* V:4.3 f can
be described without him." For instance, in Herm. *Sim.* 7,

> Hermas' family has sinned against the angel, but it is God who can give
> forgiveness. The angel has handed Hermas over to be punished, but it
> is God who has decided to show him the reason for it...We seem to be
> nearer to the OT understanding of the 'malak Yahweh' more than to any
> specific angelic figure in later developments of angelology.[37]

3. Πνεῦμα in the Fifth Similitude

The validity of the ideas formulated so far depends in large measure
on whether the outlined understanding about the *Shepherd*'s use of
"spirit" language can account for the complex problems of Herm.
Sim. 5. More specifically, there are at least two major difficulties to be
addressed: (a) Herm. *Sim.* 5 mentions "Son of God" and "Holy Spirit" as
seemingly distinct entities, which would contradict my conclusions; (b)
Herm. *Sim.* 5.6.4b–5.6.7 seems to present an adoptionistic christology,
impossible to reconcile with the high "preexistent Spirit" christology
discussed so far.

(a) The second interpretation of the parable (Herm. *Sim.* 5.5.2–3)
attempts to extract a christological meaning from a parable that, essentially, is a parable about fasting.[38] This determines a number of changes.
Not only does the text draw on certain characters of the parable, which
had held only secondary importance in the first interpretation (the son

---

Son of God for the purpose of preserving (συντηρεῖν) and strengthening (συγκρατεῖν)
each individual.

[37] Moxnes, "God and His Angel in the Shepherd of Hermas," *ST* 28 (1974): 54
n. 41, 55.

[38] There can be no doubt that the fundamental theme of the parable is fasting. It is
important to recall the very beginning of Herm. *Sim.* 5 (νηστεύοντός μου), the subsequent "Fastengespräch" and, especially the emphatic introduction of the parable as a
"similitude...relative to fasting" (Herm. *Sim.* 5.2.1).

of the master, the friends/ counselors); it also proposes a set of identifications that differ from those of the first interpretation.[39]

To determine the *Shepherd's* theology at this point, it is helpful to appeal once more to the distinction between real and symbolic identity (or rather, "parabolic" identity, given that we are no longer dealing with visions but with a parable). "Slave," "son," and "counselors" are such symbolic/parabolic identities; their corresponding realities are, according to the *Shepherd*, the Son of God, the Holy Spirit and the first-created angels, respectively.

The difficulty occurs when the technical use of "spirit," discussed above, is applied to the affirmations at hand. If the Son of God is, technically, a "holy spirit," one is led to the following equation in Herm. *Sim.* 5.2.2: "son" (in the parable) = "holy spirit" = Son of God. But how can both the "slave" and the "son" in the parable represent the Son of God? The solution consists in positing the coexistence of a "servant christology" similar to that of Philippians 2, and a "spirit christology." When the text speaks about the incarnate Christ and his work of redemption, it portrays him as a slave; when it speaks about Christ as God's eternal counselor and chief of the first-created angels (cf. Herm. *Sim.* 9.12.2), he is identified as "holy spirit."[40] The awkwardness consists in the presentation of two distinct characters in the parable to designate the two *aspects* of Christ. Henne explains it as the unfortunate result of squeezing a christological meaning out of a parable that was initially about fasting. Wilson proposes a polemical background. Finding precedent in the appropriation and reinterpretation of Jesus' parables by the Gospel tradition, he argues that Herm. *Sim.* 5 has taken up a parable from oral tradition, has "reshaped that source into his own language" (which explains the linguistic consistency of the source and the redactional additions), and has provided an interpretation meant to substitute the starkly adoptionistic christology of the original parable with the redactor's own pneumatic christology.[41] In the exchange between Hermas and the angelic shepherd, the "correct" interpretation

---

[39] While the slave and his actions earlier represented the ideal Christian engaged in true fasting and worship, the *Shepherd* now identifies the slave that is εὐάρεστος (Herm. *Sim.* 5.2.2) as the Son of God that is ἀγαπητός (Herm. *Sim.* 5.2.6). The redistribution of the master's food is no longer an image of almsgiving, but of the Son imparting God's law.

[40] Similarly Haas ("Die Pneumatologie des Hirten," 571 n. 64); Loofs, *Theophilus*, 185.

[41] Wilson, *Reassessment*, 131.

of the parable (hence, the "better" christology) is ascribed to the angelic teacher and thereby made authoritative.

These two explanations need not be seen as mutually exclusive: Wilson offers a hypothetical background to Herm. *Sim.* 5, while Henne discusses the literary means by which the *Shepherd* makes certain theological statements.

(b) The main obstacle to the "preexistent Spirit" christology seems to be the text starting with Herm. *Sim.* 5.6.4b. Two problems require clarification at this point. The first is whether Herm. *Sim.* 5.6.4b inaugurates a new section of Herm. *Sim.* 5. As will be seen, scholars tend to agree that the verse marks some sort of turning point. The second problem is whether this new section continues the christological exposition or shifts to non-christological discourse.

In his studies of the christology of the *Shepherd*, noted above, Henne has argued that the christological reinterpretation of the parable stops at Herm. *Sim.* 5.6.4a, and that the subsequent verses are not christological but rather concerned with the ascetic reshaping of the believer. Before addressing these two questions, it is important to introduce the following principles, which are fundamental for Henne's argumentation: "the internal coherence of interpretative levels," and the so-called allegorical polysemy. These terms designate a literary technique characteristic of the *Shepherd*, which consists in ascribing to the elements of a narration several levels of allegorical interpretation that are coherent in themselves, yet often incompatible among themselves. For example: the age of the "church" can be successively explained with reference to the sins of the Christians, or to the Church's pre-eternal status; the mountains symbolize both the twelve tribes of Israel (Herm. *Sim.* 9.17.1–2) and various categories of believers; the dishes that the faithful slave imparts to his fellow slaves are used first as symbols of almsgiving, then of the divine laws that Christ proclaimed to his people.[42] Consequently, each of the successive explanations of Herm. *Sim.* 5 ought to be read in its

---

[42] This literary technique is of course not peculiar to the *Shepherd*. In the interpretation of the parable of the good shepherd, Jesus identifies himself successively with the door of the sheep (John 10:7) and with the good shepherd (John 10:11). Similarly, Rev 1:12, 13, 16 portrays Jesus as "one like the Son of Man," in the midst of seven golden lampstands; these seven lamps, "which are the seven spirits of God," are burning before the throne (Rev 4:4). At the same time, however, Rev 5:6 depicts Jesus as the lamb on the throne "having seven horns and seven eyes, which are the seven spirits of God." In Rev 5:5–6, the visionary identifies Christ almost simultaneously with "the lion of the tribe of Judah" and the "lamb standing as if it had been slaughtered."

own right, by pursuing its particular logic, rather than have its obscurities clarified in light of affirmations that belong to another level of allegory.[43]

I now return to the two problems announced above. That Herm. *Sim.* 5.6.4b inaugurates a significant change in content can hardly be disputed.[44] Brox describes a shift from christological to ethical, noting that the *Shepherd* shifts "suddenly," "surprisingly," "unexpectedly" from a precise focus on Christ to general statements applicable to all Christians.[45] Osiek observes that "in fact these verses have moved into something different with not much by way of transition."[46] In fact, certain transition markers are not lacking: the use of ἄκουε, for instance, marks other (undisputed) articulations of Herm. *Sim.* 5.[47] If, then, Herm. *Sim.* 5.6.4b "begins a new explanation that has its own logic," how is this explanation to be understood?[48]

The angel takes up the several characters of the parable ("the Lord"/κύριος, "his son," "the glorious angels," and "the slave") and proceeds with his new interpretation.[49] We obtain the following scheme: the

---

[43] So Osiek (*Shepherd Commentary*, 35b): "Only by letting each passage and each image stand on its own, without assuming that comparisons made in one are valid in another, can we come to some glimpse of the whole."

[44] The reinterpretation of the parable strays farther and farther from the initial data of the story: the order of the master to his faithful slave becomes a transfer of authority over creation; the relation between the slave and his fellow-slaves mutates into one between the Lord and his people; the planting of vine-props is interpreted as the Son of God assigning angels to each of the Christians; the relation between the master and his slave is reinterpreted as one between father and son; the rooting out of the weeds becomes an image of the Passion; and the imparting of food symbolizes the giving of Christ's new law to his people. On the other hand, important elements in the parable are eliminated: the theme of supererogation—which happens to be the central element of the parable understood as paraenesis on fasting!—and the theme of exchange between the generous rich and the poor who intercedes for him.

[45] Brox, *Der Hirt*, 323.

[46] Osiek, *Shepherd Commentary*, 180a–b.

[47] The beginning of each section in Herm. *Sim.* 5 is usually marked by a cluster of three elements: (i) profession of ignorance: οὐ...δύναμαι νοῆσαι (Herm. *Sim.* 5.3.1); μὴ νοῶν (Herm. *Sim.* 5.4.2); οὐ νοῶ (Herm. *Sim.* 5.6.2); (ii) negotiation to obtain "clarifications": the word family of ἐπιλύω nd δηλόω is used in Herm. *Sim.* 5.3.1–2; 5.2.4.1–3; 5.5.1; 5.7.1; (iii) angelic exhortation to receive a new explanation, often using the imperative ἄκουε (Herm. *Sim.* 5.3.2; 5.5.2; 5.6.1; 5.6.4; 5.7.1). In Herm. *Sim.* 5.6.4b, the transition to a new section is marked by ἄκουε: "But listen to how the lord took his son and the noble angels as advisors about the inheritance of the slave!"

[48] Henne, *Christologie*, 181.

[49] As Joly notes (SC 53, 238 n. 2), the line between real and symbolic identities is blurred: the text uses κύριος instead of δεσπότης, "angels" instead of "counselors," but retains the "slave." Similarly Herm. *Sim.* 5.6.7 states that God took as fellow-counselors

"master" is God; the "son" is the Holy Spirit; the "counselors" are the
angels; the "slave" is the flesh (i.e., the self, the individual).[50] Scholarship
usually proceeds by combining these data with the definitions provided
by the previous section of Herm. *Sim.* 5 (the master = God, the son =
the Holy Spirit, the slave = the Son of God). As a result, the *Shepherd*
appears incoherent in its christology. On the contrary, if Herm. *Sim.*
5.6.4b–5.6.7 is taken as a new level of explanation, internally coherent
yet independent of and parallel to previous explanations, its theology
makes perfect sense.

I now move to the second question: what is the theological content
of this new section? Does Herm. *Sim.* 5.6.4b continue the christological
explanation or does it mark the return to the earlier normative presentation of Christian ascetical and ethical life? The overwhelming majority
of scholars has opted for the first possibility, which implicitly keeps one
prisoner to the task of articulating the two divergent christological views
that seem to be thrown together in the fifth Similitude.[51] This reading of
the text underlies most presentations of its theology in major histories
of doctrine, and most secondary literature on the *Shepherd*.[52]

"his son and the glorious angels," writing "son" (the son of the master) instead of
"holy spirit" (the Son of God). Joly notes: "C'est le Saint-Esprit, symbolisé par le fils
du maître" (SC 53, 239 n. 4).

[50] The symbolic counterpart of the "holy spirit" is not stated explicitly, but can easily
be deduced from the fact that God is said to reward the flesh by assuming it as partner
with the "holy spirit". Obviously, this would correspond to the master's decision to
make the slave coheir with his son.

[51] While Herm. *Sim.* 5.6.1–5.6.4a transforms the "slave" into the bearer of supreme
divine authority, proclaimed "lord" over humans and presiding over the ministry of
the angels, in Herm. *Sim.* 5.6.4b–5.6.7 the "slave" becomes the "flesh" (= individual,
person) which is exalted in recompense for submissive service to the divine spirit.

[52] Joly (SC 53, 32; "Le milieu complexe," 542) repeats the existing verdicts (adoptionist christology, spirit christology, binitarianism, subordinationism), and refrains from
any systematization. Leutzsch (*Einleitung*, 140) rehearses all "aspects" of the *Shepherd*'s
christology (Adoptionschristologie, Geistchristologie, Engelschristologie), but points out
that the relation between the spirit and the flesh in Christ is the model set for every
Christian. Loofs (*Theophilus*, 183–89) insists on *Geistchristologie*. H. E. W. Turner
(*Pattern of Christian Truth*, 134) sees the *Shepherd* as a prime example of "dynamic
binitarianism." Grillmeier (*Christ in Christian Tradition*, 56) ranges the author of the
Shepherd with other writers (Ignatius, Melito, *2 Clem.*) in the category of "Pneuma-
sarx christology." He detects the same two christological "lines" in Herm. *Sim.* 5 and
recognizes that "Hermas' incoherence of ideas remains," in part because in the *Shepherd*
we find "a reflection of the theology of the church not clearly understood." J. N. D.
Kelly (*Early Christian Doctrines* [5th ed.; San Francisco, Ca.: Harper & Row, 1978], 94)
speaks of "an amalgam of binitarianism and adoptionism." Opitz (*Ursprünge*, 58–59;
76) mentions adoptionism and pneumatic christology. Martin Dibelius (*Der Hirt des
Hermas* [Die Apostolischen Väter 4; Tübingen: Mohr, 1923], 569, 571) distinguishes

Henne, instead, argues that the entire section Herm. *Sim.* 5.6.4b–5.6.7 is not christological. The "flesh in which the Holy Spirit dwelled" would not be the man Jesus, but rather the Christian believer. It must be noted, however, that when Henne refers ἣν ἠβούλετο back to Herm. *Sim.* 5.2.2 (ἐκλεξάμενος οὖν δοῦλόν τινα), he is revolutionary only in his conclusion, which is to deny any christological bearing to Herm. *Sim.* 5.6.4b–5.6.7.[53] The connection itself is accepted by other scholars. Cirillo, for instance, draws the same connection between ἣν ἠβούλετο and ἐκλεξάμενος οὖν δοῦλόν τινα (Herm. *Sim.* 5.2.2), albeit to the opposite end, namely to emphasize the theme of "election" in the case of the man Jesus.

The election refers to any individual (any "flesh") that has faithfully served the holy spirit and has not defiled it in any way. The parallelism between the supposedly christological statement in Herm. *Sim.* 5.6.5 and the concluding verse in Herm. *Sim.* 5.6.7 is noticeable:

> Herm. Sim 5.6.5: αὕτη οὖν ἡ σάρξ   ἐν ᾗ κατῴκησε τὸ πνεῦμα τὸ ἅγιον
> Herm. Sim 5.6.6: πᾶσα γὰρ σάρξ   ἐν ᾗ τὸ πνεῦμα τὸ ἅγιον
> ἀπολήμψεται μισθόν...   κατῴκησεν

Henne observes that the use of οὖν rather than γάρ in Herm. *Sim.* 5.6.7 supports the non-christological reading of both Herm. *Sim.* 5.6.5 and Herm. *Sim.* 5.6.7: the reward of "all flesh" does not follow from

---

between "Allegorie vom Werk Christi" and "Allegorie von Christi Person," and considers the christology to be adoptionistic. Brox (*Der Hirt*, 494) opposes the adoptionist "Sklaven- und Bewährungschristologie" of Herm. *Sim.* 5 to the preexistence christology of Herm. *Sim.* 9.12.1–3. Luigi Cirillo ("La christologie pneumatique de la cinquième parabole du 'Pasteur' d'Hermas [Par. V, 6, 5]," *RHR* 184 [1973]: 25–48) argues that the "flesh" (i.e., the man Jesus), whose depiction as a slave relies on Deutero-Isaiah's "servant of God," is set apart from all of humankind as the unique dwelling place of the Spirit. Wilson (*Reassessment*, 165) thinks it "most likely that Hermas himself originated the combination of adoptionism and pneumatic Christology." Perhaps the only scholar to abandon completely the attempt to understand the *Shepherd* through the lens of Harnack's categories of "adoptionism" and "spirit Christology" was Pernveden, who noted "the difficulty of grasping Hermas' Christology and giving it an adequate expression by using the main current concepts of Christology" (*Concept of the Church*, 52 n. 1). I have already noted the new perspective proposed by Gieschen and Barnes. Similar to these authors, Brox believes that the actual subject of the indwelling of the man Jesus is the Holy Spirit, while "Son of God" is only a designation of the Spirit, in virtue of the indwelling of the man Jesus: "Sohn Gottes ist der Name für den einwohnenden Geist" (Brox, *Der Hirt*, 493); "Sohn Gottes is der Heilige Geist insofern er den 'Leib' bewohnen wird" (Brox, *Der Hirt*, 494). Osiek (*Shepherd Commentary*, 36a) also argues that "Pneumatology is more prominent than Christology" and that "the prevailing, polymorphous presence" is that of the Holy Spirit rather than the Son.
[53] Henne, *Christologie*, 182.

the supposed divine indwelling of the man Jesus but rather from the
general principle of having cooperated with the Spirit.[54] A christological
reading would erase the distinction between Jesus' adoption as Son of
God and the exaltation available to any other "flesh."[55]

This interpretation places Herm. *Sim.* 5.6.4b–5.6.7 in line with the
views expressed in Herm. *Sim.* 9.24–25: both texts have an eschatological
bearing, both interpret the final reward as communion with the Spirit,
and both make this reward dependent upon the cooperation with the
Spirit during the earthly sojourn.[56]

Henne's proposal was flatly rejected by Brox, whose arguments
can be systematized as follows. First, Henne would fail to take into
account the special use of "flesh and spirit" in this section.[57] Specifically, ἡ σάρξ can only be meant christologically, as opposed to πᾶσα
σάρξ in Herm. *Sim.* 5.6.7, which obviously points to all believers; the
indwelling "spirit" in Herm. *Sim.* 5.6.5 is "the trinitarian Holy Spirit,"
as opposed to the "holy spirit" present in the believer as an empowering
charisma: "nicht der übliche, alltägliche in den Christen einwohnende
'heilige Geist.'"[58] Secondly, the fact that Herm. *Sim.* 5.6.5 carries on

---

[54] "Le γάρ prouve qu'il s'agit ici du principe à cause duquel 'cette chair ayant servi
l'Esprit saint sans reproche...ne parut pas perdre le salaire de ces services' (Herm. *Sim.*
V, 6, 7). Si 'cette chair' avait été celle du Fils de Dieu et que l'exaltation de la chair
du Christ soit la cause du salut promis à toute chair soumise à l'esprit, le texte eût
alors présenté la conjonction οὖν et non γάρ comme c'est réellement le cas" (Henne,
Christologie, 182).

[55] See Osiek, *Shepherd Commentary*, 179b: "the preexistent Holy Spirit by coming
to dwell in the historical, non-preexistent person of Jesus constituted him as holy
(v. 5), and subsequently exalted him to heaven (v. 6), which is to say, in terms of the
parable, that 'this flesh,' the human Christ, the slave of the parable, was rewarded for
his faithful service, as all faithful servants will be."

[56] The expressions describing those who have the Spirit preserve the ambiguous
relation between christology, pneumatology, and angelology: "always clothed with the
holy spirit of these young women" (Herm. *Sim.* 9.24.2); "you have received something
of his [the Lord's] spirit" (Herm. *Sim.* 9.24.4); "they received the Holy Spirit" (Herm.
Sim. 9.25.2). See my discussion about the "virgins" in paragraph (c) of the section "The
Holy Spirit as the Son of God."

[57] "Henne macht den gravierenden Fehler, den redaktionellen Beitrag des H im
Gebrauch seiner Stoffe (hier: 'Fleisch und Geist') nicht einzukalkulieren" (Brox, *Der
Hirt*, 320).

[58] Brox, *Der Hirt*, 320. See also 323–25, 488. Cf. Joly, "Le millieu complexe," 534:
"l'esprit saint qui vient habiter en lui [Jésus] se distingue de celui d'autres hommes parce
qu'il est préexistant et créateur de toute la création." According to Osiek (*Shepherd
Commentary*, 180–81 n. 43) there is no textual warrant for Brox's distinction between
"Heiliger Geist" and "heiliger Geist." Scholars generally do not distinguish the spirit
indwelling the slave/flesh from the spirit present in other human beings. They differ,
however, in their assessments of the personal or impersonal nature of the Spirit. For

the christological exposition is made evident by its use of the same character of the slave.[59]

It must be noted, first, that Brox fails to criticize Henne on Henne's own terms. His arguments conveniently overlook the principles underlying the latter's interpretation (the principle of internal coherence, the allegorical polysemy). As already noted by Osiek, there is no reason to accept the assertion that the "trinitarian holy spirit" indwelling the "flesh" in Herm. Sim. 5.6.5 is different from the "holy spirit" dwelling in the believers. For Brox, the supposed distinction between "Heiliger Geist" and "heiliger Geist," and the christological interpretation of Herm. Sim. 5.6.4b–5.6.7 reinforce each other in a somewhat circular reasoning. Osiek also points to the weakness of the "singular versus plural" argument by noting the use of collective singular in Ps 65:2; 145:21; Joel 2:28; Zech 2:13.[60]

It would seem that there is little left to oppose Henne's non-christological interpretation of Herm. Sim. 5.6.4b–5.6.7. In her commentary, Osiek reiterates Brox's arguments against Henne; at the same time, she practically dismantles these arguments in her footnotes. She even concedes that "it is not totally clear that vv. 5–6 refer exclusively, or even primarily to Christ, as most commentators assume." Indeed, "the relationship between the spirit and the 'chosen flesh' (σάρξ ἣν ἠβούλετο) could be about the relationship of humanity to the holy spirit."[61] Her solution, eventually, is a mixture of Henne and Brox: the passage is "probably" speaking of Christ "as primary referent," but with a new, non-christological intention, namely "for the sake of instruction and paraenesis."[62] The net result "in a strictly christological perspective"

Pernveden (Concept of the Church, 47 n. 1), "the Holy Spirit is…not thought of as a person in the Trinity but chiefly as a power emanating from God." Wilson's opinions on this question appear contradictory. After justifying his use of the neuter personal pronoun "it" for the Spirit on the grounds that "Hermas consistently understands the Holy Spirit not as a personal being but as an impersonal force" (Reassessment, 62 n. 3), he explicitly and emphatically affirms the personal nature and relationships of the Holy Spirit ("person" and "personal" for the Holy Spirit occur at least five time in Reassessment, 131–32).

[59] Herm. Sim. 5.6.5 "[k]ündigt das folgende ausdrücklich als Erklärung einer Teilszene der vorangehenden Christologie-Parabel an und gebraucht deren Metapher („der Sklave') für den Sohn Gottes" (Brox, Der Hirt, 320).

[60] Osiek, Shepherd Commentary, 180a.

[61] Osiek, Shepherd Commentary, 180a.

[62] Osiek, Shepherd Commentary, 180b, 181a. Haas ("Die Pneumatologie des Hirten") also interprets the passage christologically (571), but then mentions, in reference to πᾶσα σάρξ, "die exemplarische Bedeutung des hier vorliegenden Jesusbildes" (572).

is the classic scholarly verdict on the *Shepherd*: adoptionism.[63] This exposes Osiek to her own critical observation, quoted earlier: "If the christology is what most interpreters say it is...it is strange that this immensely popular document of the early church was never condemned for christological heresy."[64]

Excursus: "Flesh" in the Fifth Similitude

The use of the term "flesh" in the Fifth Similitude seems to be undergoing a semantic shift, from the notion of "flesh" as designating the entire person to "flesh" as only one *part* of the human self. In Herm. *Sim.* 5.6.4b-5.6.7, the *Shepherd* mentions "flesh" independently (ἡ σάρξ αὔτη in Herm. *Sim.* 5.6.5, 6, 7; πᾶσα σάρξ in Herm. *Sim.* 5.6.7), with verbs suggesting personhood ("to serve," "to conduct oneself," "to labor," "to be rewarded"). This use of "flesh" ceases after the explicit announcement in Herm. *Sim.* 5.6.8 ("thus you now have the explanation of this parable"). In the following section (Herm. *Sim.* 5.7), σάρξ always appears determined by a possessive pronoun (τὴν σάρκα σου, five times). Hermas uses "flesh" for "self" in one section, and "flesh" as body in the next.[65]

This semantic evolution of the term "flesh" has an important bearing on the use of "spirit," which also acquires a new sense. There is no doubt that in Herm. *Sim.* 5.6.4b–5.6.7 "spirit" refers to a spiritual entity, a presence that dwells in the believer, labors together with the believer, and may become the believer's intimate companion (Herm. *Sim.* 5.6.6). The situation is slightly more ambiguous in Herm. *Sim.* 5.7. On the one hand, the spirit can "bear witness" to the believer, a view that recalls the intercession of the angelic spirit on behalf of the believer, discussed

---

[63] Osiek, *Shepherd Commentary*, 181a.

[64] Osiek, *Shepherd Commentary*, 180a.

[65] This has been duly noted by Osiek, *Shepherd Commentary* 180 n. 39, 182a. Curiously, A. Hilhorst (*Sémitismes et Latinismes dans le Pasteur d'Hermas* [Graecitas Christianorum Primaeva 5; Nijmegen: Dekker & Van De Vegt, 1976]) seems to have overlooked this obvious Semitism. He only mentions the commonplace that "in biblical language ψυχή and σάρξ do not only stand for 'soul' and 'body,' but may also designate the human as a whole" (138). See also Joly ("Le milieu complexe," 534). Cirillo ("Christologie pneumatique," 27–29), followed by Brox (*Der Hirt*, 326), notes the "anthropologie d'origine juive," in which "flesh" designated the whole of human being. To prove this point both authors point to Herm. *Mand.* 3.1 and Herm. *Mand.* 10.2.5–6, where the parallelism "spirit dwelling in the flesh"/"spirit dwelling in you" supports the identification of "flesh" with "self." Neither author seems aware of a switch from this use of "flesh" to a different one.

above. On the other hand, the insistence on the interconnectedness between "flesh" and "spirit" with respect to purity or impurity (Herm. *Sim.* 5.7.4: "They are together, and one cannot be defiled without the other. So keep both pure, and you will live in God"; cf. 1 Cor 6:16–20) is quite ambiguous, because "spirit" here could be either the heavenly "holy spirit" or part of the human self, or both.[66]

The analysis of the Fifth Similitude confirms several of the hypotheses advanced so far. First, the use of "spirit" to designate Christ remains fundamental in Herm. *Sim.* 5. Since the section describing the adoption of the "flesh" to companionship with the holy spirit (Herm. *Sim.* 5.6.4b–5.6.7) is not christological, but rather pertains to the ascetic life of the believer, reflection on the christology is no longer obliged to account for the divergent traits of a "high" and "low" christology in Herm. *Sim.* 5. In fact, with the vanishing of any basis for adoptionism, the sources of christological reflection on the *Shepherd* remain those texts that view the Son of God as the highest "spirit," the holy spirit, which have been examined earlier.

Second, Herm. *Sim.* 5 clarified the relation between the supreme "holy spirit," Christ, and the spirits "first created." References, in the same breath, to the Son and to the first-created angels (Herm. *Sim.* 5.2.6, 5.2.11, 5.6.4, 7) suggest that, even though they are clearly subordinated to the Son of God and accompany him as a celestial escort (e.g., Herm. *Sim.* 9.12.7–8; cf. Herm. *Vis.* 3.4.1; Herm. *Sim.* 5.5.3), the six are his "friends" and fellow-counselors (Herm. *Sim.* 5.5.2–3).[67]

---

[66] This ambiguity recurs in Tatian (*Or.* 13:2), as well as in no less a second-century authority than Irenaeus. In *Haer.* 5.6.1, while interpreting 1 Thess 5:23, Irenaeus talks about the human person as consisting of three elements: *caro*/σῶμα, made of dust by God but capable of partaking of incorruptibility; *anima*/ψυχή, called to open itself to the Spirit; and *Spiritus*/πνεῦμα, which communicates the incorruptible life in God to the soul and, through the soul, to the body. Critics agree that Irenaeus does not envisage a third human element, beside body and soul. "Spirit" is, throughout the entire fragment, the Spirit of God. When Irenaeus refers to the Holy Spirit as to one of the three elements mentioned in Thess 5:23, "a very precise theological instinct dictates to him the words to suggest the intimate relation between the Spirit of God and his creature and, at the same time, to safeguard God's absolute transcendence" (SC 152:229).

[67] See Bousset, *Jüdisch-christlicher Schulbetrieb*, 185. Joly ("Le milieu complexe," 542) refers to the Son of God as *primus inter pares* among the seven archangels. This depiction of the Son of God as one *among* the seven is not exceptional. According to the sermon *De centesima, sexagesima, tricesima*, God first created seven angelic princes out of fire (cf. Heb 1:7, 2 *En.* 29.3), and later made one of the seven into his Son: *Angelos enim dominus cum ex igne principum numero vii...crearet, ex his unum filium sibi constituere, quem Isaias dominum Sabaot [ut] praeconaret disposuit* (Reitzenstein, "Frühchristliche Schrift," 82). A new critical edition with English translation

Finally, the angel's successive explanations of the parable, amounting to a complex layering of moral *paraenesis*, christology, and ascetic theory, indicate clearly the intimate connection between the belief in the supreme holy spirit, Christ, and the ascetic reshaping of the believer through the indwelling spirit.

4. Further Clarifications on the *Shepherd*'s Angelomorphic Pneumatology

At this point, it appears that πνεῦμα language, although very frequent in the *Shepherd*, is used mainly christologically or in reference to the angels. What about the distinct divine person designated in Christian tradition as the Holy Spirit? It is a commonplace in scholarship to speak about the *Shepherd*'s binitarianism and *Geistchristologie*.[68] It would seem, therefore, that the *Shepherd* thinks more in terms of "Father, Son, and holy angels" (or "spirits") than as a trinitarian. Such is not the case, however.

First, as mentioned earlier, some of the angelic apparitions convey a pneumatological content (e.g., the angel of righteousness in Herm. *Mand.* 6, the virgins of Herm. *Sim.* 9 and their association with baptismal imagery).

Second, much can be gleaned from the *Shepherd*'s πρῶτοι κτισθέντες by considering this collective character in religio-historical perspective. There can be no question that Revelation's group of seven spirits/angels before the divine throne (Rev 1:4; 3:1; 4:5; 5:6; 8:2) and Clement of Alexandria's *protoctists* are an exact analogy to the *Shepherd*'s πρῶτοι κτισθέντες in echoing angelological speculations common in Second Temple Judaism. It is equally true, however, that the traditions about the highest angelic company underwent considerable modifications under the influence of the early Christian kerygma. One such modification, namely the subordination of the *protoctists* to the Son of God, is quite

---

by Philip Sellew is to be published in the near future. The dating of this text is a matter of controversy, with verdicts ranging from late second to the fourth century. The following scholarly treatments are directly relevant to the topic at hand: Barbel, *Christos Angelos*, 192–95; Daniélou, "Le traité 'De Centesima, Sexagesima, Tricesima' et le judéo-christianisme latin avant Tertullien," *VC* 25 (1971): 171–81, esp. 174–75; A. P. Orban, "Die Frage der ersten Zeugnisse des Christenlateins," *VC* 30 (1976): 214–38; Sellew, "The Hundredfold Reward for Martyrs and Ascetics: Ps.-Cyprian, *De centesima, sexagesima, tricesima*," *StPatr* 36 (2001): 94–98.

[68] See my earlier note about the scholarly views of the *Shepherd*'s Christology.

obvious in the *Shepherd*, and even more so in Revelation and Clement of Alexandria. Daniélou is convinced, moreover, that the description of the πρῶτοι κτισθέντες in Herm. *Vis.* 3.4.1 uses Zech 4:10.[69] The imagery in Zechariah is angelic (the seven eyes are the seven angels), but early Christians would not have missed the reference to πνεῦμα in Zech 4:6 ("not by mighty power, nor by strength, but by my Spirit, says the Lord Almighty"), and Zechariahs' seven eyes of the Lord were soon connected with Isaiah's seven gifts of the Spirit.

It appears, in conclusion, that together with Revelation and Clement's "elders," the *Shepherd* is part of this early Christian tradition that reworked the Second Temple notion of the seven principal angels, using it in the service of pneumatology.

As the off-hand remark in *De centesima* shows, not even the *Shepherd*'s description of the Son of God as a *primus inter pares* among the πρῶτοι κτισθέντες is exceptional in early Christianity. By comparison with the sermon, the *Shepherd* seems to have been more careful to impress upon his readers the incontestable superiority of Christ as "preexistent holy spirit" (Herm. *Sim.* 5.6.5) over against his angelic "fellow-counselors."

CONCLUSIONS

Clement's beloved *Shepherd*, which modern scholars perceive to be "bristl[ing] with problems, both literary and theological," continued to fare very well in early Christianity because it was very much part of mainstream Christian thought in the first three centuries. In keeping with the established, quasi-technical way of describing heavenly entities as "spirits," the *Shepherd* refers to the Son of God as the supreme "holy spirit," uniquely distinguished not only by his lordship over the Church but also as leader of the highest angelic company of the πρῶτοι κτισθέντες.

Since the terms "Father," "Son," and "Holy Spirit" occur in Herm. *Sim.* 5, as part of a theological reinterpretation of the initial parable, there can be no doubt that the *Shepherd* was aware of trinitarian formulas. Nevertheless, most of this writing's theology displays a marked

---

[69] Daniélou, *Gospel Message*, 459. Daniélou's assertion that the verse in Zechariah was "a text already used in the *Shepherd of Hermas*" is, however, overly confident. If there is an echo of Zech 4:10, it is quite weak.

binitarian orientation, in that it is concerned mostly with God and the supreme "holy spirit"—the Son of God. As already noted, the coexistence of trinitarian formulas with a certain binitarian orientation, and the identification of the Son as a "holy spirit" (or, in the case of more philosophically-inclined authors, the functional identity between "Logos" and "Spirit") are widespread phenomena in the first three centuries among authors writing in Latin, Greek and Syriac.

The pneumatology of the *Shepherd* is especially present in descriptions of the divine action upon the Christian ascetic. The experience of divine presence—the indwelling of the Holy Spirit—is conveyed by the language of clothing, renewal, purification, rejuvenation, strengthening, and vision, and in conjunction with angelomorphic imagery. On the other hand, a comparison with Revelation and Clement of Alexandria, suggests the possibility that the *Shepherd*'s πρῶτοι κτισθέντες represent a variant of the archaic Christian tradition that reworked the seven supreme angels into an angelomorphic representation of the Holy Spirit.

Under the heading "Πνεῦμα as the Son of God," I discussed the *Shepherd*'s views of divine indwelling, noting that the distinction is often blurred between the presence of the Son of God as supreme "holy spirit" and that of the angelic "spirits." Further investigation is necessary to determine the relationship between these views of the *Shepherd* and the New Testament traditions about the ascended Christ and the Holy Spirit. For the purpose of my argument, however, it was sufficient to revisit the theology of the *Shepherd of Hermas* in light of Jewish traditions on the angelomorphic Spirit. This reading of the *Shepherd* sustains itself within the text, does justice to this text's Second Temple roots and early Christian context, and provides a reasonable enough explanation of its positive reception by Clement of Alexandria and, more generally, in patristic literature.

CHAPTER FIVE

THE SON OF GOD AND THE ANGELOMORPHIC
HOLY SPIRIT IN JUSTIN MARTYR[1]

INTRODUCTION

The fact that Justin Martyr[2] articulated his trinitarian faith by means of a problematic trinitarian theology is a commonplace in scholarship. Some scholars go so far as to claim that there simply is no doctrine of the Trinity in the *Apologies* and the *Dialogue with Trypho*.[3] Others prefer to speak of a "rudimentary" theology of the Trinity.[4] Still other scholars argue that, since the very term "Trinity" had not yet been invented for Christian discourse, discussing Justin's alleged "trinitarian theology" betrays a fundamentally misguided approach.[5]

---

[1] This section is a slightly revised version of Bucur, "The Angelic Spirit in Early Christianity: Justin, the Martyr and Philosopher," *JR* 88 (2008): 190–208.

[2] Critical editions: Charles Munier, ed. and trans., *Justin: Apologie pour les chrétiens* (SC 507; Paris: Cerf, 2006); Philippe Bobichon, ed. and trans., *Justin Martyr: Dialogue avec Tryphon* (Paradosis 47/1–2; Fribourg; Academic Press Fribourg, 2003).

[3] "Doctrine of the Trinity Justin had none.... The Logos was divine, but in the second place; the Holy Spirit was worthy of worship, but in the third place. Such words are entirely incompatible with a doctrine of the Trinity" (Erwin R. Goodenough, *The Theology of Justin Martyr* [Jena: Frommannsche Buchhandlung, 1923], 186). Cf. Leslie W. Barnard, *Justin Martyr: His Life and Thought* (Cambridge: Cambridge University Press, 1967), 105: "Justin had no real doctrine of the Trinity," because his statement about Father, Son, and Spirit are "the language of Christian experience rather than theological reflection." For scholarship prior to 1923, see Goodenough, *Theology of Justin*, 176 n. 2.

[4] Charles Munier, *L'Apologie de Saint Justin Philosophy et Martyr* (Paradosis 37; Fribourg: Éditions Universitaires Fribourg Suisse, 1994), 109. For similar positions, see José Pablo Martín, *El Espíritu Santo en los origenes del Cristianismo: Estudio sobre I Clemente, Ignacio, II Clemente y Justino Martir* (Zürich: PAS Verlag, 1971), 253–54; Santos Sabugal, "El vocabulario pneumatológico en la obra de S. Justino y sus implicaciones teológicas," *Aug* 13 (1973): 467.

[5] For instance, Graham Stanton, "The Spirit in the Writings of Justin Martyr," in *Holy Spirit and Christian Origins*, 321: "All too often...discussion of the teaching on the Spirit of this outstanding second-century Christian philosopher and martyr has been dominated by fourth-century rather than second-century agendas. Is Justin's theology binitarian? Does Justin understand the Spirit in personal terms? Does Justin conceive the relationship among Father, Son, and Spirit in triadic or embryonic Trinitarian ways?"

The problem most often associated with Justin's trinitarian theology is its subordinationism.[6] Even more troubling is Justin's view of the Holy Spirit. Erwin R. Goodenough's observation, that "[t]here is no doctrine of Justin more baffling than his doctrine of the Holy Spirit, and no doctrine which has been more differently understood," remains as true today as it was in 1923.[7] His writings contain numerous references to "the spirit," "the holy spirit," "the divine spirit," "the prophetic spirit," "the holy prophetic spirit," "God's prophetic spirit," or "the divine, holy, prophetic spirit."[8] Nevertheless, Justin offers "very few clear ideas about the person and nature of the Prophetic Spirit."[9] Even though verdicts about Justin's pneumatology "se mantienen sensiblemente distanciadas," especially on the issue of deciding whether *pneuma* is a personal or impersonal entity in the *Apologies* and the *Dialogue*,[10] scholars generally agree that, by contrast to his extensive discussion about the Father and the Son, Justin is quite "discreet" about the Spirit.[11] In the words of André Wartelle, "one is tempted to write that Justin has the Spirit intervene only when he cannot do otherwise."[12] It has been said, again and again, that Justin's all-encompassing theory of the seminal Logos precludes the articulation of a robust pneumatology: "in strict logic there is no place in Justin's thought for the person of the Holy Spirit because the logos carries out his functions."[13]

---

[6] According to Bobichon (*Dialogue avec Tryphon*, 5), Justin's subordinationism may in fact explain the very meager manuscript tradition of the *Dialog with Trypho*.

[7] Goodenough, *Theology of Justin*, 176. Sixty years later, Justin's pneumatology was still viewed as "one of the most difficult features of his teaching to evaluate" (J. E. Morgan-Wynne, "The Holy Spirit and Christian Experience in Justin Martyr," *VC* 38 [1984]: 172).

[8] Sabugal ("Vocabulario Pneumatológico," 460) counts thirty-three references in the first *Apology*, and fifty-seven in the *Dialogue with Trypho*. For a list and classification of the relevant passages, see Martín, *Espíritu Santo*, 316–20.

[9] Goodenough, *Theology of Justin*, 180. For a similar formulation, see Willy Rordorf, "La Trinité dans les écrits de Justin Martyr," *Aug* 20 (1980): 296.

[10] Sabugal, "Vocabulario Pneumatológico," 658 (with a survey of scholarly positions).

[11] Munier, *L'Apologie*, 108.

[12] Wartelle, ed. and trans., *Saint Justin: Apologies* (Paris: Études augustiniennes, 1987), 62. For Stanton ("The Spirit in the Writings of Justin," 330), the "imbalance" between Justin's rich Logos doctrine and relatively meager pneumatology is due to the fact that "Christian views of the Spirit were not the subject of ridicule, so elaboration was not called for." Cf. Goodenough, *Theology of Justin*, 188: the notion of the Holy Spirit "was too well known to need an introduction, was too traditional to need defence."

[13] Barnard, *Justin*, 106. Cf. Munier, *L'Apologie*, 109–10: "le christomonisme instauré par Justin tend inévitablement à oculter non seulement le rôle prophétique de l'Esprit-Saint...mais aussi son action même dans l'Eglise...." See also André Benoit, *Le baptême*

This observation, although true to a large extent, is not entirely fair to Justin. As José Pablo Martín has shown, since Justin's thought is determined by several "conceptual schemes" or "systems," a study of his christology cannot be reduced to the "Logos-scheme," but must also take into consideration his extensive speculations about notions such as the angels, the divine δύναμις, or the Messiah as bearer of the Spirit.[14] Similarly, a study of Justin's pneumatology cannot be reduced to the observation that the Logos-framework allows almost no place for a theology of the Spirit.

In what follows, I shall attempt to place Justin's understanding of the Spirit in the larger tradition of angelomorphic pneumatology, illustrated by Revelation, the *Shepherd of Hermas*, and some of Clement of Alexandria's writings. In doing so, I am treading in the footsteps of Christian Oeyen, who suggested this direction in an article published in 1972 and suggestively entitled "The Teaching about the Divine Powers in Justin."[15]

1. DIFFICULTIES WITH JUSTIN MARTYR'S USE OF πνεῦμα

References to the Holy Spirit as a distinct entity occur several times in Justin's works. In *Apol.* 1.67.2, Christians are said to "bless the Maker of all through his Son Jesus Christ, and through the Holy Spirit." In *Apol.* 1.13.3, Justin states that Christ holds the second place after "the true God," while "the prophetic Spirit" holds the third place. A similar subordinationist scheme occurs in *Apol.* 1.60.6–7, this time supported by a statement attributed to Plato:

> And as to his [Plato's] speaking of a third, he did this because he read, as we said above, that which was spoken by Moses, *that the Spirit of God moved over the waters....* For he gives the second place to the Logos which is with God...and the third place (τὴν δὲ τρίτην [χώραν]) to the Spirit who was said to be borne upon the waters, saying, *and the third things around the third* (τὰ δὲ τρίτα περὶ τὸν τρίτον).

---

chrétien au second siècle: la théologie des pères (Paris: Presses Universitaires de France, 1953), 171.

[14] Martín, *Espíritu Santo*, 303–4: "Así nos encontramos con diversos <<sistemas>> o eschemas conceptuales de cristología, en torno a conceptos como λόγος, ἄγγελος, χριστός, υἱός, δύναμις...Debemos tener en cunta también el <<sistema>> del ἄγγελος, el del χριστός etc."

[15] Oeyen, "Die Lehre von den göttlichen Kräften bei Justin."

Arthur Droge notes that "the statement about 'the third' comes not from the *Timaeus*, as Justin seems to imply, but from the Pseudo-Platonic *Second Epistle* 312e."[16] There is no mention of πνεῦμα in *Ep.* 2; nevertheless, like many of the apologists (and their Jewish predecessors), Justin (*Apol.* 1.59.1–6) is convinced that Plato plagiarized the text of Genesis, and that his reference to a third principle in *Ep.* 2 (312e) refers to the πνεῦμα of Gen 1:2.[17]

Justin's references to the Holy Spirit occur mainly in biblical quotations, or are borrowed from catechesis or liturgy. In other words, they always constitute "prefabricated" elements of received tradition.[18] Such are the numerous references to the "prophetic spirit," or the various formulas related to baptismal rites, the Eucharist, or the blessing of food.[19] Even the use of the pseudoplatonic *Ep.* 2 is a *topos* in both Middle Platonism and early Christian literature.[20]

Sometimes, however, Justin attempts to give a more personal account of the received faith; this is when difficulties of all kinds start accumulating. Here are a few examples.

---

[16] Arthur J. Droge, "Justin Martyr and the Restoration of Philosophy," *CH* 56 (1987): 309. The *Second Epistle* reads καὶ τρίτον περὶ τὰ τρίτα; Justin has τὰ δὲ τρίτα περὶ τὸν τρίτον. The scholarly debate on the authenticity or inauthenticity of *Ep.* 2 is irrelevant to the topic at hand, since for Justin (and all ancients) the Platonic authorship of this writing is not questioned.

[17] As noted above, Clement of Alexandria holds the same view (*Strom.* 5.14.103.1). On the issue of Jewish models for Christian apologetics, see the exhaustive study of Monique Alexandre, "Apologétique judéo-hellénistique et premières apologies chrétiennes," in *Les apologistes chrétiens et la culture grecque* (ed. Bernard Pouderon and Joseph Doré; ThH 105; Paris: Beauchesne, 1998), 1–40.

[18] In a more general study, Adalbert Gauthier Hamman ("La Trinidad en la catechesis de los Padres Griegos," *Estudios trinitarios* 12 [1978]: 73–85) outlines baptism, the Eucharistic anaphora, prayer, and martyrdom, as the four areas in which trinitarian theology finds its existential rootedness in the life of the early Church. Building on Hamman's article, Rordorf ("La Trinité dans les écrits de Justin Martyr") has demonstrated that this enumeration finds perfect confirmation in the writings of Justin, and in the *Acts* of his martyrdom. The same opinion is voiced by Sabugal ("Vocabulario Pneumatológico," 466); José Antonio de Aldama, "El Espíritu Santo y el Verbo en la exégesis de Lc 1, 35," in idem, *María en la patrística de los siglos I y II* (Madrid: BAC, 1970), 145 and n. 18; Martín (*Espíritu Santo*, 243); Wartelle (*Apologies*, 61), and Munier (*L'Apologie*, 108).

[19] *Apol.* 1.6.2; 1.13.3; 1.60.6–7; 1.61.3,13; 1.65.3; 1.67.2.

[20] See the exhaustive presentation by H. D. Saffrey and L. G. Westerink, in *Proclus: Théologie Platonicienne*, vol. 2 (Paris: Les Belles Lettres, 1974), XX–LIX. Among Christian writers, other than Justin, references to *Ep.* 2 occur in Athenagoras (*Leg.* 24), Valentinus (Irenaeus, *Haer.* 3.4.3; Hippolytus, *Haer.* 6.37.5–6), Clement of Alexandria (*Strom.* 5.14.103), Origen (Origen, *Cels.* 6.18), and Cyril of Alexandria (*C. Jul.* 1 [PG 76:553B–D]).

(a) Justin generally affirms that the prophets are inspired by the Logos. He says so in *Apol.* 1.33.9, and even offers a rather technical explanation for the phenomenon: it is the divine Logos alone who speaks in the prophetic writings, speaking as from the "character" or "person" (ὡς ἀπὸ προσώπου) of the Father, or Christ, or the people.[21] A few sentences later, however, in *Apol.* 1.38.11, Justin reverts to traditional language, and ascribes everything to the "prophetic spirit." Elsewhere (*Dial.* 25.1), the one who speaks through the mouth of David is "the Holy Spirit."

(b) Justin refers to Luke 1:35 several times. In *Dial.* 100.5, he substitutes πνεῦμα κυρίου for πνεῦμα ἅγιον in the biblical text: "the angel Gabriel announced to her [the virgin] the good tidings that the Spirit of the Lord would come upon her, and the Power of the Most High would overshadow her...." According to Raniero Cantalamessa, the alternative reading πνεῦμα κυρίου ἐπελεύσεται occurs for the first time in Justin, but is also witnessed to by Origen, Ps.-Hippolytus, and Epiphanius. Strangely enough, it is ignored by the critical editions of the New Testament.[22]

In Apol. 1.33.4, Justin paraphrases Luke 1:35 (πνεῦμα ἅγιον ἐπελεύσεται ἐπὶ σὲ καὶ δύναμις ὑψίστου ἐπισκιάσει σοι) as follows: δύναμις θεοῦ ἐπελθοῦσα τῇ παρθένῳ ἐπεσκίασεν αὐτήν. As José Antonia de Aldama observes, Justin seems to reduce the divine presence at the conception from "Spirit and Power" to "Power."[23] Finally, in *Apol.* 1.33.6, Justin furnishes an even more precise explanation of the Lukan verse:

> It is wrong, therefore, to understand "the Spirit and the power of God" as anything else than the Word, who is also the first-born of God, as the foresaid prophet Moses declared; and it was this which, when it came upon the virgin and overshadowed her, caused her to conceive.[24]

---

[21] *Apol.* 1.36.1. On Justin's "prosopographic" or "prosopological" exegesis, see Martín, *Espíritu Santo*, 291–97; Marie-Josèphe Rondeau, *Les commentaires patristiques du Psautier (3ᵉ–5ᵉ siecles)*, vol. 2: *Exégèse prosopologique et théologie* (OCA 220; Rome: Institutum Studiorum Orientalium, 1985), 21–29; Michael Slusser, "The Exegetical Roots of Trinitarian Theology," *TS* 49 (1988): 461–76, esp. 463–64, 470. For a comprehensive discussion, see Carl Andresen, "Zur Entstehung und Geschichte des trinitarischen Personenbegriffs," *ZNW* 52 (1961): 1–39; Rondeau, *Exégèse prosopologique*.

[22] Cantalamessa, "La primitiva esegesi cristologica di 'Romani' I, 3–4 e 'Luca' I, 35," *RSLR* 2 (1966): 69–80, at 73 and n. 13.

[23] De Aldama, "El Espíritu Santo y el Verbo," 143.

[24] *Apol.* 1.33.6. The same view is repeated elsewhere (*Apol.* 1.46.5; 1.66.2).

Most scholars take these passages as evidence of a confusion between πνεῦμα and λόγος. According to Leslie W. Barnard, "on the surface...for Justin spirit and logos were two names for the same person."[25] To be more precise, in fact, the equation is the following: πνεῦμα ἅγιον = δύναμις θεοῦ = λόγος.[26] Even Martín, who is quite critical of such radical solutions, concedes that the text presents a real exegetical and theological difficulty.[27] Stanton instead seems to locate the problem half-way between muddled thought and clumsy expression: "Here Justin seems to have grafted his convictions concerning the Logos rather awkwardly onto traditional phraseology concerning the role of the Spirit."[28] This comment neither acknowledges the difficulty of the passage nor offers a satisfactory explanation. *Why* does Justin proceed in such an "awkward" way?

A possible answer is furnished by Justin's use of πνεῦμα and πνεύματα for intermediate beings—the angels and the demons. Martín has documented in detail that Justin establishes an antithetic parallelism between the phenomena of inhabitation, inspiration, and endowment with "powers" (δυνάμεις) associated with the divine πνεῦμα, and the inhabitation, inspiration, and endowment with "powers" (δυνάμεις) associated with deceiving and impure πνεύματα.[29] Goodenough made a similar observation:

> [A]ll the powers and demons, even the evil ones, were to Justin also πνεύματα [*Dial.* 7.3; 30.2; 35.2; 76.6].... The Logos, like the lowest angel was ultimately a δύναμις of God [*Dial.* 61.1; *Apol.* 2.6.3].... Since the Logos was of course a Spirit and Power of God, such an identification ["Spirit" in Luke 1:35 as the Logos] was perfectly legitimate, and in no

---

[25] Barnard, *Justin*, 104. Barnard qualifies this confusion of Word and Spirit as confusion of their functions. See also De Aldama, "El Espíritu Santo y el Verbo," 142–43; Wartelle, *Apologies*, 62; Rordorf, "La Trinité dans les écrits de Justin Martyr," 293; Goodenough, *Theology of Justin*, 181–82, 185, 187, 188. Morgan-Wynne ("Holy Spirit and Christian Experience in Justin," 174) refers to the fact that "in Christian *experience* the risen Christ and the Spirit are identical and interchangeable." Sabugal ("Vocabulario Pneumatológico," 466 n. 31) attributes the overlap between λόγος and πνεῦμα to Stoic influence. For older scholarship, see Goodenough, *Theology of Justin*, 180–81; Martín, *Espíritu Santo*, 185; Barbel, *Christos Angelos*, 242 n. 268.

[26] De Aldama, "El Espíritu Santo y el Verbo," 143.

[27] Martín, *Espíritu Santo*, 185–86.

[28] Stanton, "The Spirit in the Writings of Justin," 331.

[29] Martín, *Espíritu Santo*, 313–15. The passages discussed are *Dial.* 7.1–3; 30.2; 35.2; 39.6; 76.6; 82.3; 93.1.

way effects the fact that Justin might have believed in another Spirit which was properly *the* Spirit.[30]

In other words, the passage under discussion does not support the idea that Justin completely identifies *pneuma* and *logos*, nor is it a case of occasional confusion between the two. It is rather the case that Justin uses πνεῦμα independently of any references to the third hypostasis, as a designation of the Logos.[31] This amounts to, as scholars have pointed out, "a self-incarnation of the Word."[32] Strange as it may seem to the modern reader, this view is widespread in early Christianity. In fact, the idea that the πνεῦμα in Luke 1:35 was none other than the Logos also occurs in the *Protevangelium of James*, the *Epistula Apostolorum*, Origen, Tertullian, and Lactantius.[33]

(c) In *Dial.* 54.1, Justin comments upon Gen 49:11 (Jacob's prophecy about Judah, *He shall wash his robe in wine, and his garment in the blood of the grape*). According to Justin, this passage must be taken as a reference to Christ and the Christians:

> the Holy Spirit called those whose sins were remitted by Christ, *his robe*, among whom he is always present in power (δυνάμει), but will be present manifestly (ἐναργῶς) in person at his second coming.

Jacob's prophecy about Judah is here ascribed to the Holy Spirit. This is a perfect example of what *Apol.* 1.36.1 referred to as utterances of the Logos "in the person" of various biblical characters; this time, however, Justin refers to the Spirit.

---

[30] Goodenough, *Theology of Justin*, 196, 185, 182.

[31] "Justino...interpreta el τὸ πνεῦμα como un demonstrativo: 'este espíritu' que es el Logos" (Martín, *Espíritu Santo*, 185).

[32] De Aldama, "El Espíritu Santo y el Verbo," 146 ("una explicacion de la materni-dad virginal que envuelve una autoencarnacion del Verbo"), followed by Bobichon, *Dialogue avec Tryphon*, 780 n. 5.

[33] See Cantalamessa, "Primitiva esegesi," 75–76; De Aldama, "El Espíritu Santo y el Verbo," 155–63; Aloys Grillmeier, *Christ in Christian Tradition* (2nd, rev. ed. Atlanta, Ga: John Knox, 1975), 198–99; Paul McGuckin, "Spirit Christology: Lactantius and His Sources," *HeyJ* 24 (1983): 141–48, at 144–45. The modern reader might wonder about the possible "modalistic" implications of this overlap between λόγος and πνεῦμα; for Justin, however, this type of exegesis only strengthens the thesis of a Logos distinct from the Father, and is designed, in the words of De Aldama ("El Espíritu Santo y el Verbo," 144), "de suprimir todo possible sentido modalista." In fact, Tertullian (*Prax.* 26) also uses this interpretation of Luke 1:35 and the ensuing idea of a "self-incarnation"of the Word as an anti-monarchian argument: the "Spirit of God" and the "Power of the Most High" are not "God" but God's distinctly existent Logos.

More important, however, is the distinction between Christ's presence in the Church "in power" and his eschatological manifestation ἐναργῶς. Goodenough suggests that Justin might have intended "a pun upon δυνάμει, and [to] imply that the Holy Spirit...is the presence of Christ δυνάμει."[34] He notes that Justin also uses δυνάμει when speaking of Christ's presence in the Old Testament theophanies (e.g., *Dial.* 128.1), and concludes that the meaning of the term δυνάμει remains uncertain because "the meaning of neither passage is clear, and each obscures the other."

This hypothesis is accepted by several scholars.[35] In my opinion, more can be said about δυνάμει, as will become clear in my discussion of Justin's view of the angelic powers.

(d) The following passage in *Apol.* 1.6.2, is notorious for its problematic reference to the angels:

> ἀλλ᾽ ἐκεῖνόν [the Father] τε καὶ τὸν παρ᾽ αὐτοῦ υἱὸν ἐλθόντα καὶ διδάξαντα ἡμᾶς ταῦτα, καὶ τὸν τῶν ἄλλων ἑπομένων καὶ ἐξομοιουμένων ἀγαθῶν ἀγγέλων στρατόν, πνεῦμά τε τὸ προφητικὸν σεβόμεθα καὶ προσκυνοῦμεν, λόγῳ καὶ ἀληθείᾳ τιμῶντες, καὶ παντὶ βουλομένῳ μαθεῖν, ὡς ἐδιδάχθημεν, ἀφθόνως παραδιδόντες.

I propose the following translation of the passage:

> But that one [the Father], and the Son who came from him and taught us these things and the host of the other good angels that escort him and are being made like him, and the prophetic spirit: [these] do we venerate and worship, paying [them] homage in reason and truth, and passing [them] on just as we have been taught—liberally—to anyone who wishes to learn.

It is important to note Justin's claim to transmit further notions of the Christian faith that he has himself received through teaching: ὡς ἐδιδάχθημεν, ἀφθόνως παραδιδόντες. This phrase would fit very well with the setting of a Christian "school," such as Justin is said to have presided over at Rome, in which such central doctrines were passed on "liberally" (ἀφθόνως) from the teacher to his disciples.[36] In *Dial.* 58.1, Justin refers to himself as a charismatic expositor of the Scriptures, who

---

[34] Goodenough, *Theology of Justin*, 183.
[35] Benoit, *Le baptême chrétien*, 172; Morgan-Wynne, "Holy Spirit and Christian Experience in Justin," 177 n. 7; Bobichon, *Dialogue avec Tryphon*, 729.
[36] For Justin's teaching activity at Rome, see Neymeyr, *Die christlichen Lehrer*, 16–35.

transmits the Christian faith ἀφθόνως: "God's grace alone has been granted to me to the understanding of his Scriptures, of which grace I exhort all to become partakers freely and liberally (ἀφθόνως)." This statement recalls Clement of Alexandria's description of the "Gnostic" teacher.[37]

After these preliminary observations, it is time to address the main difficulty of *Apol.* 1.6.2, namely its inclusion of the angelic host in what might otherwise be a traditional triadic formula.[38] Scholars have proposed several possible interpretations of this text.[39] According to Goodenough, "Justin is listing the divine objects of Christian worship...he puts the entire group of angelic personalities before the Holy Spirit, though in point of rank Justin ordinarily thought of the Spirit as before the other powers."[40] For other scholars, *Apol.* 1.6.2 is, in fact, a traditional "Father, Son, Spirit" formula, in which the angels are nothing but an appendix of sorts, being the Son's "bodyguards."[41] A third opinion, advocated by Kretschmar, is that Justin illustrates here a primitive stage of trinitarian thought, namely "die Trias Gott-Christus-Engel."[42] There is, finally, another view, according to which the Spirit is numbered with the angels, either as one of the angels or as subordinated to the angels.[43]

In my opinion, the phrase "the army of the other angels" is linked not to the Spirit but to the Son. Indeed, for Justin, the Son is "the angel of God" (e.g., *Dial.* 34.2; 61.1; 127.4; 128.1) and the commander-in-chief (ἀρχιστράτηγος) of all angels (*Dial.* 34.2; 61.1; 62.5; 56.22).[44]

---

[37] "As for jealousy (φθόνος δέ)—far be it from the Gnostic! This is actually why he seeks (to determine) whether it be worse to give to the unworthy or not to hand down to the worthy; and out of (so) much love he runs the risk of sharing (knowledge) not only with the person fit (for such teaching), but—as it sometimes happens—also with some unworthy person that entreats him slickly" (*Ecl.* 27.7).

[38] Martín, *Espíritu Santo*, 244.

[39] I follow the classification of scholarly positions offered by Martín, *Espíritu Santo*, 244–50. For early scholarship on this passage, see Barbel, *Christos Angelos*, 51 n. 27.

[40] Goodenough, *Theology of Justin*, 186. Other scholars who hold the same interpretation are mentioned in Martín, *Espíritu Santo*, 245.

[41] Swete, *Holy Spirit*, 37: "the angels find a place on this context as the bodyguards of the Son, reflecting His likeness...." Similarly Barbel, *Christos Angelos*, 62. For the angels as bodyguards of the Son, see Mark 8:38 (cf. 13:26–27; 14:62); Matt 26:53.

[42] Kretschmar, *Trinitätstheologie*, 213.

[43] Benoit, *Le baptême chrétien*, 171. For a critique of this position, see Swete, *The Holy Spirit*, 37; Martín, *Espíritu Santo*, 248–49.

[44] Justin exemplifies the Christian transformation of earlier Michael-traditions (cf. Matt 25:31; 13:41; Mark 13:27). See the exhaustive treatment in Hannah, *Michael and Christ*; for Justin, see esp. 202–5, 215.

Moreover, according to *Dial.* 45.4 the Son and his good angels, who are being made like him (ἐξομοιουμένων) have their evil counterpart in "the serpent that sinned from the beginning and the angels that are made like him (ἐξομοιωθέντες αὐτῷ)."

Nevertheless, the reference to the angels remains problematic because the entire phrase is governed by σεβόμεθα and προσκυνοῦμεν.[45] Justin himself states clearly that God alone is the object of worship and honor.[46] Father, Son, and Spirit are certainly included in Justin's "scalar" exposition of Christian doctrine (see *Apol.* 1.13.3). What about the angels? Martín would like to apply only σεβόμεθα to the angels, and reserve προσκυνοῦμεν for the Father, the Son, and the Spirit.[47] From a grammatical point of view, this proposal does not stand up to scrutiny. Theologically, a better solution can be found by considering Justin's notion of the "powers of the Spirit."

2. JUSTIN MARTYR ON "THE POWERS OF THE SPIRIT"

In *Dial.* 85 Justin maintains, against his Jewish opponents, that Ps 23:7 LXX (*Raise the gates, O rulers of yours! And be raised up, O perpetual gates! And the King of glory shall enter*), applies not to Hezekiah or Solomon, but to Jesus Christ.[48] More specifically, the psalm verse would refer to the ascension of Christ.[49] In Justin's view the reference to "the king of glory" and his superiority to the angelic "princes" can only apply to Jesus Christ because

> Christ alone...is the Lord of the powers (κύριος τῶν δυνάμεων),...who also rose from the dead, and ascended to heaven, as the Psalm and the other Scriptures manifested when they announced him to be *Lord of the powers*....[50]

[45] Barbel, *Christos Angelos*, 53; Stanton, "The Spirit in the Writings of Justin," 329.
[46] *Apol.* 1.16.6; *Dial.* 93.2.
[47] Martín, *Espíritu Santo*, 250.
[48] "Then, too, some of you dare to explain the following words, *Lift up your gates, O you princes, and be lifted up, O eternal gates, that the King of Glory may enter*, as if they referred to Hezekiah, while others of you apply them to Solomon. We can prove, to the contrary, that they are spoken...solely of this Christ of ours" (*Dial.* 85.1).
[49] For early Christian exegesis of Ps 23 (24 as a reference to the ascension of Christ, see Daniélou, *Jewish Christianity*, 259–62.
[50] *Dial.* 85.1.

The identity of Christ as "Lord of the powers" is further demonstrated by Ps 148:1–2, another passage depicting the angelic worship of YHWH:

> The words of David also show that there are angels and powers whom the word of prophecy, through David, ordered to *lift up the gates in order that he* who arose from the dead, Jesus Christ, *the Lord of the powers*, should enter in accordance with the Father's will…Here is the passage from which I showed that God revealed to us that there are angels and powers in heaven: *Praise the Lord from the heavens: praise him in the high places. Praise him, all his angels; praise him, all his powers.*[51]

Justin develops his argument further (*Dial.* 85.2–3) by referring to the practice of exorcism: Christians are able to cast out demons in the name of Christ, while Jewish exorcists are successful only when they invoke the God of Abraham, of Isaac and of Jacob. Implicitly, Justin equates the "Lord" of the Christians with the "Lord" revealed to the patriarchs, according to the biblical narrative.[52]

It is noteworthy that Justin consistently uses κύριος τῶν δυνάμεων, and not κύριος παντοκράτωρ and κύριος σαβαώθ, which are more prevalent in the LXX.[53] According to Oeyen, κύριος τῶν δυνάμεων was a fixed expression, with a precise referent: the "powers." Justin might have been aware, like Origen later on, of a tradition—which Origen ascribes to his famous "Hebrew"—that actually derived the title κύριος σαβαώθ from the class of angelic beings known as the "Sabai."[54]

---

[51] *Dial.* 85.4, 6.

[52] "Whereas, if any man among you should exorcise them [the demons] in the name of the God of Abraham and the God of Isaac and the God of Jacob they will in like manner (ἴσως) become subdued." Bobichon (*Dialogue avec Tryphon*, 417) renders ἴσως by "sans doute." He notes elsewhere (*Dialogue avec Tryphon*, 602 n. 24) that this use of the term is "strange," albeit documented, according to Henri Estienne's *Thesaurus Graecae Linguae* (reprint; Paris: Didot, 1831–1865), in Plato, Aristotle, and Xenophon. I prefer to use the primary sense of the adverb ("equally," "similarly" or "in like manner"), which I understand to be describing the result of Jewish exorcisms, which invoke the name of the God of Abraham, Isaac, and Jacob, as comparable to the results of Christian exorcisms in the name of Christ.

[53] For details, see T. N. D. Mettinger, "YAHWEH Zebaoth," in *Dictionary of Deities and Demons*, 920–24, esp. 920; Staffan Olofsson, *God is My Rock: A Study of Translation Technique and Theological Exegesis in the Septuagint* (ConBOT 30; Stockholm: Almqvist & Wiksell International, 1990), 121–26.

[54] Origen, *Comm. Jo.* 1.31.215 (SC 120:164). Aside from "thrones," "dominions," "rulers," and "powers" (cf. Col 1:16), Origen is convinced that there exist many other heavenly beings, "of which one kind the Hebrew called *Sabai*, from which was formed *Sabaoth*, their ruler, who is no other than God" (ὧν ἕν τι γένος ἐκάλει Σαβαὶ <ὁ>

This tradition about the "powers" is not marginal for Justin's theology, but rather crucially important, since it is related to his theory of prophetic inspiration. The expression κύριος τῶν δυνάμεων, which in *Dial.* 85 is interpreted as a reference to Christ and the subordinated angelic powers, is further connected with the seven gifts of the Spirit in Isa 11: 2–3 (LXX), termed "powers of the Holy Spirit" (*Dial.* 87) or "powers" (*Dial.* 88.1) or even, in the singular, "power" (*Dial.* 88.2). Justin's equation of the "powers" of Christ with the seven "powers of the Holy Spirit" comes in response to the following challenge from Trypho:

> …the Scripture asserts by Isaiah: *There shall come forth a rod from the root of Jesse; and a flower shall grow up from the root of Jesse; and the Spirit of God shall rest upon him, the spirit of wisdom and understanding, the spirit of counsel and might, the spirit of knowledge and piety: and the spirit of the fear of the Lord shall fill him* (Isa 11:1–2). I grant you (he said) that these words are spoken of Christ. But you also maintain that he was preexistent as God…Now, how can He be demonstrated to have been pre-existent, who is filled with the powers of the Holy Spirit, which the Scripture by Isaiah enumerates, as if He were in lack of them?

Here Trypho understands Isa 11:1–3 as a text dealing with the *reception* of the seven "powers of the Holy Spirit," which therefore would exclude Justin's idea of a preexistent "Lord," distinct from the Father and endowed with the "powers." Justin responds by interpreting the Isaiah passage as a reference to the Jordan event: the seven powers of the Spirit rested on Jesus Christ when the Spirit "fluttered down on" him (ἐπιπτῆναι, *Dial.* 88.3) at the Jordan baptism.[55] In reaction most likely to contrary views, Justin insists that Jesus' baptism was a theophany, which did not *create* Christ's identity but *revealed* it to the world.[56] In

---

Ἑβραῖος, παρ᾽ ὃ ἐσχηματίσθαι τὸν Σαβαώθ, ἄρχοντα ἐκείνων τυγχάνοντα, οὐχ ἕτερον τοῦ θεοῦ).

[55] The connection between the sevenfold Spirit of Isa 11:1–3 and the descent of the Spirit at the Jordan Baptism also occurs in Irenaeus, who seems to view it as an element of Church tradition: "Thus the Spirit of God is <active [in] manifold [ways]> (πολύεργος), and seven forms of service were counted by Isaias the prophet resting upon the Son of God, that is [on] the Word in his human advent (παρουσία). For he says, 'The Spirit shall rest upon him…[quotation from Isa 11:2–3]" (Irenaeus, *Epid.* 9).

[56] Cf. John 1:31, ἵνα φανερωθῇ τῷ Ἰσραὴλ; Rev 3:1 ὁ ἔχων τὰ ἑπτὰ πνεύματα τοῦ θεοῦ καὶ τοὺς ἑπτὰ ἀστέρας. In fact, it is the concern about subordinationist interpretations of the Jordan event that explain why, after being an essential article of faith, the baptism of Jesus was eliminated from fourth-century creeds. See Winkler, "A Remarkable Shift in Fourth-Century Creeds: An Analysis of the Armenian, Syriac, and Greek Evidence," *StPatr* 17:3 (1982): 1396–1401. Indeed, while "it is clear from both Ignatius

support of his view, he states that a fire was kindled (πῦρ ἀνήφθη) in the Jordan at the moment of the baptism.[57] For Justin, therefore, Jesus Christ preexisted as bearer of the seven "powers of the Holy Spirit," or, as he had explained earlier, as "Lord of the powers." He is thereby witnessing to the tradition that is echoed, as I have shown earlier, in Revelation, the *Shepherd of Hermas*, and Clement of Alexandria.

This theory of the "powers" proves serviceable for an account of Old Testament prophecy and New Testament charismatic endowment. According to Justin, each of the prophets received "some one or two powers from God": καὶ ὅτι οἱ παρ᾽ὑμῖν προφῆται, ἕκαστος μίαν τινὰ ἢ καὶ δευτέραν δύναμιν παρὰ τοῦ θεοῦ λαμβάνοντες. Thus Solomon had the spirit of wisdom; Daniel, that of understanding and counsel; Moses, that of strength and piety; Elijah, that of fear; Isaiah, that of knowledge.…" The seven powers of the Spirit enumerated by Isaiah were later reassembled in Jesus Christ, "the Lord of the powers" (*Dial.* 87.4). Specifically, the Spirit "ceased" (ἐπαύσατο) from being poured out fragmentarily upon the prophets when it is said to have "rested" (ἀνεπαύσατο) upon him (*Dial.* 87.3) at the Jordan baptism. After his ascension, Christ turns the prophetic powers of the Spirit into various δόματα or χαρίσματα to the Church, thus fulfilling the prophecies of Joel 3:1 (*I shall pour out my Spirit over all flesh*) and Ps 67:19, LXX (*He*

---

of Antioch and Ephrem that early authors used it as a way of speaking of the divine origins of Jesus," it is equally clear that "the baptism of Jesus as a constitutive element in the Creeds did not survive the Christological controversies" (Killian McDonnell, "Jesus' Baptism in the Jordan," *TS* 56 [1995]: 209–36, at 213, 212). See also Robert L. Wilken, "The Interpretation of the Baptism of Jesus in the Later Fathers," *StPatr* 11 (1972): 268–77.

[57] The tradition about fire and light at the Jordan baptism is widespread in early Christianity (e.g., Gospel of the Ebionites, Proclus of Constantinople, Gregory of Nazianzus, Ephrem Syrus, Jacob of Serugh, Philoxenus of Mabbug). See McDonnell, "Jesus' Baptism in the Jordan," 231–32. According to Davies and Allison (*Matthew* 1: 330), "[t]his fire or light also appears in the Old Latin mss a and g' at Mt 3.15 as well as in the Gospel of the Ebionites (Epiphanius, *Haer.* 30.13), Tatian's *Diatessaron*, the Preaching of Paul (so Ps.-Cyprian, *Tractatus de rebaptismate*); *Sib. Or.* 7.82–5; and the Syriac liturgy of Severus." Justin's association of the Jordan event with Isa 11:1–3 naturally leads to the idea that the Spirit "rested" over Christ at his baptism. This also is similar to a tradition preserved in Ephrem's *Commentary on the Diatessaron*: according to what must have been an original Syriac version of John 1:32, the Spirit "descended and *rested*" upon Jesus—rather than "descended and *dwelt*," as all Greek and Syriac witnesses have. It is however not the Syriac version of the *Commentary* that preserves this reading (most probably because later scribes adapted the New Testament quotations to the Peshittā, which here follows the Greek text), but the Armenian translation of the *Commentary*, where the quotation was "frozen" in its original form. For a detailed and extensive argumentation, see Winkler, "Bedeutsamer Zusammenhang."

ascended on high, he led captivity captive, he gave gifts to the sons of men).[58] Here Justin is most likely using a collection of *testimonia.*[59] This pushes the Christian use of Ps 67 (LXX) in connection with Christ's ascension and the giving of spiritual gifts at least one generation prior to Justin. We are not dealing, therefore, as Halperin claims, with a third-century christianization of rabbinic traditions by Origen.[60] Morray-Jones notes, in fact, that "the claim concerning Christ's status...is already implicit in Eph 4:8–12, which quotes Ps 68:19."[61]

It is noteworthy that the gifts of the Spirit received by the Church are also distributed fragmentarily "from the grace of the power of his Spirit to those who believe in him, to each one inasmuch as he deems

---

[58] Δόματα: *Dial.* 39.2, 4, 5; 87.5–6; χαρίσματα: *Dial.* 82.1; 88.1. It may be that Justin's reference to the Spirit as "third in rank" is not necessarily subordinationistic, but rather a way of stating that the gifts of the Spirit became available only *after* the Ascension, that is, chronologically last. See in this respect Stanton, "The Spirit in the Writings of Justin Martyr," 330.

[59] See in this respect Bobichon, *Dialogue avec Tryphon*, 728 n. 2; Oskar Skarsaune, *The Proof From Prophecy: A Study in Justin Martyr's Proof-Text Tradition: Text-Type, Provenance, Theological Profile* (NovTSup 56; Leiden: Brill, 1987), 100, 123; Stanton, "The Spirit in the Writings of Justin Martyr," 330. Justin quotes Ps 67:19 in a form closer to Eph 4:8 than the LXX; his quotation from Joel 3:1 begins as in the LXX (καὶ ἔσται μετὰ ταῦτα) rather than Acts 2:17 (καὶ ἔσται ἐν ταῖς ἐσχάταις ἡμέραις), but then speaks of "my servants," as in Acts 2:18, rather than "servants," as in Joel 3:2. Some of the gifts listed in *Dial.* 39.2, namely "healing," "foreknowledge," and "teaching," echo 1 Corinthians 12, which also explains the shift from δόματα to χαρίσματα. Stanton ("The Spirit in the Writings of Justin Martyr," 332) has no doubt that the three Pauline terms are "woven into the list." Pierre Prigent (*Justin et l'Ancien Testament: L'argumentation scripturaire du traité de Justin contre toutes les hérésies comme source principale du Dialogue avec Tryphon et de la première Apologie* [Paris: Librairie Lecoffre, 1964], 112–13) and Martín (*Espíritu Santo*, 204) are more reserved, although both agree that the loose treatment of Isa 11:2 allows Justin to incorporate certain "réminiscences pauliniennes" into the list of spiritual gifts. Prigent (*Justin et l'Ancien Testament*, 114) shows that Justin's quotation from Ps 67:19 is very close to Eph 4:8, but he denies any influence from Acts 2.

[60] Halperin ("Origen, Ezekiel's Merkabah, and the Ascension of Moses," 269, 271, 272, 275) argues that Origen is reworking a "Shabuot homiletic complex," originally formulated in "a Greek-speaking Jewish community which was within the rabbinic orbit but whose ordinary folk were entirely or almost entirely ignorant of Hebrew." Origen (*Hom. Ezech.* 1; *Hom. Luc.* 27.5; *Comm. Jo.* 6.287–294) would have replaced Moses with Jesus, as the character who ascended to heaven and brought back spiritual gifts, and also expanded the exegetical between Ezek 1:1 and Ps 68:19 to include the Jordan Baptism.

[61] Morray-Jones, "The Temple Within: The Embodied Divine Image and its Worship in the Dead Sea Scrolls and Other Early Jewish and Christian Sources," SBLSP 37 (1998): 413.

him worthy."[62] Although Justin admits a general spiritual endowment of the Christian people, those who are "deemed worthy" seem to represent a particular group within the community, as Justin suggests in the immediately subsequent passage: "now, if you look around, you can see among us Christians both male and female endowed with charismata from the Spirit of God" (*Dial.* 88.1).[63] In fact, in the report of his conversion, Justin seems to present himself as such a charismatic individual.[64] He may have seen himself as especially endowed with the πνεῦμα διδασκαλίας, one of the special gifts mentioned in *Dial.* 39.2.[65]

Trypho finds nothing objectionable in Justin's pneumatology. This is not because "Trypho" would be nothing more than a literary construct of Justin's—a position that Timothy J. Horner has challenged quite convincingly.[66] It seems rather that Justin and Trypho *share a pneumatology*.[67] As a case in point, Justin's interpretation of Isaiah 11 finds its

---

[62] *Dial.* 87.5. Compare ἀπὸ τῆς χάριτος τῆς δυνάμεως τοῦ πνεύματος ἐκείνου...ὡς ἄξιον ἕκαστον ἐπίσταται with the statement about the "powers of the Spirit" received by the prophets: ἕκαστος μίαν τινὰ ἢ καὶ δευτέραν δύναμιν παρὰ τοῦ θεοῦ λαμβάνοντες.

[63] According to Morgan-Wynne ("Holy Spirit and Christian Experience in Justin," 176, 177 n. 13), "it is clear that Justin has in mind particular, specific, and special gifts" and "particular individuals," perhaps Christian exorcists.

[64] After meeting with the mysterious old man, whom certain scholars have argued is none other than Christ (Andrew Hofer, "The Old Man as Christ in Justin *Dialogue with Trypho*," *VC* 57 [2003]: 1–21), "a fire was kindled (πῦρ ἀνήφθη) in my soul"—cf. the fire kindled (πῦρ ἀνήφθη) at the Jordan, accompanied by the Spirit's "fluttering down" (*Dial.* 88.3)—creating in him a passionate, possessive desire "for the prophets, and for those great men who are friends of Christ" (*Dial.* 8.1).

[65] In *Dial.* 119.1, Justin asserts the necessity of grace for the correct understanding of the Scriptures; and in *Dial.* 58.1, he openly presents himself as such a grace-filled exegete: "this grace alone was given me from God to understand his Scriptures, in which grace I invite everyone to share freely and liberally (ἀφθόνως)." The reference to ἀφθόνως places him in line with those from whom he has also received instruction into the Christian faith (see my earlier discussion of ὡς ἐδιδάχθημεν, ἀφθόνως παραδιδόντες in Apol 1.6.2). For Justin's self-understanding as a charismatic *didaskalos*, see Neymeyr, *Die christlichen Lehrer*, 33–34.

[66] Horner, *Listening to Trypho: Justin Martyr's Dialogue Reconsidered* (Biblical Exegesis and Theology 28; Leuven/Paris: Peeters, 2001). This study demonstrates, in my opinion convincingly, that the current *Dialogue*, composed around 155–160 C.E., is an expansion of an older document, dated around 135 C.E., which is very likely to have documented a real encounter between Justin and a well-educated non-Rabbinic Jew from Asia Minor.

[67] Barnes, "Early Christian Binitarianism": "Justin and Trypho regularly refer to the Holy Spirit, neither of them question this terminology, and they both seem to understand what the other means by this term.... Justin and Trypho don't argue over 'Spirit' because they share—in a broad but functional way—a Pneumatology."

counterpart in the ps.-Philonic synagogal homily "On Samson."[68] This text is at pains to explain how it was possible that Samson committed sins even though he was possessed by the Spirit. The argument is that the prophets only received one or the other of the "spirits" mentioned in Isa 11:2. Moving away from the wording of the verse, the homilist gives some examples: Abraham received the spirit of righteousness, Joseph the spirit of self-restraint, Simeon and Levi the spirit of zeal, and Judah the spirit of discernment. As for Samson, he only received "the spirit of strength"—which explains his utter lack of wisdom![69] Despite the fact that "On Samson" enumerates only six spirits in Isa 11:2, the resemblance with Justin is obvious.[70]

Justin's theory of a fragmentary giving of "one or two" powers to the prophets, as opposed to Christ's fullness of the sevenfold Spirit, also parallels the better known distinction between the "fragmentary" manifestation of the Logos to pre-Christian humanity and his "complete" manifestation at the Incarnation.[71] Even though in this particular instance (*Dial.* 85–88) Justin retains the terms of "spirit," "powers," and "Lord of powers"—most likely because they are too traditional to change—he usually "translates" the scriptural references to πνεῦμα into his own theological idiom, which gives preference to λόγος. Such is the case, as noted earlier, in his exegesis of Luke 1:35, where Justin takes the phrase "spirit and power" as a reference to the Logos.

The language of δυνάμεις, δυνάμεις τοῦ πνεύματος, and κύριος τῶν δυνάμεων, and the connection between the seven gifts of the Spirit

---

[68] This homily was most likely composed in Alexandria, in the first century C.E. It survives in a very literal Armenian translation, dated to the early sixth century, alongside the genuine works of Philo. See Folker Siegert, Jacques de Roulet, with Jean-Jacques Aubert and Nicolas Cochand, eds. and trans., *Pseudo-Philon: Prédications synagogales* (SC 345; Paris: Cerf, 1999), 19–20, 38–39, 41; Siegert, ed. and trans., *Drei hellenistisch-jüdische Predigten: Ps.-Philon, "Über Jona", "Über Jona" <Fragment> und "Über Simson"* (WUNT 61; Tübingen: Mohr Siebeck, 1992), 51.

[69] Ps.-Philo, "On Samson," 24.

[70] It should be noted that there are no literary connections between the homily and early Christian literature prior to the Armenian translation (Siegert, *Drei hellenistisch-jüdische Predigten*, 48; Siegert and de Roulet, *Pseudo-Philon*, 38–39).

[71] "Our religion is clearly more sublime than any teaching of man for this reason, that the Christ who has appeared for us men represents the Logos principle in its totality (τὸ λογικὸν τὸ ὅλον), that is, both body, and reason, and soul. For whatever either lawgivers or philosophers uttered well, they elaborated by finding and contemplating some part of the Word (κατὰ Λόγου μέρος)....but in Christ, who was partially (ἀπὸ μέρους) known even by Socrates...not only philosophers and scholars believed, but also artisans and people entirely uneducated" (*Apol.* 2.10.1). For a brief discussion of the topic, see Osborn, *Justin Martyr*, 36–40; Munier, "Introduction," 59–62.

(Isa 11:2–3) and the "powers" are not accidental. I conclude that Justin understands the Old Testament phrase κύριος τῶν δυνάμεων such that the "Lord" is Jesus Christ and the "powers" are, at the same time, certain angelic beings (*Dial.* 85) and the seven "powers of the Spirit" referred to in Isaiah 11 (*Dial.* 87). It is also significant that Justin can easily switch from the plural "Lord of the powers" and "powers of the Spirit" to the singular "power" (*Dial.* 88.2). Assuming that he is not simply collating distinct earlier traditions without any serious attempt at a synthesis, I conclude that the Logos and the Spirit are, for Justin, the same reality, which presents itself in a complex and paradoxical relation of simultaneous unity and multiplicity, and with definite angelomorphic traits.

CONCLUSIONS

Justin is well acquainted with the Christian trinitarian profession of faith. To give an account of the Son, he deploys a christological reading of biblical theophanies, which enables him to proclaim Christ as the "Lord" who appeared to the patriarchs and prophets before being incarnate from the Virgin. To speak about the Spirit, he adopts a variety of approaches, one of which is the adaptation of early Jewish and Christian angelological speculations. More specifically, he identifies the seven gifts of the Spirit (Isa 11:2–3) with a select group of high angelic "powers."

Similarly to Clement of Alexandria, Justin uses angelic imagery to convey his teaching about the Holy Spirit. He is therefore a witness to the early Christian tradition of angelomorphic pneumatology. To paraphrase Martín, angelomorphic pneumatology is one of several "schemes" determining Justin's reflection on the topic.

I have also argued that Justin's angelomorphic pneumatology occurs in tandem with his spirit christology, within a binitarian theological framework. This places Justin in a larger tradition illustrated by texts such as Revelation, the *Shepherd of Hermas*, and Clement of Alexandria's *Excerpta ex Theodoto, Eclogae Propheticae*, and *Adumbrationes*.

PART THREE

A WITNESS FROM THE EAST:
APHRAHAT THE PERSIAN SAGE

CHAPTER SIX

ANGELOMORPHIC PNEUMATOLOGY IN APHRAHAT

INTRODUCTION

So far, I have discussed the occurrence of an angelomorphic pneumatology in Clement of Alexandria and several of his predecessors, namely Revelation, the *Shepherd of Hermas*, and Justin Martyr. In what follows, I shall pursue the occurrence of the "angelic spirit" in the writings of Aphrahat the Persian Sage, a literature "representing Christianity in its most semitic form, still largely free from Greek cultural and theological influences."[1] It is the unanimous judgment of scholars that Aphrahat is "entirely traditional," in the sense that "he transmits the teaching that he received, lays out *testimonia* pertaining to each topic, in order to convince or reassure a reader whose intelligence functions according to this logic of faith."[2] His *Demonstrations* are noted for their "archaism" or "traditionalism," and represent, as has been said, a unique treasure-trove of older exegetical and doctrinal traditions.[3] This is why, even though he flourished in the fourth century, Aphrahat provides invaluable insight into earlier Christian doctrines and practices.

---

[1] Kuriakose Valavanolickal, *Aphrahat: Demonstrations* (Catholic Theological Studies of India 3; Changanassery: HIRS, 1999), 1.

[2] Marie-Joseph Pierre, "Introduction," in *Aphraate Le Sage Persan: Les Exposés* (SC 349; Paris: Cerf, 1988), 66. For the difference between Aphrahat and Ephrem on the issue of "traditionalism," see Robert Murray, "Some Rhetorical Patterns in Early Syriac Literature," in *A Tribute to Arthur Vööbus* (ed. R. H. Fischer; Chicago: The Lutheran School of Theology at Chicago, 1977), 110. Aphrahat represents "an *unicum* in the history of Christian dogma, because his "singularly archaic" christology is "independent of Nicaea and... of the development of Greco-Roman Christology." See Loofs, *Theophilus*, 260; Peter Bruns, trans., *Aphrahat: Unterweisungen* (FC 5/1; Freiburg: Herder, 1991), 208–9; Ortiz de Urbina, "Die Gottheit Christi bei Aphrahat," *OCP* 31 (1933): 5, 22. More recently, William L. Petersen argued the same thesis, even though his views of Aphrahat's christology are quite different: Aphrahat is "untouched by the Hellenistic world and Nicaea"; he represents a subordinationist christology, which is the "Christology confessed by early Syrian Christians, a relic inherited from primitive Semitic or Judaic Christianity" ("The Christology of Aphrahat, the Persian Sage: An Excursus on the 17th *Demonstration*," *VC* 46 [1992]: 241, 251).

[3] Arthur Vööbus, "Methodologisches zum Studium der Anweisungen Aphrahats," *OrChr* 46 (1962): 32.

Aphrahat's pneumatology has not been a neglected topic in scholarship. The pioneering studies by Loofs and Ignatius Ortiz de Urbina, which to this day remain indispensable for the study of Aphrahat's christology, contain much material of pneumatological relevance.[4] The above-mentioned study by Fredrikson on the opposition between the good and the evil spirits in the *Shepherd of Hermas* also discusses Aphrahat's treatment of this topic.[5] Winfrid Cramer's book on early Syriac pneumatology dedicates some thirty pages to Aphrahat, which were hailed as "the most thorough and…without doubt the best study on this aspect of Aphrahat's theology."[6] More recently, Stephanie K. Skoyles Jarkins makes some valuable observations on the Sage, including his views on the Holy Spirit.[7]

In what follows I shall take my cue from a critique of Aphrahat's pneumatology contained in a seventh-century letter addressed by George, the monophysite bishop of the Arabs, to a certain hieromonk Išo.[8] The third chapter of this epistle bears the following title: "Third Chapter, concerning that which the Persian writer also said, that, when people die, the animal spirit (ܪܘܚܐ ܢܦܫܢܝܬܐ = τὸ πνεῦμα τὸ ψυχικόν) is buried in the body, being [lit. "which (= the animal spirit) is"] unconscious."[9] It is not, however, the sleep of the soul in Syriac tradition (a topic already treated in scholarship) that I intend to discuss

---

[4] Loofs, *Theophilus*, 257–99: "Die trinitarischen und christologischen Anschauungen des Afraates"; Ortiz de Urbina, "Die Gottheit Christi bei Aphrahat," esp. 124–38: "Der göttliche Geist der in Christus wohnt." See also Francesco Pericoli Ridolfini, "Problema trinitario e problema cristologico nelle 'Dimostrazioni' del 'Sapiente Persiano,'" *SROC* 2 (1979): 99–125, esp. 109–10, 120–21.

[5] Fredrikson, "L'Esprit Saint et les esprits mauvais," esp. 273–75.

[6] Cramer, *Der Geist Gottes und des Menschen in frühsyricher Theologie* (MBT 46; Münster: Aschendorff, 1979), 59–85; see Robert Murray's review in *JTS* n.s. 32 (1981): 260–61.

[7] Skoyles Jarkins, *Aphrahat the Persian Sage and the Temple of God: A Study of Early Syriac Theological Anthropology* (Piscataway, NJ: Gorgias, 2008), 55–57, 122–37.

[8] *Georgii Arabum episcopi epistula*, in *Analecta Syriaca* (ed. Paul Lagarde; Osnabrück: Otto Zeller, 1967 [1858]), 108–34. George became bishop of Akoula in 686 and died in 724. He translated Aristotle's *Organon*, composed a treatise "On the Sacraments of the Church," wrote scholia on the Scriptures and Gregory of Nazianzus, and brought to completion Jacob of Edessa's *Hexaemeron*. His long epistle to Išo, dated 714–718, is part of a rich epistolary activity. See William Wright, *A Short History of Syriac Literature* (Piscataway, NJ: Gorgias, 2001 [1887]), 156–59); Anton Baumstark, *Geschichte der syrischen Literatur mit Ausschluss der christlich-palästinensischen Texte* (Berlin: de Gruyter, 1968 [1922]), 257–58.

[9] Lagarde, *Analecta Syriaca*, 117.4–6.

here.[10] I shall rather expand upon a remark in bishop George's letter, and argue that Aphrahat offers a valuable witness to the early Christian phenomenon discussed above in reference to Clement of Alexandria, namely the exegesis of Zech 3:9, Isa 11:2–3, and Matt 18:10 in support of an angelomorphic pneumatology. Finally, I shall integrate Aphrahat's angelomorphic pneumatology within the larger theological framework described by earlier scholarship, that is, in relation to spirit christology, and within a theological framework of marked binitarian character.

1. APHRAHAT'S VIEWS: "MANY ABERRATIONS AND VERY CRASS STATEMENTS"

According to the seventh-century Bishop George of the Arabs, one should not waste much sleep over the writings of the "Persian Sage."[11] This otherwise unknown writer cannot have been Ephrem's disciple, he says, because the character [ܩܠܐ = εἰκών] of his teaching is unlike that of Mār Ephrem's.[12] Indeed, Aphrahat is "not among those who confessed the approved teachings (ܬܘܕܝܬܐ ܬܪܝܨܬܐ) of the teachers that were approved."[13] His writings contain "many aberrations and very crass statements."[14]

Clearly, Bishop George does not think very highly of the Persian Sage. His addressee, on the other hand, has read the *Demonstrations* front to back, and is most likely an admirer of Aphrahat's. This is why the bishop proceeds with caution: he concedes that the Persian writer was of a "sharp nature," and that he studied (lit. "ploughed") the Scriptures

---

[10] In fact, "there is hardly any feature of the teaching of Aphrahat which has occasioned so universal comment" (Frank Gavin, "The Sleep of the Soul in the Early Syriac Church," *JAOS* 40 [1920]: 104). See also Marie-Joseph Pierre, "Introduction," in *Aphraate le Sage Persan: Les Exposés*, 1:191–99; Ridolfini, "Note sull'antropologia e sul' escatologia del 'Sapiente Persiano,'" *SROC* 1/1 (1978): 5–17. See also Nicholas Constas, "An Apology for the Cult of Saints in Late Antiquity: Eustratius Presbyter of Constantinople, On the State of Souls after Death (CPG 7522)," *JECS* 10 (2002): 267–85.

[11] "It befits your Fraternity's wisdom not to consider or number that man, the Persian writer, among the approved writers, and [his writings] among the writings that are approved, so as to wear yourself out with questions and become clouded over in your mind in order to make sense of and understand the import of all the words written in the book of the *Demonstrations*" (Lagarde, *Analecta Syriaca*, 117.18–22).

[12] ܠܐ ܓܝܪ ܩܠܐ ܕܠܐܝܟܝܘܬܗ ܕܡܢ ܬܠܡܝܕܘ ܘܡܢ ܐܦܪܝܡ (Lagarde, *Analecta Syriaca*, 111.1–2).

[13] Lagarde, *Analecta Syriaca*, 117.24–25.

[14] ܣܓܝܐ ܦܗ̈ܝܐ ܘܡ̈ܠܐ ܕܝܬܝܪ ܥܒ̈ܝܢ (Lagarde, *Analecta Syriaca*, 117.27–28).

with great diligence. Some of the flaws, such as, for instance, the grave misunderstanding of Pauline statements in 1 Corinthians 15, might be due to the fact that Aphrahat did not have access to correct versions of the Scriptures.[15] Or perhaps, in his time and place, he did not have the possibility "to apply himself (ܡܣܝܡ ܠܟܡ) and conform his opinions (ܘܢܣܝܒ)" to the teachings of more trustworthy writers.[16]

At one point, however, Bishop George seems to have run out of sugarcoating, for he bluntly states that Aphrahat's views about the Holy Spirit are both stupid and blasphemous. Just as the ideas about the animal spirit are an example of "crassness and boorish ignorance (ܕܚܣܝܪܘܬ ܘܠܐ ܒܠܝܠܘܬ ܘܩܪܝܘܬܐ)," so also are those statements that seem to equate the Holy Spirit with the angels:

> You see, my brother, the crassness of the conceptions (ܥܘܒܝܘܬ ܪܥܝܢܐ); what sort of honor they ascribe to the Holy Spirit; how he understands the angels of the believers, of whom our Lord has said that they always see the face of his Father. He also holds this opinion in that which he says towards the end of the *Demonstration* On the Resurrection of the Dead.[17]

Bishop George refers, first, to *Dem.* 6.15, where, as I shall show later, Aphrahat uses Matt 18:10 to illustrate the intercessory activity of the Holy Spirit. "The crassness of the conceptions" (ܥܘܒܝܘܬ ܪܥܝܢܐ) does not refer to words or expressions but to Aphrahat's notion of the Holy Spirit as interceding like an angel, and the underlying exegesis of Matt 18:10.

The second reference is most likely to *Dem.* 8.23 (I/404), a text using the same imagery of the Spirit as intercessor before the throne of God, albeit without the reference to Matt 18:10. Bishop George's point is that Aphrahat's bothersome connection between the angels of Matt 18:10 and the Holy Spirit was not a slip of the pen, due to lack of attention or doctrinal vigilance, but rather a case of repeated, consistent, and therefore characteristic "crassness and boorish ignorance."

---

[15] Lagarde, *Analecta Syriaca*, 118.1–12.

[16] Lagarde, *Analecta Syriaca*, 117.26–27. This, of course, does not mean that Aphrahat should be "excused" for some of his views on grounds that he represents an earlier stage of theological reflection. Such an interpretation would reflect the mindset of modern Patristics more than the mind of patristic authors. The bishop's note about the difficult circumstances of Aphrahat is rather a rhetorical maneuver designed to pacify those fond of Aphrahat.

[17] Lagarde, *Analecta Syriaca*, 119.10; 120.2–6.

So much for the reception of the Sage's pneumatology by the guardians of later orthodoxy. Needless to say, the advice not to waste much time over the Persian Sage offers just the right incentive for us to start looking more closely at Aphrahat, and specifically at the passages that caused the most outrage.

2. The Seven Operations of the Spirit are Six

The following passage occurs in Aphrahat's first *Demonstration*:

> And concerning this Stone he stated and showed: *on this stone, behold, I open seven eyes* [Zech 3:9]. And what are the seven eyes opened on the stone other than the Spirit of God that dwelt (ܕܚܝܬ) upon Christ with seven operations (ܣܘܥܪ̈ܢܝܢ)? As Isaiah the prophet said, *There will rest* (ܘܬܬܢܝܚ) *and dwell* (ܘܬܫܪܐ) *upon him God's Spirit of wisdom and of understanding and of counsel and of courage, and of knowledge, and of the fear of the Lord* (Isa 11:2–3). These are the seven eyes that were opened upon the stone (Zech 3:9), and *these are the seven eyes of the Lord which look upon all the earth* (Zech 4:10).[18]

Aphrahat combines Isaiah's seven gifts of the Spirit with Zechariah's seven eyes on the stone (Zech 3:9), and "the eyes of the LORD [i.e., his angelic servants], which look upon all the earth" (Zech 4:10). Isaiah 11:2 is quoted in a distinctly Syriac form, with an additional verb (*šrā*) complementing the single "to rest" in the Hebrew and Greek.[19] Nothing

---

[18] Aphrahat, *Dem.* 1.9 (I/20). The numbers between square brackets indicate volume and page in Jean Parisot, ed., *Aphraatis Sapientis Persae Demonstrationes* (PS I; Paris: Firmin-Didot, 1894).

[19] Aside from Isa 11:2, *šrā* is used in the OT, in passages describing the Spirit's intimate relationship with certain individuals (Num 11:26; 2 Kgs 2:15; 2 Chr 15:1; 20:14). In the NT, it is not used in this sense. *Šrā* as "indwelling" occurs, however, in the invocations of the Holy Spirit over baptismal water, the eucharistic elements, or the baptismal oil, in the *Acts of Thomas* (chs. 27, 133, 156, 157), and in later patristic quotations from and allusions to Luke 1:35. After examining the divergence between the use of *aggen 'al-* in all Syriac versions of Luke 1:35, and the use of *šrā b-* for the same verse in Ephrem and Philoxenus, Sebastian Brock ("The Lost Old Syriac at Luke 1:35 and the Earliest Syriac Terms for the Incarnation," in *Gospel Traditions in the Second Century: Origins, Recensions, Text, and Transmission* [ed. W. Petersen; Notre Dame, Ind.: University of Notre Dame Press, 1989], 117–31) concluded that *šrā b-* does not reflect the lost Old Syriac of Luke 1:35 but rather a Jewish Aramaic background to the *oral* Syriac kerygma. Columba Stewart (*"Working the Earth of the Heart": The Messalian Controversy in History, Texts, and Language to A.D. 431* [Oxford Theological Monographs; Oxford: Clarendon, 1991], 212) also thinks that the occurrence of *šrā* in later authors, such as Aphrahat or Ephrem, points to "a common liturgical or catechetical source."

extraordinary here; except that, on closer examination, Aphrahat's "seven operations" of the Spirit are only six: wisdom, understanding, counsel, courage, knowledge, and fear of the Lord![20]

Neither the Hebrew of Isa 11:2–3 (whether MT or the *Great Isaiah Scroll* at Qumran), nor the Peshittā, nor the Syriac quoted by Aphrahat, nor the Targum Jonathan, mention a seventh "spirit" at Isa 11:3.[21] While the messianic interpretation of Isa 11:1–2 is not unknown in rabbinic Judaism,[22] the use of this verse to support the notion of the *sevenfold* spirit resting on the Messiah seems absent from both Second Temple apocalyptic writings and rabbinic literature.[23]

It is noteworthy that, similar to "On Samson" 24, which enumerates six spirits by referring to the "fear of the Lord" only once, as πνεῦμα φόβου θεοῦ, the *Midrash Rabbah* uses Isa 11:2 in a speculation about the *six* spirits on the Messiah.[24] This seems to be a Jewish precursor of

---

[20] Schlütz (*Isaias 11:2*, 35) thinks that Aphrahat might have counted "the Spirit of God" as one of the seven gifts of the Spirit. I find this very unlikely. First, Aphrahat speaks about two terms: the Spirit and the seven operations of the Spirit. Second, there is an obvious parallelism between "the Spirit of God that abode on Christ with seven operations," and the immediately following proof text from Isa 11:2–3: *The Spirit of God shall rest and dwell upon him*, followed by the "seven" (in reality six) gifts of the Spirit. Finally, all patristic writers who echo this tradition count, without exception, *seven* gifts of the Spirit as distinct from "the Spirit of God."

[21] Schlütz (*Isaias 11:2*, 2–11) provides a detailed treatment of the versions and their relationship. For Qumran, I have consulted *The Dead Sea Scrolls Bible* (ed. M. Abegg Jr., P. Flint, E. Ulrich; San Francisco, Calif.: HarperSanFrancisco, 1999); for *Tg. Isa.* 11:2–3, see John F. Stenning, ed., *The Targum of Isaiah* (Oxford: Clarendon, 1949), 41.

[22] See references in Bobichon, *Justin Martyr*, 803 n. 4.

[23] Schlütz, *Isaias 11:2*, 8. In *1 En.* 61.11 the sevenfold angelic praise is said to rise up "in the spirit of faith, in the spirit of wisdom and patience, in the spirit of mercy, in the spirit of justice and peace, and in the spirit of generosity." Yet, as Schlütz (*Isaias 11:2*, 20) notes, this is in no way connected to Isa. 11:2–3. Moreover, in *1 En.* 49.3 the Spirit resting over the coming Messiah is fivefold: "In him dwells the spirit of wisdom, the spirit which gives thoughtfulness, the spirit of knowledge and strength, and the spirit of those who have fallen asleep in righteousness" (*OTP* 1.36). The numerous patristic references to Isaiah 11 and the Holy Spirit adduced by Schlütz have no counterpart in the rabbinic literature surveyed by Peter Schäfer, in his work *Die Vorstellung vom Heiligen Geist in der rabbinischen Literatur* (SANT 28; Munich: Kösel, 1972).

[24] "Furthermore, in connection with the offering of Nahshon of the tribe of Judah it is written, And his offering was one silver dish (Num 7:13); whereas in connection with all the others it states, 'his offering.' Thus a *waw* was added to Nahshon, hinting that six righteous men would come forth from his tribe, each of whom was blessed with six virtues. [Next, the text enumerates David, the three youths, Hezekiah, and Daniel, each of which are shown to have been endowed with six virtues]. Finally, of the royal Messiah it is written, *And the spirit of the Lord shall rest upon him, the spirit of wisdom and understanding, the spirit of counsel and might, the spirit of knowledge and of the fear of the Lord* (Isa 11:2)" (*Gen. Rab.* 97; English version from *Midrash Rabbah*:

the idea of seven spirits resting on the Messiah in Isa 11:2–3, universally disseminated among Christian writers, which opens up the possibility of combining this text with Zech 3:9 and 4:10.[25] It is the very strong Christian tradition about the seven spirits resting on the Messiah that functions as Aphrahat's hermeneutical presupposition, allowing him to speak of seven operations of the Spirit, even though his biblical text only mentions six.[26]

3. "The Spirit is not always found with those that receive it..."

I now move to a text that provoked Bishop George's outrage.

> Anyone who has preserved the Spirit of Christ in purity: when it [the Spirit] goes to him [Christ], it [the Spirit] speaks to him thus: *the body to which I went and which put me on* [ܠܒܫܬ] *in the waters of baptism, has preserved me in holiness.* And the Holy Spirit entreats [ܡܦܝܣܐ] Christ for the resurrection of the body that preserved it in a pure manner.... And anyone who receives the Spirit from the waters [of baptism] and wearies [ܘܡܐܢ] it: it [the Spirit] departs from that person...and goes to its nature, [namely] unto Christ, and accuses that man of having grieved it... And, indeed, my beloved, this Spirit, which the Prophets have received, and which we, too, have received, is not at all times found with those that receive it; rather it sometimes goes to him that sent it, and sometimes it goes to him that received it. Hearken to that which our Lord said, *Do not despise any one of these little ones that believe in me, for their angels in heaven always gaze on the face of my Father.* Indeed, this Spirit is at all times on the move [ܐܝܬ ܒܡܗܠܟܐ], and stands before God and beholds his face; and it will accuse before God whomsoever injures the temple in which it dwells.[27]

These passages are usually discussed in reference to Aphrahat's doctrine of "the sleep of the soul" and his distinction between the "animal spirit"

Genesis [tr. H. Freedman; London: Soncino, 1983], 2:902. According to Siegert, this text constitutes an exception, inasmuch as the Rabbis had ceased to use Isa 11:2.

[25] For the patristic exegesis of the passage, see Schlütz, *Isaias 11:2*, passim. Siegert (*Drei hellenistisch-jüdische Predigten*, 2:275) refers to the homily's use of Isa 11:2 as "eine jüdische Vorstufe" to the Christian tradition.

[26] The Vulgate of Isa 11:2–3 also follows the Greek, and Jerome's attachment to the tradition of the seven spirits resting on the Messiah is evident in his commentaries (*Comm. Isa.* 4.11; *Comm. Zach.* 1.3; *Comm. Job* 38.31; 41). For details, see Schlütz, *Isaias 11:2*, 16.

[27] Aphrahat, *Dem.* 6.14–15 (I/293, 296, 297).

(ܪܕܗܠܪܘܝ ܪܘܐܝ) that slumbers in the grave with the body and the "holy spirit" (ܪܬܝܐܘܫ ܪܘܐܝ)—or "heavenly spirit" (ܪܕܗܠܝܙܪ ܪܘܐܝ), or "spirit of Christ" (ܪܗܠܪܫܘܫ ܪܘܐܝ)—which clothes "the spirituals" (ܪܠܘܐܝ = οἱ πνευματικοί) at baptism and later returns "to its nature, unto Christ."[28]

One must not lose sight, however, of the fact that the passage is part of the *Demonstration* "On the Sons of the Covenant," and that Aphrahat argues here one of the axioms of his ascetic theory, namely that the Holy Spirit departs from a sinful person and goes to accuse that person before the throne of God. According to the Sage, Christians receive the Spirit at Baptism. If one keeps the Spirit in purity, the latter will advocate for that person before the throne of God; if, on the contrary, one indulges in sinful behavior, the Spirit leaves the house of the soul—which allows the adversary to break in and occupy it (*Dem.* 6.17)—and goes to accuse the person before God.[29]

Indication that this is an inherited tradition can be found in the striking similarities with the *Shepherd of Hermas*.[30] There are, however, no Syriac manuscripts of the *Shepherd*, and no references to this work among Syriac writers.[31] Fredrikson raises the hypothesis of a common source behind both Aphrahat and the *Shepherd*, a source whose views of spiritual dualism and divine indwelling would have been similar to

---

[28] Bishop George is the first to ponder these questions. He does so in his usual dismissive style: "And there is also another thing that he said, that, as soon as people die, the holy spirit, which people receive when they are baptized, goes to its nature, [namely] to Christ. And that which goes to the Lord is the Spirit of Christ; since I do not know what he understands by 'to our Lord' other than Christ. Now, this is crassness and boorish ignorance" (Lagarde, *Analecta Syriaca*, 119.6–10).

[29] According to Skoyles Jarkins (*Aphrahat and the Temple of God*, 129), "[t]he Spirit may be either, as it were, a defense lawyer or a prosecuting attorney before the tribunal of the Lord." Cf. Pierre, *Aphraate le Sage Persan*, 402 n. 93: "L'Esprit saint est à la fois intercesseur et procureur."

[30] According to the *Shepherd*, the πνεῦμα inhabits the believer (Herm. *Mand.* 10.2.5) and, under normal circumstances, intercedes *on behalf* of that person. Yet, the *Shepherd* warns that the Holy Spirit is easily grieved and driven away by sadness (Herm. *Mand.* 10.1.3; 10.2.1); in such a case he will depart and intercede to God *against* the person (Herm. *Mand.* 10.41.5).

[31] Leutzsch, *Papiasfragmente. Hirt des Hermas*, 120–21. According to Baumstark (*Geschichte der syrischen Literatur*), 75–77, the pre-Nicene writers translated into Syriac starting with the early decades of the fifth century—that is, decades after Aphrahat—are Ignatius, Clement of Rome, Barnabas, Aristides, Gregory Thaumaturgs, Hippolytus, and Eusebius of Caesarea. Meanwhile, "Hermas, Justin, Irenaeus, Clement of Alexandria and Origen are conspicuous by their absence" (Brock, "The Syriac Background to the World of Theodore of Tarsus," in his volume *From Ephrem to Romanos* [Aldershot/Brookfield/Singapore/Sydney: Ashgate Variorum, 1999], 37).

that of the Community Rule at Qumran.[32] We should consider the idea of a massive Palestinian-Syriac cluster of ascetic vocabulary and imagery, passed on by the earliest Christian missionaries to communities in Syria and Alexandria.[33] In fact, there is good reason to suppose that early Christian asceticism originated with Jesus himself.[34]

For Aphrahat, then, the notion that the Spirit can be present in the believer, and subsequently leave, being driven away by evil spirits, was part of a traditional ascetic theory. In the course of the Messalian controversy this view became highly controversial. Most significant in this respect is the treatise *On the Inhabitation of the Holy Spirit* composed by Philoxenus of Mabbug (+ 523) with the express aim of showing that "the Holy Spirit whom, by the grace of God, we have received from the waters of baptism at the moment when we were baptized, we did not receive so that he would sometimes remain with us and some other times abide afar from us...."[35] According to Philoxenus, the Spirit "does not flee from the soul in which he dwelled at the moment of sin and return when it would repent, as was the assertion of one who blurted out stupidly."[36]

---

[32] Fredrikson, "L'Esprit saint et les esprits mauvais," 273, 277, 278. Cf. also the older studies by Pierre Audet ("Affinités littéraires et doctrinales du Manuel de Discipline," *RB* 59 [1953]: 218–38; 60 [1953]: 41–82), and A. T. Hanson ("Hodayoth vi and viii and Hermas Herm. *Sim.* VIII," *StPatr* 10 [1970]/ TU 107: 105–8). The similarities between Aphrahat's ascetic theology and the Qumran documents have been further investigated in Golitzin's ample study entitled "Recovering the 'Glory of Adam': 'Divine Light' Traditions in the Dead Sea Scrolls and the Christian Ascetical Literature of Fourth-Century Syro-Mesopotamia," published in *The Dead Sea Scrolls as Background to Postbiblical Judaism and Early Christianity: Papers from an International Conference at St. Andrews in 2001* (ed. J. R. Davila; STDJ 46; Leiden: Brill, 2003), 275–308.

[33] A fresh and compelling view has been proposed recently by DeConick, *Recovering The Original Gospel of Thomas: A History of The Gospel And Its Growth* (LNTS 286; Edinburgh: T&T Clark, 2005), 236–41. See also Kretschmar, "Ein Beitrag zur Frage nach dem Ursprung frühchristlicher Askese," *ZTK* 64 (1961): 27–67; Peter Nagel, *Die Motivierung der Askese in der alten Kirche und der Ursprung des Mönchtums* (TU 95; Berlin: Akademie Verlag 1966); Murray, "An Exhortation to Candidates for Ascetical Vows at Baptism in the Ancient Syriac Church," *NTS* 21 (1974): 59–80; idem, "The Features of the Earliest Christian Asceticism," in *Christian Spirituality: Essays in Honour of E. G. Rupp* (ed. P. Brooks; London: SCM, 1975), 65–77.

[34] See the extensive argumentation in Allison, *Jesus of Nazareth: Millenarian Prophet* (Minneapolis, Minn.: Fortress, 1998), 172–216.

[35] ܠܐ (Antoine Tanghe, "Memra de Philoxène de Mabboug sur l'inhabitation du Saint-Esprit," *Mus* 73 [1960], 43).

[36] ܐܝܟ (Tanghe, "Memra de Philoxène," 50). The doctrine attacked here is abundantly illustrated by Aphrahat and the *Liber Graduum*. Could the author whose explanations Philoxenus finds awkward or idiotic

It is noteworthy, however, that even while he writes to dismantle the
ascetic theories espoused in the *Demonstrations*, Philoxenus continues
to use the very same imagery and biblical passages (albeit to opposite
ends), thus confirming the traditional character and widespread appeal
of the theology set forth by the Sage.[37]

What seems to have been overlooked is the intimate link between
Aphrahat's notion of the Spirit departing to intercede for or against
the believer, on the one hand, and the angelomorphic representation of the Holy Spirit, on the other. Indeed, Aphrahat describes the
work of the Holy Spirit in unmistakably angelic imagery: the Spirit "is
always on the move," he stands before the divine throne, beholds the
Face of God, entreats Christ on behalf of the worthy ascetics, accuses
the unworthy, etc. It is significant that the action of carrying prayers
from earth to the throne of God is sometimes ascribed to the archangel Gabriel.[38] This is again similar to the *Shepherd* (Herm. *Sim.* 8.2.5),
where the archangel Michael states that, in addition to the inspection
of the believers' good deeds by one of his angelic subordinates, he will
personally test every soul again, at the heavenly altar (ἐγὼ αὐτοὺς ἐπὶ
τὸ θυσιαστήριον δοκιμάσω). Both Aphrahat and the *Shepherd* deploy
the traditional imagery of angels carrying up the prayer of humans to
the heavenly altar.

In the case of Aphrahat, the angelomorphic element is even more
pronounced, given that the Spirit's toing-and-froing between earth
and heaven, and his intercession before the divine throne, are "documented" with an unlikely proof-text, namely Matt 18:10 ("their angels
in heaven always behold the face of my Father"). In his commentary on
the Diatessaron, Ephrem Syrus interprets "the angels of the little ones"

(ܕܐܝܬܘܗܝ, derived from ἰδιωτεία) be Aphrahat? The connection with Bishop
George's verdict of "crassness and boorish ignorance" is tempting.

[37] Particularly striking is his description of the "mechanics" of temptation and sin
(Tanghe, "Memra de Philoxène," 50). When tempted by sin, the believer's conscience
has a choice of accepting or rejecting the inner admonition coming from the Holy Spirit.
If the admonition is accepted, the believer will refrain from sinning, and will be filled
with light and joy from the Spirit. In the opposite case, even though the Spirit does not
leave, the house of the soul becomes dim and is filled with smoke and sadness.

[38] "You who pray should remember that you are making an offering before God:
let not Gabriel who presents the prayers be ashamed by an offering that has a blemish...In such a case...Gabriel, who presents prayers, does not want to take it from
earth because, on inspection, he has found a blemish in your offering...he will say to
you: *I shall not bring your unclean offering before the sacred throne*" (*Dem.* 4.13; trans.
Brock, in his *The Syriac Fathers on Prayer and the Spiritual Life* [Kalamazoo, Mich.:
Cistercian Publications, 1987], 17–18, 19).

as a metaphor for the prayers of the believers, which reach up to the highest heavens. Later Syriac authors (Jacob of Edessa, Išodad of Merv, Dionysius Bar Salibi) use Matt 18:10 as a proof-text for the existence of guardian angels.[39] For Aphrahat, however, the angels of Matt 18:10 illustrate the intercessory activity *of the Holy Spirit.*

4. An Older Exegetical Tradition

Cramer versus Kretschmar

Scholars disagree on how the data presented above are to be interpreted. According to Kretschmar, Aphrahat does not distinguish clearly between the guardian angel, the many (angelic) spirits, and the one Spirit of God; neither does he distinguish between "spirit" as impersonal gift and "spirit" as a personal angel. The Sage's use of Matt 18:10 would be an instance in which the Spirit is placed on the same level as the angels: "der Geist [wird] also mit den Engeln gleichgesetzt."[40]

Cramer reacted sharply, asserting that Kretschmar had completely misunderstood the relevant texts and misrepresented Aphrahat's thought by means of infelicitous formulations, which led to further unwarranted and aberrant conjectures.[41] In his view, the equation between angels and the Spirit is improbable, because Aphrahat never uses ܪܘܚܐ for angelic entities; moreover, the Sage does not use Matt 18:10 in a literal sense, but rather understands "the angels of the little ones" as a metaphorical expression for the Spirit.[42]

I agree with some elements in Cramer's critique, but disagree with much of what he affirms. Kretschmar's association with the guardian angel is indeed textually unfounded, although the confusion is perhaps understandable.[43] An earlier scholar of Aphrahat, Paul Schwen,

---

[39] Cramer, "Mt 18, 10 in frühsyrischer Deutung," *OrChr* 59 (1975): 130–46.

[40] Kretschmar, *Trinitätstheologie*, 75, 76, 119.

[41] "Daß man Aphrahat...völlig mißverstehen kann, zeigt Kretschmar...." (Cramer, *Geist Gottes*, 81 n. 65); " Kretschmar...sieht die Beziehung zwischen *ruḥā* und *malakē*, formuliert aber unglücklich.... Daß Kretschmar die Engel, die—nach seiner Meinung— dem Geist gleichgesetzt werden, außerdem noch unbegründet als Schutzengel versteht, führt ihn dann zu abwegigen Kombinationen" (Cramer, "Mt 18, 10 in frühsyrischer Deutung," 132 n. 8).

[42] Cramer, Geist Gottes, 60 n. 3; "Mt 18, 10 in frühsyrischer Deutung," 132.

[43] Aphrahat draws a connection between the angels of Matt 18:10 and the Holy Spirit, but does not refer to the guardian angel. This was already noted by Loofs (*Theophilus*, 270 n. 3). Other patristic writers use Matt 18:10 as a proof-text for the existence of

proceeds with more caution, writing that the notion of the guardian angel contributes occasionally to Aphrahat's "hesitant and inconsistent" pneumatology.[44] It is also true that a simple "Gleichstellung" of the Holy Spirit with the angels, as in Kretschmar's formulation, does not account for the complexity of the Sage's thought. More precisely, even though *Dem.* 6 uses the angels of Matt 18:10 to illustrate the intercessory activity *of the Holy Spirit*, this is neither the only way in which Aphrahat interprets Matt 18:10, nor the only image he uses for the Holy Spirit.[45]

I doubt, however, that Cramer's use of the phrases "literal sense," "proper sense," and "metaphorical expression" is any more felicitous or appropriate for describing Aphrahat's exegesis. After all, the Sage's statements about the Spirit were later deemed scandalous precisely because of their handling of "the angels of the believers" in Matt 18:10 and "the sort of honor they ascribed to the Holy Spirit." At least in the eyes of Bishop George, the problem was that Aphrahat interpreted the angels of the little ones quite "properly" and "literally," to use Cramer's words, as the Holy Spirit. As for the argument that Aphrahat did not call angels "spirits," the widespread occurrence of the "angelic spirit" (in the Hebrew Bible, the LXX, the Dead Sea Scrolls, various authors of the Alexandrian diaspora, and the New Testament), which I have mentioned repeatedly in this study, suggests the existence of a tradition that the Sage would have considered authoritative. Whether the *Demonstrations* explicitly call angels "spirits" becomes irrelevant.

---

guardian angels, but make no reference to the Spirit (e.g., Basil, *Eun.* 3.1; Cramer's article also refers to later Syriac authors: Jacob of Edessa, Išodad of Merv, Dionysius Bar Salibi). Finally, in Valentinian quarters (and later in certain strands of Islam), the guardian angel seems to have been identified as the Holy Spirit—but with no reference to Matt 18:10. See Quispel, "Das ewige Ebenbild des Menschen: Zur Begegnung mit dem Selbst in der Gnosis," in *Gnostic Studies* I, esp. 147–57; Henry Corbin, *L'Ange et l'homme* (Paris: Albin Michel, 1978), 64–65; idem, *L'archange empourpré: quinze traités et récits mystiques de Shihâboddîn Yahyâ Sohravardî.* Traduits du persan et de l'arabe, présentés et annotés par Henry Corbin (Paris: Fayard, 1976), xviii–xix, 215 n. 9, 224, 258 n. 7.

[44] Paul Schwen, *Afrahat: Seine Person und sein Verständnis des Christentums* (Berlin: Trowitz & Sohn, 1907), 91: "so daß schließlich die Vorstellung des Schutzengels hineinspielt."

[45] In *Dem.* 2.20, a loose combination of Matt 18:3 and Matt 18:10 is used to exhort the readers to not despise the little ones, whose angels in heaven behold the Father. See Cramer, "Mt 18, 10 in frühsyrischer Deutung," 130–31. As Cramer shows, Aphrahat also views the Spirit as God's "spouse," as "mother" of the Son and of all creation, as "medicine," and as the "breath" constituting the divine image imparted to Adam.

It is interesting that Cramer is ready to speak of "anthropomorphic traits" in Aphrahat's depiction of the Spirit's eschatological actions.[46] The imagery of the relevant passage (*Dem*. 6.14 [I/296]), however, is clearly angelomorphic rather than anthropomorphic: the end-time ministry of the Spirit includes going before Christ, opening the graves, clothing the resurrected in glorious garments, and leading them to the heavenly king.[47] This description is immediately followed by the reference to "this Spirit" being constantly on the move between heaven and earth, and the biblical proof text—Matt 18:10!

I conclude, agreeing with Kretschmar, that the Sage does provide a witness to the tradition of angelomorphic pneumatology. "Tradition" is the proper term to use, because Aphrahat is by no means an exception in his time. As I mentioned earlier, this way of envisioning the Holy Spirit was still an option in the fourth century.[48] Aphrahat's contemporary, Eusebius of Caesarea, could write the following in secure conviction of affirming traditional Christian teaching:

> ...the Holy Spirit is also eternally present at the throne of God, since also "thousands of thousand are present before him," according to Daniel (Dan 7:10); he also was sent, at one time in the form of a dove over the Son of man, at another time over each of the prophets and apostles. Therefore he also was said to come forth from the Father. And why are you amazed? About the devil it was also said, "and the devil went forth from the Lord" (Job 1:12); and again, a second time, was it said "so the devil went forth from the Lord" (Job 2:7). And you would also find about Ahab where the Scripture adds "and a spirit came forward and stood before the Lord and said 'I will entice him'" (3 Rgns [1 Kgs] 22:21). But these are adverse spirits, and now is not the proper time to investigate just how and in what way this was said.[49]

Eusebius' imagery here is angelic. It is significant that one of the biblical passages quoted, 3 Rgns (1 Kgs) 22:19–22, together with the language of "Holy Spirit and angelic spirit," had been earlier problematized by

---

[46] Cramer, *Geist Gottes*, 68, 81. Cf. Ridolfini, "Note sull'antropologia e sul' escatologia del 'Sapiente Persiano,'" *SROC* 1/1 (1978): 12–13: the Spirit belongs "ontologically" to God, but manifests itself as a *divine* angelic guardian.

[47] *Pace* Bruns (*Das Christusbild Aphrahats des Persischen Weisen* [Bonn: Borengässer, 1990], 188 n. 20), who dismisses the passage as simply "a literary device" of no theological relevance.

[48] See the brief summary in Richard Paul Vaggione, *Eunomius of Cyzicus and the Nicene Revolution* (Oxford Early Christian Studies; Oxford: Oxford University Press, 2000), 122–23 and n. 270.

[49] Eusebius of Caesarea, *Eccl. theol.* 3.4.7–8 (GCS 14:159).

Origen (*Comm. Jo.* 20.29.263).[50] Like Origen, Eusebius is aware of traditions that failed to distinguish the Holy Spirit from the angels; however, as several statements in the same work make it clear, he distinguishes unequivocally between the two.[51]

Similar ideas occur a few decades later in the *Apostolic Constitutions*, a pseudepigraphic compilation redacted in the area of Antioch around 377–393 from sources "that are themselves compilations, and seem originally to have been written also as a manual of church life."[52] Several passages in the *Apostolic Constitutions* paint a hierarchical worldview featuring the Father and the Son, followed by the Holy Spirit and "the orders of ministering holy spirits"—that is, the various angelic ranks.[53] These passages offer unmistakable indications of the redactor's pneumatomachian leanings: rather than being numbered with the Father and the Son, the Holy Spirit is counted with the cherubim, seraphim, aeons, armies, powers, authorities, principalities, thrones, archangels, and angels.[54] In this respect, the *Apostolic Constitutions* are character-

---

[50] See my earlier remarks on Origen's awareness of traditions relating the Holy Spirit and the angelic spirit.

[51] E.g., Eusebius of Caesarea, *Eccl. theol.* 3.5.17–21 (GCS 14:162–163). For an examination of Eusebius' pneumatology, see Holger Strutwolf, *Die Trinitätstheologie und Christologie des Euseb von Caesarea: Eine dogmengeschichtliche Untersuchung seiner Platonismusrezeption und Wirkungsgeschichte* (FKDG 72; Göttingen: Vandenhoeck & Ruprecht, 1999), 184–237.

[52] David A. Fiensy, *Prayers Alleged to Be Jewish: An Examination of the Constitutiones Apostolorum* (BJS 65; Chico, Ca: Scholars, 1985), 19. For details on the composite character of this work, and questions of dating and authorship, see Marcel Metzger, "Introduction: Le genre littéraire et les origines des *CA*" (SC 320:13–62); Joseph G. Mueller, *L'ancien Testament dans l'ecclésiologie des pères: une lecture des "Constitutions apostoliques"* (IPM 41; Turnhout: Brepols, 2004), 36–53; 86–91.

[53] *Const. ap.* 8.4.5 (SC 336:142): The ordaining bishop asks all the faithful if they are certain of the worthiness of the candidate, "as if they were at the tribunal of God and of Christ and in the presence also of the Holy Spirit and of all the ministering holy spirits (ὡς ἐπὶ δικαστῇ Θεῷ καὶ Χριστῷ, παρόντος δηλαδὴ καὶ τοῦ ἁγίου Πνεύματος καὶ πάντων τῶν ἁγίων καὶ λειτουργικῶν πνευμάτων); *Const. ap.* 6.11.2 (SC 329:324): We confess "one God, Father of one Son and not of more, the maker, through Christ, of the one Paraclete and of the other orders" (ἑνὸς παρακλήτου διὰ Χριστοῦ καὶ τῶν ἄλλων ταγμάτων ποιητήν); *Const. ap.* 8.12.8 (SC 336:182): Through the Son, God has created, before all else, "the Spirit of Truth, the interpreter and minister of the Only Begotten," and after him the various heavenly choirs (πρὸ πάντων ποιήσας τὸ Πνεῦμα τῆς ἀληθείας, τὸν τοῦ μονογενοῦς ὑποφήτην καὶ διάκονον, καὶ μετ' αὐτὸν τὰ Χερουβὶμ καὶ τὰ Σεραφίμ, αἰῶνάς τε καὶ στρατιάς, δυνάμεις τε καὶ ἐξουσίας, ἀρχάς τε καὶ θρόνους, ἀρχαγγέλους τε καὶ ἀγγέλους).

[54] Mueller, *Une lecture des "Constitutions apostoliques,"* 101–105.

ized, much like Aphrahat, by "a certain archaism" that is perfectly understandable for a compilation of older traditions.[55]

To return to Aphrahat, the use of Matt 18:10 as a pneumatological proof-text does not mean, however, that the Sage himself consciously and actively promoted an angelomorphic pneumatology. First, the angelomorphic Spirit is one representation of the Holy Spirit among several others in the *Demonstrations*. To paraphrase Bruns' presentation of Aphrahat's christology, it could be said that the Sage's pneumatology is "open," inasmuch as the accumulation of symbols (mother, spouse, medicine, angels of the face) moves asymptotically towards the inexhaustible experience of the Spirit, resulting in a multicolored picture book of pneumatological impressions, rather than a unitary theology of the Holy Spirit.[56]

Second, it is quite obvious, from the way he writes, that Aphrahat does not see himself as proposing anything new or unusual. This is in keeping with the general character of his theology. It is very likely, therefore, that Aphrahat's use of Matt 18:10 is one such received tradition.

The passages from *Dem.* 6 and *Dem.* 1, quoted above, share the same theme (the Holy Spirit), and the same formal structure (both provide scriptural proof for the activity of the Holy Spirit). The connection between Zech 4:10, Isa 11:1-3, and Matt 18:10 illustrates very well what Pierre calls a "network of scriptural traditions," which Aphrahat inherited from earlier Christian tradition.[57] That this is indeed the case, is made clear by the occurrence of the same cluster of biblical verses

---

[55] Metzger, "Introduction: La théologie des *CA*" (SC 329: 10–39, at 32). This does not preclude Mueller's recent and original thesis that the low pneumatology of the *Const. ap.* is a distinct element of the redactor's theological agenda, and is intimately linked with his "hyper-episcopal ecclesiology," with his refusal of any soteriology of deification, and with the very pseudepigraphic nature of these writings (*Une lecture des "Constitutions apostoliques,"* 104, 107–110, 547–50, 560–61, 577).

[56] Bruns speaks of the "open character" of Aphrahat's christology, noting that the accumulation of symbols (e.g., *Dem.* 17.2, 11) "moves asymptotically towards the inexhaustible reality of Christ," resulting in "a multicolored picture book of christological impressions," rather than a unitary christological vision. Bruns, *Christusbild*, 183, 214. See also Vööbus, "Methodologisches," 27; Cramer, *Geist Gottes*, 67.

[57] Some of these traditions were embodied in a "series of *testimonia* that might have circulated orally and been transmitted independently from the known biblical text." In fact, Aphrahat is "one of the richest witnesses" to the use of *testimonia*, with *Dem.* 16 furnishing "the largest collection ever realized by a Father." See Pierre, "Introduction," in *Aphraate, "Les Exposés,"* 115, 138, 68. See also Murray, "Rhetorical Patterns," 110; idem, *Symbols of Church and Kingdom: A Study in Early Syriac Tradition* (2nd ed.; London/New York: T&T Clark International, 2004), 289–90; Schlütz, *Isaias 11:2*, 33–34, 40, 58.

and echoes of angelomorphic pneumatology in Clement of Alexandria. As I have shown earlier, Clement identifies the angels of Matt 18:10 with the "thrones" of Col 1:16 and "the seven eyes of the Lord" (Zech 3:9; 4:10; Rev 5:6), and understands all these passages as descriptions of the seven "first-born princes of the angels" (πρωτόγονοι ἀγγέλων ἄρχοντες), elsewhere called the seven πρωτόκτιστοι.[58]

The exegeses of Clement of Alexandria and Aphrahat offer a surprising convergence. Both writers use the same cluster of biblical verses: "the seven eyes of the Lord" (Zech 3:9; 4:10), "the seven gifts of the Spirit" (Isa 11:2–3), and "the angels of the little ones" (Matt 18:10); both echo the tradition about the highest angelic company; finally, both use angelic imagery to express a definite pneumatological content. This is one of several convergences between Aphrahat and earlier writers in the West, which, as I have stated earlier, cannot be explained by direct literary connection.[59] Gilles Quispel was convinced that behind both Clement and Aphrahat lies a tradition that goes back to Jewish Christian missionaries "who brought the new religion to Mesopotamia," and were also "the founding fathers of the church in Alexandria."[60] Be this as it may, the angelomorphic pneumatology detected in the writings of Clement and Aphrahat represents an echo of older views, which in their times were still acceptable.

5. THE LARGER THEOLOGICAL FRAMEWORK FOR APHRAHAT'S ANGELOMORPHIC PNEUMATOLOGY

At this point it is important to inquire about the place of angelomorphic pneumatology in the larger theological framework of the *Demonstrations*. I am especially interested in the relationship between angelomorphic pneumatology, on the one hand, and other theologi-

---

[58] *Strom.* 5.6.35; *Ecl.* 57.1; *Exc.* 10.

[59] I have already mentioned the resemblance with the *Shepherd of Hermas*. Another case refers to the striking resemblance between the exegesis of Judg 7:4–8 by Aphrahat (*Dem.* 7.19–21) and Origen (*Hom. Judic.* 9.2). R. H. Connolly ("Aphraates and Monasticism," *JTS* 6 [1905]: 538–39) hypothesized that the Sage might have read Origen. In response, Loofs (*Theophilus*, 258–59) stated that a common source is a far more likely explanation.

[60] Quispel, "Genius and Spirit," 160, 164. See also Schlütz, *Isaias 11:2*, 33–34: "die Sicherheit der Aussage bei Aphraat [kann] am besten mit der theologischen Tradition aus den Tagen der palästinensischen Gemeinde erklärt werden."

cal phenomena discussed by students of the *Demonstrations*, namely Aphrahat's *Geistchristologie* and binitarianism.[61]

Difficulties of Aphrahat's Pneumatology

How does Aphrahat think about God as Trinity? He does not know the terms *tlitāyutā* (τρίας) and *qnomā* (ὑπόστασις), and holds a non-philosophical notion of *kyanā* (οὐσία; φύσις).[62] It is rather a soteriological and history-of-salvation perspective that comes to be expressed in the various formulas of Aphrahat:

> Glory and honor to the Father, and to his Son, and to his living and holy Spirit, from the mouth of all who glorify him there above and here below, unto ages of ages, Amen and Amen!
> We know only this much, that God is one, and one his Christ, and one the Spirit, and one the faith, and one the baptism.
> ...the three mighty and glorious names—Father, and Son, and Holy Spirit—invoked upon your head when you received the mark of your life...[63]

Aphrahat is undoubtedly familiar with the liturgical usage of the terms "Father," "Son," and "Holy Spirit." Occasionally, as noted by Bruns, the *taxis* underlying such creedal statements seems to be Father—Spirit—Christ.[64] For instance:

> Now, this is the faith: one should believe in God, the Lord of all, who made heaven and earth and the seas and all that is in them, and made Adam in his image, and gave the Law to Moses, and sent [a portion] of his Spirit upon the prophets [ܪܘܚܗ ܡܢ ܫܕܪ], and, moreover [ܘܬܘܒ], sent his Christ into the world.... This is the faith of the Church of God.[65]

Such formulaic statements allow only limited insight into the Sage's theology. It is certain that "trinitarian elements" are present in Aphrahat's various doxologies.[66] Yet to say that *Dem.* 23.63, for instance, which I

---

[61] Some of the major scholars writing about Aphrahat, such as Schwen and Loofs, have used "binitarian," "binitarianism," "ditheism," "binity" (*Zweieinigkeit*), and *Geistchristologie* in ways that could easily lead to confusion. I ask the reader to refer to the definitions of these terms that I proposed in the Introduction.

[62] Bruns, *Christusbild*, 99, 143; Alois Grillmeier, *Christ in Christian Tradition* (2nd, rev. ed.; tr. J. Bowden; Atlanta, Ga.: John Knox, 1975), 216–17; Pierre, "Introduction," 162 n. 58; Ridolfini, "Problema trinitario e problema cristologico," 99.

[63] *Dem.* 23.61 (II/128); 23.60 (II/124); 23.63 (II/133).

[64] Bruns, *Christusbild*, 97.

[65] *Dem.* 1.19 (I/44).

[66] Bruns, *Christusbild*, 94.

have quoted earlier, offers "[a]n example of Aphrahat being obviously Trinitarian," is to overlook the fact that such passages are derived from liturgical practice.[67] If these are, in the words of Schwen, "eben nur Formeln, übernommene Bruchstücke fremder Anschauung," they tell us very little about Aphrahat's theological thought.[68]

Still formulaic, but more elaborate and personal, is the following passage in the *Letter to an Inquirer*.

> As for me, I just believe firmly that God is one, who made the heavens and the earth from the beginning...and spoke with Moses on account of his meekness, and himself spoke with all the prophets, and, moreover [ܘܬܘܒ], sent his Christ into the world.[69]

It is noteworthy that this passage contains nothing about the Holy Spirit, and that the similar composition in *Dem.* 1.19, quoted earlier, contains merely an oblique reference to Christ sending from his Spirit into the prophets.[70] It is true, on the other hand, that when Aphrahat elsewhere treats the "moments" preceding the sending of the Spirit in the Creed (namely cosmogony, anthropogony, the giving of the Law, and the inspiration of the prophets) he usually mentions the Spirit.[71] The fact remains, however, that the Creed refers to the Spirit only in its fourth article, and that this reference does not contain anything specifically Christian. As Cramer notes, the statement could just as well have been made by Philo.[72]

As early as 1907, Schwen noted that Aphrahat's notion of the Spirit was hesitant and inconsistent.[73] Far from being conceived of as a divine person, on par with the Father and the Son, Aphrahat's "Holy Spirit" is at times indistinguishable from the ascended Christ (e.g., *Dem.* 6.10 [I/281]), at other times simply an impersonal divine power, similar to the rays of the sun (e.g., *Dem.* 6.11 [I/284]), and occasionally merged with

---

[67] Skoyles Jarkins, *Aphrahat and the Temple of God*, 56 n. 208.
[68] Schwen, *Afrahat*, 91.
[69] Aphrahat, *Letter to an Inquirer* 2 (I/4).
[70] Loofs, *Theophilus*, 260 n. 9: "...ist des Geistes nur in dem Satzteile gedacht." Note the parallel that obtains between *Letter to an Inquirer* 2 (I/4) and *Dem.* 1.19 (I/44):
"he spoke in all the prophets   and sent his Christ into the world"
"he sent from his Spirit upon the prophets   and sent his Christ into the world."
[71] Pierre, "Introduction," 165 n. 70.
[72] Cramer, *Geist Gottes*, 70.
[73] Schwen, *Afrahat*, 90.

the notion of the guardian angel (e.g., *Dem.* 6.14 [I/296]).[74] For Bruns also, and even for Ortiz de Urbina, who is a defender of Aphrahat's fundamental orthodoxy, many passages in the *Demonstrations* present the Spirit as an impersonal divine "grace" or "power."[75] The personal elements would only occur in the "dramatism" of the eschatological scene, the "saddening" of the spirit, and the mother-image.[76]

In several instances (*Dem.* 6.11 [I/286]; 20.16 [I/919]), Aphrahat focuses exclusively on "God and his Christ" so that, according Loofs, "there is no place left for the Spirit."[77] Moreover, the *Demonstrations* seem to use "Spirit," "Spirit of Christ," and "Christ" interchangeably. Especially with respect to the inhabitation of God in the believers, any distinction vanishes.[78] Cramer noted that the Sage "almost" identifies Christ and the Spirit—"almost," because the use of "spirit" in trinitarian formulas would prevent full identification.[79] In light of my earlier

---

[74] Schwen, *Afrahat*, 91: "Als besondere göttliche Person im Sinne des ökumenischen Konzils von 381, dem Vater und dem Sohne gleichgeordnet, ist er nicht gedacht."

[75] Bruns, *Christusbild*, 188; Ortiz de Urbina, "Die Gottheit Christi bei Aphrahat," 137. Similarly Ridolfini, "Problema trinitario e problema cristologico," 109–10, 121.

[76] Ortiz de Urbina, "Die Gottheit Christi bei Aphrahat," 134–35.

[77] Loofs, *Theophilus*, 260. At one point (*Dem.* 18.10 [I/839]), however, God is represented as "divine couple"—God as Father and the Spirit as Mother. Loofs (*Theophilus*, 275 n. 6) explains that "für die erbauliche Verwendung von Gen. 2, 24, an der ihm hier lag, allein der Geist, weil im Syrischen ein Femininum, sich eignete, nicht aber ,der Messias' (Christus)." In fact, as the context shows, Aphrahat's interest is more than vaguely "edifying": he is here thinking of God and his Spirit-consort as genitors of the transformed ascetics, and is interested in linking the "spirituals" with their "mother," the Spirit. Moreover, he is also bowing to the pressure of an already traditional reading of Gen 2:24 in the Syriac milieu (e.g., *Acts Thom.* 110), which connects Eve and the Holy Spirit and, implicitly, adopts the *taxis* Father—Spirit—Son. Other texts can be adduced from *Gos. Heb.*, Tatian, and Ps.-Macarius. See Quispel, *Makarius, das Thomasevangelium, und das Lied der Perle* (NovTSup 15; Leiden: Brill, 1967), 9–13; Winkler, "Die Tauf-Hymnen der Armenier: Ihre Affinität mit Syrischem Gedankengut," in *Liturgie und Dichtung* (2 vols; ed. H. Becker and R. Kaczynski; Munich: St. Ottilian, 1983), 1:381–420; Susan Ashbrook Harvey, "Feminine Imagery for the Divine: The Holy Spirit, the Odes of Solomon, and Early Syriac Tradition," *SVTQ* 37 (1993): 111–40; Brock, "The Holy Spirit as Feminine in Early Syriac Literature," in *After Eve* (ed. Janet Martin Soskice; London: Collins, 1990),73–88; Emmanuel Kaniyamparampil, "Feminine-Maternal Images of the Spirit in Early Syriac Tradition," *Letter & Spirit* 3 (2007): 169–88.

[78] Skoyles Jarkins (*Aphrahat and the Temple of God*, 56 n. 207) suggests that this "may be due to the influence of Pauline texts (e.g., Rom 8:9 in *Dem.* 23.47 [II/91.24–25] and *Dem.* 8.5 [I/370.9–10]) upon Aphrahat. This does not explain much about Aphrahat, but simply moves Pandora's box in the field of biblical studies, where the issue of Pauline "spirit christology" happens to be a fiercely debated issue. For an introduction to the debate, see Fatehi, *Relation*, 23–43; Fee, *God's Empowering Presence*, 831–45.

[79] Cramer, *Geist Gottes*, 65, 67.

statements above, I find Cramer's recourse to formulas unconvincing.
At first sight at least, it is more accurate to conclude with Schwen that
the Sage had no doctrine of the Trinity "in the sense of later Church
dogma," and that his thought would be better termed "binitarian" than
"trinitarian."[80]

Loofs attempted to place Aphrahat's "Geistchristologie" and "binitarianism" in a larger religio-historical perspective. In his interpretation,
"spirit" is, for Aphrahat, simply a way of referring to the divinity
of Christ prior to the Incarnation. "Spirit" should not, however, be
understood by analogy with the Logos-hypostasis of other patristic
writers, as a second hypostasis alongside the Father since, for Aphrahat,
the differentiation of the Spirit from the Father occurred only at the
Incarnation. Prior to the Incarnation, the Spirit represents, by analogy
with Power, Wisdom, or Presence in pre-Christian Jewish thought, a
divine attribute rather than a distinct entity.[81] Aphrahat distinguishes
"Spirit" and "Christ" only when speaking about the man Jesus, and it
is this historical Jesus Christ that Aphrahat has in mind when he uses
the phrase "God and his Christ." According to Loofs, the Sage's perspective switches back and forth between the preexisting πνεῦμα and
the historical Jesus Christ.[82] Finally, this formula does not introduce
any alteration of strict monotheism, given that the reign of the Son
is seen as temporary, ultimately to end by being delivered to the sole

---

[80] Schwen, *Afrahat*, 91; 92: "Man darf wohl sagen daß die Anschauung Afrahats
nicht trinitarisch, sondern binitarisch ist: 'Gott und sein Christus' oder 'Gott und
der heilige Geist.'" Skoyles Jarkins also notes that "Aphrahat uses Spirit, Holy Spirit,
Spirit of Christ, and Christ almost interchangeably for identification of the Divine
who may dwell within a person"; in her judgment, however, this does not preclude a
trinitarian concept of indwelling: "The Spirit of Christ is the same as the Holy Spirit
or third person of the Trinity in Aphrahat's writings. So in *Dem.* 6:14 we have two of
the persons of the Trinity indwelling. The Sage also writes in *Dem.* 4:11 that wherever
Christ dwells so the Father does also; here are the first and second persons of the
Trinity dwelling within people. Therefore, we may state that Aphrahat does have a
Trinitarian concept of indwelling in a human being" (Skoyles Jarkins, *Aphrahat and
the Temple of God*, 55, 56).
[81] Loofs, *Theophilus*, 273 n. 2, 274, 278.
[82] Loofs, *Theophilus*, 270 n. 3, 274, 275: "vor seinem geistigen Auge steht die ein-
heitliche Person des geschichtlichen und erhöhten Herrn, aber Aphrahat sieht in ihr,
abwechselnd, hier das πνεῦμα, dort den Menschen"; Loofs, *Theophilus*, 277 n. 5: "In
einem Satze kann die Betrachtungsweise wechseln: Unser Herr (hier: das πνεῦμα) nahm
von uns ein Pfand (die σάρξ, das Menschsein) und ging (hier der ganze Christus) und
ließ uns ein Pfand von dem Seinen (den Geist) und wurde erhöht (das gilt nur vom
Menschen in ihm)."

God (*Dem.* 6.12 [I/287]).[83] Loofs' conclusions were severely criticized by Ortiz de Urbina, later also by Vööbus and Bruns, who all argued that Aphrahat views Christ as pre-existent with the Father prior to the Incarnation, and that he has a clear understanding of the distinction between the risen Christ and the Spirit.[84]

The texts remain, however, ambiguous. One of the passages invoked by Ortiz de Urbina, *Dem.* 6.10 [I/281], is quite telling. Aphrahat speaks here about the Logos becoming flesh (quoting John 1:14), then returning to God with "that which he had not brought with him"—thus raising humanity to heaven (quoting Eph 2:6)—and sending the Spirit in his stead. This seems to affirm the preexistence of Christ as Logos, as well as the clear distinction between the ascended Christ and the Spirit he sends to his disciples. Yet the sending of the Spirit is documented not with a reference to the paraclete, but rather with Matt 28:20, a christological text: "when he went to his Father, he sent to us his Spirit and said to us *I am with you until the end of the world.*"[85]

What, then, of the relation between "Christ," "the Spirit of Christ," and "the Holy Spirit" in Aphrahat? Bruns notes that "the sending of the Spirit is identical with the presence of Christ," and suggests that the Spirit is the medium through which Christ dwells in the believers and, especially, in the prophets.[86] In other words, Christ dwells in the Spirit, and the Spirit dwells in the human being—which suggested Skoyles Jarkins' phrase "matroshki-doll christology."[87] More needs to be said, however, about this indwelling.

---

[83] Loofs, *Theophilus*, 280. For similarities with "dynamic monarchianism," see Loofs, *Theophilus*, 278; Schwen (*Afrahat*, 83) notes a similarity with Paul of Samosata. *Contra*, convincingly, Ortiz de Urbina, "Die Gottheit Christi bei Aphrahat," 123.

[84] Ortiz de Urbina, "Die Gottheit Christi bei Aphrahat," 80–88, 136–37; Vööbus, "Methodologisches," 24–25; Bruns, *Christusbild*, 133–44.

[85] This recalls *Ep. Apos.* 17: "'Will you really leave us until your coming? Where will we find a teacher?' And he answered and said to us, 'Do you not know that until now I am both here and there with him who sent me?…I am wholly in the Father and the Father in me.'" The long treatment of the relation between Christ and his disciples after the ascension, even though heavily indebted to the farewell discourse in the Gospel of John, diverges from the latter precisely on the problem of the paraclete. According to Julian Hills (*Tradition and Composition in the Epistula Apostolorum* [HDR 24; Minneapolis, Minn.: Fortress, 1990], 123), "[t]he crisis of the Lord's departure is resolved in the Fourth Gospel by the coming of the Spirit…In the Epistula it turns on the presence of the risen Lord among the disciples…" Instead of the paraclete, *Ep. Apos.* insists on the perfect unity of Christ with the Father and, implicitly, on Christ's ubiquity.

[86] Bruns, *Unterweisungen*, 200 n. 21; *Christusbild*, 187.

[87] Skoyles Jarkins, *Aphrahat and the Temple of God*, 55 n. 206.

The Holy Spirit and the Move from Unity to Multiplicity

The difficulties outlined in the previous section never seem to have existed as such for Aphrahat. The reason is quite simple: the Sage's point of departure is not metaphysical—God in Godself, or the "*ad intra*" relation of "divine Persons"—but rather, to use Bruns' very apt phrase, "die Anrufbarkeit und liturgische Erfahrbarkeit des einen Gottes in drei Namen."[88] For Aphrahat, then, the "problem" of explaining the relation between the Father and the Spirit, or between Christ (whether "preincarnate" or "post-resurrectional") and the Spirit simply did not present itself as such. His statements about the Spirit come in response to a different set of questions:

> Since Christ is one, and one his Father, how is it that Christ and his Father dwell in the believers?
>
> Now, Christ is seated at the right hand of his Father, and Christ dwells in human beings...And though he dwells among many, he is seated at the right hand of his Father.[89]

Aphrahat's notion of the Spirit will become more easily understandable if we consider these questions, and inquire about the role of the Holy Spirit in the multiplicity of creation and the charismatic life of the Church. Although it is certainly not a novelty in scholarship, this perspective has thus far not been given enough attention.[90] I now return to Aphrahat:

> Our Lord...left us a pledge of his own (ﬤﬠﬥ ﬡﬥ ﬠﬤﬠﬥﬡ) when he ascended...it behooves us also to honor that which is his, which we have received...let us honor that which is his, according to his own nature. If we honor it, we shall go to him.... But if we despise it, he will take away from us that which he has given us; and if we abuse his pledge (ﬡﬤ ﬠﬤﬠﬥﬡ ﬥﬠ ﬤﬥﬠﬥ), he will there take away that which is his, and will deprive us of that which he has promised us.[91]

---

[88] Bruns, *Christusbild*, 156.

[89] *Dem.* 6.11 (I/284); 6.10 (I/281).

[90] Cf. Ortiz de Urbina, "Die Gottheit Christi bei Aphrahat," 129 n. 16: "Bei Afrahat vermehrt sich Christus durch seinen Geist"; Bruns, *Christusbild*, 188: "der Heilige Geist hat vornehmlich die Funktion, die Universalisierung und individuelle Aneignung der Christusgeschehens zu garantieren."

[91] *Dem.* 6.10 (I/279–280). The root of ﬤﬠﬥ means "to cover up, conceal." Hence, the verb can mean "to appropriate secretly," "to defraud," "to refuse to return," "to keep in or suppress until the thing is spoiled."

It is quite evident that "the pledge" (ܪܗܒܘܢܐ, ἀρραβών) refers to the Spirit. There is, first, the allusion to biblical texts (2 Cor 1:22; 5:5; Eph 1:14); then, also, the obvious parallels with statements made elsewhere in *Dem.* 6, where the same is said in reference to the Holy Spirit.[92]

To explain how it is that Christ is divided among believers and dwells in them without thereby forsaking his unity and dignity, Aphrahat suggests several comparisons. Just as the one sun is manifested to a multiplicity of receivers in that "its power is poured out in the earth"—that is, by means of the multiplicity of his rays—so also "God and his Christ, though they are one, yet dwell in human beings, who are many."[93]

Excursus: "Wisdom" and "Power" as Pneumatological Terms

Towards the end of his comparison between Christ and the sun, Aphrahat mentions the power of God (ܚܝܠܐ ܕܐܠܗܐ): "the sun in heaven is not diminished when it sends out its power upon the earth. How much greater is the power of God, since it is by the power of God that the sun itself subsists."[94] Bruns is probably right in speaking about the Spirit as (non-hypostatic) "göttlich-dynamische Kraft" mediating between the transcendent God and the world.[95] Earlier, Aphrahat had stated that Christ, even though one, "is able to [be] above and beneath" and "dwell in many," by means of his Father's wisdom (ܒܚܟܡܬܐ ܕܐܒܘܗܝ).[96] This prompted Ortiz de Urbina to suggest that Aphrahat may have equated ܪܘܚܐ (πνεῦμα) with ܚܟܡܬܐ (σοφία), two words that were feminine in his time.[97]

I think that more can be added to this discussion. In *Dem.* 10.8, "wisdom" seems to constitute a divine gift imparted freely to the Christian

---

[92] In the text just quoted, Christ leaves his pledge upon his ascension, just as in another passage "when he went to his Father, he sent to us his Spirit" (*Dem.* 6.10 [I/282]); the exhortation to "honor the pledge" finds counterpart in an earlier exhortation, to "honor the spirit of Christ, that we may receive grace from him" (*Dem.* 6.1 [I/241]); the characterization of the pledge as "that which is of his [Christ's] own nature" is very similar to the statement about the Spirit going "to its nature, [namely] unto Christ" (*Dem.* 6.14 [I/296]); the "two-way" discourse on the required attitude towards the pledge corresponds perfectly to the ascetic theory of the same *Demonstration*, which opposes those who "preserve the Spirit of Christ in purity" and those who defile the Spirit (*Dem.* 6.14–15).

[93] *Dem.* 6.11 (I/285).

[94] *Dem.* 6.11 (I/285).

[95] Bruns, *Christusbild*, 205.

[96] *Dem.* 6.10 (I/281).

[97] Ortiz de Urbina, "Die Gottheit Christi bei Aphrahat," 128.

"shepherds," which, therefore, calls for generous transmission from the clergy to the Christian people. Christ is "the steward of wisdom." This fits well with the earlier statement in *Dem.* 6: "And Christ received the Spirit not by measure (John 3:34), but his Father loved him and delivered all into his hands, *and gave him authority over all his treasure.*"[98] Moreover, just as Aphrahat had said earlier about the Spirit of Christ,

> this wisdom is divided among many (ܐܬܚܠܩܬ ܠܣܓܝܐܐ) yet is in no way diminished, as I have shown to you above: the prophets received of the Spirit of Christ (ܡܢ ܪܘܚܗ ܕܡܫܝܚܐ ܢܣܒܘ ܢܒܝܐ), yet Christ was in no way diminished.[99]

Obviously, the Sage takes "wisdom" and "Spirit of Christ" as synonyms.

In conclusion, "wisdom" refers to the Spirit understood as divine power, presence, gift, etc., while Christ is the treasurer and giver of the Spirit. Aphrahat seems to have felt a certain tension between this view and that expressed in 1 Cor 1:24, because he feels compelled to quote this verse, without, however offering any explanation: "And while he is the steward of the wisdom, again, as the Apostle said: *Christ is the power of God and his wisdom.*"

Aphrahat has of course much more to offer than comparisons drawn from nature. His argumentation from Scripture is particularly interesting. According to *Dem.* 14, the believers are like the fertile ground that accepted the seed sown by the Lord (Luke 8:15). The seeds are nothing else than the Spirit of the Lord, poured out over all the flesh (Joel 3:1), but accepted only by a few.[100] The prophets "received [a portion] from the Spirit of Christ, each one of them as he was able to bear."[101] In the new dispensation, "[a portion] from the Spirit of Christ (ܘܡܢ ܪܘܚܗ ܕܡܫܝܚܐ ܬܘܒ ܡܬܐܫܕ) is again poured forth today upon all flesh [Joel 3:1]."[102] As a result, Christ now overshadows all believers—each of them severally (ܚܕ ܚܕ).[103]

Obviously, for Aphrahat the Spirit "multiplies" Christ, making him available to the prophets and all believers. The imagery is quite crude, as the Sage seems particularly fond of "part-to-whole" explanations.

---

[98] *Dem.* 6.12 (I/288).
[99] *Dem.* 10.8 (I/464). Cf. *Dem.* 6.10–12.
[100] *Dem.* 14.47 (I/716).
[101] ܡܛܠ ܕܡܢ ܪܘܚܗ ܕܡܫܝܚܐ ܢܣܒ ܟܠܚܕ ܡܢܗܘܢ ܐܝܟ (*Dem.* 6.12 [I/288]).
[102] *Dem.* 6.12 (I/288).
[103] *Dem.* 6.10 (I/281).

Several times he refers to God sending "[a portion] of his Spirit upon the prophets": the prophets received [a portion] from the Spirit of Christ; John the Baptist, the greatest among prophets, still received the Spirit "according to measure" (ܪܕܟܠܝܣܐ); [a portion] from the Spirit of Christ is again poured forth today upon all flesh [Joel 3:1]; Christ overshadows each of the believers severally; at Baptism, believers receive the Holy Spirit "from a little portion of the Godhead."[104] The insertion of "portion" in my English rendering of the phrase is justified. In his footnotes to the German translation of the *Demonstrations*, Bruns points to the "exceedingly materialistic" imagery of expressions such as ܪܕܟܠܝܣܐ ܪܕܟܠܝܣܐ ("severally," "one by one") for the presence of the Spirit in the prophets, or ܪܕܟܠܐܡܐܟܐ ܪܝܣܐ ܡܐ ("a little portion/particle of the Godhead"), for the gift of the Spirit received at Baptism.[105]

The difference between the Spirit present in the prophets and the Spirit in the historical Jesus Christ is one of degree: partially present in the prophets, the Spirit is fully present in Christ.[106] In *Dem.* 6.12 [I/285], the proof-text for Christ is John 3:34: "it was not by measure that his Father gave the Spirit unto him." For the partial presence of the Spirit in the prophets, on the other hand, Aphrahat quotes Num 11:17 (God taking "from the Spirit" of Moses to endow the seventy elders).[107] But he also refers to something that "the blessed apostle said": *God distributed from the Spirit of Christ and sent it into the prophets.*[108]

Even though scholarship is not unanimous on this point, I find it indisputable that Aphrahat is quoting "the blessed apostle" according to *3 Corinthians*, an apocryphal text that Aphrahat and Ephrem seem to have regarded as canonical.[109] The relevant verse (*3 Cor.* 2.10) reads as follows:

---

[104] *Dem.* 6.12 (I/288); 10.8 (I/464); 1.19 (I/44); 6.13 (I/288); 6.12 (I/288); 6.10 (I/281); 6.14 (I/293).

[105] Bruns, *Unterweisungen*, 200 n. 22, 205 n. 26. The passages are *Dem.* 6.10 (I/281) and *Dem.* 6.14 (I/293).

[106] Similarly Ortiz de Urbina, "Die Gottheit Christi bei Aphrahat," 127; Bruns, *Christusbild*, 140.

[107] On the "massive presence" of this verse in rabbinic literature, see Pierre, *Exposés*, 395 n. 73.

[108] ܪܕܟܠܝܣܐ ܒܣܪ ܡܫܝܚܐ ܪܘܚܐ ܡܢ ܐܠܗܐ ܦܠܓ (Dem. 6.12 [I/285]).

[109] See Vahan Hovhanessian, *Third Corinthians: Reclaiming Paul for Christian Orthodoxy* (Studies in Biblical Literature 18; New York: Peter Lang, 2000); Loofs, *Theophilus*, 148–53. Pierre expresses extreme reservation on the issue of Aphrahat's use of *3 Corinthians*. She notes ("Introduction," 139 n. 73) that the Sage may "perhaps" have known *3 Corinthians*, but does not think that Aphrahat's Creed (*Dem.* 1.19 [I/44]) echoes this text. Nowhere in the critical apparatus to the *Demonstrations* is there any reference to *3 Cor.* On the contrary, Bruns (*Christusbild*, 187 n. 13) states

"For he [God] desired to save the house of Israel. Therefore, distributing from the Spirit of Christ, he sent it into the prophets" (μερίσας οὖν ἀπὸ τοῦ πνεύματος τοῦ Χριστοῦ ἔπεμψεν εἰς τοὺς προφήτας).[110]

The notion of a partial endowment of the prophets with the gifts of the Spirit, and the comparison of this partial charismatic endowment with the complete and sovereign possession of the Spirit by Jesus Christ, are ancient and widespread themes. Aside from *3 Cor.*, I have already mentioned its use in Justin Martyr's *Dialogue with Trypho* (and the latter's striking similarities to the Ps.-Philonic homily "On Samson"). It appears that the Persian Sage bears witness to the existence of the same tradition in the early Syriac milieu. If Aphrahat identifies the "pledge" or the "Spirit" as the spiritual gifts that the Church received from the ascended Christ in fulfillment of Joel 3:1 ("I shall pour out my Spirit on all flesh"), Justin articulates the very same idea by combining Joel 3:1 with Isa 11:2–3 (the gifts of the Spirit) and Ps 67/68:19 (the ascension: "He ascended on high, he led captivity captive, he gave gifts to the sons of men").[111]

The texts I have discussed so far lead to the conclusion that Aphrahat's pneumatology can be considered from at least two vantage-points. On the one hand, the *Demonstrations* are passing on received formulas, most of which contain references to "spirit." On the other hand, the meaning of "spirit" in these formulas is given by reflection on the charismatic endowment of the prophets and the "pledge" of Christ received at Baptism. In this light, "spirit" is understood as divine "operations" (ܡܥܒܕܘܬܐ) in the believer, which convey the presence of Christ, with all that derives from such presence.

In Aphrahat's thought, the intimate relation between Christ and the Spirit is likened to the relation between the sun and the rays of the sun, the sower and the seeds, or the treasure-holder and the riches of the treasure-house. In more abstract terms, it is the relationship between simple unity and unity-as-multiplicity, i.e., divine unity become

---

that Aphrahat is "very obviously" quoting *3 Cor.* 3.10. In *Dem.* 23 (II/64) also, where Aphrahat again mentions "the Apostle who bears witness: Jesus Christ was born of the Holy Spirit by Mary of the house of David," Pierre believes this to be an echo of Rom 1:3–4. Yet, *3 Cor.* 2.5 offers a closer match: "Christ Jesus [some mss: Jesus Christ] was born of Mary of the seed of David by the Holy Spirit." Cf. Ignatius, *Eph.* 18.2: Jesus Christ was "borne by Mary according to God's providence, namely from (ἐκ) the seed of David, but from the Holy Spirit."

[110] Greek text in Hovhanessian, *Third Corinthians*, 149.
[111] Justin, *Dial.* 87.6.

accessible to the religious experience. For further elucidation of this aspect, it is necessary to return briefly to the topic of angelomorphic pneumatology.

6. The "Fragmentary" Gift of the Spirit and Angelomorphic Pneumatology

It may seem that the angelomorphic pneumatology discussed in the first part of this section and the pneumatological conceptions presented in the second part are not necessarily related. Such is not the case, however.

In *Dem.* 6.10 (I/277–280), Christians are asked not to *despise* "the pledge"—i.e., the gift of the Holy Spirit—received at Baptism. The notion of "despising" the Spirit is significant here. Aphrahat returns to it later in the same *Demonstration*, also supplying a fitting Scriptural proof: "the Spirit that the prophets received, and which we, too, have received" is indicated by something "that our Lord said, *Do not despise any of these little ones that believe in Me, for their angels in heaven always gaze on the face of my Father.*"[112]

Aphrahat's notion of "fragmentary" Spirit-endowment and his angelomorphic pneumatology should be considered jointly, as in the case of Justin and Clement. As I have shown, Justin and Clement understand the seven gifts of the spirit in the Isaiah passage as seven highest angelic powers; Clement even identified the seven spirits with the "angels" of Matt 18:10. In Aphrahat this identification is not explicit. Unlike Justin Martyr, who uses Isa 11:1–3 to contrast the "partial" outpouring of the Spirit over the prophets and Christ's "full" and sovereign possession of the Spirit, Aphrahat only uses the Isaiah verse to illustrate the latter.[113] In other words, Isa 11:2 serves, in *Dem.* 1, the same role as John 3:34 in *Dem.* 6. Aphrahat does say that the prophets received only "[a portion] from the Spirit of Christ, each one of them as he was able to bear"— but he prefers to use *3 Cor.* 2.10 rather than Isa 11:2 in support of this statement. Matthew 18:10 is therefore never connected with Isa 11:2 to

---

[112] *Dem.* 6.14–15 (I/292, 297).

[113] *Dem.* 1.9 (I/20): "And concerning this Stone he stated and showed: *on this stone, behold, I open seven eyes* (Zech 3:9). And what are the seven eyes opened on the stone other than the Spirit of God that abode on Christ with seven operations? As Isaiah the Prophet said…(Isa. 11:2–3)."

affirm the dynamism of divine indwelling, the partial endowment of prophets and baptized Christians, and the intercessory activity of the Spirit. In Aphrahat, Matt 18:10 is instead linked to other texts such as 2 Cor 1:22; 5:5; Eph 1:14; *3 Cor.* 2.10; Num 11:17; 1 Sam 16:14–23 (the evil spirit sent to Saul).

It is true that this particular arrangement of the proof-texts is determined by the necessities of the discourse, and that, in other contexts, Aphrahat would most likely have furnished a different "constellation" using the same passages. As the texts stand, however, the scriptural support for Aphrahat's doctrine of "partial versus complete" possession of the Spirit differs slightly from that of Justin and Clement. By way of consequence, the link between the notion of "fragmentary Spirit" and angelomorphic pneumatology is also less clear than it is in these authors.

Conclusions

In the first part of this chapter I argued that Aphrahat witnesses to the existence of angelomorphic pneumatology in the early Syriac tradition, which was supported by an exegesis of biblical texts (Matt 18:10; Zech 3:9; 4:10; Isa 11:2–3) very similar to that occurring in Justin Martyr and Clement of Alexandria.

The connection, in Aphrahat's *Demonstrations*, between the ascetic doctrine of the indwelling Spirit, on the one hand, and the angelomorphic representation of the Spirit, on the other, is also significant from a history-of-ideas perspective. As mentioned above, the idea that the Spirit would depart from the sinful person was rejected in the course of the Messalian controversy. The ascetic doctrine, however, survived in an altered form, as can be seen in Isaac of Nineveh: if the Holy Spirit, once received in baptism, does not leave, it is the guardian angel who is driven away by one's sins, and this departure leaves the house of the soul open to demonic influences.[114] In other words, the angelomorphism

---

[114] Isaac of Nineveh, *Hom.* 57: "First a man withdraws his mind from his proper care and thereafter the spirit of pride approaches him. When he tarries in pride, the angel of providence, who is near him and stirs in him care for righteousness, withdraws from him. And when a man wrongs his angel and the angel departs from him, then the alien [the devil] draws nigh him, and from henceforth he has no care whatever for righteousness." The English translation is that of Dana Miller (*The Ascetical Homilies of Saint Isaac the Syrian* [Boston, Mass.: Holy Transfiguration Monastery, 1984], 283).

of the older pneumatology was relegated to a "real" (guardian) angel, while the pneumatological content was conformed to the conciliar theology of the Spirit and the sacraments.

In the second part of the chapter I discussed Aphrahat's treatment of the Spirit in relation to Christ, and concluded that the blurring of lines between "Christ," "Spirit of Christ," and "Holy Spirit" is best understood as an attempt to convey the "multiplication" of Christ in the world in (or through) the work of the Spirit. In all likelihood, Aphrahat did not view the angelic imagery and the notion of "particles of the Spirit" as distinct elements. I submit that this represents one of the layers of tradition that Aphrahat has preserved, and which can be identified more specifically with the primitive stage of trinitarian thought proposed by Kretschmar, namely "die Trias Gott-Christus-Engel."[115] This theological complex is still visible in Aphrahat's *Demonstrations*, and it can be verified by recourse to earlier authors, most notably Justin Martyr and Clement of Alexandria.

I have shown how Aphrahat's angelomorphic pneumatology is an integral part of his ascetic theory. It is true that the angelomorphism of the Spirit is one way (among several others) of expressing the subordination of pneumatology to christology, which is one of the characteristic features of Aphrahat's thought.[116] There is no doubt that Aphrahat is aware of trinitarian formulas. In his own reflection on the Holy Spirit, however, he is mostly concerned with the Spirit's "operations" that make possible the experience of divine indwelling. In agreement with Loofs and Bruns, I conclude that he speaks of the Holy Spirit not as an independent hypostasis, but rather as divine power from Christ. Within this overall binitarian framework of the *Demonstrations*, the experience of the Spirit is expressed by recourse to traditional angelomorphic language.

Measuring Aphrahat's angelomorphic pneumatology against the standard of later orthodoxy, Bishop George had good reason to decry

---

In his homily on Ps. 33:8 (PG 29: 364), a verse that reads "the angel of the Lord will encamp around those who fear him and will deliver them" (LXX), Basil writes: "An angel attends to anyone who has believed unto the Lord, unless we chase him away (ἀποδιώξωμεν) ourselves by evil deeds. Just as smoke drives away (φυγαδεύει) bees, and foul odor repels (ἐξελαύνει) doves, so also does the ill-smelling and lamentable sin remove (ἀφίστησιν) the angel who is the guardian of our life."

[115] Kretschmar, *Trinitätstheologie*, 213.

[116] Bruns, *Christusbild*, 186, 188, 204. Cf. Cramer (*Geist Gottes*, 65), who speaks of the "christological anchoring of the doctrine of the Spirit."

the heretical "aberrations," "crassness," and "boorish ignorance" of the *Demonstrations*. Considered from a different perspective, however, these same writings are the invaluable "treasure trove" described by Vööbus. It is therefore imperative to do just what the good bishop counseled against, namely "wear ourselves out with questions and become clouded over in our minds in order to make sense of and understand the import of all the words written in the book of the *Demonstrations*." In my opinion the reward for doing so is quite substantial, since we have found in Aphrahat a witness to the early Christian tradition of angelomorphic pneumatology.

GENERAL CONCLUSIONS

This work started by pointing out certain gaps in early Christian studies: the need for a study of angelomorphic pneumatology to complement the already existing research on angelomorphic christology; the need to advance the discussion on Clement of Alexandria's understanding of the Holy Spirit; finally, the need for more attentive consideration of Clement's *Hypotyposeis*. I have argued that these areas of study are intimately related, and that research on angelomorphic pneumatology ought to give special attention to the so-called other Clement.

"THE OTHER CLEMENT"

"The other Clement" is a rhetorical term which I have used, both in this work and in two earlier studies, as a designation for those works that are usually left out in most scholarly treatments of Clement of Alexandria: the *Adumbrationes*, the *Eclogae propheticae*, and, to a lesser degree, the *Excerpta ex Theodoto*. The importance of these writings lies, first, in their traditional character. They often quote or in other ways present teachings inherited from the earlier generation of charismatic "elders," which Clement holds up as paradigms of "Gnostic" biblical exegesis and doctrinal exposition. Secondly, they represent the pinnacle of Clement's mystagogical curriculum, whose purpose is to communicate the highest mysteries of Christian doctrine by means of advanced biblical exegesis. Finally, and most relevant for my purpose here, the *Excerpta*, *Eclogae*, and *Adumbrationes* contain much material of pneumatological relevance. I have demonstrated that these Clementine writings contain elements of early Christian reflection on the Holy Spirit and the angels, which are best designated as angelomorphic pneumatology, and that Clement's angelomorphic pneumatology occurs in a larger theological articulation, namely in tandem with binitarianism and spirit christology.

All of this is not Clement's own creation, but part of the older tradition that Clement reworked and integrated into his account of Christian thought. To prove my overall thesis about the existence of a vigorous and relatively widespread tradition of angelomorphic pneumatology in early Christianity, I have discussed Revelation, the *Shepherd of Hermas*,

190 GENERAL CONCLUSIONS

Justin Martyr's *Apologies* and *Dialogue*, and the *Demonstrations* of Aphrahat of Persia. The first three are writings that Clement would have read and considered authoritative. Aphrahat, on the other hand, is relevant because he provides access to early Syriac exegetical and doctrinal traditions very similar to those echoed by Clement.

ANGELOMORPHIC PNEUMATOLOGY AND THE HISTORY OF CHRISTIAN THOUGHT

From a religio-historical perspective, angelomorphic pneumatology constitutes a significant phase in Christian reflection on the Holy Spirit. Generally speaking, early Christian reflection on Christ and the Spirit was carried out within the categories inherited from Jewish apocalyptic literature. I have discussed the ways in which the apocalyptic themes of the divine Face and the angels before the Face, which were part of the Second Temple matrix of Christian thought, were used as building blocks for an emerging doctrine of Christ and the Holy Spirit. In some of the authors under discussion (Justin, Clement, Aphrahat), I was able to point to an exegetical tradition using specific biblical texts (Matt 18:10; Zech 3:9; 4:10; Isa 11:2–3), and the resulting "Face" christology and angelomorphic pneumatology.

"Face" christology never became a major player in classic definitions of faith. Like "Name" christology, "Wisdom" christology, or "Glory" christology—once crucial categories in the age of Jewish Christianity—this concept went out of fashion, giving way to a more precise vocabulary shaped by the christological controversies of the third and fourth centuries. Angelomorphic pneumatology, however, and the associated exegesis of Matt 18:10 illustrated by Clement and Aphrahat, became problematic with the advent of the Arian and Pneumatomachian confrontations, and were eventually discarded.

The *Shepherd of Hermas* and Aphrahat illustrate the link between angelomorphic pneumatology and early Christian ascetic theory, which is also significant from a history-of-ideas perspective. The idea that the Spirit would depart from the sinful person was rejected in the course of the Messalian controversy. The ascetic doctrine, however, survived in an altered form: the angelomorphism of the older pneumatology was relegated to a "real" (guardian) angel, while the pneumatological content was conformed to the conciliar theology of the Spirit and the sacraments.

Given the limitations of this study, I have referred only very briefly to Eusebius of Caesarea and the *Apostolic Constitutions*, to some of the anti-Pneumatomachian statements by Basil of Caesarea and Gregory of Nyssa, and to the Ps-Dionysian Corpus. There would also be much to add by taking into account the Latin-speaking authors, perhaps especially Lactantius, studied in great detail by Macholz. It is my intention to discuss these and other texts of the fourth, fifth, and sixth century in a separate work.

Brief Theological Assessment

So much can be said from a historical perspective. A few notes from a systematic theological point of view are now in order. First, it is useful to remind ourselves constantly of the fact that in using terms such as "angelomorphic pneumatology" or "spirit christology" we affirm something about the author's theological *language*, not about the theological *reality* signified by the language. These terms are not meant as descriptions of the divine, but rather as an aid to understand how an author or a text chooses to speak about things divine.

Second, it would be helpful to distinguish between a "creedal" and a "functional" level of theology, and to evaluate a given Christian text by the manner and degree to which the two levels are in correspondence. By "creedal" I mean those elements of received tradition, such as formulas of faith, liturgical formulas, blessings, letter greetings and endings, etc., which are passed on to the readers in the same "prefabricated" form in which they have been received by the writer. The "functional" level of theology would represent the author's personal effort of reflection upon and formulation of the data of Christian faith. The evidence presented in this work illustrates a certain incongruence, in early Christianity, between the "creedal" level of theology (i.e., *what* is defined as normative faith) and the "functional" level of theology (i.e., *how* faith is expressed theologically). Obviously, articulating a trinitarian doctrine, in order to reflect a trinitarian experience of God, took longer than the introduction of trinitarian formulas. In the words of H. E. W. Turner, "Christians lived Trinitarianly before the doctrine of the Trinity began to be thought out conceptually."[1]

---

[1] Turner, *Pattern of Christian Truth*, 474. See also 134–35: "If, however, there is a persistent tendency in the early centuries to interpret the Christian doctrine of the

Third, any interpretation of the overlap of Christ and the Spirit ("spirit christology"), and the overlap of divine and angelic manifestation ("angelomorphic Spirit") must take into consideration the *functional identity* of Christ, the Holy Spirit and the angel as grasped by religious experience. Indeed, many of the texts illustrating angelomorphic pneumatology center around the phenomenon of prophecy. In the hierarchical worldview shared by the texts that I have discussed, the lowest angelic rank, and, by consequence, the one closest to the human world, transmits the divine "movement" to the prophet, who represents the highest level in the human hierarchy and its link with the celestial realm.

To take the "Father, Son/Spirit, and angelomorphic Spirit" scheme as a (very deficient) statement on *theologia* rather than *oikonomia* would be not only an anachronism, but also a theological misinterpretation. In the words of Basil of Caesarea, these texts "do not set forth the Spirit's nature [τὴν φύσιν], but…the variety of the effectual working [τῆς ἐνεργείας]."[2]

Finally, the prophetic-visionary context of the writings discussed in this study should also lead the reader to recognize their mystagogic role. This aspect is most explicit in the *Shepherd*: again and again we see that with Hermas' spiritual development his perception of celestial realities and his ability to comprehend their meaning also improve.[3]

Godhead in a bi-personal rather than in a tri-personal manner… [t]here is no reason to believe that those who worked normally with a Binitarian phrasing in their theology were other than Trinitarian in their religion. There is no trace, for example, of an alternative Twofold Baptismal Formula."

[2] Basil the Great, *Spir.* 8.17. Along the same lines, I find it interesting that the angelomorphism of the Spirit reemerges in the writings of no less than the champion of Byzantine theology in the fourteenth century, Gregory Palamas. This author is uninhibited in using precisely those biblical verses that had once supported angelomorphic pneumatology. In his *Fifth Antirhetikos against Akindynos* (chs. 15; 17), Gregory Palamas identifies the seven gifts of the Spirit in Isaiah 11 with the seven eyes of the Lord (Zech 4:10), the seven spirits of Revelation, and the "finger/spirit of God" (Luke 11:20; Matt 12:28). All of these, he says, designate the divine *energies* referred to in Scripture as seven, and should therefore not be considered created. The exact same cluster of passages occurs also in Palamas' *One Hundred and Fifty Chapters* (chs. 70–71), and in his *Dialogue between an Orthodox and a Barlaamite* (ch. 27).

[3] "The angel of repentance, he came to me and said, 'I wish to explain to you what the Holy Spirit that spoke with you in the form of the Church showed you, for that Spirit is the Son of God. For, as you were somewhat weak in the flesh, it was not explained to you by the angel. *When, however, you were strengthened by the Spirit, and your strength was increased, so that you were able to see the angel also, then accordingly was the building of the tower shown you by the Church.* In a noble and solemn manner did you see everything as if shown you by a virgin; but now you see [them] through

Revelation, the *Shepherd*, and the Clementine writings are simply not designed to be approached like extraneous objects. Their function is rather to draw the reader into reenacting the same type of dynamic message-appropriation which they narrate. What, then, of the angelomorphic description of the Spirit? One is tempted to respond by quoting Goethe's *Faust*:

> I have, alas! Philosophy,
> Medicine, Jurisprudence too,
> and to my cost Theology,
> with ardent labour studied through.
> And here I stand, with all my lore,
> poor fool, no wiser than before.
> Magister, doctor styled, indeed,
> already these ten years I lead
> up, down, across, and to and fro
> my pupils by the nose—and learn
> that we in truth can nothing know!

For my part, I prefer to borrow a page from Hermas: *Sir, I do not see the meaning of these similitudes, nor am I able to comprehend them, unless you explain them to me* (Herm. Sim. 5.3.1).

---

the same Spirit as if shown by an angel. You must, however, learn everything from me with greater accuracy..." (Sim 9.1.1, *ANF*; emphasis added).

BIBLIOGRAPHY

1. Primary Sources

Andrew of Caesarea

Schmid, Josef, ed. *Studien zur Geschichte des griechischen Apokalypse-Textes. Vol. 1: Der Apokalypse-Kommentar des Andreas von Kaisareia*. Münchener Theologische Studien 1. Munich: Zink, 1955.

Anon. De centesima

Reitzenstein, Richard. "Eine frühchristliche Schrift von den dreierlei Früchten des christlichen Lebens." *Zeitschrift für die neutestamentliche Wissenschaft* 15 (1914): 60–90.

Aphrahat

Bruns, Peter, trans. *Aphrahat: Unterweisungen*. Fontes christiani 5/1–2. Freiburg/New York: Herder, 1991.

Gwynn, John. *Selections translated into English from the Hymns and Homilies of Ephraim the Syrian and from the Demonstrations of Aphrahat the Persian Sage*. The Nicene and Post-Nicene Fathers, Second Series, vol. 13/2. Oxford: Parker & Co, 1898. Repr. Grand Rapids, Mich.: Eerdmans, 1983.

Parisot, Jean, ed. *Aphraatis Sapientis Persae Demonstrationes*. Patrologia Syriaca 1/1–2. Paris: Firmin-Didot, 1894; 1907.

Pierre, Marie-Joseph, trans. *Aphraate le Sage Persan: Les Exposés*. Sources chrétiennes 349, 359. Paris: Cerf, 1988–1989.

Ridolfini, Francesco Pericoli. *Le "Dimostrazioni" del "Sapiente Persiano": Traduzione italiana con introduzione e note*. Verba Seniorum 14. Brescia: Studium, 2006.

Valavanolickal, Kuriakose. *Aphrahat: Demonstrations*. Catholic Theological Studies of India 3. Changanassery: HIRS, 1999.

Apostolic Constitutions

Marcel Metzger, ed. and trans. *Les Constitutions Apostoliques*. 3 vols. Sources chrétiennes 320, 329, 336. Paris: Cerf, 1985–1987.

Basil of Caesarea

Benoît Pruche, ed. and trans. *Basile de Césarée: Sur le Saint-Esprit*. Sources chrétiennes 17bis. Paris: Cerf, 1968.

Bernard Sesboüé, ed. and trans. *Basile de Césarée: Contre Eunome*. 2 vols. Sources chrétiennes 299, 305. Paris: Cerf, 1982, 1983.

Cassiodorus

Bürsgens, Wolfgang, ed. and trans. *Cassiodor: Einführung in die geistlichen und weltlichen Wissenschaften*. Fontes christiani 39/1–2. Freiburg/New York: Herder, 2003.

Clement of Alexandria

Casey, Robert P., ed. and trans. *The Excerpta ex Theodoto of Clement of Alexandria*. London: Christophers, 1934.

Descourtieux, Patrick, ed. and trans. *Clément d'Alexandrie: Stromate VI*. Sources chrétiennes 446. Paris: Cerf, 1999.

Le Boulluec, Alain, ed., Pierre Voulet, trans. *Clément d'Alexandrie: Stromate V*. Vol. 1: *Introduction, text and index*. Vol. 2: *Commentary, bibliography, and index*. Sources chrétiennes, 278, 279. Paris: Cerf, 1981.

Le Boulluec, Alain, ed. and trans. *Clément d'Alexandrie: Stromate VII*. Sources chrétiennes 428. Paris: Cerf, 1997.

Mondésert, Claude, ed., Marcel Caster, trans. *Clément d'Alexandrie: Stromate I*. Sources chrétiennes 30. Paris: Cerf, 1951.

Mondésert, Claude, ed. and trans. *Clément d'Alexandrie: Stromate II*. Sources chrétiennes 38. Paris: Cerf, 1954.

Nardi, Carlo, ed. and trans. *Estratti profetici*. Biblioteca patristica 4. Florence: Centro internazionale del libro, 1985.

Sagnard, François, ed. and trans. *Clément d'Alexandrie: Extraits de Théodote*. Sources chrétiennes 23. Paris: Cerf, 1948.

Stählin, Otto, Ludwig Früchtel, and Ursula Treu, eds. *Clemens Alexandrinus 1: Protrepticus und Paedagogus*. Die griechischen christlichen Schriftsteller der ersten drei Jahrhunderte 12. 3rd edition. Berlin: Akademie-Verlag, 1972.

———. *Clemens Alexandrinus 2: Stromata I–VI*. Die griechischen christlichen Schriftsteller der ersten drei Jahrhunderte 52. 4th edition. Berlin: Akademie-Verlag, 1985.

———. *Clemens Alexandrinus 3: Stromata VII–VIII, Excerpta ex Theodoto, Eclogae Propheticae, Quis dives salvetur, Fragmente*. Die griechischen christlichen Schriftsteller der ersten drei Jahrhunderte 17. 2nd edition. Berlin: Akademie-Verlag, 1970.

Van den Hoek, Annewies, ed., Claude Mondésert, trans. *Clément d'Alexandrie: Stromate IV*. Sources chrétiennes 463. Paris: Cerf, 2001.

George of the Arabs

Lagarde, Paul, ed. "Georgii Arabum episcopi epistula." Pages 108–34 in *Analecta Syriaca*. Osnabrück: Otto Zeller, 1967 [1858].

Eusebius of Caesarea

Klostermann, Erich, Günther Christian Hansen, ed. *Eusebius' Werke 4: Contra Marcellum, De ecclesiastica theologia*. Die griechischen christlichen Schriftsteller der ersten drei Jahrhunderte 14. 3rd ed. 1991.

Georgius Monachus

De Muralto, Eduard, ed. Georgius Monachus (Hamartolos). *Chronicon Breve*. Patrologia graeca 110.

Gregory of Nyssa

Mueller, Friedrich, ed. *Gregorii Nysseni Opera* 3/1. Leiden: Brill, 1958.

Irenaeus of Lyon

Behr, John, trans. *Irenaeus of Lyons: On the Apostolic Preaching*. Crestwood, N.Y.: Saint Vladimir's Seminary Press, 1997.

Rousseau, Adelin, Louis Doutreleau, and Charles Mercier, eds. and trans. *Irénée de Lyon: Contre les hérésies*. Sources chrétiennes 100x–100xx, 152–153, 210–211, 263–264, 293–294. Paris: Cerf, 1965–1979.

Rousseau, Adelin, ed. and trans. *Irénée de Lyon: Démonstration de la prédication apostolique*. Sources chrétiennes 406. Paris: Cerf, 1995.

Justin Martyr

Bobichon, Philippe, ed. and trans. *Justin Martyr: Dialogue avec Tryphon.* Paradosis 47/1–2. Fribourg: Academic Press Fribourg, 2003.

Munier, Charles, ed. and trans. *Justin: Apologie pour les chrétiens.* Sources chrétiennes 507. Paris: Cerf, 2006.

Wartelle, André, ed. and trans. *Saint Justin: Apologies.* Collection des études augustiniennes, Série Antiquité 117. Paris: Études Augustiniennes, 1987.

Oecumenius

Groote, Marc de, ed. *Oecumenii Commentarius in Apocalypsin.* Traditio Exegetica Graeca 8. Leuven: Peeters, 1999.

Suggit, John N., tr. *Oecumenius: Commentary on the Apocalypse.* Washington, D.C.: Catholic University of America Press, 2006.

Origen

Bammel, Hammond, ed. *Der Römerbriefkommentar des Origenes: Kritische Ausgabe der Übersetzung Rufins.* Vetus Latina 34. Freiburg: Herder, 1998.

Blanc, Cécile, ed. and trans. *Origène: Commentaire sur saint Jean.* 5 vols. Sources chretiennes 120, 157, 222, 290, 385. Paris: Cerf, 1966–1982.

Brésard, Luc, and Henri Crouzel, with Marcel Borret, eds. and trans. *Origène: Commentaire sur le Cantique des Cantiques.* Sources chrétiennes 375, 376. Paris: Cerf, 1991.

Doutreleau, Louis, ed. and trans. *Origène: Homélies sur les Nombres.* Sources chrétiennes 442. Paris: Cerf, 1996.

Lawson, R. P., trans. *Origen: The Song of Songs, Commentary and Homilies.* Ancient Christian Writers, 26. New York: Newman, 1956.

Rowan A. Greer, trans. *Origen.* Classics of Western Spirituality 11. New York: Paulist, 1979.

Philoxenus of Mabbug

Tanghe, Antoine. "Memra de Philoxène de Mabboug sur l'inhabitation du Saint-Esprit." *Le Muséon* 73 (1960): 39–71.

Ps.-Clementine Writings

Rehm, Bernhard, and Georg Strecker, eds. *Die Pseudoklementinen 1: Homilien.* Die griechischen christlichen Schriftsteller der ersten drei Jahrhunderte 42. 3d, rev. ed. Berlin: Akademie-Verlag, 1992.

Ps.-Philo

Siegert, Folker, trans. *Drei hellenistisch-jüdische Predigten: Ps.-Philon, "Über Jona", "Über Jona" "Fragment" und "Über Simson."* Wissenschaftliche Untersuchungen zum Neuen Testament 2/61. Tübingen: Mohr Siebeck, 1992.

Siegert, Folker, and Jacques de Roulet, with Jean-Jacques Aubert and Nicolas Cochand, trans. *Pseudo-Philon: Prédications synagogales.* Sources chrétiennes 345. Paris: Cerf, 1999.

Ps.-Dionysius

Suchla, Beate Regina, ed. *Corpus Dionysiacum 1: Pseudo-Dionysius Areopagita, De divinis nominibus.* Patristische Texte und Studien 33. Berlin: Walter de Gruyter, 1990.

Heil, Günter, Adolf Martin Ritter, eds. *Corpus Dionysiacum 2: Pseudo-Dionysius Areopagita, De coelesti hierarchia, de ecclesiastica hierarchia, de mystica theologia, epistulae.* Patristische Texte und Studien 36. Berlin: Walter de Gruyter, 1991.

Revelation

Dulaey, Martine, ed. and trans. *Victorin de Poetovio: Sur L'Apocalypse et autres écrits.* Sources chrétiennes 423. Paris: Cerf, 1997.
Dyobouniotes, Constantine I., and Adolf von Harnack. *Der Scholien-Kommentar des Origenes zur Apokalypse Johannis.* Pages 21–44 in Texte und Untersuchungen zur Geschichte der altchristlichen Literatur 38.3. Leipzig: Hinrichs, 1911.
Gryson, Roger, ed. *Variorum auctorum commentaria minora in Apocalypsin Johannis.* Corpus Christianorum: Series latina 107. Turnhout: Brepols, 2003.
Turner, C. H. "The Text of the Newly Discovered Scholia of Origen on the Apocalypse." *Journal of Theological Studies* 13 (1912): 386–97.
———. "Origen, Scholia in Apocalypsin." *Journal of Theological Studies* 25 (1924): 1–15.

Rufinus

Amacker, René, and Éric Junod, eds. and trans. *Rufin d'Aquilée: Sur la falsification des livres d'Origène.* Sources chrétiennes 464. Paris: Cerf, 2002.

Shepherd of Hermas

Körtner, Ulrich H. J., and Martin Leutzsch, eds. and trans. *Papiasfragmente. Hirt des Hermas.* Schriften des Urchristentums 3. Darmstadt: Wissenschaftliche Buchgesellschaft, 1998.

2. Secondary Sources

Adam, Karl. "Die Lehre von dem hg Geiste bei Hermas und Tertullian." *Theologische Quartalschrift* 88 (1906): 36–61.
Aldama, José Antonio de. *María en la patrística de los siglos I y II.* Madrid: Editorial Biblioteca de Autores Cristianos, 1970.
Alexandre, Monique. "Apologétique judéo-hellénistique et premières apologies chrétiennes." Pages 1–40 in *Les apologistes chrétiens et la culture grecque.* Edited by Bernard Pouderon and Joseph Doré. Théologie historique 105. Paris: Beauchesne, 1998.
Allison, Dale C. *Jesus of Nazareth: Millenarian Prophet.* Minneapolis, Minn.: Augsburg Fortress, 1998.
Andia, Ysabel de. *Homo Vivens: Incorruptibilité et divinisation de l'homme selon Irénée de Lyon.* Paris: Études Augustiniennes, 1986.
Andres, Friedrich. "Die Engel- und Dämonenlehre des Klemens von Alexandrien." *Römische Quartalschrift für christliche Altertumskunde und Kichengeschichte* 34 (1926): 13–27, 129–40, 307–29.
Andresen, Carl. "Zur Entstehung und Geschichte des trinitarischen Personenbegriffs." *Zeitschrift für die neutestamentliche Wissenschaft* 52 (1961): 1–39.
Arnim, Hans Friedrich August von. "De octavo Clementis Stromateorum libro." Ph.D. diss. University of Rostock. Rostock: Adler, 1894.
Audet, Pierre. "Affinités littéraires et doctrinales du Manuel de Discipline." *Revue Biblique* 59 (1952): 218–38; 60 (1953): 41–82.
Aune, David E. *Revelation.* 3 vols. Word Biblical Commentary 52. Dallas, Tex.: Word Books, 1997.

Baarda Tijtze. *The Gospel Quotations of Aphrahat the Persian Sage.* Amsterdam: Vrije Universiteit, 1975.

Barbel, Joseph. *Christos Angelos: Die Anschauung von Christus als Bote und Engel in der gelehrten and volkstümlichen Literatur des christlichen Altertums. Zugleich ein Beitrag zur Geschichte des Ursprungs und der Fortdauer des Arianismus.* Theophaneia: Beiträge zur Religions- und Kirchengeschichte des Altertums 3. Bonn: Peter Hannstein, 1941. [Fotomechanischer Nachdruck mit einem Anhang, 1964].

Bardy, Gustave. *Clément d'Alexandrie.* Paris: Gabalda, 1926.

———. "Aux origines de l'école d'Alexandrie." *Recherches de science religieuse* 27 (1937): 65–90.

———. "Pour l'histoire de l'école d'Alexandrie." *Vivre et penser* 2 (1942): 80–108.

Barnard, Leslie W. *Justin Martyr: His Life and Thought.* Cambridge: Cambridge University Press, 1967.

———. "The Shepherd of Hermas in Recent Study." *Heythrop Journal* 9 (1968): 29–36.

———. "God, the Logos, the Spirit and the Trinity in the Theology of Athenagoras." *Studia Theologica* 24 (1970): 70–92.

Barnard, Percy Mordaunt. *The Biblical Text of Clement of Alexandria: In the Four Gospels and the Acts of the Apostles.* Cambridge: Cambridge University Press, 1899.

Barnes, Michel R. *The Power of God: Δύναμις in Gregory of Nyssa's Trinitarian Theology.* Washington, D.C.: The Catholic University of America Press, 2001.

———. "Early Christian Binitarianism: The Father and the Holy Spirit." Paper presented at the 2001 Annual Meeting of the North American Patristics Society (online: www.mu.edu/maqom/barnes).

———. "The Visible Christ and the Invisible Trinity: Mt. 5:8 in Augustine's Trinitarian Theology of 400." *Modern Theology* 19 (2003): 329–55.

Bauckham, Richard. "The Role of the Spirit in the Apocalypse." *Evangelical Quarterly* 52 (1980): 66–83.

———. "The Fall of Angels as the Source of Philosophy in Hermias and Clement of Alexandria." *Vigiliae christianae* 39 (1985): 313–30.

———. *Jude. 2 Peter.* Word Biblical Commentary 50. Dallas, Tex.: Word Books, 1993.

———. *The Climax of Prophecy: Studies on the Book of Revelation.* Edinburgh: T&T Clark, 1993.

Becker, Adam H., and Annette Y. Reed, eds. *The Ways that Never Parted.* Texte und Studien zum antiken Judentum 95. Tübingen: Mohr Siebeck, 2003.

Beckwith, Isbon Thaddeus. *The Apocalypse of John: Studies in Introduction with a Critical and Exegetical Commentary.* New York: Macmillan, 1919. Repr. Grand Rapids, Mich.: Baker, 1967.

Benoit, André. *Le baptême chrétien au second siècle: la théologie des pères.* Paris: Presses Universitaires de France, 1953.

Berthold, George C. "Origen and the Holy Spirit." Pages 444–48 in *Origeniana Quinta: Papers of the 5th International Origen Congress, Boston College, 14–18 August 1989.* Edited by Robert J. Daly. Bibliotheca ephemeridum theologicarum lovaniensum 105. Leuven: Leuven University Press, 1992.

Boeft, Jan den, and David T. Runia, eds. *ARCHE: A Collection of Patristic Studies by J. C. M. van Winden.* Supplements to Vigiliae Christianae 41. Leiden: Brill, 1997.

Bos, Abraham P. *Cosmic and Meta-Cosmic Theology in Aristotle's Lost Dialogues.* Brill's Studies in Intellectual History 16. Leiden/New York: Brill, 1989.

———. *The Soul and Its Instrumental Body: A Reinterpretation of Aristotle's Philosophy of Living Nature.* Brill's Studies in Intellectual History 112. Leiden/Boston: Brill, 2003.

Bousset, Wilhelm. *Jüdisch-christlicher Schulbetrieb in Alexandria und Rom: Literarische Untersuchungen zu Philo und Clemens von Alexandria, Justin und Irenäus.* Göttingen: Vandenhoeck & Ruprecht, 1915.

Boyarin, Daniel. *Border Lines: The Partition of Judaeo-Christianity.* Philadelphia, PA.: University of Pennsylvania Press, 2004.

Braun, François Marie. *Jean le Théologien et son évangile dans l'église ancienne.* Paris: Gabalda, 1959.

Brock, Sebastian. *The Syriac Fathers on Prayer and the Spiritual Life.* Kalamazoo, Mich.: Cistercian Publications, 1987.

———. "The Priesthood of the Baptized: Some Syriac Perspectives." *Sobornost* 9 (1987): 14–22.

———. *Spirituality in the Syriac Tradition.* Kerala, India: St. Ephrem Ecumenical Research Institute, 1989.

———. "The Holy Spirit as Feminine in Early Syriac Literature." Pages 73–88 in *After Eve.* Edited by Janet Martin Soskice. London: Collins, 1990.

———. "Fire from Heaven: From Abel's Sacrifice to the Eucharist: A Theme in Syrian Christianity." *Studia Patristica* 25 (1993): 229–43.

———. *From Ephrem to Romanos: Interactions Between Syriac and Greek in Late Antiquity.* Brookfield: Ashgate Variorum, 1999.

Broek, Roelof van den. *Studies in Gnosticism and Alexandrian Christianity.* Nag Hammadi and Manichaean Studies 39. Leiden: Brill, 1996.

Brooks, James A. "Clement of Alexandria as a Witness to the Development of the New Testament Canon." *The Second Century* 9 (1992): 41–55.

Brox, Norbert. *Der Hirt des Hermas.* Kommentar zu den Apostolischen Vätern, 7. Göttingen: Vandenhoek & Ruprecht, 1991.

Bruce, F. F. "The Earliest Latin Commentary on the Apocalypse." *Evangelical Quarterly* 10 (1938): 352–66.

———. "The Spirit in the Apocalypse." Pages 333–344 in *Christ and Spirit in the New Testament: In Honour of C. F. D. Moule.* Edited by Barnabas Lindars and Stephen S. Smalley. Cambridge: Cambridge University Press, 1973.

Bruns, Peter. *Das Christusbild Aphrahats des Persischen Weisen.* Bonn: Borengässer, 1990.

Bucur, Bogdan G. "The Other Clement: Cosmic Hierarchy and Interiorized Apocalypticism." *Vigiliae christianae* 60 (2006): 251–68.

———. "Observations on the Ascetic Doctrine of the Shepherd of Hermas." *Studia Monastica* 48 (2006): 7–23.

———. "The Son of God and the Angelomorphic Holy Spirit: A Rereading of the Shepherd's Christology." *Zeitschrift für die neutestamentliche Wissenschaft* 98 (2007): 121–43.

———. "Revisiting Christian Oeyen: 'The Other Clement' on Father, Son, and the Angelomorphic Spirit." *Vigiliae christianae* 61 (2007): 381–413.

———. "Hierarchy, Prophecy, and the Angelomorphic Spirit: A Contribution to the Study of the Book of Revelation's Wirkungsgeschichte." *Journal of Biblical Literature* 127 (2008): 183–204.

———. "The Angelic Spirit in Early Christianity: Justin, the Martyr and Philosopher," *Journal of Religion* 88 (2008): 190–208.

———. "Matt. 18:10 in Early Christology and Pneumatology: A Contribution to the Study of Matthean *Wirkungsgeschichte.*" *Novum Testamentum* 49 (2007): 209–31.

Burge, Gary M. *The Anointed Community: the Holy Spirit in the Johannine Tradition.* Grand Rapids, Mich.: Eerdmans, 1987.

Butterworth, G. W. "The Deification of Man in Clement of Alexandria." *Journal of Theological Studies* 17 (1916): 157–69.

Cantalamessa, Raniero. "La primitiva esegesi cristologica di 'Romani' I, 3–4 e 'Luca' I, 35." *Rivista di storia e letteratura religiosa* 2 (1966): 69–80.

———. *L'omelia in S. Pascha dello pseudo-Ippolito di Roma: Ricerche sulla teologia dell'Asia Minore nella seconda metà del II secolo.* Milan: Vita e pensiero, 1967.

Caragounis, Chris. *The Development of Greek and the New Testament*. Wissenschaftliche Untersuchungen zum Neuen Testament 2/167. Tübingen: Mohr Siebeck, 2004.

Carlson, Stephen C. "Clement of Alexandria on the 'Order' of the Gospels." *New Testament Studies* 47 (2001): 118–25.

Carrell, Peter R. *Jesus and the Angels: Angelology and the Christology of the Apocalypse of John*. Society for New Testament Studies Monograph Series 95. Cambridge/New York: Cambridge University Press, 1997.

Casurella, Anthony. *The Johannine Paraclete in the Church Fathers: A Study in the History of Exegesis*. Beiträge zur Geschichte der biblischen Exegese 25. Tübingen: Mohr Siebeck, 1983.

Casey, Robert P. "Clement and the Two Divine Logoi." *The Journal of Theological Studies* 25 (1923): 43–56.

———. "Clement of Alexandria and the Beginnings of Christian Platonism." *Harvard Theological Review* 18 (1925): 39–101.

Charles, R. H. *A Critical And Exegetical Commentary on The Revelation of St. John*. 2 vols. Edinburgh: T&T Clark International, 1920.

Charlesworth, James H. "The Portrayal of the Righteous as an Angel." Pages 135–51 in *Ideal Figures in Ancient Judaism; Profiles and Paradigms*. Edited by John J. Collins and George W. E. Nickelsburg. Society of Biblical Literature Septuagint and Cognate Studies 12. Chico, Ca.: Scholars, 1980.

Choufrine, Arkadi. *Gnosis, Theophany, Theosis: Studies in Clement of Alexandria's Appropriation of His Background*. New York/London: Peter Lang, 2002.

Coleborne, W. "A Linguistic Approach to the Problem of Structure and Composition of the Shepherd of Hermas." *Colloquium* 3 (1969): 133–42.

———. "The Shepherd of Hermas: A Case for Multiple Authorship and Some Implications." *Studia Patristica* 10 (1970): 65–70.

Collomp, Paul. "Une source de Clément d'Alexandrie et des Homélies Pseudo-Clémentines." *Revue de philologie de littérature et d'histoire anciennes* 37 (1913): 19–46.

Connolly, R. H. "Aphraates and Monasticism." *Journal of Theological Studies* 6 (1905): 522–39.

Corbin, Henry. *L'Ange et l'homme*. Paris: Albin Michel, 1978.

Cosaert, Carl. P. "The Text of the Gospels in the Writings of Clement of Alexandria." Ph.D. diss. University of North Carolina at Chapel Hill, 2005.

Cramer, Winfrid. *Die Engelvorstellungen bei Ephräm dem Syrer*. Rome: Pontificium Institutum Orientalium Studiorum, 1965.

———. "Mt 18, 10 in frühsyrischer Deutung." *Oriens christianus* 59 (1975): 130–46.

———. *Der Geist Gottes und des Menschen in frühsyrischer Theologie*. Münsterische Beiträge zur Theologie 46. Münster: Aschendorff, 1979.

Crouzel, Henri. "Le thème platonicien du 'véhicule de l'âme' chez Origène." *Didaskalia* 7 (1977): 225–38.

Daley, Brian. *The Hope of the Early Church: A Handbook of Patristic Eschatology*. Peabody, Mass.: Hendrickson, 2003 [1991].

Daniélou, Jean. "Trinité et angélologie dans la théologie judéo-chrétienne." *Recherches de science religieuse* 45 (1957): 5–41.

———. "Les traditions secrètes des Apôtres." *Eranos Jahrbuch* 31 (1962): 199–215.

———. *The Theology of Jewish Christianity*. London: Darton, Longman & Todd, 1964 [1958].

———. "Le traité 'De Centesima, Sexagesima, Tricesima' et le judéo-christianisme latin avant Tertullien." *Vigiliae christianae* 25 (1971): 171–81.

———. "La tradition selon Clément d'Alexandrie." *Augustinianum* 12 (1972): 5–18.

Davey, D. M. "Justin Martyr and the Fourth Gospel." *Scripture* 17 (1965): 117–22.

Davies, W. D., and Dale C. Allison, Jr., *A Critical and Exegetical Commentary on the Gospel According to Saint Matthew*. International Critical Commentary 1. London: T&T Clark, 1989.

Davison, James E. "Structural Similarities and Dissimilarities in the Thought of Clement of Alexandria and the Valentinians." *The Second Century* 3 (1983): 201–17.

Dawson, David. *Allegorical Readers and Cultural Revision in Ancient Alexandria.* Berkeley: University of California Press, 1992.

DeConick, April D. *Seek to See Him: Ascent and Vision Mysticism in the Gospel of Thomas.* Supplements to Vigiliae Christianae 33. Leiden: Brill, 1996.

———. "Heavenly Temple Traditions and Valentinian Worship: A Case for First-Century Christology in the Second Century." Pages 308–41 in *The Jewish Roots of Christological Monotheism.* Edited by C. C. Newman, J. R. Davila, and G. S. Lewis. Supplements to the Journal for the Study of Judaism 63. Leiden: Brill, 1999.

———. "The Great Mystery of Marriage: Sex and Conception in Ancient Valentinian Traditions." *Vigiliae christianae* 57 (2003): 307–42.

———. *Recovering The Original Gospel of Thomas: A History of the Gospel and Its Growth.* Library of New Testament Studies 286. Edinburgh: T&T Clark, 2005.

Deutsch, Nathaniel. *Guardians of the Gate: Angelic Vice Regency in Late Antiquity.* Brill's Series in Jewish Studies 22. Leiden: Brill, 1999.

Dibelius, Martin. *Der Hirt des Hermas.* Die Apostolischen Väter 4. Tübingen: Mohr, 1923.

Di Benedetto, Filippo. "Un nuovo frammento delle *Ipotiposi* di Clemente Alessandrino." *Sileno* 9 (1983): 75–82.

Dix, Gregory. "The Seven Archangels and the Seven Spirits: A Study in the Origin, Developement, and Messianic Associations of the Two Themes." *Journal of Theological Studies* 28 (1927): 233–50.

Droge, Arthur J. "Justin Martyr and the Restoration of Philosophy." *Church History* 56 (1987): 303–19.

Duckworth, Colin, and Eric Osborn. "Clement of Alexandria's Hypotyposeis: A French Eighteenth-Century Sighting." *Journal of Theological Studies* n.s. 36 (1985): 67–83.

Dunn, James D. G. "Once More, ΠΙΣΤΙΣ ΧΡΙΣΤΟΥ." Society of Biblical Literature Seminar Papers 30 (1991): 730–42.

Dünzl, Franz. *Pneuma: Funktionen des theologischen Begriffs in frühchristlicher Literatur.* Jahrbuch für Antike und Christentum, Ergänzungsband 30. Münster, Westfalen: Aschendorffsche Verlagsbuchhandlung, 2000.

Echle, Harry A. "The Baptism of the Apostles: A Fragment of Clement of Alexandria's Lost Work *Hypotyposeis* in the *Pratum Spirituale* of John Moschus." *Traditio* 3 (1945): 365–68.

Edwards, Mark J. "Clement of Alexandria and His Doctrine of the Logos." *Vigiliae christianae* 54 (2000): 159–77.

Eijk, Ton H. C. "Gospel of Philip and Clement of Alexandria: Gnostic and Ecclesiastical Theology on the Resurrection and the Eucharist." *Vigiliae christianae* 25 (1971): 94–120.

Elior, Rachel. *The Three Temples: On the Emergence of Jewish Mysticism.* Oxford/ Portland: The Littman Library of Jewish Civilization, 2005.

Farkasfalvy, Denis M. "The Presbyters' Witness on the Order of the Gospels as Reported by Clement of Alexandria." *Catholic Biblical Quarterly* 54 (1992): 260–70.

Fatehi, Mehrdad. *The Spirit's Relation to the Risen Lord in Paul.* Wissenschaftliche Untersuchungen zum Neuen Testament 2/128. Tübingen: Mohr Siebeck, 2000.

Faye, Eugène de. *Clément d'Alexandrie: étude sur les rapports du christianisme et de la philosophie grecque au IIe siècle.* Paris: Leroux, 1898.

Fee, Gordon D. *God's Empowering Presence: The Holy Spirit in the Letters of Paul.* Peabody, Mass.: Hendrickson, 1994.

———. "Christology and Pneumatology in Romans 8:9–11 and Elsewhere: Some Reflections on Paul as a Trinitarian." Pages 312–31 in *Jesus of Nazareth: Lord and Christ: Essays in the Historical Jesus and New Testament Christology.* Edited by Joel B. Greene and Max Turner. Grand Rapids, Mich.: Eerdmans, 1994.

Ferguson, John. "The Achievement of Clement of Alexandria." *Religious Studies* 12 (1976): 59–80.

Feulner, Rüdiger. *Clemens von Alexandrien: sein Leben, Werk und philosophisch-theologisches Denken.* Frankfurt am Main/New York: Peter Lang, 2006.

Fiensy, David A. *Prayers Alleged to Be Jewish: An Examination of the Constitutiones Apostolorum.* Brown Judaic Studies 65. Chico, Ca: Scholars, 1985.

Fletcher-Louis, Crispin. *Luke-Acts: Angels, Christology and Soteriology.* Wissenschaftliche Untersuchungen zum Neuen Testament 2/94. Tübingen: Mohr Siebeck, 1997.

Fontaine, J., and M. Perrin, eds. *Lactance et son temps: recherches actuelles.* Actes du IVᵉ Colloque d'études historiques et patristiques, Chantilly, 21–23 septembre 1976. Paris: Beauchesne, 1978.

Förster, Niclas. *Marcus Magus: Kult, Lehre und Gemeideleben einer valentinianischen Gnostikergruppe: Sammlung der Quellen und Kommentar.* Wissenschaftliche Untersuchungen zum Neuen Testament 2/114. Tübingen: Mohr Siebeck, 1999.

Fortin, E. L. "Clement and the Esoteric Tradition." *Studia Patristica* 9 (1966)/Texte und Untersuchungen zur Geschichte der altchristlichen Literatur 94: 41–56.

Fossum, Jarl. "Jewish-Christian Christology and Jewish Mysticism." *Vigiliae christianae* 37 (1983): 260–87.

——. "Colossians 1.15–18a in the Light of Jewish Mysticism and Gnosticism." *New Testament Studies* 35 (1989): 183–201.

——. "Glory." Pages 348–352 in *Dictionary of Deities and Demons in the Bible.* Edited by K. Van der Toorn, B. Becking, and P. W. van der Horst. Leiden: Brill, 1999.

Foster, Edgar G. *Angelomorphic Christology and the Exegesis of Psalm 8:5 in Tertullian's Adversus Praxean: An Examination of Tertullian's Reluctance to Attribute Angelic Properties to the Son of God.* Lanham, Md.: University Press of America, 2005.

Frangoulis, Johannes. *Der Begriff des Geistes Πνεῦμα bei Clemens Alexandrinus.* Leipzig: Robert Noske, 1936.

Fredrikson, Nadia Ibrahim. "L'Esprit saint et les esprits mauvais dans le *Pasteur* d'Hermas: Sources et Prolongements." *Vigiliae christianae* 55 (2001): 262–80.

Frend, W. H. C. *Martyrdom and Persecution in the Early Church: A Study of a Conflict from the Maccabees to Donatus.* Garden City, N.Y.: Doubleday, 1967 [1965].

Gavin, Frank. "The Sleep of the Soul in the Early Syriac Church." *Journal of the American Oriental Society* 40 (1920): 103–20.

Gieschen, Charles. *Angelomorphic Christology: Antecedents and Early Evidence.* Arbeiten zur Geschichte des antiken Judentums und des Urchristentums 42. Leiden: Brill, 1998.

——. "The Divine Name in Ante-Nicene Christology." *Vigiliae christianae* 57 (2003): 115–58.

Giet, Stanislas. *Hermas et les Pasteurs: les trois auteurs du Pasteur d'Hermas.* Paris: Presses Universitaires de France, 1963.

Golitzin, Alexander. *Et introibo ad altare Dei: The Mystagogy of Dionysius Areopagita, with Special Reference to Its Predecessors in the Eastern Christian Tradition.* Analekta Vlatadon 59. Thessalonica: Patriarchal Institute of Patristic Studies, 1994.

——. "Earthly Angels and Heavenly Men: the Old Testament Pseudepigrapha, Nicetas Stethatos, and the Tradition of Interiorized Apocalyptic in Eastern Christian Ascetical and Mystical Literature." *Dumbarton Oaks Papers* 55 (2001): 125–53.

——. "Recovering the 'Glory of Adam': 'Divine Light' Traditions in the Dead Sea Scrolls and the Christian Ascetical Literature of Fourth-Century Syro-Mesopotamia." Pages 275–308 in *The Dead Sea Scrolls as Background to Postbiblical Judaism and Early Christianity: Papers from an International Conference at St. Andrews in 2001.* Edited by James R. Davila. Studies on the Texts of the Desert of Judah 46. Leiden: Brill, 2003.

——. "The Place of the Presence of God: Aphrahat of Persia's Portrait of the Christian Holy Man." Pages 391–47 in *ΣΥΝΑΞΙΣ ΕΥΧΑΡΙΣΤΙΑΣ: Studies in Honor of*

Archimandrite Aimilianos of Simonos Petras, Mount Athos. Edited by the Holy Monastery of Simonos Petras of the Holy Mount. Athens: Indiktos, 2003.

———. "Dionysius Areopagita: A Christian Mysticism?" *Pro Ecclesia* 12 (2003): 161–212.

Goodenough, Erwin R. *The Theology of Justin Martyr.* Jena: Frommannsche Buchhandlung, 1923.

Grillmeier, Aloys. *Christ in Christian Tradition.* 2nd, revised edition. Atlanta, Ga: John Knox, 1975.

Groote, Marc de. "*Die Quaestio Oecumeniana.*" *Sacris Eruditi: Jaarboek voor Godsdienstwetenschappen* 36 (1996): 67–105.

Gundry, Robert H. *Matthew: A Commentary On His Handbook For A Mixed Church Under Persecution.* Grand Rapids, Mich.: Eerdmans, 1994.

———. "Angelomorphic Christology in Revelation." *Society of Biblical Literature Seminar Papers* 33 (1994): 662–78.

Haas, Cornelis. "Die Pneumatologie des 'Hirten des Hermas.'" *Aufstieg und Niedergang der Römischen Welt* II/27.1 (1993): 552–86.

Hadot, Ilsetraut. *Art libéraux et philosophie dans la pensée antique.* Paris: Études Augustiniennes, 1984.

———. "Les introductions aux commentaries exégétiques chez les auteurs néoplatoniciens et les auteurs chrétiens." Pages 99–119 in *Les règles de l'interprétation.* Edited by Michel Tardieu. Paris: Cerf, 1987.

Hadot, Pierre. "Les divisions des parties de la philosophie dans l'Antiquité." *Museum helveticum* 36 (1979): 201–23.

Hägg, Henny Fiskå. *Clement of Alexandria and the Beginnings of Christian Apophaticism.* Oxford Early Christian Studies. Oxford: Oxford University Press, 2006.

Hagner, Donald A. *Matthew.* Word Biblical Commentary 33A. Dallas, Tex.: Word Books, 1993.

Halperin, David J. "Origen, Ezekiel's Merkabah, and the Ascension of Moses." Church History 50 (1981): 261–75.

Hamman, Adalbert Gauthier. "La Trinidad en la catechesis de los Padres Griegos." *Estudios trinitarios* 12 (1978): 73–85.

Hannah, Darrell D. *Michael and Christ: Michael Traditions and Angel Christology in Early Christianity.* Wissenschaftliche Untersuchungen zum Neuen Testament 2/109. Tübingen: Mohr Siebeck, 1999.

Hanson, Anthony Tyrrell. "Hodayoth vi and viii and Hermas Herm. Sim. VIII." *Studia Patristica* 10 (1970)/Texte und Untersuchungen zur Geschichte der altchristlichen Literatur 107: 105–8.

Harl, Marguerite. "Les prologue des commentaries sur le Cantique des Cantiques." Pages 249–269 in *Texte und Textkritik: Eine Aufsatzsammlung.* Edited by J. Dummer et al. Texte und Untersuchungen zur Geschichte der altchristlichen Literatur 133. Berlin: Akademie-Verlag, 1987.

Harnack, Adolf von. *Geschichte der altchristlichen Literatur bis Eusebius* I–II. Hinrichs: Leipzig, 1958 [1893–1904].

Harvey, Susan Ashbrook. "Feminine Imagery for the Divine: the Holy Spirit, the Odes of Solomon, and Early Syriac Tradition." *Saint Vladimir's Theological Quarterly* 37 (1993): 111–40.

Hauck, Robert J. "The Great Fast: Christology in the Shepherd of Hermas." *Anglican Theological Review* 75 (1993): 187–98.

Hauschild, Wolf-Dieter. *Gottes Geist und der Mensch: Studien zur frühchristlichen Pneumatologie.* Beiträge zur evangelischen Theologie 63. Munich: Kaiser, 1972.

Hays, Richard B. *The Faith of Jesus Christ: The Narrative Substructure of Galatians 3:1–4:11.* 2nd edition. Grand Rapids, Mich.: Eerdmans/Dearborn, Mich.: Dove, 2002.

Heine, Ronald E. "The Alexandrians." Pages 117–30 in *The Cambridge History of Early Christian Literature*. Edited by Francis Young, Lewis Ayres, and Andrew Louth. Cambridge: Cambridge University Press, 2004.

Henne, Philipe. "La cohérence des niveaux d'explication dans la Cinquième Similitude." *Revue des sciences philosophiques et théologiques* 72 (1988): 569–78.

———. "La polysémie allégorique dans le Pasteur d'Hermas." *Ephemerides theologicae lovanienses* 65 (1989): 131–5.

———. "La véritable christologie de la Cinquième Similitude du Pasteur d'Hermas." *Revue des sciences philosophiques et théologiques* 74 (1990): 182–204.

———. *La Christologie chez Clément de Rome et dans le Pasteur d'Hermas*. Paradosis 33. Fribourg: Éditions Universitaires, 1992.

Hennessey, Lawrence R. "A Philosophical Issue in Origen's Eschatology: The Three Senses of Incorporeality." Pages 373–80 in *Origeniana Quinta: Papers of the 5th International Origen Congress, Boston College, 14–18 August 1989*. Edited by Robert J. Daly. Bibliotheca ephemeridum theologicarum lovaniensum 105. Leuven: Leuven University Press, 1992.

Héring, Jean. "Un texte oublié: Mt 18, 10. À propos des controverses récentes sur le pédobaptisme." Pages 95–102 in *Aux sources de la tradition chrétienne: FS Maurice Goguel*. Edited by O. Cullmann et al. Neuchâtel: Delachaux & Niestlé, 1950.

Hernans, Theo. *Origène: Théologie sacrificielle du sacerdoce des chrétiens*. Théologie historique 88. Paris: Beauchesne, 1996.

Heussi, Carl. "Die Stromateis des Clemens Alexandrinus und ihr Verhältnis zum Protreptikos und Pädagogos." *Zeitschrift für wissenschaftliche Theologie* 45 (1902): 465–512.

Hilhorst, Antonius. *Sémitismes et Latinismes dans le Pasteur d'Hermas*. Graecitas Christianorum Primaeva 5. Nijmegen: Dekker & Van de Vegt, 1976.

Hills, Julian. *Tradition and Composition in the Epistula Apostolorum*. Harvard Dissertations in Religion 24. Minneapolis, Minn.: Fortress, 1990.

Hofer, Andrew. "The Old Man as Christ in Justin *Dialogue with Trypho*." *Vigiliae christianae* 57 (2003): 1–21.

Hoffmann, Matthias Reinhard. *The Destroyer and the Lamb: The Relationship Between Angelomorphic and Lamb Christology in the Book of Revelation*. Wissenschaftliche Untersuchungen zum Neuen Testament 2/203. Tübingen: Mohr Siebeck, 2005.

Hooker, Morna D. "Πίστις Χριστοῦ." *New Testament Studies* 35 (1989): 321–42.

Hovhanessian, Vahan. *Third Corinthians: Reclaiming Paul for Christian Orthodoxy*. Studies in Biblical Literature 18. New York: Peter Lang, 2000.

Hurtado, Larry. *At the Origins of Christian Worship*. Grand Rapids, Mich.: Eerdmans, 1999.

———. *Lord Jesus Christ: Devotion to Jesus in Earliest Christianity*. Grand Rapids, Mich.: Eerdmans, 2003.

Jakab, Attila. *Ecclesia Alexandrina: Evolution sociale et institutionnelle du christianisme alexandrin (IIᵉ et IIIᵉ siècles)*. Christianismes anciens 1. Bern: Peter Lang, 2004.

Jefford, Clayton N. "Clement of Alexandria and Gnosis: A Dissertation in Review." *Perspectives in Religious Studies* 20 (1993): 381–96.

Jeremias, Joachim. *New Testament Theology*. London: SCM, 1971.

Joly, Robert. "Hermas et le Pasteur." *Vigiliae christianae* 21 (1967): 201–18.

———. "Le milieu complexe du Pasteur d'Hermas." *Aufstieg und Niedergang der Römischen Welt* II/27.1 (1993): 524–51.

Jones, F. Stanley. "The Pseudo-Clementines: A History of Research." *The Second Century* 2 (1982): 1–33, 63–96.

Junod, Éric. "À propos des soi-disants scolies sur l'Apocalypse d'Origène." *Rivista di storia e letteratura religiosa* 20 (1984): 112–21.

Kaniyamparampil, Emmanuel. "Feminine-Maternal Images of the Spirit in Early Syriac Tradition." *Letter and Spirit* 3 (2007): 169–88.

Kiddle, Martin. *The Revelation of St. John.* London: Hodder and Stoughton, 1963 [1940].

Kimelman, Reuven. "Rabbi Yohanan and Origen on the Song of Songs: A Third-Century Jewish-Christian Disputation." *Harvard Theological Review* 73 (1980): 567–95.

Kindiy, Oleh. *Christos Didaskalos: The Christology of Clement of Alexandria.* Saarbrücken: VDM Verlag Dr. Müller, 2008.

Kirchmeyer, J. "Origène, Commentaire sur le Cantique, prol. (GCS Origenes 8, Baehrens, p. 75, ligne 8)." *Studia Patristica* 10 (1970)/Texte und Untersuchungen zur Geschichte der altchristlichen Literatur 107: 230–35.

Knauber, Adolf. "Die patrologische Schätzung des Clemens von Alexandrien bis zu seinem neuerlichen Bekanntwerden durch die ersten Druckeditionen des 16. Jahrhunderts." Pages 289–308 in *Kyriakon: Festschrift Johannes Quasten.* Edited by Patrick Granfield and Josef A. Jungmann. Münster: Aschendorff, 1970.

Knight, Jonathan. *Disciples of the Beloved One: The Christology, Social Setting, and Theological Context of the Ascension of Isaiah.* Journal for the Study of the Pseudepigrapha: Supplement Series 18; Sheffield: Sheffield Academic Press, 1996.

Kovacs, Judith. "Divine Pedagogy and the Gnostic Teacher According to Clement of Alexandria." *Journal of Early Christian Studies* 9 (2001): 3–25.

Kovacs, Judith and Christopher Rowland. *Revelation: The Apocalypse of Jesus Christ.* Malden, Mass.: Blackwell, 2004.

Kretschmar, Georg. *Studien zur frühchristlichen Trinitätstheologie.* Beiträge zur historischen Theologie 21. Tübingen: Mohr, 1956.

——. "Ein Beitrag zur Frage nach dem Ursprung frühchristlicher Askese." *Zeitschrift für Theologie und Kirche* 64 (1961): 27–67.

Ladaria, Luis. *El Espíritu en Clemente Alejandrino: Estudio teológico antropológico.* Madrid: Universidad Pontificia Comillas de Madrid, 1980.

Lamoreaux, John C. "The Provenance of *Ecumenius*' Commentary on the. Apocalypse." *Vigiliae Christianae* 52 (1998): 88–108.

Lattey, Cuthbert. "The Deification of Man in Clement of Alexandria: Some Further Notes." *Journal of Theological Studies* 17 (1916): 257–62.

Lazzati, Giuseppe. *Introduzione allo studio di Clemente Alessandrino.* Milan: Vita e pensiero, 1939.

Le Boulluec, Alain. "L'école d'Alexandrie: de quelques aventures d'un concept historiographique." Pages 403–417 in *Alexandrina: Héllenisme, Judaisme et christianisme à Alexandrie. Mélanges offerts à Claude Mondésert.* Edited by Marguerite Harl. Paris: Cerf, 1987.

——. "Extraits d'oeuvres de Clément d'Alexandrie: La transmission et le sens de leur titres." Pages 287–300 in *Titres et articulations du texte dans les oeuvres antiques.* Actes du colloque international de Chantilly 13–15 décembre 1994. Edited by Jean-Claude Fredouille et al. Paris: Institut d'Études Augustiniennes, 1997.

——. "Pour qui, pourquoi, comment? Les 'Stromates' de Clément d'Alexandrie." Pages 23–36 in *Entrer en matière: Les prologues.* Edited by Jean-Daniel Dubois and Bernard Roussel. Paris: Cerf, 1998.

Lebreton, Jules. "Le désaccord entre la foi populaire et la théologie savante dans l'Église chrétienne du IIe siècle." *Revue d'histoire ecclésiastique* 19 (1923): 481–506; 20 (1924): 5–37.

——. "La théologie de la Trinité chez Clément d'Alexandrie." *Recherches de science religieuse* 34 (1946): 55–76, 142–79.

Levison, John R. "The Angelic Spirit in Early Judaism." *Society of Biblical Literature Seminar Papers* 34 (1995): 464–93.

——. "The Prophetic Spirit as an Angel According to Philo." *Harvard Theological Review* 88 (1995): 189–207.

——. *The Spirit in First Century Judaism.* Arbeiten zur Geschichte des antiken Judentums und des Urchristentums 29. Leiden: Brill, 1997.

Lilla, Salvatore. *Clement of Alexandria: A Study in Christian Platonism and Gnosticism.* Oxford: Oxford University Press, 1971.

Longenecker, Richard N. "Some Distinctive Early Christological Motifs." *New Testament Studies* 14 (1968): 526–45.

Loofs, Friedrich. *Theophilus von Antiochien Adversus Marcionem und die anderen theologischen Quellen bei Irenaeus.* Texte und Untersuchungen zur Geschichte der altchristlichen Literatur 46. Leipzig: Hinrichs, 1930.

Lueken, Wilhelm. *Michael: Eine Darstellung und Vergleich der jüdischen und morgen-ländisch-christlichen Tradition vom Erzengel Michael.* Göttingen: Vandenhoeck & Ruprecht, 1898.

Lupieri, Edmondo F. *A Commentary on the Apocalypse of John.* Grand Rapids, Mich.: Eerdmans, 2006.

Lusini, Gianfrancesco. "Nouvelles recherches sur le texte du Pasteur d'Hermas." *Apocrypha* 12 (2001): 79–97.

Luz, Ulrich. *Matthew 8–20: A Commentary.* Hermeneia. Minneapolis, Minn.: Augsburg Fortress, 2001.

Mach, Michael. Entwicklungsstadien des jüdischen Engelglaubens in vorrabbinischer Zeit. Texte und Studien zum Antiken Judentum 34. Tübingen: Mohr Siebeck, 1992.

Macholz, Waldemar. *Spuren binitarischer Denkweise im Abendlande seit Tertullian.* Jena: Kämpfe, 1902.

Markschies, Christoph. *Alta Trinità Beata: Gesammelte Studien zur altkirchlichen Trinitätstheologie.* Tübingen: Mohr Siebeck, 2000.

———. *Origenes und sein Erbe: Gesammelte Studien.* Texte und Untersuchungen zur Geschichte der altchristlichen Literatur 160. Berlin/New York: Walter de Gruyter, 2007.

Marrou, Henri-Irenée. *A History of Education in Antiquity.* Madison, Wis.: University of Wisconsin Press, 1982 [1956].

Martin, José Pablo. *El Espíritu Santo en los orígenes del Cristianismo: Estudio sobre I Clemente, Ignacio, II Clemente y Justino Martir.* Zürich: PAS Verlag, 1971.

McDonough, Sean. *YHWH at Patmos.* Wissenschaftliche Untersuchungen zum Neuen Testament 2/107. Tübingen: Mohr Siebeck, 1999.

McGuckin, John Anthony. "Lactantius as Theologian: An Angelic Christology on the Eve of Nicaea." *Rivista di storia e letteratura religiosa* 22 (1986): 492–97.

McGuckin, Paul. "Spirit Christology: Lactantius and His Sources." *Heythrop Journal* 24 (1983): 141–48.

McNamara, Martin. *The New Testament and the Palestinian Targum to the Pentateuch.* Analecta Biblica 27. Rome: Pontifical Biblical Institute: 1966.

Mees, Michael. *Die Zitate aus dem Neuen Testament bei Clemens von Alexandrien.* Quaderni di "Vetera Christianorum" 2. Bari: Instituto di Letteratura Cristiana Antica, 1970.

Méhat, André. "'Apocatastase': Origène, Clément d'Alexandrie, Act. 3, 21," *Vigiliae christianae* 10 (1956): 196–214.

———. *Étude sur les "Stromates" de Clément d'Alexandrie.* Patristica Sorbonensia 7. Paris: Seuil, 1966.

———. "Θεὸς Ἀγάπη: Une hypothèse sur l'objet de la gnose orthodoxe." *Studia Patristica* 9 (1966)/Texte und Untersuchungen zur Geschichte der altchristlichen Literatur 94: 82–86.

Merkel, Helmut. "Clemens Alexandrinus über die Reihenfolge der Evangelien." *Ephemerides theologicae lovanienses* 60 (1984): 382–5.

Mettinger, Tryggve N. D. "YAHWEH Zebaoth." Pages 920–24 in *Dictionary of Deities and Demons in the Bible.* Edited by K. van der Toorn, B. Becking, and P. W. van der Horst. 2nd, extensively revised edition. Leiden: Brill, 1999.

Michl, Joseph. *Die Engelvorstellungen in der Apokalypse des hl. Johannes.* Munich: Max Hueber, 1937.

Mondésert, Claude. *Clément d'Alexandrie: Introduction à l'étude de sa pensée religieuse à partir de l'écriture*. Paris: Aubier/Montaigne, 1944.
Morgan-Wynne, John Eifion. "The Holy Spirit and Christian Experience in Justin Martyr." *Vigiliae christianae* 38 (1984): 172–77.
———. "The 'Delicacy' of the Spirit in the Shepherd of Hermas and in Tertullian." *Studia Patristica* 21 (1989): 154–57.
Morray-Jones, C. R. A. "Transformational Mysticism in the Apocalyptic-Merkabah Tradition." *Journal of Jewish Studies* 43 (1992): 1–31.
———. "The Temple Within: The Embodied Divine Image and its Worship in the Dead Sea Scrolls and Other Early Jewish and Christian Sources," Society of Biblical Literature Seminar Papers 37 (1998): 400–431.
Mortley, Raoul. *Connaissance religieuse et herméneutique chez Clément d'Alexandrie*. Leiden: Brill, 1973.
———. "Mirror and I Cor 13:12 in the Epistemology of Clement of Alexandria." *Vigiliae christianae* 30 (1976): 109–120.
———. "The Theme of Silence in Clement of Alexandria." *Journal of Theological Studies* n.s. 24 (1973): 197–202.
Moser, Maureen Beyer. *Teacher of Holiness: The Holy Spirit in Origen's Commentary on the Epistle to the Romans*. Piscataway, N.J.: Gorgias, 2005.
Moxnes, Halvor. "God and His Angel in the Shepherd of Hermas." *Studia Theologica* 28 (1974): 49–56.
Mueller, Joseph G. *L'ancien Testament dans l'ecclésiologie des pères: une lecture des "Constitutions apostoliques."* Instrumenta patristica et mediaevalia 41. Turnhout: Brepols, 2004.
Mullins, Terence Y. "Papias and Clement and Mark's Two Gospels." *Vigiliae christianae* 30 (1976): 189–92.
Munck, Johannes. *Untersuchungen über Klemens von Alexandria*. Stuttgart: Kohlhammer, 1933.
Munier, Charles. *L'Apologie de Saint Justin Philosophy et Martyr*. Paradosis 37. Fribourg: Éditions Universitaires Fribourg Suisse, 1994.
Murray, Robert. "An Exhortation to Candidates for Ascetical Vows at Baptism in the Ancient Syriac Church." *New Testament Studies* 21 (1974): 59–80.
———. "The Features of the Earliest Christian Asceticism." Pages 65–77 in *Christian Spirituality: Essays in Honour of Gordon Rupp*. Edited by Peter Brooks. London: SCM, 1975.
———. "Some Rhetorical Patterns in Early Syriac Literature." Pages 109–31 in *A Tribute to Arthur Vööbus*. Edited by Robert H. Fischer. Chicago: The Lutheran School of Theology at Chicago, 1977.
———. *Symbols of Church and Kingdom: A Study in Early Syriac Tradition*. 2nd ed.; London/New York: T&T Clark International, 2004.
Muse, Robert L. "Revelation 2–3: A Critical Analysis of Seven Prophetic Messages." *Journal of the Evangelical Theological Society* 29 (1986): 147–61.
Nagel, Peter. *Die Motivierung der Askese in der alten Kirche und der Ursprung des Mönchtums*. Texte und Untersuchungen zur Geschichte der altchristlichen Literatur 95. Berlin: Akademie-Verlag, 1966.
Nardi, Carlo. *Il battesimo in Clemente Alessandrino: Interpretazione di Eclogae propheticae 1–26*. Rome: Institutum Patristicum "Augustinianum," 1984.
———. "Note di Clemente Alessandrino al Salmo 18: *EP* 51–63." *Vivens homo* 6 (1995): 9–42.
Nautin, Pierre. "Pantène." Pages 145–52 in *Tome commémoratif du millénaire de la bibliothèque patriarchale d'Alexandrie*. Edited by T. D. Mosconas. Alexandria: Publications de l'Institut d'études orientales de la bibliothèque patriarchale d'Alexandrie, 1953.

——. "La fin des *Stromates* et les *Hypotyposeis* de Clément d'Alexandrie." *Vigiliae christianae* 30 (1976): 268–302.

Neymeyr, Ulrich. *Die christlichen Lehrer im zweiten Jahrhundert: Ihre Lehrtätigkeit, ihr Selbst-verständnis und ihre Geschichte.* Supplements to Vigiliae Christianae 4. Leiden: Brill, 1989.

Niculescu, Vlad Michael. *The Spell of the Logos: Origen's Exegetic Pedagogy in the Contemporary Debate Regarding Logocentrism* (Piscataway, NJ: Gorgias, 2009).

——. "Spiritual Leavening: The Communication and Reception of the Good News in Origen's Biblical Exegesis and Transformative Pedagogy." *Journal of Early Christian Studies* 15 (2007): 447–81.

Nötscher, Friedrich. *"Das Angesicht Gottes schauen" nach biblischer und babilonischer Auffassung.* Darmstadt: Wissenschaftliche Buchgesellschaft, 1969 [1924].

Oeyen, Christian. *Eine frühchristliche Engelpneumatologie bei Klemens von Alexandrien.* Erweiterter Separatdruck aus der Internationalen Kirchlichen Zeitschrift. Bern, 1966.

——. "Eine frühchristliche Engelpneumatologie bei Klemens von Alexandrien." *Internationale Kirchliche Zeitschrift* 55 (1965): 102–120; 56 (1966): 27–47.

——. "Die Lehre von den göttlichen Kräften bei Justin." *Studia Patristica* 11 (1972): 214–21.

Olofsson, Staffan. *God is My Rock: A Study of Translation Technique and Theological Exegesis in the Septuagint.* Coniectanea biblica: Old Testament Series 30. Stockholm: Almqvist & Wiksell International, 1990.

Opitz, Helmut. *Ursprünge Frühkatholischer Pneumatologie.* Berlin: Evangelische Verlagsanstalt, 1960.

Orbán, A. P. "Die Frage der ersten Zeugnisse des Christenlateins." *Vigiliae christianae* 30 (1976): 214–38.

Orlov, Andrei. *The Enoch-Metatron Tradition.* Texte und Studien zum antiken Judentum 107. Tübingen: Mohr Siebeck, 2005.

——. *From Apocalypticism to Merkabah Mysticism: Studies in the Slavonic Pseudepigrapha.* Supplements to the Journal for the Study of Judaism 114. Leiden: Brill, 2006.

Ortiz de Urbina. "Die Gottheit Christi bei Aphrahat." *Orientalia Christiana Periodica* 31 (1933): 1–140.

Osborn, Eric Francis. *The Philosophy of Clement of Alexandria.* Cambridge: Cambridge University Press, 1957.

——. "Teaching and Writing in the First Chapter of the Stromateis of Clement of Alexandria." *Journal of Theological Studies* n.s. 10 (1959): 335–43.

——. *Justin Martyr.* Tübingen: Mohr, 1973.

——. *The Beginning of Christian Philosophy.* Cambridge: Cambridge University Press, 1981.

——. "Clement of Alexandria: A Review of Research, 1958–1982." *The Second Century* 3 (1983): 219–44.

——. "Clement's *Hypotyposeis*: Macarius Revisited." *The Second Century* 10 (1990): 233–35.

——. *The Emergence of Christian Theology.* Cambridge: Cambridge University Press, 1993.

——. "Arguments for Faith in Clement of Alexandria." *Vigiliae christianae* 48 (1994): 1–24.

——. "Philo and Clement: Quiet Conversion and Noetic Exegesis." *Studia Philonica* 10 (1998): 108–24.

——. *Clement of Alexandria.* Cambridge: Cambridge University Press, 2005.

——. "One Hundred Years of Books on Clement." *Vigiliae christianae* 60 (2006): 367–88.

Osiek, Carolyn. *Shepherd of Hermas.* Hermeneia. Minneapolis, Minn.: Augsburg Fortress, 1999.

Paget, James C. "Clement of Alexandria and the Jews." *Scottish Journal of Theology* 51 (1998): 86–97.

Pearson, Birger. *Christianity in Roman and Coptic Egypt.* New York: T&T Clark, 2004.

Pépin, Jean. *Théologie cosmique et théologie chrétienne (Ambroise, Exam. I 1, 1–4).* Paris: Presses Universitaires de France, 1964.

Pernveden, Lage. *The Concept of the Church in the Shepherd of Hermas.* Studia Theologica Lundensia 27. Lund: Gleerup, 1966.

Petersen, William L. "The Christology of Aphrahat, the Persian Sage: An Excursus on the 17th *Demonstration*." *Vigiliae christianae* 46 (1992): 241–56.

Peterson, Erik. *Frühkirche, Judentum und Gnosis.* Rome: Herder, 1959.

——. *The Angels and the Liturgy: The Status and Significance of the Holy Angels in Worship.* London: Darton, Longman & Todd, 1964.

Pohlenz, Max. *Klemens von Alexandreia und sein hellenisches Christentum.* Göttingen: Vandenhoeck & Ruprecht, 1943.

Pratt, Andrew L. "Clement of Alexandria: Eucharist as Gnosis." *Greek Orthodox Theological Review* 32 (1987): 163–78.

Prigent, Pierre. *Commentary on the Apocalypse of St. John.* Tübingen: Mohr Siebeck, 2001.

——. *Apocalypse et liturgie.* Cahiers Théologiques 52. Neuchâtel: Delachaux et Niestlé, 1964.

——. *Justin et l'Ancien Testament: L'argumentation scripturaire du traité de Justin contre toutes les hérésies comme source principale du Dialogue avec Tryphon et de la première Apologie.* Paris: Librairie Lecoffre, 1964.

Pryor, John W. "Justin Martyr and the Fourth Gospel." *The Second Century* 9 (1992): 153–69.

Quatember, Friedrich. *Die christliche Lebenshaltung des Klemens nach seinem Pädagogus.* Vienna: Herder, 1946.

Quispel, Gilles. *Gnostic Studies* I–II. Istanbul: Nederlands Historisch-Archaeologisch Instituut in het Nabije Oosten, 1974.

——. "Genius and Spirit." Pages 155–69 in *Essays on the Nag Hammadi Texts in Honour of Pahor Lahib.* Edited by Martin Krause. Leiden: Brill, 1975.

——. "The Original Doctrine of Valentinus the Gnostic." *Vigiliae christianae* 50 (1996): 327–52.

——. "Jewish-Christian Gospel Tradition." *Anglican Theological Review* 3 (1974): 112–16.

——. "Gnosticism and the New Testament." *Vigiliae christianae* 19 (1965): 65–85.

——. "L'Evangile selon Thomas et les Clementines." *Vigiliae christianae* 12 (1958): 181–96.

Rainbow, Paul A. "Jewish Monotheism as the Matrix for New Testament Christology: A Review Article." *Novum Testamentum* 33 (1991): 78–91.

——. "Monotheism—A Misused Word in Jewish Studies?" *Journal of Jewish Studies* 42 (1991): 1–15.

Reiling Jannes. *Hermas and Christian Prophecy: A Study of the Eleventh Mandate.* Supplements to Novum Testamentum 37. Leiden: Brill, 1973.

Reuss, Joseph. *Matthäus-Kommentare aus der griechischen Kirche aus Katenenhandschriften gesammelt und herausgegeben.* Texte und Untersuchungen zur Geschichte der altchristlichen Literatur 61. Berlin: Akademie-Verlag, 1957.

Ridolfini, Francesco Pericoli. "Note sull'antropologia e sul' escatologia del 'Sapiente Persiano.'" *Studi e ricerche sull'Oriente cristiano* 1/1 (1978): 5–17; 1/2 (1978): 5–16.

——. "Problema trinitario e problema cristologico nelle 'Dimostrazioni' del 'Sapiente Persiano.'" *Studi e ricerche sull'Oriente cristiano* 2 (1979): 99–125.

Riedinger, Utto. "Pseudo-Dionysius Areopagites, Pseudo-Kaisarios und die Akoimeten." *Byzantinische Zeitschrift* 52 (1959): 276–96.

——. "Neue Hypotyposenfragmente bei Ps.-Caesarius und Isidor von Pelusium." *Zeitschrift für die neutestamentliche Wissenschaft* (1960): 154–96.

——. "Eine Paraphrase des Engel-Traktates von Klemens von Alexandreia in den Erotapokriseis des Pseudo-Kaisarios." *Zeitschrift für Kirchengeschichte* 73 (1962): 253–71.

Riedweg, Christoph. *Mysterienterminologie bei Platon, Philon und Klemens von Alexandrien. Untersuchungen zur altern Literatur und Geschichte 26.* Berlin/New York: de Gruyter, 1986.

Rizzerio, Laura. *Clemente di Alessandria e la "φυσιολογία veramente gnostica". Saggio sulle origini e le implicazioni di un'epistemologia e di un'ontologia "cristiane."* Recherches de théologie ancienne et medievale, Supplementa 6. Leuven: Peeters, 1996.

Roberts, Colin. *Manuscript, Society, and Belief in Early Christian Egypt.* London: Oxford University Press, 1979.

Roberts, Louis. "The Literary Form of the Stromateis." *The Second Century* 1 (1981): 211–22.

Roques, René. *L'univers dionysien: structure hiérarchique du monde selon le Pseudo-Denys.* Paris: Cerf, 1983.

Romanides, John. "Justin Martyr and the Fourth Gospel." *Greek Orthodox Theological Review* 4 (1958): 115–34.

Roncaglia, Martiniano Pellegrino. *Histoire de l'église copte.* Vol. 1: *Introduction générale: Les origines du christianisme en Égypte: du judéo-christianisme au christianisme hellénistique, Ier–IIe siècles.* Beirut: Dar al-Kalima, 1987 [1966].

——. "Pantène et le didacalée d'Alexandrie: du Judéo-Christianisme au Christianisme Hellénistique." Pages 211–23 in *A Tribute to Arthur Vööbus: Studies in Early Christian Literature and Its Environment, Primarily in the Christian East.* Edited by Robert H. Fisher. Chicago: The Lutheran School of Theology, 1977.

Rondeau, Marie-Josèphe. *Les commentaires patristiques du Psautier (3e–5e siecles).* Vol. 2: *Exégèse prosopologique et théologie.* Orientalia Christiana Analecta 220. Rome: Institutum Studiorum Orientalium, 1985.

Roose, Hanna. *"Das Zeugnis Jesu": seine Bedeutung für die Christologie, Eschatologie und Prophetie in der Offenbarung des Johannes.* Texte und Arbeiten zum neutestamentlichen Zeitalter 32. Tübingen: Francke, 2000.

Rordorf, Willy. "La Trinité dans les écrits de Justin Martyr." *Augustinianum* 20 (1980): 285–97.

Rorem, Paul, and John C. Lamoreaux. *John of Scythopolis and the Dionysian Corpus: Annotating the Areopagite.* Oxford: Clarendon, 1998.

Rowland, Christopher. "A Man Clothed in Linen: Daniel 10.6 ff. and Jewish Angelology." *Journal for the Study of the New Testament* 24 (1985): 99–110.

——. "Apocalyptic, the Poor, and the Gospel of Matthew." *Journal of Theological Studies* n.s. 45 (1994): 504–18.

Ruben, Paul. "Clementis Alexandrini Excerpta ex Theodoto." Ph.D. diss. University of Bonn. Leipzig: Teubner, 1892.

Runia, David T. "Clement of Alexandria and the Philonic Doctrine of the Divine Power(s)." *Vigiliae christianae* 58 (2004): 256–76.

——. "Why Does Clement of Alexandria Call Philo 'The Pythagorean'?" *Vigiliae christianae* 49 (1995): 1–22.

Saake, Helmut. *Pneumatologica: Untersuchungen zum Geistverständnis im Johannesevangelium, bei Origenes und Athanasios von Alexandreia.* Frankfurt am Main: Diagonal, 1973.

Sabugal, Santos. "El vocabulario pneumatológico en la obra de S. Justino y sus implicaciones teológicas." *Augustinianum* 13 (1973): 459–67.

Sanders, J. N. *The Fourth Gospel in the Early Church, Its Origin and Influence on Christian Theology up to Irenaeus.* Cambridge: Cambridge University Press, 1943.

Schäfer, Peter. *Die Vorstellung vom Heiligen Geist in der rabbinischen Literatur.* Studien zum Alten und Neuen Testament 28. Munich: Kösel, 1972.

Schibli, Hermann S. "Origen, Didymus, and the Vehicle of the Soul." Pages 381–91 in *Origeniana Quinta: Papers of the 5th International Origen Congress, Boston College, 14–18 August 1989.* Edited by Robert J. Daly. Bibliotheca ephemeridum theologicarum lovaniensum 105. Leuven: Leuven University Press, 1992.

Schimanowski, Gottfried. *Die himmlische Liturgie in der Apokalypse des Johannes.* Wissenschaftliche Untersuchungen zum Neuen Testament 2/154. Tübingen: Mohr Siebeck, 2002.

Schlütz, Karl. *Isaias 11:2 (Die sieben Gaben des Heiligen Geistes) in den ersten vier christlichen Jahrhunderten.* Münster: Aschendorff, 1932.

Schneider, Ulrich. *Theologie als christliche Philosophie: zur Bedeutung der biblischen Botschaft im Denken des Clemens von Alexandria.* Arbeiten zur Kirchengeschichte 73. Berlin: Walter de Gruyter, 1999.

Scholem, Gershom. *Jewish Gnosticism, Merkabah Mysticism, and Talmudic Tradition.* New York: Jewish Theological Seminary of America, 1965.

Scholten, Clemens. "Die Alexandrinische Katechetenschule." *Jahrbuch für Antike und Christentum* 38 (1995): 16–37.

Schwartz, Jacques. "Survivances littéraires païennes dans le ,Pasteur' d'Hermas." *Revue Biblique* 72 (1965): 240–47.

Schweizer, Eduard R. *Spirit of God.* Bible Key Words from Gerhard Kittel's *Theologisches Wörterbuch zum Neuen Testament.* London: Adam & Charles Black, 1960.

Schwen, Paul. *Afrahat: Seine Person und sein Verständnis des Christentums.* Berlin: Trowitz & Sohn, 1907.

Segal, Alan F. *Two Powers in Heaven: Early Rabbinic Reports about Christianity and Gnosticism.* Studies in Judaism in Late Antiquity 25. Leiden: Brill, 1977.

——. *The Other Judaisms of Late Antiquity.* Brown Judaic Studies 127. Atlanta, Ga.: Scholars Press, 1987.

——. *Paul the Convert: The Apostolate and Apostasy of Saul the Pharisee.* New Haven/London: Yale University Press, 1990.

Seitz, O. J. F. "Antecedents and Signification of the Term *Dipsychos.*" *Journal of Biblical Literature* 66 (1947): 211–19.

——. "Afterthoughts on the Term *Dipsychos.*" *New Testament Studies* 4 (1957–1958): 327–34.

Sekki, Arthur E. *The Meaning of Ruach at Qumran.* Society of Biblical Literature Dissertation Series 110. Atlanta, Ga.: Scholars Press, 1989.

Sellew, Philip. "The Hundredfold Reward for Martyrs and Ascetics: Ps.-Cyprian, *De centesima, sexagesima, tricesima.*" *Studia Patristica* 36 (2001): 94–98.

Seow, C. L. "Face." Pages 322–25 in *Dictionary of Deities and Demons in the Bible.* Edited by K. van der Toorn, B. Becking, and P. W. van der Horst. 2nd, extensively revised edition. Leiden: Brill, 1999.

Simonetti, Manlio. "Note di cristologia pneumatica." *Augustinianum* 12 (1972): 201–32.

Siniscalco, Paolo. "Ἀποκατάστασις e ἀποκαθίστημι nella tradizione della Grande Chiesa fino ad Ireneo." *Studia Patristica* 3 (1961)/Texte und Untersuchungen zur Geschichte der altchristlichen Literatur 78:380–396.

Skarsaune, Oskar. *The Proof from Prophecy: A Study in Justin Martyr's Proof-text Tradition: Text-type, Provenance, Theological Profile.* Supplements to Novum Testamentum 56. Leiden: Brill, 1987.

Skoyles Jarkins, Stephanie K. *Aphrahat the Persian Sage and the Temple of God: A Study of Early Syriac Theological Anthropology.* Piscataway, NJ: Gorgias, 2008.

Škrinjar, Albin. "Les sept esprits (Apoc. 1, 4; 3, 1; 4, 5; 5, 6)." *Biblica* 16 (1935): 1–24, 113–40.

Slusser, Michael. "The Exegetical Roots of Trinitarian Theology." *Theological Studies* 49 (1988): 461–76.

Smelik, Willem F. "On Mystical Transformation of the Righteous into Light in Juda-ism." *Journal for the Study of Judaism* 26 (1995): 122–44.

Stanton, Graham. "The Spirit in the Writings of Justin Martyr." Pages 321–34 in *The Holy Spirit and Christian Origins: Essays in Honor of James D. G. Dunn*. Edited by G. N. Stanton, B. W. Longenecker, and S. C. Barton. Grand Rapids, Mich.: Eerd-mans, 2004.

Stead, Christopher. *Philosophy in Christian Antiquity*. Cambridge: Cambridge University Press, 1994.

Stewart, Columba. *"Working the Earth of the Heart": The Messalian Controversy in History, Texts, and Language to A.D. 431*. Oxford Theological Monographs. Oxford: Clarendon, 1991.

Strecker, Georg. *Das Judenchristentum in den Pseudoklementinen*. 2d rev. and enl. ed. Texte und Untersuchungen zur Geschichte der altchristlichen Literatur 70. Berlin: Akademie Verlag, 1981.

Stroumsa, Gedaliahu A. G. *Hidden Wisdom: Esoteric Traditions and the Roots of Christian Mysticism*. Studies in the History of Religions 70. Leiden: Brill, 1996.

———. "Form(s) of God: Some Notes on Metatron and Christ." *Harvard Theological Review* 76 (1983): 269–88.

———. "Le Couple de l'Ange et de l'Esprit: Traditions juives et chrétiennes." *Revue Biblique* 88 (1981): 42–61.

Strutwolf, Holger. *Die Trinitätstheologie und Christologie des Euseb von Caesarea: Eine dogmengeschichtliche Untersuchung seiner Platonismusrezeption und Wirkungsges-chichte*. Forschungen zur Kirchen- und Dogmengeschichte 72. Göttingen: Vanden-hoeck & Ruprecht, 1999.

Stuckenbruck, Loren T. *Angel Veneration and Christology*. Wissenschaftliche Untersu-chungen zum Neuen Testament 2/70. Tübingen: Mohr Siebeck, 1994.

———. "The Holy Spirit in the Ascension of Isaiah." Pages 309–320 in *The Holy Spirit and Christian Origins: Essays in Honor of James D. G. Dunn*. Edited by G. N. Stanton, B. W. Longenecker, and S. C. Barton. Grand Rapids, Mich.: Eerdmans, 2004.

Studer, Basil. "La sotériologie de Lactance." Pages 252–71 in *Lactance et son temps: Recherches actuelles*. Actes du IVe Colloque d'études historiques et patristiques, Chantilly 21–23 septembre 1976. Edited by J. Fontaine and M. Perrin. Paris: Beauchesne, 1978.

Sullivan, Kevin P. *Wrestling with Angels: A Study of the Relationship Between Angels and Humans in Ancient Jewish Literature and the New Testament*. Arbeiten zur Geschichte des antiken Judentums und des Urchristentums 55. Leiden, Brill 2004.

Swarat, Uwe. *Alte Kirche und Neues Testament: Theodor Zahn als Patristiker*. Wup-pertal: Brockhaus, 1991.

Swete, Henry Barclay. *The Apocalypse of St. John: The Greek Text with Introduction, Notes and Indices*. 3rd ed. London: Macmillan, 1909.

———. *The Holy Spirit in the Ancient Church: A Study of Christian Teaching in the Age of the Fathers*. London: Macmillan, 1912.

Tite, Philip L. "The Holy Spirit's Role in Origen's Trinitarian System: A Comparison with Valentinian Pneumatology." *Theoforum* 32 (2001): 131–64.

Tollinton, Richard B. *Clement of Alexandria: A Study in Christian Liberalism*. 2 vols. London: Williams and Norgate, 1914.

Treu, Ursula. "Etymologie und Allegorie bei Klemens." *Studia Patristica* 4 (1961)/Texte und Untersuchungen zur Geschichte der altchristlichen Literatur 79: 190–211.

Tuilier, André. "Les évangelistes et les docteurs de la primitive église et les origines de l'École d'Alexandrie." *Studia Patristica* 17 (1982): 738–49.

Turner, H. E. W. *The Pattern of Christian Truth: A Study in the Relations between Orthodoxy and Heresy in the Early Church*. Bampton Lectures 1954. London: Mow-bray & Co., 1954.

Tuzlak, Sibel Ayse. "Service and Performance: 'Leitourgia' and the Study of Early Christian Ritual." Ph.D. diss., Syracuse University, 2001.

Vaggione, Richard Paul. *Eunomius of Cyzicus and the Nicene Revolution.* Oxford Early Christian Studies. Oxford: Oxford University Press, 2000.

Van den Hoek, Annewies. *Clement of Alexandria and His Use of Philo in the Stromateis: An Early Christian Reshaping of a Jewish Model.* Supplements to Vigiliae Christianae 3. Leiden: Brill, 1988.

———. "How Alexandrian was Clement of Alexandria? Reflections on Clement and his Alexandrian Background." *Heythrop Journal* 31 (1990): 179–94.

———. "Divergent Traditions in Clement of Alexandria,' and other Authors of the 2nd century." *Apocrypha* 7 (1996): 43–62.

———. "The 'Catechetical' School of Early Christian Alexandria and Its Philonic Heritage." *Harvard Theological Review* 90 (1997): 59–87.

———. "'I Said, You Are Gods...': The Significance of Psalm 82 for Some Early Christian Authors." Pages 203–19 in *The Use of Sacred Books in the Ancient World.* Edited by Leonard Victor Rutgers et al. Contributions to Biblical Exegesis and Theology 22. Louvain: Peeters, 1998.

VanderKam, James C. *The Book of Jubilees.* Guides to Apocrypha and Pseudepigrapha. Sheffield: Sheffield Academic Press, 2001.

Verbeke, Gérard. *L'évolution de la doctrine du pneuma, du stoicisme à s. Augustin: étude philosophique.* Bibliothèque de l'Institut supérieur de philosophie, Université de Louvain. Paris: Desclée de Brouwer/Louvain: Institut supérieur de philosophie, 1945.

Vignaux, Paul, ed. *In Principio: Interprétations des premiers versets de la Genèse.* Collection des études augustiniennes, Série Antiquité 51. Paris, Études Augustiniennes, 1973.

Völker, Walther. *Der wahre Gnostiker nach Clemens Alexandrinus.* Texte und Untersuchungen zur Geschichte der altchristlichen Literatur 57. Berlin: Akademie-Verlag, 1952.

Vööbus, Arthur. "Methodologisches zum Studium der Anweisungen Aphrahats." *Oriens christianus* 46 (1962): 25–32.

Waddell, Robby. *The Spirit in the Book of Revelation.* Journal of Pentecostal Theology Supplement Series 30. Dorset, UK: Deo, 2006.

Wagner, Walter H. "Another Look at the Literary Problem in Clement of Alexandria's Major Writings." *Church History* 37 (1968): 251–60.

———. "A Father's Fate: Attitudes Toward and Interpretations of Clement of Alexandria." *Journal of Religious History* 6 (1971): 209–31.

Wallis, Ian G. *The Faith of Jesus Christ in Early Christian Traditions.* Society for New Testament Studies Monograph Series 84. Cambridge/New York: Cambridge University Press, 1995.

Waszink, Jan Hendrik. "Bemerkungen zum Einfluss des Platonismus im frühen Christentum." *Vigiliae christianae* 19 (1965): 129–62.

Westcott, Brooke Foss. "Clement of Alexandria." Pages 559–66 in *A Dictionary of Christian Biography, Literature, Sects, and Doctrines.* Edited by W. Smith and H. Ware. London: Murray, 1877.

Whittaker, John. "ΕΠΕΚΕΙΝΑ ΝΩΥ ΚΑΙ ΟΥΣΙΑΣ." *Vigiliae christianae* 23 (1969): 91–104.

Wilken, Robert. "Alexandria: A School for Training in Virtue." Pages 15–30 in *Schools of Thought in the Christian Tradition.* Edited by Patrick Henry. Philadelphia: Fortress, 1984.

Wilson, J. Christian. *Toward a Reassessment of the Shepherd of Hermas: Its Date and Pneumatology.* Lewiston, N.Y.: Mellen, 1993.

———. *Five Problems in the Interpretation of the Shepherd of Hermas: Authorship, Genre, Canonicity, Apocalyptic, and the Absence of the Name "Jesus Christ."* Lewiston, N.Y.: Mellen, 1995.

Winkler, Gabriele. "Ein bedeutsamer Zusammenhang zwischen der Erkenntnis und Ruhe in Mt 11, 27–29 und dem Ruhen des Geistes auf Jesus am Jordan: Eine Analyse zur Geist-Christologie in Syrischen und Armenischen Quellen." *Le Muséon* 96 (1983): 267–326.

———. "Die Tauf-Hymnen der Armenier: Ihre Affinität mit syrischem Gedankengut." Pages 1: 381–420 in *Liturgie und Dichtung.* 2 vols. Ed. H. Becker and R. Kaczynski. Munich: St. Ottilian, 1983.

———. "A Remarkable Shift in Fourth-Century Creeds: An Analysis of the Armenian, Syriac, and Greek Evidence." *Studia Patristica* 17/3 (1982): 1396–1401.

Wolfson, Harry Austryn. "Clement of Alexandria on the Generation of the Logos. *Church History* 20 (1951): 72–81.

———. *The Philosophy of the Church Fathers.* 3d, rev. ed. Cambridge, Mass.: Harvard University Press, 1970.

Wytzes, Jelle. "The Twofold Way: Platonic Influences in the Work of Clement of Alexandria." *Vigiliae christianae* 11 (1957): 226–45; 14 (1960): 129–53.

Zahn, Theodor. *Forschungen zur Geschichte des neutestamentlichen Kanons und der altkirchlichen Literatur 3: Supplementum Clementinum.* Erlangen: Andreas Deichert, 1884.

Ziebritzki, Henning. *Heiliger Geist und Weltseele: das Problem der dritten Hypostase bei Origenes, Plotin und ihren Vorläufern.* Beiträge zur historischen Theologie 84. Tübingen: Mohr Siebeck, 1994.

INDEX OF TERMS

angel,
  angelic hierarchy, 35–41, 172 (*see also*
    hierarchy)
  relative corporality, 40–41
  "Father, Son, holy angels" taxis, x, 32,
    39–40, 147
  group of seven first created angels,
    xxii, 31–32, 38–39, 39n145, 40n146,
    42, 49, 51, 56–58, 69–70, 95ff,
    135–137, 149–150, 174 (see also
    protoctists)
  the angels called "Sabai", 149n54
  angelus interpres, 106, 109n68
  danger of angelolatry, 106
  angelic spirit, xxi–xxii, 60n220, 81–82,
    98–99, 107n61, 110n69, 115–119,
    123–124, 132n56, 135
  as guardian angel, 169–170,
    176–177, 186–187
  angels as the powers of the Logos,
    29–32, 79–80, 147, 149–150
  stars as angels, 93
  transformation of humans into angels,
    45–48, 59n217 (*see also* deification)
angelomorphic, angelomorphism,
  xxi–xxii
  in tandem with spirit christology
    and binitarianism, xxiii, 75, 141,
    174–175
apokatastasis, 42n156
apocalyptic ("interiorized apocalyptic"),
  50–51

binitarian, binitarianism, xxvii–xviii,
  73–74, 100–101, 136, 137–138, 155,
  178, 187

christology
  Face Christology, 37, 68, 69–70
  spirit Christology, 75, 79, 102–104,
    120–126, 132n56, 135, 143–145,
    177–179, 187, 192

deification, 49, 59n217. *See also* angel:
  transformation of humans into angels

exalted patriarchs, xxviii

hierarchy
  of angels, 35–41, 172 (*see also* angel)
  (see also *protoctists*)
  in Jewish and Christian apocalyptic
    writings, 33, 35
  in Ps.-Dionysius, 31–32, 34, 37n138
    (*see* Ps.-Dionysius)
  role in prophetic inspiration,
    52–55, 79–80, 109–110, 116–118,
    125n36, 138
  relative corporality, 40–41
  ecclesiastic hierarchy (imitates angelic
    h.), 49–50

Logos
  Logos-theology precluding a robust
    pneumatology, ix, 4, 73, 140
  relation to Spirit (*see* christology:
    spirit christology) (*see* spirit:
    powers of the spirit)
  powers of the Logos, 29–32, 79–80
  Logos as commander-in-chief of the
    angels, 147
  Logos as Lord of the angelic powers
    (κύριος τῶν δυνάμεων), 149–150,
    155

power, 76, 77n17, 80, 144, 149–155
protoctists, xxii, 31–32, 38–39 (esp.
  39n145), 40n146, 42, 49, 51, 56–58,
  69–70, 97–99, 135–138, 174
  heavenly liturgy of the, 38, 56, 70, 81
  as the two paracletes, 57
  as the sevenfold Holy Spirit, 61, 92
  relation to Holy Spirit, 57–61, 77–78,
    79, 80–83, 92, 136–137

spirit,
  Logos-theology precluding a robust
    pneumatology, ix, 4, 73, 140 (*see
    also* christology: spirit christology)
  Wisdom as spirit, 121n23–24,
    181–182
  in relation to angel, xxi–xxii, 60n220,
    81–82, 98–99, 107n61, 110n69,
    115–119, 123–124, 132n56, 147,
    162, 167, 169–173, 185–187

as guardian angel, 169–170,
  176–177, 186–187
Holy Spirit as choirmaster, 70
Holy Spirit as feminine, 76–77n14,
  170n45, 177n77
"powers of the Spirit", 29–32, 79–80,
  144, 154–155
  as charismata, 151–153, 182–185
seven gift of the Holy Spirit, 95ff,
  135–137, 163–165, 174, 185
  spirit as charisma, 107–109

as divine energies, 184, 192
  "heptad of the spirit", 61, 81
angelic, xxi–xxii, 81–82
  role in prophetic inspiration and
  indwelling the saints, 52–55,
  79–80, 109–110, 116–118,
  125n36, 138, 171, 186
  seven spirits (see *protoctists*)
relation of Holy Spirit to *protoctists*,
  57–61, 77–78, 79, 80–83

INDEX OF SOURCES

A. Hebrew Bible

Genesis
1:26   45
18:2   *xxvii*n11
18:5–6   55
32:31–32   24
49:11   145

Exodus
13:21   93
14:19   93, 94
23:20   93
30:22   116n11
33:14–15   94n21
34:29–35   122n27
40:38   93

Numbers
7:13   164n24
11:17   183, 186
11:26   163n19
12:8   24
18:6   116n11

Deuteronomy
4:37   94

Judges
6:34   123n30
7:4–8   174n59

1 Samuel
3   53
16:14   118n17
16:14–23   186

1 Kings
18:15   125
22:19–22   81, 171
22:21   171

2 Kings
2:15   163n19
3:14   125

1 Chronicles
9:13   116n11

2 Chronicles
15:1   163n19
18:18–21   81
20:14   163n19

Nehemiah
9:19   93

Tobit
12:15   39n145, 95, 98
12:16–22   106n56

Job
1:12   171
2:7   171

Psalms
18:2   52
18:5   45
23:7   148
23:10   125
33:16   79
45:8   125
45:12   125
50:13   94n21
50:14   82
67   152
67:19   151, 184
68:19   152
78:14   93
81:6   45, 46n173
104:4   40n146
105:39   93
138:7   94n21
148:1–2   149

Proverbs
8:12–16   95

Isaiah
6:1   53n196
9:11   94n24
11   96, 153, 155
11:1–2   32, 164
11:1–3   68, 150, 151n57,
            173, 185

11:2	95, 152n59, 154, 185	*Joel*	
11:2–3	97, 150, 155, 161, 163, 164, 165, 174, 184, 186, 190	3:1	151, 152n59, 182, 183, 184
		3:2	152n59
11:34	95n25	*Zephaniah*	
63:9–10	60n220, 94, 116n10	2:9	125
63:14	94	*Zechariah*	
		3:9	38, 62, 68, 95, 97, 161, 163, 165, 174, 186, 190
Jeremiah			
40:12	125		
		4:2	32
Ezekiel		4:6	111, 137
1:1	152n60	4:10	32, 38, 62, 68, 95, 97, 111, 137, 163, 165, 173, 174, 186, 190
1:26	24		
9:2–3	39n145		
44:26	43		
Daniel			
7:10	171		

B. New Testament

Matthew		*Luke*	
1:20	117	1:23	116n11
1:24	117	1:35	78n18, 143, 144, 145, 154, 163n19
2	93		
3:15	151n57	11:20	192n2
12:28	192n2	20:36	47
13:41	147n44		
18:3	170	*John*	
18:10	38, 61–71, 98, 99, 161, 162, 168, 169, 170, 171, 173, 174, 185, 186, 190	1:3	74n4
		1:4–8	75n12
		1:14	179
		1:18	77n14
		1:31	150n56
18:30	65	1:32	151n57
22:30	47	3:8	77
25:31	147n44	3:34	183, 185
25:31–46	66	4:24	77
25:40	63, 65	8:56	75n12
25:45	63, 65	10:7	128n42
26:53	147n41	10:11	128n42
28:20	179	16:13–14	81
Mark		*Acts*	
8:38	147n41	2:17	152n59
9:1–2	48n179	2:18	152n59
13:26–27	147n41	7:35	54n197
13:27	147n44	7:38	54n197
14:62	147n41	7:53	54n197
15:34	45	8:26	60n220

8:29	60n220	*1 Timothy*	
8:39	60n220	5:21	96n27
13:2	116n11		
		Hebrews	
Romans		1:1	79
3:22	105n55	1:3	68, 69, 70
3:26	105n55	1:7	40n146, 135n67
8:9	177n78	1:14	116n11
8:26	115n9	9:21	116n11
8:38	125n34	10:11	116n11
15:7	116n11	12:9	60n220, 108, 125
1 Corinthians		*1 Peter*	
1:24	182	3:12	79
6:16–20	135	3:22	125n34
10:4	121	4:14	54n199, 55
12	152n59		
12:11	76	*1 John*	
12:4–6	92	4:1–3	102n47
15	162		
15:24	125n34	*Revelation*	
15:51	47	1:1	106n57, 109, 110n69
2 Corinthians		1:1–3	91n10
1:22	181, 186	1:4	30, 32, 40, 91, 93, 96, 97n30, 98, 99, 100, 101, 111
3:17	122		
5:5	181, 186		
13:13	96–97n30	1:4–5	100
13:14	92	1:5	91, 105
		1:8	30, 100
Galatians		1:10	101
2:16	105n55	1:12	128n42
2:20	105n55	1:13	128n42
3:22	105n55	1:16	128n42
		1:20	93
Ephesians		2–3	102
1:14	181, 186	2:7	101
1:21	125n34	3:1	40, 91, 93, 101, 111, 150n56
2:6	179		
3:12	105n55	3:14	105
4:812	152	4:2	101
		4:4	128n42
Philippians		4:5	40, 91, 101, 111
3:9	105n55	4:8	100
3:20–21	47	4:11	100
		4:17	100
Colossians		5:5	128n42
1:15	66n241, 68, 121	5:6	32, 38, 40, 68, 91, 96, 100, 101, 111, 128n42, 174
1:16	38, 62, 68, 70, 99, 149n54, 174		
2:18	106n56	5:13–14	100n43
		8:2	30, 32, 40, 93, 111
1 Thessalonians			
5:23	135n66	10:1	95n24, 110n69

10:3	94	19:9–10	104–105
11:11	101	19:10	101, 105, 106, 107
11:15	101n43	19:15	100
12:3	92	20:6	100n43
13:1	92	21:6	30
13:15	101	21:10	101
14:4	100n43	21:22	100
14:13	99	21:22–23	100n43
15:13	100	22:5	101n43
16:6	109	22:6	101, 106n57, 107,
16:7	100		108
16:13	92, 101	22:8–19	105
16:13–14	98	22:9	109
16:14	100, 101	22:13	30
17:3	101	22:16	91, 110n69
18:2	98, 101	22:16–17	108
18:24	109	22:17	101
19:6	100	22:21	91n10
19:9	99		

C. Early Christian Writings

Andrew of Caesarea
Comm. Apoc.
3.7	94n23	14.47	182
4.12	96n28	16	173n57
28	94n24	20.16	177
		23.47	177n78
		23.60	175
		23.61	175
		23.63	175

Aphrahat
Letter to an Inquirer Dem.
2	176		
1	173, 185	*Apostolic Constitutions*	
1.9	163, 185n113	6.11.2	172n53
1.19	175, 183	8.4.5	172n53
2.20	170n45	8.12.8	172n53
4.13	168n38		
6	170, 173, 181,	Arethas	
	182, 185	*Comm. Apoc.*	
6.1	181	1	95n26, 96n27
6.10	176, 179, 180,	10	95n26, 97n33
	181, 182, 185	12	96n28
6.11	176, 177, 180, 181	28	94n24
6.12	182, 183		
6.13	183	Athenagoras	
6.14	171, 177, 178n80,	*Leg.*	
	181n92, 183	24	142n20
6.14–15	165, 185		
6.15	162	Basil of Caesarea	
6.17	166	*Spir*	
8.5	177n78	8.17	192n2
8.23	162	16.38	69
10.8	181, 182, 183		
14	182	*Eun*	
		3.1	170n43

Cassiodorus
  Div. litt.
    Praef. 4   90n6
    1.8.4   91n9

Clement of Alexandria
  Strom.
    1.1.15   16, 20n70
    1.24.158   5
    1.28.176   22
    1.29.181   78n17
    2.2.3   78n17
    2.2.5   77–78n17
    4.1.3   22, 23n83
    4.13.93   5
    4.25.156   28–29, 32, 78, 80,
                    89
    4.25.157   29
    4.25.158   43
    4.25.159   43
    4.26.172   77
    5.1.8   55
    5.6   30–32, 76, 79
    5.6.35   32, 68, 79, 97n31,
                    110, 174n58
    5.14.89   74n4
    5.14.91   63
    5.14.103   61, 81, 142n17
    6.3.32   54n197
    6.5.41   106n56
    6.13.106   48
    6.13.107   36, 49, 50
    6.14.113   48
    6.16.138   75n12
    6.16.142–143   32, 44, 68, 98
    6.16.143   97n33
    6.16.148   37n138
    6.18.166   78n17
    6.18.168   19, 20
    7.1.3   48n180
    7.2.2   36n132
    7.2.6   54n198
    7.2.7   76n14
    7.2.9   37n138
    7.2.12   54n198
    7.3.13   44, 45
    7.10.56   48
    7.10.56–57   44, 45
    7.10.57   48
    7.10.58   44
    7.15.89   21
    7.16.101   48
    7.18.110   20–21
    7.58.3–6   68

Paed.
    1.1.3   12
    1.6.43   75n12
    1.8.71   36n132
    2.1.8   52n191
    2.2.19–20   78
    2.12.126   52n191
    2.12.129   52n191
    3.12.87   60, 61, 68, 81,
                    99
    3.12.97   12
    3.12.101   74, 77

Protr.
    1.5.3   52
    1.8   49n182
    9.82   60
    10.94   27
    11.114   48n180

Adumbr.
    1 John 2:1   53n196, 56, 58,
                    59, 61
    Jude 5.24   38n141, 45
    Jude 9   53n195, 58
    1 Peter   58
    1 Peter 1:10–12 56
    1 Peter 2:3   55n200
    1 Peter 4:14   60

Exc.
    4.2   76n14
    10   38n142, 53,
                    58, 68, 97n31,
                    174n58
    10.1   40n148
    10.2–3   40n149
    10.3   42
    10.3–4   38n143
    10.4   45n172, 70
    10.6   39, 63
    11   53
    11.1   39, 63
    11.3   41n151
    11.4   39, 42
    12.3   76n14
    17   76
    19.2   76
    23.4   63
    24.2   52n191, 56, 76
    27   53
    27.2   39
    27.3.6   76n13

Ecl.
27.1–2   87n1
27.4–7   87n1
27.7   147n37
51–52   53, 110
56.5   42
57.1   38n142, 42, 68,
         97n31, 174n58
57.3   45
57.5   42

Quis div.   31.1   63
34.1   75n10
37.1–3   76–77n14
42.20   75n9

Cyprian
Fort.
11   39n144, 95n26

Cyril of Alexandria
In Ioann.
1.7   *xxvii*n11

C. Jul.
1   142n20

Epistula Apostolorum
17   179n85

Eusebius of Caesarea
Eccl. theol.
3.4.7–8   171n49
3.5.17–21   172n51

Evagrius
Gnost.
1.11   40n146

Georgius Monachus
Chronicon Breve
26; 140   25n92

George of the Arabs
Ep. (in *Analecta Syriaca*)
111.1–2   161n12
117.18–22   161n11
117.24–25   161n13
117.26–27   162n16
117.27–28   161n14
118.1–12   162n15
119.6–10   166
119.10   162n17
120.2–6   162n17

Gregory of Nyssa
Trin.   68–69

Gregory Palamas
One Hundred and
  Fifty Chapters   192n2
Dialogue with a
  Barlaamite   192n2

Hippolytus
Haer.
6.37.5–6   142n20

Irenaeus of Lyon
Haer
1.13.6   67n248
1.14.3   66
1.14.4   66
1.14.8   67
3.4.3   142n20
3.23.5   124n32
4.33.4   66n241
4.36.6   124n32
5.6.1   135n66
5.36.6   48n180

Dem.
9   97–98n36,
         150n55
96   116n11

Isaac of Nineveh
Hom.
57   186n114

Jerome
Comm. Isa.
4.11   165n26

Comm. Zach.
1.3   165n26

Comm. Job
38.31; 41   165n26

John Chrysostom
Hom. Matt.
6.3   93n20
59.4–5   62n228

John of Scythopolis
Scholia   33–34, 90n5, 97

Justin Martyr
Dial

4	36n132
7.3	144
8.1	153n64
25.1	143
30.2	144
34.2	147
35.2	144
39.2	152n58, 153
39.4	152n58
39.5	152n58
45.4	148
54.1	145
58.1	153n65
56.22	147
61.1	144, 147
62.5	147
76.6	144
85	148, 150, 155
85.1	148
85.2–3	149
85.4	149
85.6	149
87	150, 155
87.3	151
87.4	151
87.5	153n62
87.5–6	152n58
87.6	184
88.1	150, 153
88.2	150, 155
88.3	150, 153n64
93.2	148n46
100.5	143
119.1	153n65
127.4	147
128.1	146, 147

Apol.

1.6.2	142n19, 146, 147
1.13.3	141, 142n19, 148
1.16.6	148n46
1.33.4	143
1.33.6	78n18, 143
1.33.9	143
1.36.1	143n21, 145
1.38.11	143
1.46.5	143n24
1.60.6–7	141, 142n19
1.61.3	142n19
1.61.13	142n19
1.65.3	142n19
1.66.2	143n24
1.67.2	141, 142n19

2.6.3	144
2.10.1	154n71

Marcus Magus	66–68

Oecumenius
Comm. Apoc.

1	109n68
1.1	95n26
1.9	96n27
2.11	94n23
3.5	97n33
3.7	95n26
3.14	96n28
4.10	95n26

Origen
Comm. Jo.

1.31.215	149n54
2.23.145–146	*xxvii*n11
6.287–294	152n60
13.17	106n56
20.29.263	82, 172

Comm. Rom.

7.1	82

Hom. Num.

18.4	94n22

Hom. Ezech.

1	152n60

Hom. Luc.

27.5	152n60

Comm. Cant. prol.

3.1,4	19n68

Cels.

6.18	142n20

Philoxenus of Mabbug
*On the Inhabitation
of the Holy Spirit* 167–168

Photius
Cod.

109	25–26, 27n99, 90n5–6

Ps.-Clementine Homilies

5.49,53,61	64n236
5.62–65	65
11.4	66n241

17.7.1–4	63–64	Sim. 5.5.2	122, 127, 129n47
17.7.4–6	65	Sim. 5.5.2–3	126, 135
17.7.7–10	64	Sim. 5.5.3	40, 121n22, 135
17.10.5	63–64	Sim. 5.6.1	129n47, 130n51
18.22	65	Sim. 5.6.2	125n36, 129n47
		Sim. 5.6.4	121n22, 126, 128,
Ps.-Dionysius the			129, 135
Areopagite	10n33, 32–34,	Sim. 5.6.4–5.6.7	126, 130–135
	35n128, 37n138,	Sim. 5.6.5	121, 131, 133,
	50, 53n196, 80,		134, 137
	83n30, 90n5, 111	Sim. 5.6.6	134
		Sim. 5.6.7	129n49, 131, 132,
Ps.-Philo			134, 135
On Samson	154	Sim. 5.6.8	134
		Sim. 5.7	134
Ps.-Plato		Sim. 5.7.1	129n47
Ep. 2		Sim. 5.7.4	135
312E	142	Sim. 6.1.2	126
		Sim. 7	126
Rufinus		Sim. 7.4	126
Apol. adv. Hier.		Sim. 7.6	116n11
4	25n90	Sim. 8.1.2	119
		Sim. 8.2.5	116, 168
Shepherd of Hermas		Sim. 9	120, 121, 124
Vis. 1.3.2	126	Sim. 9.1.1	120, 122, 123, 192
Vis. 1.4.3	125	Sim. 9.1.1–2	120
Vis. 2.2.5	121n22	Sim. 9.1.2	118, 125
Vis. 2.2.8	121n22	Sim. 9.2.4	119
Vis. 2.4.1	121	Sim. 9.4.5–6	124
Vis. 2.6.7	48n180	Sim. 9.6.1	119
Vis. 3.1.2	120	Sim. 9.11	119
Vis. 3.1.9–10.1	120	Sim. 9.12.1–2	121
Vis. 3.4.1	40, 135, 137	Sim. 9.12.1–3	131n52
Vis. 3.6.11	125	Sim. 9.12.2	127
Vis. 3.12.3	125, 126	Sim. 9.12.7–8	135
Vis. 3.16.4	125	Sim. 9.13.2	119, 123, 124
Vis. 3.17.8	125	Sim. 9.13.5	124, 125
Vis. 3.20.2	125	Sim. 9.14.5	121n22
Vis. 3.20.3	125	Sim. 9.17.1–2	128
Vis. 3.22.3	125n36	Sim. 9.24–25	132
Vis. 5.7	117	Sim. 9.24.2	123, 132n56
Sim. 5	121, 126–130,	Sim. 9.24.4	48n180, 124,
	135, 137		132n56
Sim. 5.1.3	125n36	Sim. 9.25.2	48n180, 124,
Sim. 5.2.2	131		132n56
Sim. 5.2.6	135	Sim. 9.27.3	116n11
Sim. 5.2.7–8	48n180	Sim. 9.32.2	124
Sim. 5.2.11	135	Sim. 9.32.4	124
Sim. 5.3.1	129n47, 193	Mand. 3.1	134n65
Sim. 5.3.2	129n47	Mand. 3.28.1	125n36
Sim. 5.3.8	116n11	Mand. 5	118
Sim. 5.4.2	129n47	Mand. 5.1.2	116n11
Sim. 5.4.3	125n36, 126	Mand. 5.1.4	118
Sim. 5.5.1	129n47	Mand. 5.2.1–3	118

Mand. 5.2.6	118, 119	Mand. 11.17	118
Mand. 5.2.7	118	Mand. 12.6.4	126
Mand. 5.33.1	125n36	Mand. 21	118
Mand. 6	118		
Mand. 6.2	118	Tertullian	
Mand. 6.2.1	117n14, 118	*Carn. Chr.*	
Mand. 6.2.3	119	14	*xxvii*n11
Mand. 6.2.3–4	118		
Mand. 6.2.5	117n14	*Marc*	
Mand. 6.2.7	118	3.9	40n146
Mand. 10.1.3	115, 166n30	3.9.4, 7	47n178
Mand. 10.2.1	115, 166n30		
Mand. 10.2.5	115, 166n30	Victorinus	
Mand. 10.2.5–6	134n65	*Comm. Apoc.*	
Mand. 10.41.5	115–116, 166n30	1.1	94n24
Mand. 11	110	1.6	94n24
Mand. 11.9	53n194, 116–117,	1.1	94n24
	125n36	1.2	94n24

D. DEAD SEA SCROLLS, TARGUMS, PHILO, PSEUDEPIGRAPHA, AND APOCRYPHA

4QSb 4.25	46	*2 Baruch*	
4Q403 20–21–22 10	40n146	21.6	40n146
		51.12	48n180
Tg. Job		55.3	117n14
25.2	40n146		
		3 Baruch	
Philo		11.7	117n14
Leg. All.			
3.177	78n17	*3 Corinthians*	
Mos.		2.5	184n109
1.166	93	2.10	183–184, 185
Conf.		3.10	184n109
168–182	125n34		
		Apoc. Abr.	
1 Enoch		19.6	40n146
10.1–9	39n145		
14.11		*Apoc. Zeph.*	
20	39n145	6.13–15	106n56
37.2	108		
39.12	108	*Gos. Pet.*	
71.11	46	10.39–40	119
90.20–21	95		
90.21	39n145	*Jubilees*	
		2.2	39n145
2 Enoch		15.27	39n145
19.6	39n145		
28.11	46	*Mart. Asc. Isa.*	
29.1–3	40n146	7.21–23	106n56
29.3	135n67	7.23	117n14
39.5	40n146	8.4–5	106n56
		8.12	117n14
		9.36	117

9.39	117n14	*Test. Levi*	
9.40	117n14	4.2	46
11.4	117	7.4–8.3	39n145

Sib. Or.
7.82–5   151n57

E. Mishna, Talmud, Hekhalot and Later Jewish Literature

m. Hag.		*Pirq. R. El.*	
2.1	23	22	40n146
b. Hag.		*3 Enoch*	
13b–14a	40n146	10.2–6	39n145, 47
		12	47
Gen. Rab.		15.84C	46
78.1	40n146		
97	164n24	*Hekhalot Zutarti*	
		§§396–397	37n136
Deut. Rab.			
11.4	40n146		

INDEX OF MODERN AUTHORS

Adam, K., 114n5
Afinogenov, D., 25n92
Alexandre, M., 142n17
Allison, D., 93, 94n23, 151n57, 167n34
Andresen, C., 143n21
Arnim, H., 8
Audet, P., 167n32
Aune, D., 91n11, 94n23, 95n26m, 96n29, 100n42, 101n44m, 102n46, 105n55, 106n57, 107n60

Barbel, J., xxixn19, 57n207, 58n211, 136n67, 144n25, 147n39, 148n45
Bardy, G., 15
Barker, M., xxviiin17
Barnard, L., 113n2, 139n3, 140n13, 144
Barnard, P., 63n230
Barnes, M., 69n256, 78n17, 122, 153n67
Bauckham, R., 74n5, 95n24, 101n44, 102n46, 111n70
Baumstark, A., 160n8, 166n31
Beckwith, I., 107n60
Benoit, A., 140n13, 146n35, 147n43
Berthold, G., 81n25
Bobichon, P., 145n32, 146n35, 149n52, 152n59, 164n22
Bos, A., 41n152
Bousset, W., 9, 18n62, 34, 35n130, 81, 135n67
Boyarin, D., xxvii
Brock. S., 163n19, 166n31, 177n77
Brox, N., 114n3, 117n13, 121n24, 122n27, 129, 131n52, 132n57, 133, 134n65
Bruce, F. F., 102n49
Bruns, P., 159n2, 171n47, 173n56, 175, 177, 179, 180, 181, 183n105, 187
Brütsch, C., 103n50
Bunsen, C., 8–10, 90n5
Burge, G., 103n52
Butterworth, G. W., 48n180

Caird, B., 101n44
Cambe, M., 106n56
Cantalamessa, R., xxviiin18, 76n12, 77n16, 78n18, 143n22, 145n33
Caragounis, C., 45n169
Carlson, S., 7n19

Carrell, P., xxvin8, 95n24
Casey, R., 26n94
Charles, R. H., 92n17, 95n26
Charlesworth, J., 46n174
Cirillo, L., 131n52, 134n65
Coleborne, W., 113n2
Collins, J. J., 51n188, 106n58
Collomp, P., 17n62, 35n130, 36n132, 41n154, 61n226, 64n235, 68n250
Connolly, R. H., 174n59
Constas, N., 161n10
Corbin, H., 170n43
Cosaert, C., 63n230
Cramer, W., 160, 169, 170, 171n46, 176, 177, 178, 187n116
Crouzel, H., 41n152
Culianu, I.-P., 43n162, 64n236

Daley, B., 48n181
Daniélou, J., xxiin4, xxv, xxviin10, 35n130, 41n155, 57n210, 119, 121n22, 136n67, 137n69, 148n49
Davies, W. D., 46n174, 151n57
Dawson, D., 63n232
de Aldama, J., 78n18, 142n18, 143n23, 144n25, 145n32
de Andia, Y., 48n180, 124n32
DeConick, A., 36n134, 37n137, 67n248, 167n33
de Faye, E., 11, 12n39, 14–16
De Groote, M., 97n32
Descourtieux, P., 10, 20, 25n91
Deutsch, N., 37n136, 46n174
Dibelius, M., 130n52
di Benedetto, F., 6, 7n19
Dix, G., 93n17
Droge, A., 142n16
Duckworth, C., 7n19, 17n58
Dulaey, M., 89n2
Dunn, J. D. G., 105n55
Dünzl, F., 61n224
Dyobouniotes, C. I., 89n3

Echle, H., 7n19
Edwards, M. J., 26n94
Elior, R., 39n145, 47
Farkasfalvy, D., 7n1
Fatehi, M., xxii, 103n52, 104n53, 177n78

Fee, G., 92n13, 177n78
Fekkes III, J., 106n57, 108n64
Feulner, R., 18n64
Fiensy, D., 172n52
Fletcher-Louis, C., xxvin8, 46n174, 61, 99, 119
Förster, N., 66n243, 67n247
Fortin, E. L., 15, 16n54, 24n88
Fossum, J., 24n87, 66n242
Foster, E., xxvin8
Frangoulis, J., 3, 57n207, 77n17
Fredrickson, N., 115, 118n17, 160, 166, 167n32
Frend, W. H. C., 3, 73

Gavin, F., 161n10
Gieschen, C., xxii, xxvin8, 37n137, 60n220, 66n242, 94n24, 95n26, 99n38, 100, 102n46, 110n69, 118n15, 121n22, 122, 125n34
Giet, S., 114n7
Golitzin, A., 34, 35n128, 50–51, 167n32
Goodenough, E., 139n3, 140, 144n25, 145n30, 146, 147
Grillmeier, A., 78n18, 119n19, 130n52, 145n33
Gundry, R., xxvin8, 94n24

Haas, C., 116n11, 118n16, 127n40
Hadot, I., 19n69, 20n71, 24n85
Hadot, P., 18n65
Hägg, H., 4n8, 18n64, 28n102, 29–30, 36n132, 77n16, 78n17
Halperin, D., 22n80, 152, 152n60
Hamman, A., 142n18
Hannah, D., xxvin8, 147n44
Hanson, A. T., 167n32
Hanson, P., 51n188
Harl, M., 22n80
Harnack, A., xxvii, 8, 18n64, 89n3, 114n3, 131n52
Harvey, S., 177n77
Hauck, R., 113
Hauschild, W.-D., 3, 4, 55n201, 57n207, 59, 81n25
Hays, R., 105n55
Heine, R., 7, 18n64
Henne, P., xxvin10, 114, 122n27, 123n28, 127, 128, 129n48, 131n53, 132n54, 133
Hennessey, L., 41n152
Héring, J., 62n229
Hernans, T., 116n11

Heussi, C., 11n35, 15
Hilhorst, A., 134n65
Hofer, A., 153n64
Hoffmann, M., 95n24
Hooker, M., 105n55
Horner, T., 153
Hovhanessian, V., 183n109, 184n110
Hurtado, L., 74n5, 100

Jakab, A., 35n130, 49n185, 50n186
Joly, R., 114n7, 129n49, 130n52, 134n65, 135n67
Jones, F., 64n234
Joseph-Pierre, M., 159n2
Junod, E., 89n3

Kaniyamparampil, E., 177n77
Kelly, J. N. D., 130n52
Kiddle, M., 106n57, 109n65
Kimelman, R., 22n80
Kindiy, O., 26n94, 75n8
Knauber, A., 25n89, 26n94
Knight, J., xxvin10
Kovacs, J., 12n39, 13–14, 16
Kretschmar, G., xxiiin5, xxviiin19, 4, 35n130, 57, 58, 61, 77n15, 81n25, 147, 167n33, 169, 170, 187

Ladaria, L., xxviin13, 3, 4n9, 57n207, 59, 60, 77n15, 78n20
Lagarde, P., 160n9
Lamoreaux, J., 97n32
Layton, B., 64n236
Lazatti, G., 11n35,
Le Boulluec, A., 5n14, 10, 18, 27n100, 35n129, 38n142, 45n171, 51
Lebreton, J., 3, 9
Légasse, S., 62n228
Levison, J., xxi, 60n220, 73, 108n61, 118, 123n30
Lilla, S., xxviiin18, 15, 26n94, 29–30, 42n158
Longenecker, R., xxvin8
Loofs, F., xxvii, xxviiin18, xxixn19, 127n40, 130n52, 159n2, 160, 169n43, 174n59, 176n70, 177n77, 178, 183n109, 187
Lueken, W., 57, 58, 61
Lupieri, E., 92, 94n23, 95n24, 99n39, 109, 110
Lusini, G., 113n1
Luttikhuizen, G., 64n236
Luz, U., 62n229

Mach, M., 46n174
Macholz, W., xxviiin19
Markschies, C., 26n94, 81n25
Martín, J., 139n4, 141, 142n18, 144, 145n31, 147n38, 148n47, 152n59
McDonnell, K., 151n56
McDonough, S., 100n42
McGuckin, J. A., xxvin8
McGuckin, P., xxviiin18, xxixn19, 78n18, 145n33
McNamara, M., 100n42
Mees, M., 55n202, 63n230
Méhat, A., 5n14, 6, 9, 15–17, 20–21, 23n84, 27n98, 42n156, 83n30
Merkel, H., 7n19
Mettinger, T. N. D., 149n53
Metzger, M., 172n52, 173n55
Michl, J., 92n12, 95n26, 96n30, 97n35
Moberly, R. W. L., 102n47
Mondésert, C., 13n43, 14n47
Montefiore, C., 62n228
Morgan-Wynne, J. E., 114n5, 118n17, 144n25, 153n63
Morray-Jones, C. R. A., 47n177, 152n61
Mortley, R., 26n94, 36n132
Moser, M., 82n27
Moxnes, H., 126
Mueller, J., 172n52
Munck, J., 11
Munier, C., 139n4, 140n11, 154n71
Murray, R., 159n2, 160n6, 167n33, 173n57
Muse, R., 91n11

Nagel, P., 167n33
Nardi, C., 6n16, 7n17, 10, 21, 41n154, 43
Nautin, P., 6, 9–11, 18, 21, 35n130
Neymeyr, U., 13n44, 18n64, 146n36, 153n65
Niculescu, M.-V., 19n69
Nötscher, F., 36n134

Oeyen, C., 3–5, 28, 30, 36n132, 38n139, 41n154, 42n158, 51, 55n201, 57, 58, 59, 60, 61, 73, 83, 141, 149
Olofsson, S., 149n53
Opitz, H., 117n13, 118n17, 130n52
Orban, A. P., 136n67
Orlov, A., 36n134, 37n135, 46n174, 47n175, 70n257
Ortiz de Urbina, I., 159n2, 160, 177, 179, 180, 181, 183n106

Osborn, E., xxvin10, 3n5, 7n19, 12n38, 15, 17, 26n94, 28–30, 33, 35n130, 43n160, 52, 54, 73–74, 75n7, 77n16, 80, 81, 154n71
Osiek, C., 113n1, 114n4, 115n7, 121n22, 122n27, 129, 131n52, 132n55, 133, 134

Pearson, B., 64n236
Pépin, J., 40n146, 41n153, 78n17
Pernveden, L., 121n23, 131n52m, 133n58
Pesch, W., 62n228
Petersen, W., 159n2
Pierre, M.-J., 161n10, 166n29, 173, 176n71, 183n107
Plátová, J., 7n19
Prigent, P., 91n11, 93, 100n40, 101n44, 106n57, 107, 108n64, 152n59

Quatember, F., 13
Quispel, G., xxviiin17, 61n227, 65n239, 170n43, 174, 177n77

Rainbow, P., xxviiin17
Reiling, J., 117n14
Reitzenstein, R., 40n146
Ridolfini, F., 160n4, 161n10
Riedinger, U., 7n19, 34
Riedweg, C., 12n39
Rizzerio, L., 18n65, 24, 36n132
Roberts, C., 68n250
Robinson, J. A. T., 115n7
Roncaglia, M., 35n130, 50n186
Rondeau, M.-J., 143n21
Roose, H., 106n56
Roques, R., 33n121
Rordorf, W., 140n9, 142n18, 144n25
Rowland, C., xxvin10, 62n228
Ruben, P., 8
Runia, D., 30n112
Russell, N., 46n173, 48n180

Sabugal, S., 139n4, 140n8, 142n18, 144n25
Saffrey, H. D., 142n20
Sagnard, F., 37n139, 57n208, 66n244, 76n14
Schäfer, P., 37n136, 164n23
Schibli, H., 41n152
Schimanowski, G., 95n26
Schlütz, K., 32n116, 57n209, 60, 95n25, 164n20, 165n25, 174n60

Scholem, G., 22n80, 65n239
Schweizer, E., 96n29, 102n48, 103n51
Schwen, P., 169, 170n44, 176, 177n74, 178n80, 179n83
Segal, A., xxvii–xxviii, 24n87
Sellew, P., 136n67
Seow, C. L., 36n134
Siegert, F., 154n68
Simonetti, M., xxvii, 76n12, 77n16
Skarsaune, O., 152n59
Skoyles Jarkins, S., 160, 166n29, 176n67, 177n77, 178n80, 179
Škrinjar, A., 95n26, 97n35
Slusser, M., 143n21
Smelik, W., 39n145, 47n177
Stanton, G., 139n5, 144n28, 148n45, 152n58
Stead, C., xxviiin18, 75n11
Stenning, J., 164n21
Stewart, C., 163n19
Strecker, G., 64n234
Stroumsa, G., xxiin4, xxiiin5, 23, 51n189, 65n239
Stuckenbruck, L., xxiiin5, xxvin8, 101n43, 106n56, 116n11
Strutwolf, H., 172n51
Studer, B., xxixn19
Sullivan, K., 46n174
Swarat, U., 18n64
Swete, H., 4n9, 95n26, 109n65, 147n41

Tanghe, A., 167n35, 168n37
Termini, C., 78n17
Thomson, W. G., 62n228
Tite, P., 82n27
Tollinton, R., 16n57, 18n62
Treu, U., 45n168
Turner, C. H., 89n3
Turner, H. E. W., xxviiin18, 9, 130n52, 191

Turner, J. D., 65n236
Turner, M., 104n54
Tuzlak, S., 116n11

Vaggione, R., 171n48
Valavanolickal, K., 159n1
van den Broek, R., 64n236
van den Hoek, A., 10–11, 21, 23n82, 31n113, 35n130, 46n173, 63n230
Verbeke, G., 3n5
Völker, W., 11, 18n62
von Balthasar, H., 10n33
von Bunsen, C., 8
Vööbus, A., 159n3, 173n56, 179

Waddell, R., 95n24, 102n46, 108n62, 110n69
Wagner, W., 13n43, 14n47, 25n89, 26n95
Wallis, I., 105n55
Wartelle, A., 140, 144n25
Wasznik, J., 77n16
Westcott, B. F., 8, 57, 58
Westerink, L. G., 142n20
Whittaker, J., 36n132, 77n16
Wilson, J., 115n7, 117n13, 118n18, 122n25, 123, 124, 127, 131n52
Winkler, G., 119, 150n56, 151n57, 177n77
Witherington III, B., 100n42, 107n60
Wolfson, H., xxviiin18, 76n12
Wright, W., 160n8

Yarbro-Collins, A., 43n162

Zahn, T., 4, 8–10, 14n48, 18n64, 25n89, 38n140, 55n202, 57, 58, 61, 77n15, 90, 91n8
Ziebritzki, H., 4–5, 57, 59, 74n4, 75n8, 80, 81n25, 209

SUPPLEMENTS TO VIGILIAE CHRISTIANAE

1. Tertullianus. *De idololatria.* Critical Text, Translation and Commentary by J.H. Waszink and J.C.M. van Winden. Partly based on a Manuscript left behind by P.G. van der Nat. 1987. ISBN 90 04 08105 4
2. Springer, C.P.E. *The Gospel as Epic in Late Antiquity.* The *Paschale Carmen* of Sedulius. 1988. ISBN 90 04 08691 9
3. Hoek, A. van den. *Clement of Alexandria and His Use of Philo in the* Stromateis. An Early Christian Reshaping of a Jewish Model. 1988. ISBN 90 04 08756 7
4. Neymeyr, U. *Die christlichen Lehrer im zweiten Jahrhundert.* Ihre Lehrtätigkeit, ihr Selbstverständnis und ihre Geschichte. 1989. ISBN 90 04 08773 7
5. Hellemo, G. *Adventus Domini.* Eschatological Thought in 4th-century Apses and Catecheses. 1989. ISBN 90 04 08836 9
6. Rufin von Aquileia. *De ieiunio* I, II. Zwei Predigten über das Fasten nach Basileios von Kaisareia. Ausgabe mit Einleitung, Übersetzung und Anmerkungen von H. Marti. 1989. ISBN 90 04 08897 0
7. Rouwhorst, G.A.M. *Les hymnes pascales d'Éphrem de Nisibe.* Analyse théologique et recherche sur l'évolution de la fête pascale chrétienne à Nisibe et à Édesse et dans quelques Églises voisines au quatrième siècle. 2 vols: I. Étude; II. Textes. 1989. ISBN 90 04 08839 3
8. Radice, R. and D.T. Runia. *Philo of Alexandria.* An Annotated Bibliography 1937–1986. In Collaboration with R.A. Bitter, N.G. Cohen, M. Mach, A.P. Runia, D. Satran and D.R. Schwartz. 1988. repr. 1992. ISBN 90 04 08986 1
9. Gordon, B. *The Economic Problem in Biblical and Patristic Thought.* 1989. ISBN 90 04 09048 7
10. Prosper of Aquitaine. *De Providentia Dei.* Text, Translation and Commentary by M. Marcovich. 1989. ISBN 90 04 09090 8
11. Jefford, C.N. *The Sayings of Jesus in the Teaching of the Twelve Apostles.* 1989. ISBN 90 04 09127 0
12. Drobner, H.R. and Klock, Ch. *Studien zu Gregor von Nyssa und der christlichen Spätantike.* 1990. ISBN 90 04 09222 6
13. Norris, F.W. *Faith Gives Fullness to Reasoning.* The Five Theological Orations of Gregory Nazianzen. Introduction and Commentary by F.W. Norris and Translation by Lionel Wickham and Frederick Williams. 1990. ISBN 90 04 09253 6
14. Oort, J. van. *Jerusalem and Babylon.* A Study into Augustine's *City of God* and the Sources of his Doctrine of the Two Cities. 1991. ISBN 90 04 09323 0
15. Lardet, P. *L'Apologie de Jérôme contre Rufin.* Un Commentaire. 1993. ISBN 90 04 09457 1
16. Risch, F.X. *Pseudo-Basilius: Adversus Eunomium IV-V.* Einleitung, Übersetzung und Kommentar. 1992. ISBN 90 04 09558 6
17. Klijn, A.F.J. *Jewish-Christian Gospel Tradition.* 1992. ISBN 90 04 09453 9

18. Elanskaya, A.I. *The Literary Coptic Manuscripts in the A.S. Pushkin State Fine Arts Museum in Moscow.* ISBN 90 04 09528 4
19. Wickham, L.R. and Bammel, C.P. (eds.). *Christian Faith and Greek Philosophy in Late Antiquity.* Essays in Tribute to George Christopher Stead. 1993. ISBN 90 04 09605 1
20. Asterius von Kappadokien. *Die theologischen Fragmente.* Einleitung, kritischer Text, Übersetzung und Kommentar von Markus Vinzent. 1993. ISBN 90 04 09841 0
21. Hennings, R. *Der Briefwechsel zwischen Augustinus und Hieronymus und ihr Streit um den Kanon des Alten Testaments und die Auslegung von Gal. 2,11-14.* 1994. ISBN 90 04 09840 2
22. Boeft, J. den & Hilhorst, A. (eds.). *Early Christian Poetry.* A Collection of Essays. 1993. ISBN 90 04 09939 5
23. McGuckin, J.A. *St. Cyril of Alexandria: The Christological Controversy.* Its History, Theology, and Texts. 1994. ISBN 90 04 09990 5
24. Reynolds, Ph.L. *Marriage in the Western Church.* The Christianization of Marriage during the Patristic and Early Medieval Periods. 1994. ISBN 90 04 10022 9
25. Petersen, W.L. *Tatian's Diatessaron.* Its Creation, Dissemination, Significance, and History in Scholarship. 1994. ISBN 90 04 09469 5
26. Grünbeck, E. *Christologische Schriftargumentation und Bildersprache.* Zum Konflikt zwischen Metapherninterpretation und dogmatischen Schrift-beweistraditionen in der patristischen Auslegung des 44. (45.) Psalms. 1994. ISBN 90 04 10021 0
27. Haykin, M.A.G. *The Spirit of God.* The Exegesis of 1 and 2 Corinthians in the Pneumatomachian Controversy of the Fourth Century. 1994. ISBN 90 04 09947 6
28. Benjamins, H.S. *Eingeordnete Freiheit.* Freiheit und Vorsehung bei Origenes. 1994. ISBN 90 04 10117 9
29. Smulders s.j., P. (tr. & comm.). *Hilary of Poitiers' Preface to his* Opus historicum. 1995. ISBN 90 04 10191 8
30. Kees, R.J. *Die Lehre von der* Oikonomia Gottes in der Oratio catechetica *Gregors von Nyssa.* 1995. ISBN 90 04 10200 0
31. Brent, A. *Hippolytus and the Roman Church in the Third Century.* Communities in Tension before the Emergence of a Monarch-Bishop. 1995. ISBN 90 04 10245 0
32. Runia, D.T. *Philo and the Church Fathers.* A Collection of Papers. 1995. ISBN 90 04 10355 4
33. DeConick, A.D. *Seek to See Him.* Ascent and Vision Mysticism in the Gospel of Thomas. 1996. ISBN 90 04 10401 1
34. Clemens Alexandrinus. *Protrepticus.* Edidit M. Marcovich. 1995. ISBN 90 04 10449 6
35. Böhm, T. *Theoria – Unendlichkeit – Aufstieg.* Philosophische Implikationen zu *De vita Moysis* von Gregor von Nyssa. 1996. ISBN 90 04 10560 3
36. Vinzent, M. *Pseudo-Athanasius, Contra Arianos IV.* Eine Schrift gegen Asterius von Kappadokien, Eusebius von Cäsarea, Markell von Ankyra und Photin von Sirmium. 1996. ISBN 90 04 10686 3

37. Knipp, P.D.E. *'Christus Medicus' in der frühchristlichen Sarkophagskulptur*. Ikonographische Studien zur Sepulkralkunst des späten vierten Jahrhunderts. 1998. ISBN 90 04 10862 9
38. Lössl, J. *Intellectus gratiae*. Die erkenntnistheoretische und hermeneutische Dimension der Gnadenlehre Augustins von Hippo. 1997. ISBN 90 04 10849 1
39. Markell von Ankyra. *Die Fragmente. Der Brief an Julius von Rom*. Herausgegeben, eingeleitet und übersetzt von Markus Vinzent. 1997. ISBN 90 04 10907 2
40. Merkt, A. *Maximus I. von Turin*. Die Verkündigung eines Bischofs der frühen Reichskirche im zeitgeschichtlichen, gesellschaftlichen und liturgischen Kontext. 1997. ISBN 90 04 10864 5
41. Winden, J.C.M. van. *Archè*. A Collection of Patristic Studies by J.C.M. van Winden. Edited by J. den Boeft and D.T. Runia. 1997. ISBN 90 04 10834 3
42. Stewart-Sykes, A. *The Lamb's High Feast*. Melito, *Peri Pascha* and the Quartodeciman Paschal Liturgy at Sardis. 1998. ISBN 90 04 11236 7
43. Karavites, P. *Evil, Freedom and the Road to Perfection in Clement of Alexandria*. 1999. ISBN 90 04 11238 3
44. Boeft, J. den and M.L. van Poll-van de Lisdonk (eds.). *The Impact of Scripture in Early Christianity*. 1999. ISBN 90 04 11143 3
45. Brent, A. *The Imperial Cult and the Development of Church Order*. Concepts and Images of Authority in Paganism and Early Christianity before the Age of Cyprian. 1999. ISBN 90 04 11420 3
46. Zachhuber, J. *Human Nature in Gregory of Nyssa*. Philosophical Background and Theological Significance. 1999. ISBN 90 04 11530 7
47. Lechner, Th. *Ignatius adversus Valentinianos?* Chronologische und theologiegeschichtliche Studien zu den Briefen des Ignatius von Antiochien. 1999. ISBN 90 04 11505 6
48. Greschat, K. *Apelles und Hermogenes*. Zwei theologische Lehrer des zweiten Jahrhunderts. 1999. ISBN 90 04 11549 8
49. Drobner, H.R. *Augustinus von Hippo:* Sermones ad populum. Überlieferung und Bestand – Bibliographie – Indices. 1999. ISBN 90 04 11451 3
50. Hübner, R.M. *Der paradox Eine*. Antignostischer Monarchianismus im zweiten Jahrhundert. Mit einen Beitrag von Markus Vinzent. 1999. ISBN 90 04 11576 5
51. Gerber, S. *Theodor von Mopsuestia und das Nicänum*. Studien zu den katechetischen Homilien. 2000. ISBN 90 04 11521 8
52. Drobner, H.R. and A. Viciano (eds.). *Gregory of Nyssa: Homilies on the Beatitudes*. An English Version with Commentary and Supporting Studies. Proceedings of the Eighth International Colloquium on Gregory of Nyssa (Paderborn, 14-18 September 1998) 2000 ISBN 90 04 11621 4
53. Marcovich, M. (ed.). *Athenagorae qui fertur* De resurrectione mortuorum. 2000. ISBN 90 04 11896 9
54. Marcovich, M. (ed.). *Origenis: Contra Celsum Libri VIII*. 2001. ISBN 90 04 11976 0

55. McKinion, S. *Words, Imagery, and the Mystery of Christ.* A Reconstruction of Cyril of Alexandria's Christology. 2001. ISBN 90 04 11987 6

56. Beatrice, P.F. *Anonymi Monophysitae* Theosophia, *An Attempt at Reconstruction.* 2001. ISBN 90 04 11798 9

57. Runia, D.T. *Philo of Alexandria:* An Annotated Bibliography 1987-1996. 2001. ISBN 90 04 11682 6

58. Merkt, A. *Das Patristische Prinzip.* Eine Studie zur Theologischen Bedeutung der Kirchenväter. 2001. ISBN 90 04 12221 4

59. Stewart-Sykes, A. *From Prophecy to Preaching.* A Search for the Origins of the Christian Homily. 2001. ISBN 90 04 11689 3

60. Lössl, J. *Julian von Aeclanum.* Studien zu seinem Leben, seinem Werk, seiner Lehre und ihrer Überlieferung. 2001. ISBN 90 04 12180 3

61. Marcovich, M. (ed.), adiuvante J.C.M. van Winden, *Clementis Alexandrini* Paedagogus. 2002. ISBN 90 04 12470 5

62. Berding, K. *Polycarp and Paul.* An Analysis of Their Literary and Theological Relationship in Light of Polycarp's Use of Biblical and Extra-Biblical Literature. 2002. ISBN 90 04 12670 8

63. Kattan, A.E. *Verleiblichung und Synergie.* Grundzüge der Bibelhermeneutik bei Maximus Confessor. 2002. ISBN 90 04 12669 4

64. Allert, C.D. *Revelation, Truth, Canon, and Interpretation.* Studies in Justin Martyr's Dialogue with Trypho. 2002. ISBN 90 04 12619 8

65. Volp, U. *Tod und Ritual in den christlichen Gemeinden der Antike.* 2002. ISBN 90 04 12671 6

66. Constas, N. *Proclus of Constantinople and the Cult of the Virgin in Late Antiquity.* Homilies 1-5, Texts and Translations. 2003. ISBN 90 04 12612 0

67. Carriker, A. *The Library of Eusebius of Caesarea.* 2003. ISBN 90 04 13132 9

68. Lilla, S.R.C., herausgegeben von H.R. Drobner. *Neuplatonisches Gedankengut in den 'Homilien über die Seligpreisungen' Gregors von Nyssa.* 2004. ISBN 90 04 13684 3

69. Mullen, R.L. *The Expansion of Christianity.* A Gazetteer of its First Three Centuries. 2004. ISBN 90 04 13135 3

70. Hilhorst, A. (ed.). *The Apostolic Age in Patristic Thought.* 2004. ISBN 90 04 12611 2

71. Kotzé, A. *Augustine's* Confessions: *Communicative Purpose and Audience.* 2004. ISBN 90 04 13926 5

72. Drijvers, J.W. *Cyril of Jerusalem: Bishop and City.* 2004. ISBN 90 04 13986 9

73. Duval, Y.-M. *La décrétale* Ad Gallos Episcopos: *son texte et son auteur.* Texte critique, traduction Française et commentaire. 2005. ISBN 90 04 14170 7

74. Mueller-Jourdan, P. *Typologie spatio-temporelle de l'*Ecclesia *byzantine.* La Mystagogie de Maxime le Confesseur dans la culture philosophique de l'Antiquité. 2005. ISBN 90 04 14230 4

75. Ferguson, T.J. *The Past is Prologue.* The Revolution of Nicene Historiography. 2005. ISBN 90 04 14457 9

76. Marjanen, A. & Luomanen, P. *A Companion to Second-Century Christian "Heretics".* 2005. ISBN 90 04 14464 1

77. Tzamalikos, P. *Origen – Cosmology and Ontology of Time.* 2006. ISBN 90 04 14728 4

78. Bitton-Ashkelony, B. & Kofsky, A. *The Monastic School of Gaza*. 2006. ISBN-13: 978 90 04 14737 9, ISBN-10: 90 04 14737 3

79. Portbarré-Viard, de la G.H. *Descriptions monumentales et discours sur l'édification chez Paulin de Nole. Le regard et la lumière (epist. 32 et carm. 27 et 28)*. 2006. ISBN 90 04 15105 2

80. Ziadé, R. *Les martyrs Maccabées: de l'histoire juive au culte chrétien*. Les homélies de Grégoire de Nazianze et de Jean Chrysostome. 2007. ISBN-13: 978 90 04 15384 4, ISBN-10: 90 04 15384 5

81. Volp, U. *Die Würde des Menschen*. Ein Beitrag zur Anthropologie in der Alten Kirche. 2006. ISBN-13: 978 90 04 15448 3, ISBN-10: 90 04 15448 5

82. Karfíková, L., S. Douglass and J. Zachhuber (eds.). *Gregory of Nyssa: Contra Eunomium II*. An English Version with Supporting Studies Proceedings of the 10th International Colloquium on Gregory of Nyssa (Olomouc, September 15-18, 2004). 2007. ISBN-13: 978 90 04 15518 3, ISBN-10: 90 04 15518 X

83. Silvas, A.M. *Gregory of Nyssa: The Letters*. Introduction, Translation and Commentary. 2007. ISBN-13: 978 90 04 15290 8, ISBN-10: 90 04 15290 3

84. Tabbernee, W. *Fake Prophecy and Polluted Sacraments*. Ecclesiastical and Imperial Reactions to Montanism. 2007. ISBN-13: 978 90 04 15819 1, ISBN-10: 90 04 15819 7

85. Tzamalikos, P. *Origen: Philosophy of History & Eschatology*. 2007. ISBN-13: 978 90 04 15648 7, ISBN-10: 90 04 15648 8

86. Maspero, G. *Trinity and Man*. Gregory of Nyssa's Ad Ablabium. 2007. ISBN-13: 978 90 04 15872 6

87. Otten, W. & Pollmann, K. (eds.) *Poetry and Exegesis*. Modes of Interpretation in Late Antique and Medieval Latin Christian Poetry. 2007. ISBN-13: 978 90 04 16069 9

88. Schmid, H. *Die Eucharistie ist Jesus*. Anfänge einer Theorie des Sakraments im koptischen Philippusevangelium (NHC II 3). 2007. ISBN-13: 978 90 04 16096 5

89. Weedman, M. *The Trinitarian Theology of Hilary of Poitiers*. 2007. ISBN 978 90 04 16224 2

90. Graves, M. *Jerome's Hebrew Philology*. A Study Based on his Commentary on Jeremiah. 2007. ISBN 978 90 04 16204 4

91. Steenberg, M. *Irenaeus on Creation*. The Cosmic Christ and the Saga of Redemption. 2008. ISBN 978 90 04 16682 0

92. Allen, J.S. *The Despoliation of Egypt* in Pre-Rabbinic, Rabbinic and Patristic Traditions. 2008. ISBN 978 90 04 16745 2

93. Wessel, S. *Leo the Great and the Spiritual Rebuilding of a Universal Rome*. 2008. ISBN 978 90 04 17052 0

94. McGowan, A.B., B.E. Daley S.J. & T.J. Gaden (eds.). *God in Early Christian Thought*. Essays in Memory of Lloyd G. Patterson. 2009. ISBN 978 90 04 17412 2

95. Bucur, B.G. *Angelomorphic Pneumatology*. Clement of Alexandria and Other Early Christian Witnesses. 2009. ISBN 978 90 04 17414 6

96. Loon, H. van. *The Dyophysite Christology of Cyril of Alexandria*. 2009. ISBN 978 90 04 17322 4

97. Itter, A.C. *Esoteric Teaching in the* Stromateis *of Clement of Alexandria.* 2009. ISBN 978 90 04 17482 5
98. Ernst, A.M. *Martha from the Margins.* The Authority of Martha in Early Christian Tradition. 2009. ISBN 978 90 04 17490 0